Heart of
Iron

The Philippine Archipelago in Geographical Context

Lt. Col. Harley F. Hieb
AUS (Ret.)

Heart of Iron

PACIFICA PUBLISHING
LODI, CALIFORNIA

Designed by Rick Chafian, San Francisco

Printed and bound by The Murray Printing Company
Westford, Massachusetts

Text printed on Warren's Olde Style, a permanent paper

Edited and produced by Cornelia P. Hunt, San Francisco

Pacifica Publishing, Box 2282, Lodi, CA 95241

Published 1987
Printed in the United States of America

The Central University Library of the University of California
at San Diego has generously permitted the use of maps necessary
to the proper preparation of this book.

Library of Congress Cataloging-in-Publication Data

Hieb, Harley F., 1914–
   Heart of iron.

   Bibliography: p.
   1. Hieb, Harley F., 1914–   2. World War,
1939–1945—Underground movements—Philippines.
3. World War, 1939–1945—Personal narratives,
American. 4. Guerrillas—Philippines—Biography.
5. Guerrillas—United States—Biography.
6. Soldiers—United States—Biography.
7. United States. Army—Biography. I. Title.
D802.P5H55 1987   940.53'599   87-2475
ISBN 0–935109–00–5 (alk. paper)

To my wife Elaine;
my daughters Cynthia and Candace;
and my grandchildren.

Acknowledgements

At the outset, I would like to acknowledge my gratitude to the Phil-Americans of the Philippine Islands, both soldiers and civilians, who suffered the miseries and tragedies of the Second World War and the attendant enemy occupation, and who have been suffering again recently in another kind of war.

There is another group of men and women to whom I also say a special thank you: the men and women of the American Armed Services who have participated in our country's wars.

Especially, I offer my grateful thanks to the servicemen and women who were involved in the wars in Korea and Vietnam, where in both actions, the hell was the same as the hell of all wars, but the usual clear mandate to defeat the enemy was withheld, and the concept of victory was so redefined that satisfaction in achieving this was denied those who fought to the inconclusive ends.

In acknowledging a debt of gratitude at the completion of such an undertaking as the endeavor to write this story of "my" war, there are so many intangibles that to properly thank all those who deserve my heartfelt thanks is logistically impossible. Such a list properly would span the better part of a century and include now-forgotten places and people whose full names I perhaps never knew. If these go unacknowledged on this page, they do not go unacknowledged in my heart. Family, friends, in-laws, teachers, mentors, associates, casual acquaintances—all these have contributed in many important, if different, ways. I am immensely grateful for those intangible—and priceless—contributions that have not only resulted in this book but have enriched all the experiences of my life.

In my enumeration of tangibles, I would like to thank C. M. Nielson of Salt Lake City for his magnificent kindness in supplying me with much information, both general and specific, pertaining to the Philippine Islands during World War II, including a variety of extremely useful maps and documentation of many kinds. In particular I thank him for giving me a copy of Col. John Horan's handwritten diary.

M/Sgt. Leon Beck, USAF (Ret.), and Maj. Dave Fisher, USAR (Ret.), were also generous in providing me with information.

That my effort to locate photographs from an era when a photograph itself represented a special event did not fail entirely is due in large measure to the gracious and enthusiastic cooperation of several people. Among those who came to my rescue are my old friend Garret Zenk; my aunt Helen and her husband, Elmer Holman; my cousin Madelyn and her husband, Don Nunn; and my cousin Carl Hieb.

I would also be remiss if I did not mention the great assistance provided during the early stages of this project by our good family friend Madeleine Newman.

No list of tangibles would be acceptable nor would my debt be discharged without the inclusion of my niece Barbara Pruden, who was unstinting in providing invaluable advice as the actual writing progressed and who helped me through several periods when thoughts would not easily translate into written communication.

A word of special thanks is due Adele Horwitz, Senior Editor, Presidio Press, Novato, California, whose recommendation resulted in my placing this project in the sympathetic and persevering hands of Cornelia P. Hunt, independent editor and production manager, without whose help and knowledge this book would never have been completed.

Certainly very special loving thanks are reserved for my daughters, Cynthia and Candace, and their husbands, Jeffrey McFarland-Johnson and Boyd Wilson.

The one person above all to whom I owe the most is my beloved wife, Elaine. To her, I offer my inadequate acknowledgement of help far beyond the call of duty. There seems no way to express fully, or even adequately, my thanks for her unselfish gifts of time, energy, concern, patience, and loving encouragement throughout the project's long duration. For reasons tangible and intangible, that debt, which I accept with love and gratitude, can never be discharged.

Contents

Maps

Preface

Life in a small midwestern town during the 1930s did not seem to promise much future for a restless sixteen-year-old boy. The desire for a better life prompted me to leave home, rich in dreams but with very little money. Like many other young men of that time, I joined the depression era's growing number of vagabonds. Hitchhiking, riding the freights, sleeping in jails, and going hungry eventually led me to seek a way to better myself—and a way that would include three meals a day.

I decided a career in the army would provide me with the basic necessities of life—shelter, clothing, and, above all, regular meals—and with the structure that to me seemed necessary to a well-planned future. Had I known in 1933 that nine years later none of these basics would be forthcoming and that for two and a half years I would find myself foraging for food in the jungles of the Philippines with my future very much in doubt, I might have reconsidered my choice of careers.

Had it not been for the discipline instilled in me by my German-American parents and my own stubborn nature, the unexpected turn of events in 1941 might have led to a different ending. The trapping and tracking skills I learned as a boy also helped me survive those years of jungle life when I was forced to exist on rats, monkeys, wildcats, lizards, bats, snails—even the liver of a python—with bamboo shoots and wild berries for salad and dessert. During that time, my weight dropped to eighty pounds, and malaria, beriberi, and jaundice haunted me constantly. But through it all self-discipline, the will to live, and prayer, helped me to prevail.

At the outbreak of World War II, we in the Philippines believed that the Japanese Imperial Forces could not conquer that multi-island commonwealth. The Filipino and American soldiers fought bravely and with confidence, until lack of ammunition and debilitating hunger forced the surrender of Bataan and Corregidor. Our war came to a temporary halt; the trials many of us would endure over the next few years began.

When I reflect on World War II, the war in Europe seems to have taken precedence over the war in the Pacific. Our Allies there received most of our attention and resources. The United States government gave priority to the European Theater of Operations, and only one-quarter of the war effort was allocated for the defeat of Japan. Those of us who were left behind in the Philippines without ammunition or supplies felt ignored and forgotten. But even thus handicapped, we continued the struggle by engaging in guerrilla warfare, until MacArthur's return to the islands and the eventual landing of American forces on Luzon in 1945.

Ten thousand Americans were taken prisoner on Bataan and Corregidor in 1942, of whom only four thousand survived to be liberated in 1945. Six thousand died in the prison camps, on the Death March, and on the Japanese ships that were sunk while taking them to Formosa, Japan, and Korea to be used as slave laborers. They were the true heroes.

Heroes too were the patriotic Filipino people who risked their lives to aid those of us who organized the guerrilla fighters during the Japanese occupation. By harassing and demoralizing the enemy, these guerrilla forces helped to undermine the hard core of fanatics within the Japanese Imperial Forces and bring the Bushido-lovers to their knees ready to surrender.

We returned home, victorious and filled with the hope that war had been ended for all time.

Yet, seven years later we were fighting again, this time against communist aggression in Korea. Only now it wasn't called a war; a new name had been coined: "police action." But to those of us under fire, it was a war, though certainly a singular and counterproductive one—for it ended exactly where it began: on the 38th parallel. (During this Korean action I was first assigned to the 2d Battalion, 5th RCT, as executive officer. Later I commanded this battalion.)

Five years after the signing of the peace treaty in Korea, news from Vietnam gradually began to capture the headlines, and another name for war was added to the list: "conflict." I had retired from the army by then, but after watching with growing dismay the war that television was bringing into our homes and listening with growing anger to the political manuevering that accompanied this war, I felt compelled in 1965 to request a return to active service. I was rejected as physically unfit. Thereafter, I watched the unfolding conflict, and its inconclusive end, from the sidelines.

With the passage of time and the accompanying continuous reports of conflicts, hot spots, and escalating terrorism, I began to feel the need to tell the story of "my" war. The issues of that war were clear to every soldier in it. We knew who we were fighting and why, and that knowledge gave us strength and determination.

While searching through my papers in preparation for the task of writing this book, I found and read again the poem Rosa Leaño sent me from the Philippines after the war. Her tribute reminded me anew of the warmth and generosity those courageous people had shown me. I thought again of her father, the brave patriot Teniente Leaño, and of all the soldiers of that war on Luzon who had fought with "the invincible strength of a Heart of Iron" for freedom from oppression.

I can only hope—indeed, this is my sincere prayer—that if America sees fit to send her soldiers off to war again, they will go with that same clarity of vision, invincible spirit, and belief that if a cause is just and worth a soldier's life, it is worth winning.

A HEART OF IRON

Hail to the soldier brave!
In whose bosom a heart of iron beats.
In reverent silence we pause and praise,
While warm tears alight. We feel a grip in our throats,
As we offer bouquets of honor in grateful mood
To the heart that defends our nation.

Do we speak of thy hardships, we know not the word.
Under the sky where bullets rained,
You advanced beneath bursting shells;
Amidst reverses of battle you beheld thy comrades dead;
With prayers on your lips,
You went to fight behind.

More bitter these the tears you shed,
Heavier to the sufferings you had,
Yet how steady and firm thy heart throbbed
As the ray of victory gleamed from afar,
Assuring the coming of the blessed day
As the dawn ascertains the coming daylight.

Then to live and bow under the enemy's yoke!
What sacrifice can equal yours?
May your faith to the glorious cause
Be a guiding star to all your young
Whose faith must last from day to day.
The tide mounts higher as onward we move

Towards the goal of our hopes and prayers.
Behold thy country is ever alert and ready
To bask under the rays of victory,
But always in our breasts we feel the might
Of the invincible strength of a Heart of Iron.

Rosa R. Leaño
Manuri, Jones, Isabela
10 August 1946

Prologue

The jungle was in full bloom. Coming from a cloudless summer sky, rays of sunlight penetrated the dense undergrowth and fell on a colorful variety of wild shrubs and orchids. A deceptive serenity pervaded the foliage-scented air. Under any other circumstances, the peaceful setting would have been delightful. But there was nothing at all peaceful about our world. We were at war.

On this hot, humid day in 1943, I was in the jungle on the Philippine island of Luzon intent on the task of trapping game. Bataan and Corregidor had fallen. News of the outside world was sparse and unreliable. For me and the gaunt, hunger-ridden men with me who had escaped from the infamous Death March and the Pinappagan raid, life had become a daily battle against starvation, fatigue, and illness. At the moment, our hopes were focused on the makeshift traps and snares that would provide our evening meal, if we were successful.

The Japanese garrison in Isabela Province's municipality of Jones was ten or fifteen miles away. It numbered from five thousand to ten thousand troops. Enemy patrols were sent out daily to look for guerrilla forces, gather intelligence information, and commandeer food.

The Japanese normally seized one-half to two-thirds of all food they found in the barrios, or small villages. This eventually reduced the residents to a half-ration diet, and the hardship was carried to us since then they could not supply us with rice—only with year-old corn, which the Japanese didn't like and left behind, but which we shelled and boiled for twelve hours to make an unappetizing mushlike soup.

My men and I had been on a starvation diet for some time.

1

Ninety-nine percent of our food supply consisted of what we could forage from the jungle, which meant anything that could walk, crawl, or fly. Weakened by hunger, we had little reserve strength to fight the malaria, dysentery, jaundice, and beriberi prevalent in our camp, and we had only barks, herbs, and roots to use for medicines.

It was my responsibility as the ranking officer to see that the forty-five men with me were fed, clothed, and provided with medical care. It was a nearly impossible task; however, my German-American background with its emphasis on hard work and discipline, my experience in trapping and tracking as a youth, and my ten years of military combat training had toughened me so that I was prepared to endure the hardships of jungle existence.

I knew the Japanese soon would begin penetrating deeper into our jungle territory looking for us. I had prepared my men for this eventuality by instructing them daily in various guerrilla tactics. One such technique involved a surprise ambush and quick retreat. In practice, this usually caused the enemy patrols to regroup as quickly as possible. Our quick retreat to another good concealment-and-cover area would draw them on, and we would be ready for another ambush and fast retreat. This process could be continued all day, inflicting heavy casualties, and eventually wearing down the enemy and breaking his morale.

We were prepared for the possibility of being tracked down in our hidden campsites, but the Japanese patrols were not the only source of danger. We were well inside the tribal territory of the Ilongots, and these feared and vicious headhunters were another ever-present threat.

Surrounded by the thick tropical underbrush, I watched the trap lines that day, feeling the same anticipation I had felt as a boy when I checked my snares, hoping and praying for some catch—only this time whatever we caught would be eaten. The Twenty-third Psalm kept going through my mind. "The Lord is my shepherd, I shall not want. . . . Yea though I walk through the valley of the shadow of death, I will fear no evil, for Thou art with me. . . ." I had a feeling that somehow my men and I would survive anything the Japanese or the headhunters could throw at us.

My thoughts turned back to my boyhood, and I reflected on the various circumstances of my life that had culminated in this daily struggle for survival in a Luzon jungle far from the small midwestern town where my journey to this place began.

PART ONE

THE RESTLESS YEARS: EUREKA TO MANILA 1914–1935

CHAPTER 1

A Born Traveler

I guess you could say I was a born traveler. My instinct to see the world first asserted itself one summer-scented June morning in 1918, when I was four years old. Having tired of playing on the front porch of the large three-story home my father had built to accommodate his expanding family, I set off down the sun-warmed sidewalk toward Main Street. I trudged along, unnoticed by the neighbors, stopping occasionally in the shade of the cottonwoods that lined the neat front lawns. My journey was momentarily sidetracked when I paused to inspect the fascinating variety of insect life hidden deep within the crevices of the rough bark. Some of this life found its way inside my shirt as I attempted, unsuccessfully and for no particular reason, to reach around the broad, scratchy trunks.

Dragging a small cottonwood branch behind me, which alternately scraped the pavement and clicked pleasantly in and out of the sidewalk's cracks, I eventually reached my father's place of business near downtown Eureka, a small farming community situated in the midst of the windswept grass and wheat fields of the rolling South Dakota prairie. My adventure came to an abrupt end when one of my father's customers noticed me going by and asked Father if I wasn't a bit young to be striking out on my own.

Unappreciative of the wanderlust that had prompted my excursion—and interrupted his business transaction—Father administered an on-the-spot spanking, and taking me firmly by the hand, marched me home. Depositing me once more in Mother's care, he added a further scolding for the worry my disappearance had caused her. She had

7

been frantically searching the neighborhood for me. This was the first of several confrontations that would take place between my father and me in connection with my desire to travel and assert my independence. I did mend my ways, however—for the time being—and for several years did not leave the yard again without asking permission.

Father should not have been surprised by my first impromptu journey. It was an early manifestation of a family trait that ran back through several generations of adventurers and seekers after a better way of life. In 1812 his own great-grandfather, Adam Hieb, left Württemberg, Germany, in the company of his parents, to settle in the Black Sea region of Russia. In 1874, Adam's son Jacob journeyed with his family from Russia to America and settled on a farm near Yankton, South Dakota. From there, Jacob's son George, my grandfather, embarked on his own adventure, while Jacob himself, after his first wife, Klara Schnabel, died, moved still farther west. He and his equally adventurous cousin "Columbus" Hieb eventually reached Lodi, in California's San Joaquin Valley, where Columbus went into business, providing German immigrant labor for that region's vineyards. No one seems to know exactly what Jacob's later occupation was, other than marrying women of means. Perhaps my grandparents knew more than they divulged; possibly, they were ashamed of his career after he left farming in Yankton and moved west. My grandfather George was a very religious and settled man, and a lifestyle of adventure and monied marriages might not have impressed him. Jacob returned to South Dakota as an old man and lived out the rest of his many days with George.

In May of 1884, George and his bride of a few months, Katharina Perman, traveled northwest from Yankton to McPherson County, South Dakota. There, on a small hill overlooking a lake, some miles from the site that would eventually become the town of Eureka, he pitched a tent and began his first homestead. Over the years, he homesteaded sixteen 160-acre claims, one for each of his sixteen children, including my father, John, his eldest son, who was born on that first farm.

After staking his claim, Grandfather's immediate concern had been to build a shelter before the fierce winter of the plains set in. Toward this end, like so many of the early pioneers who homesteaded the

8

Dakota prairies, he used the land itself to build this first crude home. He dug out a cellar and then used the sod to build up the sides, finishing off the structure with a roof that sloped almost to the ground at the rear. Remnants of this sod house, which eventually became a root and storage cellar, were still visible one hundred years later.

Those first few years were spent in backbreaking work. The sod was broken and prepared for farming with a plow and the aid of two oxen and a pair of horses. Times were difficult and cash was scarce. Needing a source of income until the crops could be harvested, Grandfather and Grandmother would gather buffalo bones, which still could be found in abundance on the prairie, and sell them for eight dollars a load.

Diligence, frugality, and almost unceasing labor gradually brought prosperity, and Grandfather built a house to replace the soddy. Finally, in 1920 he built one more house: a modern, four-bedroom one with running water and generator-powered electric lights, comforts still rare in farm homes at that time, and an indoor toilet, a practically unheard of luxury. Grandmother insisted on having one further luxury: two groves of trees.

The old house became the summer kitchen. As families increased in size and larger homes were needed, the smaller, outgrown houses were used in the summer months for extra kitchens, thus the term "summer kitchen." Here the produce from the garden—Grandmother's pride and joy—was canned or preserved for the coming winter, and the large, nourishing meals required during planting and harvesttime were prepared.

Eureka and many of the surrounding communities were settled for the most part by German immigrants like my grandfather. These hardworking farmers and tradesmen brought with them the traditional family values of the old country. Families were large and discipline was strict. Religion played a major role in community and family life, and the work ethic was instilled early. Frivolity and laziness were sins akin to such evils as card playing and public drunkenness. The greatest accolade the community could give one of its members was "hard worker." To be told "You are a hard worker" meant more than to be told "I love you."

I was born on my father's farm, six miles east of Eureka, on 15 January 1914. The fifth of thirteen children, three of whom died early (two, Robert and Elsie, at birth; one, Johnny, at the age of fifteen years), like my father was, I am the eldest son. Nine of us are still alive in 1987: my sisters Ella, Ann, Frances, Agnes, Florence, and Colleen; my brothers Harry and Max; and myself. Verna died 6 July 1982.

When I was a year old, Father sold his farm and moved us to Eureka, where he entered the farm implement business. Most of my early memories date from the time when our new home there was built. Our yard was beautifully landscaped, and as soon as I was old enough, one of my chores was caring for it. I spent many hours diligently mowing, trimming, and weeding, perpetually—it seemed—striving for perfection, until, at last, my efforts would meet Father's exacting demands. My mother, Eva Bauer, was as lavish with her praise as Father was reticent with his, and she would take time from her household chores to survey my handiwork and compliment me on the care I gave her vegetable garden and brightly colored flower beds.

In the summer, I worked for Grandfather, then the largest landowner in McPherson County, raking hay or driving the header box. We worked from sunup to sundown, and the work was hard, but hunger was certainly not part of the daily routine.

Starting with an early breakfast of hot cereal, eggs, bacon, ham, sausage, potatoes, homemade bread, jellies, jams, butter, milk, and coffee, there were large meals of some kind scheduled throughout the day. Nine o'clock in the morning called for a midmorning lunch. Noon brought a second lunch. Four o'clock in the afternoon brought lunch number three. At sundown the evening meal was served.

Many times I was too weary to eat my supper, for arduous as the day's work may have been, all the livestock had to be fed and bedded down before any of the family sat down to eat. Work was second nature to our sturdy family. I learned very early in my life that part of growing up includes learning to tackle a job, no matter how difficult or distasteful, and see it through to the end.

Life on the farm was not all work, however, and I enjoyed those summers. In the company of my happy-go-lucky young uncles who seemed to live such interesting lives, I felt quite a grown-up and like one of the boys. On Saturday evenings there was always an air of hardly suppressed excitement as I helped with the chores so that Bill, Emil, and Gust could get ready for their weekly night out, a doubly special occasion because Grandfather allowed them to use the Model T touring car, a rare possession in a time when horse-drawn vehicles provided the transportation for most people. They would rush through the work while Grandfather kept a watchful eye on them so they wouldn't cut corners, and I would do my utmost to help speed things along for them.

These Saturday night outings included another extra for the *buben* (German for boys), as they were called despite their young-adult status. Grandfather made large quantities of rhubarb, plum, and chokecherry wine, and he kept a good supply of this in the cellar in fifty-gallon barrels. He also kept a stick marked for measuring the barrels' contents. Having discovered this stick, my ever-resourceful uncle Bill would take some wine from each barrel, carefully changing the markings on the gauge in accordance with the new levels. To the best of my knowledge, Grandfather never found out that his buben were taking along his wine to liven up the barn dances.

Sunday morning on the farm called for early rising in order to get the necessary chores done before church—hangovers and lack of sleep notwithstanding. The remainder of the day was spent resting. No work was done that wasn't absolutely essential. Noisy children were frowned upon and sternly warned to be quiet and stay out of mischief, which was not easy for us considering how many we were when my brothers and sisters and children brought along by Sunday guests were added to those in my grandparents' large brood who were still at home, including my young aunts Katie, Emma, and Helen. Our community took seriously the admonition "on the seventh day, shalt thou rest." Working on Sunday was not only sinful; it was a sign of poor management—itself a sin. As far as possible, grandmother even prepared for the huge Sunday meals on Saturday. In town, the stores were locked tight; the churches were full.

The German Reformed Church, which my grandparents attended, was about five miles from the farm. Uncle Bill would run the Model T into the creek so the wooden spokes could swell and tighten on the tire rims, and then as many as nine of us would pile in for the ride to church. The car almost drove itself; the road consisted of two deep ruts, which exerted an effect similar to that of a railroad track. In the summer, there was no need for heat as we drove to and from church, but cars did not come equipped with heaters. In the winter, the cold could be numbing, and I remember my father used to heat a large stone to place on the backseat floor of his Buick in order to give his passengers a way to warm their feet.

My grandparents were extremely religious, and they were very strict in observing the church's tenets. Even with so many meals each day, my grandfather, still red of hair, but slightly stooped from his years of hard work, and always serious of eye and manner, never failed to read—always in German—from the family Bible before every one of these. I remember vividly one particular episode that illustrates the serious observance of religious teaching.

One day, a sudden downpour of rain turned the furrows into instant mud and field work became impossible: the horses were unable to pull the tiller. After working a while in the harness shed repairing tack, my uncles Bill, Emil, and Gust decided to take a real raincheck. They went back to the house with, as usual, me tagging along after them. Outside, the rain continued unabated. Inside, up in Bill's room, a lively—and forbidden—nickel-a-hand card game commenced. While I watched spellbound and Bill and Gust grew more and more aggravated, Emil hit a lucky streak and began to win every hand, crowing delightedly each time he raked in another pot. The proceedings grew boisterous, and we were so absorbed in them, we didn't notice Grandmother poised in the doorway. In a voice vibrant with mixed horror and anger, she announced, "Das ist einen Sünde! Der Teufel steht dahinter." (That's a sin! The devil is behind such a game.) That was the end of that rainy day's diversion.

Angry with her sons, who meanwhile beat a hasty retreat back to the safety of the harness shed, and perturbed mightily by the evil to which she felt my impressionable young mind had been exposed, Grandmother took me by the hand and led me out into the garden. The rain had stopped, and the sun was shining. All the lush, rain-brightened green plants sparkled with water droplets. I can still remember the concern for my welfare in Grandmother's eyes as we stood there surrounded by the scent of rain-fresh, garden-sweet air. Maintaining her firm grip on my hand, she explained earnestly how playing cards was a sinful activity, sinful even to watch, and enjoined me never again to involve myself with such a game. (I am afraid her warning came too late. The seed already had been sown and poker was to become my game!)

Later, Grandmother found one card inadvertently dropped by Bill as he fled her wrath. She picked it up gingerly by one corner, held it away from herself as if it were contaminated, and consigned it to the flames in the large black kitchen stove. To me, young and impressionable as I was, it seemed that she was sending that card back to the devil. Grandmother, who was quite heavy set in build, had a very kind and loving nature; she saw only people's good points. But der Teufel and the Sünde he encouraged were other matters.

When I started school, I spoke very little English. Eureka was almost 100 percent German and German was the language of choice. It was spoken in the homes, in churches, at work, and on the streets. Luckily, my first grade teacher, Miss Gerdes, was able to help me through my transition to bilingualism. Most of the young people I knew were bilingual and interchanged German and English words, often without realizing they were mixing the two languages. To this day, our family gatherings are spiced with a sprinkling of the German expressions each of us has carried from childhood, and when we are all together these familiar phrases bring back memories of long ago days and far away homes.

Among other things, growing up in my hometown meant looking forward to Christmas, the Fourth of July, and the county fair. With reasonable luck, a circus would come to town once a year. Like most young people, I was fascinated with the circus; it exuded excitement in the form of promised adventure. I used to dream of the day when I could leave home to travel—not necessarily with the circus and quite in spite of father's disapproval of any such plans. My early wanderlust began to reassert itself, and I became an ardent fan of Horatio Alger. I read most of his books, avidly devouring them word by word. I also spent many hours daydreaming, sometimes when I would have been

13

better occupied paying attention in class. When I wasn't preoccupied with thoughts of adventure in exotic places, I did devote time to history and geography, then, as now, my favorite subjects. And when these topics were not uppermost in my mind, I was afflicted with a tendency to fall in—and out—of love, especially with my teachers, who I like to think were ever unsuspecting.

Although in April and May my friends and I looked forward with longing to the time when we would be free from school and could enjoy the summer, sometimes small-town living could be too placid for restless boys by the time August rolled around. The tedium of the long, hot summer days occasionally led to pranks that had unexpected results.

One day when I was eleven years old, a fifteen-year-old neighborhood boy, Kelly Quast, caught me meandering down the sidewalk next to the city park, about a block from home. Having nothing pressing to do at the moment, he amused himself by tying me to a tree in the park. I did quite a bit of kicking and indignant yelling, but to no avail. I suppose the neighbors thought we were playing, though from the blood-curdling howls I was producing, our play could have been nothing less than a reenactment of Custer's Last Stand. When the rescue party showed up, unfortunately it wasn't the cavalry. It was Father, furious at having his lunch interrupted. After administering his usual antidote, an on-the-spot spanking, he added insult to injury by asking me how I could have been so stupid as to let another kid tie me to a tree.

Smarting from the spanking, wounded in pride, and with revenge lurking in my soul, I awaited my opportunity. Find and attack the enemy's weak spot is the first rule of war. I knew Kelly's weakness. Kelly loved to bet. In fact, Kelly couldn't resist betting and would bet on absolutely anything—this was definitely his weak spot. I plotted my revenge and enlisted my friend Maynard Schamber's help. We placed a Cracker Jack box containing a small brick on the sidewalk near the scene of my humiliation. With our trap set, we waited gleefully for the enemy. After a while, like a hog on ice, Kelly came sauntering along the walk with a jaunty air and filled with the glory of all his fifteen years—to find Maynard and me in the midst of an earnest discussion concerning which of us could kick the Cracker Jack box farther. Graciously including him in our debate, we bet Kelly a dime we could kick that box farther than he could. With unprecedented generosity we even allowed him first kick. Predictably, he found the bet irresistible.

As he took his thirty-foot running start, Kelly must have been spending that ten cents already. He was wearing tennis shoes, a detail we had not included in our plot. Together, the running start, the brick, and those shoes produced more than the desired effect. While Kelly was occupied clutching his foot and hopping around on one leg, the time seemed perfect for an evacuation of the area. Maynard and I were not seen downtown again for some days. In later years, Kelly admitted my friend and I had had a large hand in curing him of his betting habit.

At eleven, I also joined the business world and was proudly self-employed shining shoes in the local barbershop on Friday and Saturday evenings. The economy was good at that time, and tips were generous. For two nights' work, I earned as much as ten dollars, which I gave to Father. He allowed me to keep a quarter; the rest was put in a savings account opened for me at the bank.

During the winter months, I put out trap lines a few blocks from our home along the frozen shoreline of Lake Eureka. To set the traps, I chipped through the thick ice and placed them inside the mounds where the muskrats lived. Trapping muskrats meant either getting up by six in the morning to check the traps before school began, or seeing my efforts wasted; to free itself from a trap, a muskrat will chew off a leg and escape.

On weekends I trapped for skunk, mink, and weasel. After skinning my catch, I hung the pelts in our garage to dry. One day not long after I had gone into the trapping business, a neighbor, Mr. H. I. Bauer, dropped in to visit me. At some point in our conversation, Mr. Bauer asked me casually if I had any skunk pelts for sale. Using my best salesmanship, I eagerly showed him my whole line of muskrat, weasel, and skunk. Expressing interest only in the skunk pelts, he agreed to buy them all. I was so delighted, it was not until some time later that I made the connection between his sudden interest in skunk pelts and the fact that he lived downwind from our garage. Since then, I have reflected with gratitude on Mr. Bauer's investment in those pelts, which I suspect he quickly buried in his backyard, and particularly on his kindness in not discouraging my venture into the free enterprise system.

Ever alert for a chance to make money, I involved myself in another business at about this same time. As an incentive to rid the area of gophers because these pesky animals caused considerable damage to crops and pastures, the McPherson County Treasurer paid a bounty of two cents for each gopher tail received. My sister Ann and I joined forces in a gopher elimination enterprise more memorable for its competitiveness than for its humaneness. One of the methods we used in this venture was drowning. We would fill our buckets at the freshwater spring on Uncle Emil Mehlhaff's farm and carry them to the pasture next to his wheat fields. Chasing the frantic gophers as they scurried in and out of the holes riddling that pasture was hot, sweaty work punctuated by shouts of "That one's mine! I saw him first!"

One day as we jostled each other and ran after the same gopher, with water sloshing out of our buckets and warfare dominating our spirits, Ann gave me a shove. I tripped, spilled what was left of my water, landed on the empty bucket, and knocked out a front tooth. Dripping blood down the front of my shirt, I made the trip back home, where I sat dejectedly on the back porch steps, gopherless and toothless, waiting for Father to come home from work. When he did, to my great surprise Ann got the spanking instead of me. What I did get, from Mr. Bauer's son Ted, was the nickname "Toothless," and that sobriquet was mine until I left home several years later. Father eventually gave me the money to have the tooth replaced some years after it was knocked out—and Ann and I have since made up!

Trouble seemed to locate me without difficulty, and often in the most unlikely places, even though Father was an expert at finding chores to keep me busy and out of mischief. One warm summer morning, he decided it was time to clean out the cistern. Because the water in our region was of poor quality, quite a few families, including ours, had deep cement reservoirs called cisterns. Runoff from the roofs was funneled from the eaves into these, and the water was used as an alternative to the iron-laden, rusty red liquid that came from the town waterpipe. Often the cisterns also were used to keep perishable foods cool at a time when it was not uncommon for a household to be without an icebox or refrigerator. The items to be kept cool usually were placed in a wooden or metal bucket, which was lowered a few inches into the water.

Grumbling about my latest unsavory assignment, which this time was to crawl down into the cistern, scoop out the six or so inches of water left in it, and scrub the filter, I reluctantly hauled the ladder out of the garage, and, as reluctantly, descended into the gradually darkening dankness. After numerous trips up and down to empty the bucket, and after lowering the water level by about three inches, my diligence reaped an unexpected reward.

Father was in the habit of keeping a few bottles of his homebrew beer inside a gunnysack immersed in the water and tied to the side of the cistern. After repeated use, these sacks would rot through and have to be replaced. In the dim light that came from the small circle of blue sky above me, I noticed the sheen of smooth, brown, beer bottles resting unbroken and inviting in the gently lapping water on the cistern's floor. Glistening and cool, they were impossible to resist after my Sisyphus-like exertion. I shinned up the ladder with renewed energy to find an opener and soon was back down sampling my find.

The ensuing singing and joviality echoed up from the cistern, which amplified my bell tones—and brought Mother to investigate. An analysis of the situation was quickly accomplished. Firmly telling me to stay put and not attempt climbing the ladder, she sped off to return shortly with Father, who came down after me fuming with anger. He hauled me out, and when he had finished applying the usual deterrent—neither sparing the rod nor spoiling the child—and in addition dosing me with castor oil and a lecture, I was sober.

Another time, Father sent me and his partner's son Harold out to hoe a potato patch at the edge of town. He let us use the company car, a Model T Ford coupe. Instead of going directly to the potato patch as instructed, on the way I drove out to Uncle Emil's farm. On the drive back from there to the potato patch, I thought I heard a car in back of us. The road was narrow and when I turned around to look, our car started for the ditch. Harold screamed; I jerked the steering wheel and flipped the car over on its side. Luckily, the only damage was a bent

17

fender and a broken door window, and a farmer and his son came along with a wagon and a team of horses and helped us right the car. We drove it back to the implement shop, where I told Dad the wheels locked; although I had no idea what that meant, I'd heard this terminology some place and thought it sounded good. Dad bought my story, and I didn't get a whipping. I never again wrecked a car.

When I was thirteen, Father decided it would be good for me to learn to play a musical instrument. I asked the school's music teacher, Mr. Liefeld, what instrument he thought would be easiest for me to play. He suggested the French horn. By chance, just such a horn had been lying in a dust-covered case on a back shelf in Father's store, left there by the business's former owner. I had no problem convincing Father this was the ideal instrument for me, and I practiced with great enthusiasm in the early mornings, until the neighbors began to complain.

I was busier than ever now, and my days were filled with jobs I found for myself and ones Father found for me. I had a paper route; shined shoes; trapped, and shoveled snow in the winter; did yard work, and worked on Grandfather's farm in the summer. Now that I also played in the city band, I had to allow room in my schedule for the band concerts in the park, at the county fairs, and on the Fourth of July, and for the out-of-town trips we took to such places as Leola, South Dakota, where we played at the dedication ceremony for the new courthouse—a real high point in my life at that time. These travel experiences served to fan my smouldering wanderlust, something I am certain Father hadn't foreseen when he encouraged my musical career.

All that work left virtually no time for organized sports, but I especially liked ice skating and always looked forward to the winters when, free from chores and school, I could skim across Lake Eureka's frozen surface on Sunday afternoons.

When I was fourteen, a job soda-jerking at the local luncheonette woke my inherent passion for sales and public relations work, two inbuilt skills I have enjoyed using ever since.

My fifteenth year brought a job in a service station, and for the munificent sum of twenty dollars a month, I worked during my lunch hour, after school, in the evenings, and on weekends. When the manager of this station, Matt Mutschler, married my sister Ella, I talked

him into letting me move in with them, and the feeling of independence I gained was worth every penny of the five dollars in wages I
lost. By adding car washing and polishing to my other duties, I managed to survive nicely. The old "highway" through Eureka, a graded
dirt road wide enough for only one car at a time, by then had been replaced with a two-lane gravel highway. This amenity and the general
availability—and affordability—of the Ford Model A meant there were
plenty of cars needing my ministrations.

That year also brought a vacation shared with three friends, Irving
Pietz, Henry Ehrmann, and Elnathan Juedes. Supposedly, we were going to Big Stone Lake, South Dakota, at the Minnesota border, and
Irving Pietz, who was sixteen or seventeen years old, borrowed his father's company truck—with John J. Pietz Hardware Company boldly
advertised on both sides—for our transportation. When we got to Big
Stone Lake, Elnathan, who was a local minister's son, said, "Let's go
to Minneapolis!"

Minneapolis was only two hundred miles farther, but to us this
seemed a great distance, and to me, a great adventure because I had
never been there. We went.

On our way back, just as we recrossed the border into South Dakota, we ran out of money. This posed quite a problem since we had to
feed the truck with gas even if we went without food ourselves. Because of my experience working in Matt's filling station, however, I
knew how we could get this commodity free of charge.

In those days, gas pumps actually were hand-operated pumps. At
night they were drained, but a small amount of gas always remained in
the hoses. Sometimes, because people trusted each other then, the
pumps were even left unlocked. We traveled back to Eureka driving at
night and helping ourselves from pump to pump along the way.

Even in the summer of my fifteenth year trouble still found me—
and sometimes with a little help from my own stubborn nature. One
hot Saturday evening I was walking to work at the filling station with
some of my friends, who were keeping me company on my way. We
happened upon a noisy group of young men who had been drinking
and were by this time getting out of hand and attracting considerable
attention.

19

The mayor and the marshall came along just as we did and told the older fellows to go home. The mayor's eyes also lit on me, and he told me to go home, too. With some sense of indignation, I protested that I was only on my way to work and had had nothing to drink. Unfortunately, the mayor thought otherwise. My protest seemed to him to bear out his assessment, and he said he thought I was drunk and, as mayor, he was sending me to jail. Even when all the others came to my defense, he insisted that my destination was not Matt's filling station but jail.

Now really fired by outrage, I said that was fine; but, since I had plenty of witnesses, I wanted a proper trial. The marshall was quite reluctant to lock me up at this point. Nonetheless, I went to jail.

When Dad showed up later, and I swore I had not been drinking, he asked the marshall why I was there. When that worthy explained that the mayor had insisted and added that, at Dad's insistence, he would let me go, I remained adamant: I was going to stay in jail, I said, until my trial. I also said I hadn't had my supper yet and it was up to the city to feed me. The only way I would leave my cell would be if the mayor came down, admitted he had made a mistake, and released me himself.

Well, I got my Saturday's supper, and my Sunday breakfast—as well as what seemed like hundreds of visitors, who all told me to stick to my guns. At last, about ten o'clock on Sunday morning, the mayor arrived. After telling me he had investigated and found I was telling the truth, he said the best thing was to forget the whole affair, and he released me.

As time went on and I matured, I acquired a taste for nice things, particularly for good clothes. I began to dream of a future in which, as a successful businessman, I would drive a luxury car, live in a lovely home, and possess all the accoutrements of financial success. The idea of going into business for myself also appealed to my well-developed sense of independence; the possibility of a military career had not occurred to me yet.

Dreams are one thing. Reality is another. The depression was deepening, and by the early 1930s it was hurting everyone, including my father. A government program for young men, the Citizens Military Training Camp (CMTC), paid thirty dollars for completion of a one-month training course, and I decided to enroll. My brother-in-law Matt agreed to let me take a one-month leave from my service station job. He thought I probably would be so homesick after two or three weeks that I would come home again. Privately, I had other plans. I wanted to see other places and be on my own, anywhere there was a chance to get ahead. I didn't intend to return.

With my friends Maynard, Elnathan, and Henry, I left for the CMTC at Fort Snelling, Minnesota. After the month's training, Maynard went on to Denver; Elnathan and Henry returned home. I headed for the West Coast.

CHAPTER 2

The Runaway

I was ready to test my independence. I had thirty dollars in my pocket, a suitcase full of clothes, plenty of optimism, and two ways to travel: hitchhike or ride the freights. I chose to hitchhike, and my first attempt took me from Minneapolis to Des Moines, Iowa, where Father, and I, had some cousins, John and Herbert Hieb, who were doing well there selling radios. On a visit to their office, I found Herbert pacing back and forth, dictating a letter to his secretary. Duly impressed, I filed the busy-executive image in the back of my mind for future reference.

My unexpected arrival in Des Moines had its drawbacks. After I had been there a few days, my cousins began asking if I had enough money to return home, and if I planned to finish my last two years of high school. Uneasy about dodging all the questions—and worried that they might let Father know where I was—I said I thought it was probably about time for me to head home. I mentioned that I was running a little low on cash because the bus fare had cost more than I had anticipated. The next morning on his way to work, John dropped me off at the bus depot, handed me an envelope that contained five dollars, and said good-bye. Armed with confidence in my hitchhiking ability, I put the five dollars in my pocket; two days later I was in Tulsa, Oklahoma.

In the days and months to come, I had no problem finding rides or jobs. I managed to find rooms at night for about a dollar, and sometimes I washed dishes in return for a meal. I was sixteen, but looked fourteen. I undoubtedly benefited from a combination of luck and the fact that people felt sorry for me. If anyone asked me about myself, most often I said I was an orphan; invariably, everyone was kind. I hope the Lord has forgiven me for some of the lies I told to get both work and transportation. I always tried to give full value in return for any help I received, and I have remembered with gratitude all the kind people who helped me during my youthful travels.

In Tulsa, I met a young boy from Seattle, Dale Johnson, who had been on the East Coast. He had been riding the rails, or traveling by freight car in unauthorized fashion, and was now on his way home. We decided to team up. We worked for our meals while hitchhiking, and sometimes the drivers would buy us coffee and sandwiches. In New Mexico, we found a ride to Los Angeles with a Mr. Jack Shepherd, who agreed to take us along if we would help with the driving. We jumped at the chance.

Lunch on the road during that trip sometimes meant a sandwich made with two-day-old bread. At night, we would check the restaurants looking for any kind of a job in exchange for a hot meal. Usually we were successful, but there were times when we postponed a meal or two. We slept in Mr. Shepherd's car. Hitchhiking was not the way to travel if a hot bath at the end of the day was of major importance. Occasionally, Mr. Shepherd would let us use the shower in his room, or he would stop by a lake or river and wait for us to clean up, clothes and all.

It took us seven days to reach Los Angeles. I was headed for Lodi, California, where several of my father's brothers lived, including my uncle Gust, who had left the farm back in Eureka to try his luck in California, and my uncle George, who was the assistant manager of the Stockton Box Company. I was hoping Uncle George could help me get a job. Dale was planning to go with me as far as Fresno, where he had relatives he could stay with while he looked for a job.

We reached Fresno around the first of September, and I stayed with Dale's relatives for a few days before continuing north. They helped me launder my clothes and found me a ride to Lodi. Dale and I agreed to keep in touch. We made good traveling companions, and we thought we might be on the road again, depending on how things worked out for each of us. I didn't know how welcome I would be in Lodi, and since I had no intention of going home, it seemed a good idea to have an alternate plan in mind.

The first thing Uncle George asked was, "Do your mother and father know where you are?" Under the circumstances, it seemed best to tell him the truth; otherwise, I was sure he would write and tell them I was there. When he suggested I return to Eureka to finish my last two years of high school, I appealed to Gust to tell him how little chance there was for a young man to make something of himself during the depression in a small town like Eureka. Since Gust himself had left for similar reasons, my choice of an advocate was a good one. He must have been persuasive, because George finally agreed to let me stay and promised to help me find a job. Actually, except for my age and high-school-dropout status, my arrival in Lodi was well within the parameters of a family tradition that began when my great-grandfather Jacob went there with Columbus Hieb. George had followed, right after the end of World War I, and Gust, in the late 1920s.

Unfortunately, I wore out my welcome a little sooner than even I had anticipated. Gust owned a Harley-Davidson motorcycle, and he was very proud of it. I was enthralled with the machine and, after much coaxing, I talked him into letting me learn how to ride it; however, I was under strict orders *never* to touch it unless he was there. At sixteen that was a tough edict to follow. One afternoon, George's wife, my aunt Almira, asked me to run an errand for her. I reasoned that the fastest way to get it done would be on the motorcycle. Cocksure, enjoying the throb of the motor and the image of myself in control of all that noise and power, I was fine until I rounded a corner covered with loose gravel. The cocky image disappeared in a cloud of dirt; the motorcycle went one way, and I went another, digging up more dirt. When the cloud cleared, I had three broken toes and a sprained ankle; Gust was furious. It must have been about this time that George wrote to Father, told him I was there, and asked him to send train fare to get me back home.

I limped around for a few days, thinking the situation over and working up enough nerve to ask Gust if he would lend me ten dollars to get to Los Angeles. He had cooled off a bit and probably figured that lending me ten dollars was cheaper than another repair bill on the motorcycle. A few days later, I hopped a freight out of Lodi and got off at Fresno to look up Dale, who was still staying with his relatives, working for room and board and a few dollars of spending money. He

24

thought his welcome also had worn a bit thin, and he was ready to leave. This time, we decided to avoid staying with relatives. They put too much damper on our sense of freedom, and there were just too many pitfalls.

We caught a freight to Los Angeles, where we found a room on Main Street for two dollars a week. Fifteen cents bought a meal, and another nickel bought a piece of pie and a second cup of coffee. I found a job assembling bicycles, while Dale got one washing dishes, and we tried to save as much of our pay as we possibly could. The jobs didn't last long. After talking it over, we decided to try Texas.

We hopped a freight with that destination in mind, only to be rounded up by the railroad cops—or "bulls," as they were called— along with quite a few other fellows who were riding the rails. The bulls shook us down. Luckily, they didn't find our thirty-dollar bank-roll, but they did send us off to work for the state. After being issued clothing and boots against the December cold, we were transported to the San Bernadino mountains and put to work cutting fire trails with a medax, a tool that looked like a small pick. We were paid twenty-five cents a day and room and board. The food was great, and I would have liked to stay, but the State of California would let us work for sixty days only, just long enough to earn the bus fare to Yuma, Arizona, and a few extra dollars for pocket money. We had told the bulls we were orphans and needed work. Although they didn't believe us, they did seem to be sympathetic—perhaps they understood youthful wander-lust—but nonetheless, they advised us to go straight home. This was not advice we felt like taking.

After we were paid, we took the bus to Yuma, where we arranged to ship our suitcases to the El Paso, Texas, YMCA. This time Dale and I hit the road, not the rails, and we hitchhiked.

The weather in El Paso was nice, especially after our recent so-journ in the mountains, but that was about all that was nice. Because we were competing in the job market with Mexican labor, work was hard to find. Our living conditions were not good, either. Although the rooms we found usually had gas burners and we saved money by cook-ing our own meals, these accommodations were on Skid Row, not the most savory location even compared to boxcars and work camps. We bought our food at the farmer's market, and Dale did most of the cooking, although if necessity forced me, I was able to fry bacon, eggs, and potatoes, and slap together a cold sandwich.

It was during this time that I made my first journey outside the United States—to Juarez, Mexico. As unremarkable as this excursion was, it did serve to whet my appetite for foreign travel. Also about this time, Dale confided to me the information that he was a deserter from the navy. I asked him many questions about this, and from his answers I surmised that he had trouble adjusting to a regimented life. I decided such a life would not bother me, but since enlistees had to be eighteen years old and have parental consent and I had only just turned seventeen, whether or not I would find regimentation a problem was not of any immediate importance. That Dale was beginning to feel the strain of his deserter's status did seem important, however, and soon my life was to be affected by this fact.

We stayed in El Paso only one week. Again sending our suitcases ahead, we left for Houston, this time riding a freight. Traveling that way was pleasant enough during the daylight hours. Usually we would find something to read in the boxcars, or we would sit in the open sliding doorways and watch the scenery as we rolled by. We were fairly comfortable during the chilly nights, especially when we were lucky enough to find a boxcar that previously had held grain. Extra-heavy wrapping paper was used on the floors and walls of such cars to keep the grain from leaking through the cracks. This paper usually was left inside after the grain was unloaded. Folded and used as a bed and blanket, it provided excellent insulation against the cold.

Riding the freights provided a unique education. We discovered the old-time tramps, or railroad bums, didn't like the competition from young kids like us. They called us "sight-seeing bums." I imagine they felt they were professionals and we were just green kids horning in on what they considered their exclusive territory. They didn't really bother us, however; we kids usually outnumbered them, and we were a lot younger and stronger. Most of those tramps had never done a day's work in their lives, except for the times when they were caught by the railroad bulls and given a month of hard labor, which they hated with a passion.

26

After arriving in Houston, we picked up our luggage at the YMCA, bathed, cleaned up our clothes, and set out to find a cheap apartment. We rented a one-bedroom with a gas burner and a sofa for five dollars a week. This was luxurious compared to some of the other places we had lived; and it wasn't on Skid Row.

I was delighted with our latest arrangements, but Dale had been worrying about his unresolved situation with the navy, and after discussing it some more, he decided to turn himself in. I was sorry to see him go, but I felt he probably was doing the right thing. He figured with any luck, he would only get about six months in the brig and then he would be restored to active duty. He said good-bye, and we lost touch. I hope he was able to resume his career, and that life treated him well.

After Dale left, I set about finding a job in earnest. I didn't know this yet, but my life was about to improve considerably. Looking for work in the Sam Houston Park area one day, I happened to pass a nice house with hedges that needed trimming. I rang the bell and waited. A lovely gray-haired lady came to the door, and after introducing myself, I said I was looking for work and could trim hedges or do any other work that she needed done. The lady, Mrs. McDermitt, invited me in and began asking me questions. She wanted to know my age, where I was from, whether I had finished high school, and whether I had been brought up in a Christian home. I answered all her questions, filling in the gaps with fictitious details I had been perfecting over several months of practice. I told her, truthfully, that I had been baptized and confirmed in the German Reformed Church, but, untruthfully, that I had been orphaned at sixteen and placed with relatives. I embellished my story further, telling her how poor my relatives were, how many other children there were to care for, and how I had been left to shift for myself. To this day, I am still ashamed of the story I told. She was very concerned about my welfare, and she treated me with great kindness even though I was a stranger. Finally, she suggested we kneel and pray for guidance, which we did; but I left right after the prayer, feeling more than a little guilty and unsure whether I would come back as requested the following day.

The next day I was still very reluctant to return, but I did. Mrs. McDermitt had taken such a kind interest in me, and I felt bad enough about lying to her without adding ingratitude to my already overloaded conscience. Fidgeting at the door after I rang the bell, I was considering bolting down the street when the door opened, and a smiling Mrs. McDermitt invited me in. Once inside, I followed her into the front room, where she suggested we kneel and pray because she had good news for me. So we knelt, and she thanked the Lord for answering her prayer on my behalf. She had called some friends of hers, the Marshalls, who had a five-year-old son, Hugh, for whom I was to babysit. I was to take care of the Marshalls's yard and do some chauffeuring too, if I knew how to drive. I was happy to tell her I qualified in all respects and would do my best to justify her faith in me.

For the next three days I stayed with the McDermitts, during which time I did their yardwork. It was the best job I had ever done. When I finished, the yard looked manicured. Her husband said it was perfect, and even I thought it would have passed Father's inspection. That early training had certainly come in handy, and I was happy to have some way of showing my gratitude for what this couple had done for me. I washed their two cars and polished Mr. McDermitt's shoes. Mrs. McDermitt was going to pay me, but I refused because she had washed and ironed my clothes.

Dressed in my freshly laundered clothes, I was taken to meet the Marshalls. Considering how hard the times were, this was to be a wonderful opportunity, and I made the most of it. They entertained often since Mr. Marshall was an executive with the Home Ice Company, and sometimes when I chauffeured their guests home, I received two or three dollars in tips. And I was paid two dollars a day and room and board! My bankroll was growing.

After I had been there several months, Mr. Marshall offered to set me up in business. He said if I stayed another year, he would give me an ice route and a truck. I was grateful for the offer and for his confidence in me, but I wasn't ready to settle down to a career just yet.

Not long after this conversation, I began thinking about going home. I had been gone for over a year, hadn't written, and was homesick. Finally, I asked Mr. Marshall if I could have a month's vacation in order to go home and visit relatives. He said, "You mean your parents?" I confessed everything and he understood, but he said I should have written my parents. I wrote that same day.

I had saved three hundred dollars, which I sent ahead by money order. I said my good-byes to Mrs. Marshall and Hugh, and went with Mr. Marshall to the bus depot. As soon as he left me, I headed for the railroad yards and caught a freight going north. When the bulls asked where I was headed, I told them to the Dakotas for the harvest season. They said, "Okay, keep going, and good luck. There are too many people here now that need help, and we can't care for them all."

I got off the boxcar in Aberdeen, South Dakota. The trip had taken about ten days. I had one dollar and a pretty good coat of dirt. The first place I headed for was the post office to pick up my money order at the general delivery window. It took the clerk forever, and I was beginning to worry that my hard-earned money was lost when he finally came up with it.

My next stop was the YMCA, where I spent quite a bit of time scrubbing off my coat of dust and dirt. Then I cashed my check, headed for the local Chinese restaurant, and treated myself to a chicken chow mein dinner, a favorite to this day. I remember that one with particular relish. That night, I called home and told my mother I was all right. I discovered I had a new sister, Colleen, born after I had left home. Father promised he would come to collect me the next day.

When Father showed up, I was sitting in the lobby, dressed in the new clothes the Marshalls had bought me. He walked right by, then came back and looked again. He was more than a little surprised to see me looking so prosperous. On the way home, he asked where I had been and how I had gotten the money to buy the nice clothes. When I told him I was making sixty dollars a month plus room and board and had saved about three hundred dollars, he was so surprised I thought he would wreck the car.

Although I had run away, I was welcomed back without anger, somewhat like a post-biblical prodigal son. For one thing, my father had mellowed a little; for another, my mother, as always, exerted a forebearing influence.

In later years, Dad and I established a much better relationship.

He was proud of my many accomplishments, and the old wounds of our early warfare healed. In fact—and I still chuckle over this—he began to take credit for my successes, saying, "You see what happens when you're disciplined!"

Mother was openly proud of my resourcefulness, and she was interested in the judiciously edited stories I told her of my adventures. I was still restless and unsettled, but I decided that rather than return to Houston and the Marshalls, I would go back to high school. Matt took me back at the service station, and I moved in again with him and Ella and their daughter Barbara, who had been born while I was away, like my new little sister Colleen. (I now had a niece and a sister the same age, just as I had an aunt and a sister born in the same year! With such large families, this was not unusual.) Life settled down to a routine for a while, but I was still pondering the future and dreaming of a new life.

CHAPTER 3

United States Army: First Enlistment

In the spring of 1933, two friends of mine, Edgar Oster and Alfred Junker, who were home on leave from the army, interested me in the military service as a career. I liked the sound of the structured lifestyle, and I figured if I joined, I could retire at the age of forty-eight with a pension for the rest of my life. But, I needed my father's consent.

He said no. I said, in that case I was going to drop out of school and leave town again. Ever the peacemaker, Mother interceded, and Father consented to take me to Aberdeen for the necessary tests.

I tried for the navy first, remembering the stories about a seaman's life that my friend Dale had told me during our hitchhiking days. I passed all the tests except one; the recruiter discovered I was colorblind, and he turned me down.

In order to test for this condition, the navy used a sheet consisting of a series of circles painted in various colors. Some of these circles contained numbers outlined in other colors. Even when the numbers were pointed out and traced for me, I was unable to see them. The recruiter told me I had the worst case of color blindness he had ever seen, especially for red and green. Then he suggested I try the army and told me—on the Q.T.—by using my head, I might be able to pass that test because it consisted of identifying colored tassels. My color blindness was a surprising discovery for me. Frankly, I never had noticed colors. If something was green, to me it looked red, but all I really paid attention to was that things looked *nice*!

Unwilling to give up, I decided to take the navy recruiter's advice, and I went to Fort Lincoln, at Bismarck, North Dakota, to take the army exams. When I got to the test for color blindness, if a tassel looked red to me, I said it was green, and vice versa. I passed with flying colors.

The next hurdle was my weight. At the time I was trying to enlist, the entire armed forces consisted of about 160,000 men, and no new recruits were being taken. However, the battalion at Fort Lincoln was in the process of organizing a band, and I was accepted because they needed someone who could play the French horn. I was in—if I could gain the three pounds I needed to meet the 120-pound-minimum weight requirement. There was no weight limit at the other end of the scale. Presumably, the army thought any excess poundage very quickly would be worked off. The band director made arrangements for me to stay at the post while I gained the weight, and I tried the mess sergeant's suggested method: stuffing myself with bananas. Major Duckworth, the medical officer who weighed me every day, must have been getting tired of this because one morning, as I was getting ready to step on the scale, he said, "*Jump* on it!" Surprised, I did. "Well, how about that!" He laughed. "You made it."

I was sworn in on 2 May 1933, assigned to K Company, an infantry company, and put on special duty with the battalion band.

Fort Lincoln was a battalion post at that time. The 3d Battalion of the 4th Infantry consisted of three rifle companies, I, K, and L, and one machine-gun-and-heavy-weapons company, M. The heavier weapons were mounted on two-wheel carts pulled by mules. In the thirties, the most powerful shoulder weapon we had in the rifle company was the BAR. Tradition decreed that on a hike, the smallest man in the company carried this. "Here," someone would say, "let's make a man of you!" So, on all the hikes, while my French horn rode comfortably in a wagon, I trudged along carrying a sixteen-pound automatic weapon, with a thirty-pound full pack on my back, which trial and error taught me how to roll so it didn't bang me in the buttocks with every step.

My first army clothing was the old World War I uniform, which had to have been the most uncomfortable uniform the U.S. Army ever issued. It boasted wraparound leggings. If a soldier did a really good-looking job of wrapping, the end result effectively cut off the circulation in his legs and feet; hardly, I often thought when wrapping them, what the top brass had intended for the nation's standing army.

At the time of my enlistment, K Company consisted of sixty enlisted men and one officer. I was the one and only recruit during my basic training, which was given me by a feisty little sergeant of Italian descent. At best, Sergeant Zaperdino's English was difficult to understand; usually, it was impossible. Since I was the only recruit, I had his undivided attention. I was stumbled, pushed, and booted, all of which the army allowed at that time. I thanked my lucky stars for the bit of training I had received during the month I spent at Fort Snelling, Minnesota, in the CMTC. Eventually, after learning to understand the sergeant's orders and deciding to dig in and get through, I passed basic training with a respectable showing.

Today, complicated drills are used only for show, but in those days, the army still had the old eight-man squad; we drilled four in the front, four in the rear; squads right, squads left; left front into line; forward march, left flank march, by the right flank march, to the rear march; eyes right, eyes left, eyes front. This was beautiful to watch, and to perform it a soldier had to be on his toes at all times, with his ears open.

When I first enlisted, a private's pay was twenty-one dollars a month. Once toilet articles and laundry were paid for, a soldier was lucky to walk away from the pay table with ten dollars. We also had five dollars' worth of canteen checks and a two-dollar book of movie tickets deducted from our twenty-one dollars!

Servicemen were not allowed to vote in national elections, and we were forbidden to discuss politics around the barracks, especially during an election. Writing your congressman to complain about the service could result in being given a Section 8, or undesirable, discharge.

Soon after my enlistment, Franklin D. Roosevelt, who had been elected president that same year, approved the organization of the Civilian Conservation Corps. The young men who joined, my brother Harry among them, were to receive $30.00 a month, which was quite good pay. However, to meet the necessary appropriation for the CCC payroll, and for some other programs, an across-the-board cut in wages of 15 percent was initiated for all servicemen and government employees. My pay went from $21.00 to $17.85 a month, and with it went my estimation of the dependability of the government's promises to its servicemen.

The "bank holiday" occurred at this time. Banks everywhere were closed, including the one in Eureka. Everyone was hit hard. My grandfather George, who had retired and moved to town, lost all his savings, a considerable amount; he never recovered any of it. The depression grew more serious, and I decided to stay in the service despite my disillusion over the wage cut. There was no work on the outside, and the army provided a place to sleep, food, clothing, and medical care. I was in for the duration, and since that was the case, I was determined to finish my high school education and do my best to get ahead in the service. As I watched the economy go from bad to worse, it seemed wise to make the best of my situation.

Not only did the pay cut rankle; I discovered there were ramifications to the second-class-citizen status associated with being in military service at this time. Going to town in uniform wasn't very wise, and although the post contributed to the economy of the Bismarck area, there were places where it was stated in no uncertain terms that soldiers were not welcome—in particular some of the taverns, where prominently displayed signs read Dogs and Soldiers Not Allowed.

On an excursion into town one evening, two friends of mine wandered into a tavern for a beer before calling it a night. The bartender pointed to his sign and asked one of them, Harry Hellwig, if he could read. Harry could do more than read; he had gone to the Olympic finals as a welterweight. He mentioned rather laconically that the sign should read Little Soldiers and Dogs Not Allowed; so, it really didn't apply to him. With that, the bartender came across the bar and the fight was on. Harry and his buddy were more than a match for the bartender and the several customers who came into the beer garden to join the melee, and when they brushed themselves off to return to the post, the bar was a shambles. Harry thought it had been a pretty fine evening's entertainment and a good workout to boot.

Early the next morning, the police arrived at the post ready to make arrests. Harry was called into company headquarters. When he told the company and post commanders about the signs, the post commander told the police there would be no arrests. Then he called the mayor and the chief of police and said if the signs in bars were not taken down, he would put the city under martial law. The community at large was aware of the value of our payroll, and purchases, in aiding the sagging local economy. The bluff worked, and after this incident relations improved.

Weekly company inspections were held on Saturday mornings. Friday afternoons about four o'clock, we would begin to police the barracks, scrubbing and polishing the floors, cleaning and dusting our wall- and footlockers, and sometimes cleaning and scrubbing the sergeants' rooms if they wanted that done. Because of their rank, sergeants were privileged and had individual rooms. Many of them were married and lived off post. My incentive to make sergeant was increased by the fact that a buck sergeant's base pay was fifty-six dollars a month, plus a longevity bonus, rations, and a quarters allowance, all adding up to pretty good money for those times.

My own biggest inspection problem was with my hair. I would tell the post barber just to trim it; but the company commander wanted to see skin on the sides and back of my head, and he got what he wanted.

Weather permitting, battalion inspection was held once a month. These inspections always were held on a Saturday, which meant that week we would only have a day and a half off, provided we weren't on kitchen police (KP) or hadn't caught weekend guard duty, which meant working seven days a week.

Battalion full-field inspections were held on the parade ground. We would pitch our pup tents and display all our equipment—including in my case my French horn. Immediately following the inspection, we would roll up our gear; pack it on our backs; the band members would stack arms; and then we would pass in review.

Our hours were from 5:45 A.M. reveille to 5:00 P.M. Standing reveille in the wintertime meant getting up before the chickens to face, at attention, a frozen parade ground. A late night out sometimes led to obeying the temptation to use a shortcut getting dressed the next morning. This involved putting on your shoes, wrapping your leggings over your long johns, then putting on a shirt, tie, and overcoat. Any absence of britches under the overcoat was undetectable. But 1st Sergeant Bounds knew all the tricks. After he had taken roll call, he would say, "Take off your overcoats." Then he would leave ten or fifteen of us standing outside in our long johns for fifteen minutes, sometimes in temperatures as low as thirty degrees below zero (Fahrenheit). Occasionally, even some of the buck sergeants were caught without britches.

In addition to my other duties, the company commander, Capt. Gerald Mickel, offered me a job "dog-robbing," or acting as his orderly. This meant a chance to escape guard duty and earn an extra five dollars a month. Captain Mickel and his wife had no children to babysit, so my time was spent shining his boots, brass, and saber and helping her around the house.

About three months after my job with them began, a friend arrived from my hometown. He talked enthusiastically about taking a weekend trip of approximately 125 miles to western North Dakota and insisted it was just what I needed for a break in the routine of army life. We weren't supposed to go farther than thirty miles from the post without a pass, but he was sure I could be back by reveille Monday morning. Captain Mickel and his wife didn't need me over the weekend, so I was free to go.

Unfortunately, my friend liked a few drinks and of course I joined him. Five days after leaving the post, I began to think it might be a good idea to get back. I had been AWOL Monday, Tuesday, and Wednesday. After being AWOL for nine days, a soldier was considered to be a deserter; the penalty was usually six months in the guardhouse, and sometimes, a dishonorable discharge. I had been absent only three days, but I was facing trouble and I knew it.

On my return, I explained my situation to Captain Mickel's wife. A month in the guardhouse seemed fairly certain, but she said not to worry about it. When Captain Mickel called me in, it seemed best to tell him the truth, and I expressed regret that I hadn't used better judgment. He told me a month in the guardhouse was the appropriate penalty, but since he thought there was a good future for me in the service, he would only restrict me to the post for one month and assign me ten extra weekend KPs. I thanked him and asked if I still had my job as his "striker" (another slang term for orderly). He said, "Yes, if I want to eat my meals at home," and smiled. I knew then that Mrs. Mickle had interceded for me.

Sergeant Bounds was an early riser and was usually hanging around the kitchen on Sunday mornings. One Sunday he was in early, saw me, and asked what I was doing in the dining room. I told him it was my last extra KP. He grinned and said, "For your information, your last KP was last week, but for not checking the bulletin board you can finish this one out." So, I did eleven extra KPs; after that I read the bulletin board very carefully. I also was careful not to be AWOL again.

Our free time was spent variously. On Wednesdays, Fridays, Saturdays, and Sundays, there were movies. We had a fairly well equipped gym in which to work out or play, and all the companies participated in sports, including basketball and football. There was also a battalion baseball team.

On weekday evenings, a soldier's favorite spot for relaxing was the dayroom with its pool and card tables, sofas, easy chairs, and radio. The radio was supposed to be turned off after 9:00 P.M., but this rule usually was overlooked, as long as we kept the lights off and the radio low. Many nights we stayed up until the wee hours listening to our favorite bands—Wayne King; Jan Garber; the Dorsey Brothers; and Lawrence Welk, who is, like me, a former farm-country boy, and whose rise to fame I had followed with interest.

The first time I saw the now-legendary band leader was in Eureka when I was a youngster. He was part of a three-man group that gave a performance at the small theater in the city park, and in those days he was still living on his family's farm in Strasburg, North Dakota. Welk came on stage and did a skit and played his accordian. He was chewing sunflower seeds, or Russian seeds as we called them then. (At that time, sunflowers grew wild in great profusion and were considered almost a nuisance. People collected and roasted the seeds, which were used for chicken feed but were not sold in stores. All kids, among others, chewed them, and we thought it great sport to expel the hulls from the corners of our mouths, aiming at various targets. Kelly, of Cracker Jack–box fame, undoubtedly placed many a bet on such impromptu contests. A man in Aberdeen, South Dakota, got the idea of bagging and selling the seeds, at first with the hulls intact; then he began to hull them—at which point he made his fortune.)

Soon after I saw that Eureka performance, Welk began playing over radio station WNAX in Yankton, South Dakota. By then, he had a five- or six-piece band. From Yankton he went to Chicago, where he got his big start. While I was with the Marshalls in Houston, I drove Mrs. Marshall and her son, Hugh, to Mineral Wells, Texas, a resort some four hundred miles away, and we stayed at the Mineral Wells Hotel, where Lawrence Welk was performing in the lobby! I remember I went up and spoke with him. Bubbles were part of his act even then and had been since his radio days in Yankton.

Once a year, the battalion made a hike of approximately a hundred miles. Each man carried a full pack, a rifle, and ammunition. My first year in the service, I weighed 120 pounds, and I will never forget that first hike. A full pack included half a pup tent (its other scheduled occupant carried the other half) with ropes and stakes, mess kit, toilet articles, clothing, and extra shoes. When ammunition was attached, the pack weighed a total of 30 pounds. The BAR automatic weapon, which, because I was the company's smallest member, I carried, weighed 16 pounds. Altogether, I carried nearly half my own weight for over a hundred miles.

These annual hikes were considered quite special, and taking part on foot was such a matter of pride that even some of the old-timer sergeants with nearly thirty years of service would walk them. At night when they took off their shoes, their feet would be covered with blood blisters, but they absolutely refused to ride in the supply wagons.

Another reason I recall my first hike so clearly is because the soldier walking in front of me was constantly out of step. On a one-hundred-plus-mile hike with a full pack, that is one thing you don't need: someone out of step in front of you. I warned this man I'd walk on his heels if he didn't get in step, but he ignored me. I finally stepped heavily on his heels about three times. He got the message but mumbled something about waiting until after the hike. At the end of the day, I had just taken off my pack when he turned and—with his pack still on—took a swing at me. I ducked, swung, and knocked him down.

The brawl was beginning to escalate when Captain Mickel stepped in and made us quit and shake hands. I was happy it ended that way because if that man had ever gotten his pack off, I would have been in real trouble. As time went by, we became good friends and often laughed about our first hike together.

If a soldier didn't qualify on the rifle range, he was said to have "boloed," meaning that he should carry a bolo instead of a rifle; this was an insult. The term "bolo" came into use during the Spanish-American War when the American soldiers were fighting the Moros on the Philippine island of Mindanao. During that war, the Moros, a Muslim minority in the preponderantly Christian Philippines, carried spears and large knives, or bolos, as their only weapons. Although in my second year I qualified as an expert on the rifle range, for much of my first year I was afraid I would bolo; this was a real nightmare of mine. But one sergeant in particular took a special interest in helping me.

Sergeant Lietz repeatedly told Captain Mickel, "Hieb didn't breathe. He was right on target." But still, every time I fired, up would come "Maggie's drawers" (the red disk), which meant a miss. I was flinching or doing something else wrong, and my jaw was badly swollen from the rifle beating the hell out of the side of my face, where I braced it.

One morning Sergeant Lietz brought along a sponge and taped it to the small of my rifle stock. I had at least three coaches for my first shot that day, including Captain Mickel. When I squeezed the trigger this time, the small of the stock didn't hurt me. The sergeant had finally solved the problem. He had seen that I habitually hunched my shoulder into the rifle because it was hurting my jaw. With the help of the sponge, I was able to correct this posture. When the sponge was removed and there was no more pain, I went on to qualify as a sharpshooter.

I had been in the service about a year by this time and the depression was getting worse instead of better. Crop failures and drought throughout the center of the nation really hurt the wheat and corn states. About the only thing that seemed to grow in the early 1930s was the tumbleweed.

It was almost impossible to get a promotion in the army at this time. Privates would reenlist with just a promise that if they remained on good behavior they would get the first Pfc rating available. A number of the Pfc's were married and living off post, which entitled them to separate rations and quarters allowances. Many of them reenlisted because the employment situation in civilian life was so grim.

Several months into my second year of service, we got back 5 percent to 10 percent of the 15 percent cut that had gone into effect right after my enlistment. A year after that, we were back on the old pay scale of twenty-one dollars a month for a private.

We were allowed a thirty-day leave with pay once a year and could accumulate up to ninety days. My first year in the service I didn't have enough money to go on leave, so I postponed this and only took weekend passes, which didn't count against leave time.

One weekend I had a date but no money. I decided my father owed me some of the money he had been putting in the bank for me when I lived at home, and I wrote him saying I was in desperate need of five dollars. (This actually would have seen me through a number of dates.) He replied by asking how much money I was making a month. I answered immediately, confident he would send me the five dollars. Instead, the answer I got back asked, "Are there any vacancies?"

The depression continued and the Pfc's were reenlisting, filling their own grade vacancies. The band I was attached to had no ratings because it was a volunteer band. I could see it was almost impossible to get ahead at Fort Lincoln because of the size of the post battalion. The soldiers usually stayed put if they received any kind of rank. Some of the sergeants had been in the same battalion for twenty years. During this period, it was not possible to travel in grade (transfer to another base while retaining your grade) unless you were one of the first three grades: 1st sergeant, master sergeant, technical or staff sergeant. Even then, this was possible only if a mutual transfer was made with another sergeant of the same grade. Buck sergeants, or "three stripers" as they sometimes were called, had to take a bust to private and start over again. There were a few old-timers called "barracks-bag soldiers" who would move around from post to post, eventually getting their ranks back when vacancies occurred. The rest, those who stayed put at one post, were called "homesteaders."

Life on an army post could have its humorous occasions—if you were willing to pay the penalties. One such incident I remember vividly had to do with standing retreat. For this procedure, the various companies would line up in front of their respective barracks with the buglers positioned in front of battalion headquarters. The normal routine called for the 1st sergeant to report to the officer of the day, who was usually standing in the center of the parade ground, and to sing out "Sir, K Company all present and accounted for." The buglers also reported. Our company had an excellent bugler—when he was not in the guardhouse. Private Billingham must have put in four years trying to complete a three-year hitch because he was always pulling a thirty- or sixty-day detention. One evening at retreat when it was time for the buglers to report, Billingham, no doubt hoping to liven up the routine, phrased his report: "Sir, what the hell are you standing out there for?" Everyone started to laugh. The lieutenant who was officer of the day did not hear the question, but he came across the parade ground demanding to know why everyone was laughing; luckily for Billingham, no one told him.

On another occasion, Private Billingham was on guard duty as bugler of the day with this same officer. They were inside headquarters when the lieutenant saw a cigarette butt on the floor and asked if it was Billingham's. The private answered without thinking, "No sir, the lieutenant saw it first. He can have it." That remark cost him thirty days in the guardhouse.

Morning training consisted of close-order drill and marching in step to precise military movements. In the afternoon there would be machine-gun drill, rifle drill, and the disassembling of weapons and the naming of all their component parts. We were taught to do this blindfolded. Gas drill with our gas masks in place was another drill we would practice at least once a month.

Every two months we had a company dance. Some of our band members formed a pretty good dance band. Music was no problem. In those days, the problem was to get the local girls to come to the dances; their parents didn't trust the soldiers. As a result, we had only the married men's wives and the old-timer sergeants' daughters for dance partners. I had very few dates during my first two and a half years at Fort Lincoln, mostly because I never had the money needed in order to take a girl out.

My size often belied my capacity for food, and I remember one occasion when a friend of mine, Jimmy Miller, and I went to Bismarck one night for a few drinks and some dancing. Jimmy was somewhat under the weather, so about twelve o'clock I suggested that as long as we had enough money left for a sandwich, we could have a bite to eat at the Grand Hotel and catch the bus back to Fort Lincoln. He said he was hungry for chow mein, which we ordered. As we sat waiting for the meal to arrive, Jimmy fell asleep. When the waitress brought the food, I ate my plate of chow mein. Jimmy slept on. Still hungry, I slipped my empty plate in front of him and polished off his plateful. Waking him up, I said, "We finished eating. Let's go." He complained all the way back to the barracks that he was still hungry. I told him a few days later what had happened, took him to town, and bought him a meal.

Chances for advancement at Fort Lincoln were so rare, and it was so impossible to transfer to another post, that another friend, Richard Willer, and I decided to take a short discharge and go to the Philippine islands. If anything, my wanderlust had grown over the years. I very much wanted to travel and see as much of the world as possible. At that time, overseas opportunities in the army were limited to Tientsin, China; Panama; Hawaii; and the Philippines. My first choice was, of course, China, but to join the 15th Infantry's one battalion stationed there as part of an international military presence that included British, French, and Italian contingents, you had to have completed one full enlistment, or three years. I had only two years, and I was too impatient to wait. Panama and Hawaii were also unavailable, due to lack of openings. By the process of elimination, the Philippines became my choice; openings did exist there.

The short discharge procedure involved a real discharge. It was a formal and fully acceptable way for soldiers with at least two years of service to leave the army and reenter immediately. To ensure that a soldier would reenlist, the army would hold his discharge papers and reenlist him the very next day. When I put in for this, I didn't know I still had to have my parents' consent since I wasn't quite twenty-one. I had to ask for a weekend pass to go home for the necessary signatures.

42

This would be the second time I had been home in two and a half years. It was July 1935.

When I got home my father said, "What makes you think mother and I will sign papers so you can wander off halfway around the world?" I told him the army had a regimental band in the Philippines, and I would have a better chance there for promotion. I mentioned I would be twenty-one in another six months and then would not need his consent. I knew my mother would talk to him, which she did; and the next morning the papers were signed.

CHAPTER 4

Wanderlust Fulfilled

I arrived back at Fort Lincoln with all the necessary papers in order, and Richard Willer and I took our short discharges. We each had an accumulated ninety-day leave and received an additional thirty-day reenlistment leave. We decided to go to Eureka together to see if we could get work for the harvest season since we did not have to report to Fort McDowell, California, until the first week of October.

With great good fortune, we found farm jobs the first week we were home that paid five dollars a day and keep. Our hours were sunup to sundown, with Saturday afternoons and all of Sundays free.

Richard had no problem with the grueling physical labor involved. He had been raised on a farm in North Dakota and soon regained his former topnotch condition, which two years in the army had done nothing to maintain. I faced an altogether different situation. I had never done such heavy work, and while I could handle the job of driving the binder that cut and bundled the oats and barley, when it came to shocking these—by hand—I quickly became exhausted.

My first day on the header box throwing wheat up onto the stacks went well, but just about midafternoon of the second day, I almost passed out. At the point of collapse from this exertion, I told Henry Hausauer, my employer, he would be better off hiring someone who could do the job. Luckily, he wouldn't hear of this and said he had confidence I could learn to handle the work. We made an arrangement whereby I would drive the binder one day and shock the next. Since there were still ten acres of barley to be dealt with, he felt certain that by the time we had finished that chore, I would be in great condition.

After one day on the binder, I went back to the header box, where I worked straight through to the end of the harvest. At that point, Mr. Hausauer actually was bragging about how strong I was for my 120 pounds.

The year 1935 brought the first good crops and decent prices the farmers had seen in years. A great effort was being made to harvest every last field before hailstorms could destroy the crops. Wheat was bringing about one dollar a bushel, a considerable improvement over the price earlier in the thirties of twenty-five cents.

Five dollars a day and keep was considered a good wage, and I had been determined to do my best, even doing a little more than was expected of me. I have always been grateful for that job and for the faith shown in my ability to make the grade. The chance to prove my mettle that summer was to stand me in good stead in the future.

At last it was time for Richard and me to leave for the West Coast. Although we had been issued travel pay, we hated to spend it on transportation, and once again luck was with us. A neighbor, Mr. Nies, had just returned from the coast in order to sell his farm preparatory to moving west to Lodi. We talked to him, offering to drive his vanload of furniture to California, and he accepted our offer. The trip to Lodi took us a week. Once in Lodi, Richard and I stayed for a week with my uncle George and aunt Almeria, and I felt very good indeed when I realized my past misadventures had been forgiven and they were now proud of me.

Then it was time to report to Fort McDowell, and we took a bus to Oakland. From there, we took the ferry across the bay to San Francisco (the bridge had not been completed yet) and reported to Fort Mason, then an active military installation. From there we headed for Angel Island and Fort McDowell on an army ferry that made a stop at Alcatraz Island to pick up the laundry, which the prisoners did. Richard and I were surprised to find how cold it was out on the bay in October; after all, this was California!

Our ship to the Philippines wasn't scheduled to sail for another two weeks, and we spent much of that time doing KP at Fort McDowell. In the middle of October, we were transported back to Fort Mason where we boarded the USAT *U. S. Grant*, a former German

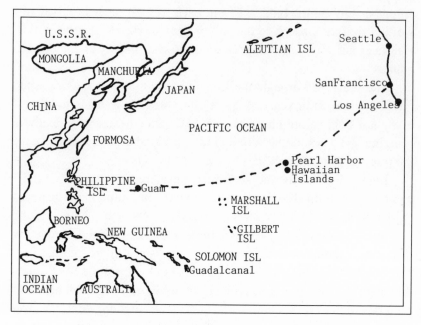

Route, U. S. Grant, *San Francisco to Philippine Islands*

passenger liner that had been captured during World War I and converted into an army transport capable of carrying about fifteen hundred troops. The army band turned out to bid us farewell. I was very excited and was looking forward to my overseas assignment, which certainly seemed my greatest adventure—yet.

The only duty that Richard and I were assigned aboard ship was, again, KP. To keep us shipbound men reasonably fit, calisthenics were held twice a day. The rest of the time, we gambled, playing either blackjack, poker, or dice. Although I was one of the youngest aboard, I was a proficient gambler, and I was lucky and made money on that voyage. Grandmother Hieb would have been appalled.

Some six days after leaving San Francisco, we arrived in Honolulu, which at that time had a population just short of twenty-six thousand. The only hotel on Waikiki Beach was the Royal Hawaiian, where I enjoyed my first legal drink of hard liquor. We were given

46

three days of shore leave in which to see the sights, and those were vastly different then than they are in 1987.

Our next destination was Guam. Because there were then no docking facilities for large ships, which therefore had to anchor out in the bay, we were ferried in small boats from the USAT *U. S. Grant* to the island for a one-day shore leave. There was one company of marines stationed on Guam; the rest of the small island's population consisted of the native people, most of whom were employed by the U.S. government.

Guam was certainly well removed from Eureka, both geographically and climatically, but Richard and I found its twenty-mile diameter somewhat lacking in adventure. My most striking recollection of that day we spent there is the veritable mountain of broken beer bottles I discovered behind the marine's bar.

After our stop at Guam, life aboard ship settled into monotony for the last lap of the journey to Manila, and gambling continued to occupy the major portion of our time.

At night, movies were shown on deck, and afterwards, because it was cool out there compared to our quarters below, Richard and I used to lie on deck and look up at the stars. The whole sky seemed to pitch back and forth—military transports were not equipped with stabilizers—and the stars seemed incredibly bright in the Southern Hemisphere. Lying out there flat on my back, I would remember how I used to dream of far-flung travel and a life of adventure; now, here I was, living such a life!

But at last the announcement came that in only a few more hours the island of Corregidor would be coming into view. Our passage from San Francisco had taken twenty-two days. We had crossed what was to become one of the theaters of the greatest, most hideous war the world has ever known; 1941 was only six years distant.

PART TWO

THE DECIDING YEARS:
1935–1941

CHAPTER 5

The Philippines:
Some Facts

During the trip to Manila, in order to satisfy some of my curiosity about this, to me unknown, world where I was headed, I had tried to learn as much as possible about the Philippines. The facts and figures I amassed through reading made me very aware that there was much more than vast mileage separating Eureka, South Dakota, from this land of islands.

The Philippine Islands, named for Philip II of Spain, were under Spanish rule from the sixteenth until the late nineteenth century. In 1889, after the Spanish-American War, the archipelago became a United States possession, which it remained until 1946, when it was given full independence as a republic.

The approximately 7,083 islands of this chain are located five hundred miles east of Asia's southeast coast. Y'Ami, the northernmost island, lies sixty-five miles south of Taiwan (Formosa). The southernmost island, Suluag, lies thirty miles northeast of Borneo.

Surrounded by the Philippine Sea and the Pacific Ocean to the east, the South China Sea to the west, the Celebes Sea to the south, and the Luzon Strait to the north, the islands extend in length for a distance of approximately 1,152 miles and in width, approximately 686 miles. The total land area is 114,830 square miles, or 6,000 square miles less than Great Britain's; the two islands of Luzon and Mindanao account for 65 percent of that total. There are altogether more than 21,500 miles of coastline.

Individually, most of the islands are quite small; only 466 have

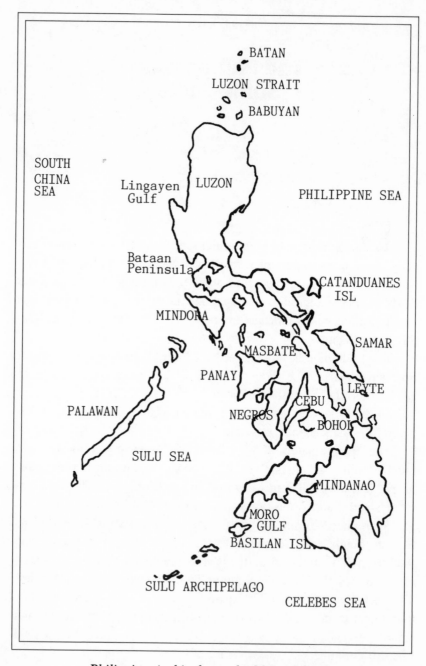

Philippine Archipelago, the Major Islands

an area of at least a square mile; a mere 11 have an area of 1,000 or more square miles; only 2,441 of the 7,083 have names.

The archipelago consists of three main island groups. Dominated by the 40,814-square-mile island of Luzon, the northern group is referred to most commonly as the Luzon group. It contains the island of Mindoro, south of Luzon, and two groups of much smaller islands, the Babuyans and the Batans, which are located in the Luzon Strait and are the chain's northernmost land masses.

The central islands are all comparatively small and include Palawan, the Visayans, Bohol, Cebu, Leyte, Masbate, Negros, Panay, and the Samars.

The southern group is dominated by the large island of Mindanao and includes the Sulu Archipelago.

The entire chain is located between the Equator and the latitude of 21°25′ north. The climate is tropical rain forest with weather conditions that vary according to season. The mean annual temperature is 80° Fahrenheit, with variations depending on altitude. Humidity is extremely high; the yearly rainfall averages approximately eighty inches, and the rainy season occurs during the summer monsoon, from May to November, when the winds blow from the southwest. The dry season is from December to April, during which time the winds blow from north to east, and from east to southeast. Typhoons strike usually between June and October, sometimes inflicting widespread and serious damage, often more the result of the torrential rainfall than of the high winds.

Most of the islands are mountainous with ranges that run north to south, parallel to, and in many cases bordering on, the coastlines. The island of Luzon has four such ranges: the Sierra Madre, which runs close to the east coast; the Ilocos or Malaya, a narrow range that lies along the west coast; the Cordillera Central chain; and, in the southern portion of the Bataan Peninsula, the Zambales Mountains. The most prominent of these ranges is the Cordillera Central, which consists of two, and in some places three, parallel ranges, each with an average height of 5,900 feet. (I will never forget the Cordillera Central. Between 1942 and 1945, I would cross all its component ranges, at one point half-starved and with bare feet, leading 173 guerrilla fighters.)

This chain joins the Sierra Madre in the province of Nueva Vizcaya to form the Caraballo Mountains.

North of the Caraballos and between the Sierra Madre and Cordillera Central lies the Cagayan River valley. Its fertile 50-mile width contains many areas of jungle; these were to be used during World War II as sites for the hidden camps of the guerrilla forces and as headquarters for the continuing resistance against the Japanese occupying forces.

The most important rivers in the Philippines are, on Luzon, the Cagayan, Agno, Bikol, Pampanga, and Pasig; and, on Mindanao, the Rio Grande de Mindanao, and the Agusan; the largest is the Cagayan River, which flows northward and drains one-quarter of Luzon's land mass. Between 1942 and 1945, I would travel this river extensively in *bangkâs,* which are boats made from hollowed-out logs, sometimes with stabilizing poles attached on either side like outriggers, and sometimes with sails as well.

The Cagayan, Rio Grande de Mindanao, and Agusan rivers are each more than 200 miles long. The Pasig River flows through the center of the capital city of Manila and is of great importance commercially. The largest lake in the Philippines is Laguna de Bay, located on Luzon near Manila.

On Luzon, dense jungle areas are found on the east coast in the Sierra Madre range running from north to south and extending west to the Cagayan River and its great valley. Another dense jungle lies in the area between Jones, in the province of Isabela, and Pinappagan, in the province of Nueva Vizcaya. There are also vast areas of jungle in the Mariveles and Zambales mountains. The five mountain provinces of northern Luzon—Kalinga-Apayao, Ifugao, Abra, Benguet, and Mountain—which lie to the west of the Cagayan River, contain many areas of forest, as opposed to jungle, and of dense junglelike groundcover.

The three main population groups in the Philippines are the Tagalogs of central Luzon; the Ilocanos of the Cagayan River valley and the northern coastal provinces of Luzon; and the Visayans of the central islands. Smaller population groups include the Moros, a Muslim minority whose religion predates the sixteenth-century Spanish conquest; the Pygmy-Negritos, who now make their homes in the jungles

54

of the Zambales, but whose ancestors migrated from Southeast Asia sometime during the last period of glaciation, preceding the Malays who are ancestral to the other Philippine population groups; and the Igorots of the mountain provinces, who once were headhunters, and who, as bolo-wielding soldiers in the Philippine army, would strike terror in the hearts of the Japanese during World War II; and the Ilongots.

The Ilongots were headhunters as recently as the Second World War. Their tribal territory encompasses the jungles of the entire Sierra Madre range. Living in tribal groups of twenty to twenty-five members, this primitive nomadic people was one of the Philippine's most feared.

For the purposes of government, the Philippines consisted of fifty-three provinces (fifty-five after 1958) with 1,078 municipalities and thirty chartered cities. The municipalities are administered by elected mayors and each has its capital city. Surrounding the cities and towns and in many cases bordering the jungles, are small villages, or *barrios*, often populated by members of one extended family; these are administered by *barrio tenientes*, or headmen. (During the period between 1942 and 1945, my survival and that of the men with me would be in large measure thanks to certain of the barrios and barrio tenientes in the provinces of Nueva Vizcaya and Isabela.)

CHAPTER 6

31st Infantry:
The Enlisted Man's West Point

On that October day in 1935, the USAT *U. S. Grant* steamed toward Manila, now less than eighty miles away, and as we approached Manila Bay, the first island we passed was the tiny El Fraile, where Fort Drum is located. In 1935, Fort Drum had one resident company of Coast Artillery and four 12-inch guns to protect the entrance to the bay.

Not long after El Fraile became a distant dot, Corregidor loomed up ahead of us. The Rock, as this fortress island is called, also had 12-inch guns to protect the bay and Manila's harbor, and the 59th and 60th Coast Artillery companies were stationed there.

Next, we passed the town of Cavite, with its naval base and four impressive-looking 12-inch guns. Those guns, vintage 1890 and 1908, were to play a key role in the future defense of the Philippines. While they were very accurate and were capable of sending shells a distance of fifteen hundred yards, their placement left them open to attack from the sky; an unimaginable eventuality when they had been set there, but an all-too-real nightmare at the onset of World War II. During the 1920s and 1930s, protective turrets were suggested at various times, but the idea was rejected for reasons of economy. In 1942, the guns' vulnerability to air attack made their effectiveness short-lived. Richard and I, however, were not worried about such problems as, spellbound and brimming with excitement, we hung over the ship's rail waiting for our first glimpse of Manila, the Pearl of the Orient.

At last that beautiful sight came into view. We steamed slowly into

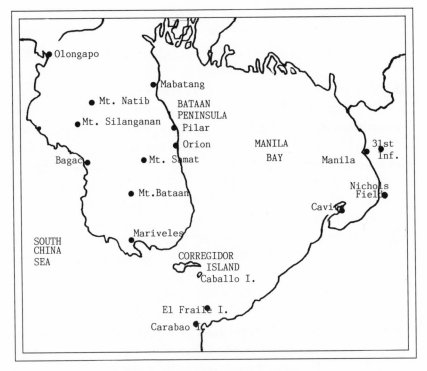

Details of the Manila Bay Region

Manila Harbor, which was clean and modern and not at all as we had expected it to be. The famous *China Clipper* seaplane was anchored in the harbor, and I was thrilled to see for the first time this then-new contraption that carried passengers and mail over the vast distances of the Pacific Ocean and took only one week to go from San Francisco to Manila.

A landing party boarded the *U. S. Grant*, and at the quay, we were greeted by an honor guard and a fifty-piece band mainly comprised of Philippine Scouts. I noticed that a good deal of rank was in evidence, as well as a multitude of hash marks on the uniforms, each one of which stood for three years of service. Some of the soldiers wore as many as seven of these on their sleeves. The band interested me because I hoped to join it, in this way assuring myself of an automatic promotion to private, first class; although, were I not to be that lucky,

I was determined to excel for the next two years at being a foot soldier.

To our great dismay, we now discovered we would be quarantined for two weeks before being assigned to our respective companies. We were transported to the stadium at Cuartel de España, the headquarters of the 31st Infantry, which was to be our home for the duration of our quarantine. Cots, bedding, mosquito nets, and mess kits were issued; our American money was exchanged for pesos; and we were given shots against every known tropical disease and quinine tablets against malaria. Strict orders were given that we were not to leave the area for any reason whatsoever during the weeks of quarantine.

The first night there, those of us who had civilian clothes waited only until dark; then we went over the fence and headed for the Mapa-hou Cabaret, where reportedly the largest dance floor in the Far East was to be found.

My first impression of life in Manila was a rather startling one because, as Richard and I walked down the city's main thoroughfare, we nearly became unwilling participants in a wild scenario akin to cops and robbers, something we had known until then only as a kids' game. Two Filipinos fled past us, one chasing the other and brandishing a long knife; close behind them was a policeman in hot pursuit. We speeded up our own progress, more interested in avoiding any confrontation with the MPs who were sure to appear than in discovering the cause and outcome of the commotion.

The Mapahou was indeed huge and had two dance bands playing simultaneously. It was filled with servicemen, most of them in civilian clothes. Richard and I danced with the dance-hall girls, who were available for ten centavos (a nickel) a dance. Later in the evening, however, we noticed MPs removing several uniformed soldiers, and we quickly decided it would be wise for us to leave and get back into quarantine. Once we were safely back over the fence, I decided not to take such a risk again and postponed further introductions to the city's nightlife.

At the end of the quarantine period, I was assigned to the 31st Infantry's K Company to replace a bugler who was returning to the States. As I would have been had I been assigned to the band, where there were no vacancies at that time, I was assured of a private, first class rating. That was the best rating a bugler could expect in the company, however, and NCO ratings were still almost impossible to get in any case.

We were welcomed by Captain Warshowsky, the company commander, who told us the 31st Infantry was the "West Point of enlisted personnel." A show outfit that stood the honor guard whenever dignitaries came to Manila, it emphasized spit and polish: close-order drill, manual of arms, and discipline. When the Philippine Commonwealth was to be inaugurated on 15 November 1935, President Roosevelt sent a delegation of fifty-four prominent American statesmen. I remember standing at attention as Vice President Garner and Secretary of War Dern inspected our honor guard with Manuel Quezon, the president of the Philippines. Douglas MacArthur, on loan to President Quezon as a military advisor and the only American to hold the rank of field marshall in the Philippine Army, was in the stand as the 31st Infantry and the Philippine Scouts passed in review.

In 1935, the Philippines epitomized a soldier's paradise. I could hardly wait to write home to tell of my good fortune, and I began to think about extending my tour of duty.

Our work day lasted from 5:30 A.M. to noon, when we could sign out, with the proviso that we had to be back—sober and ready for drill—the following morning. The short hours were necessitated by the extreme afternoon heat and humidity.

Sunday evening was movie night. The theater doubled as the church, and the movies were shown right after the services: to have a good seat for the show it was necessary to attend these. I soon formed the habit of going to church, and I have been a church-goer ever since.

Once every three months, we had twenty-mile forced marches, at night. We looked forward to these because upon returning to the barracks, we would be off duty for the next three days.

Once a year, we were taken by truck for a vacation at Baguio, a high-mountain resort and the summer capital of the Philippines. Our headquarters there, Camp John Hay, is situated next to a very beautiful nine-hole golf course, where Dwight Eisenhower, then a major and MacArthur's chief of staff, often could be seen hard at play.

We saw a good portion of northern Luzon on the trips to and from Camp John Hay, and Baguio is close to the famous rice terraces carved from the mountainsides centuries ago and still considered an engineering marvel. Some of the world's largest gold mines are also in that area.

The rate of exchange was then two pesos to the dollar, and civilians were allowed to work in the camps as barbers, barracks boys, and KPs, thus relieving the line soldiers of all duties save guard duty. Our hair was trimmed four times a month for two pesos; the barracks boys and KPs were paid four pesos a month each to do the KP, make beds, and keep the barracks clean and ready for inspections.

Our barracks, originally constructed by the Spanish during the 1600s, were open on the sides and had neither windows nor screens; nets protected us from mosquitoes, and everyone took a quinine tablet before each meal. Actually, malaria already had been eradicated in Manila, although one particular type of mosquito carried a minor malaria-like illness, dengue fever. When we caught this, we took the native cure: gin.

As bugler, I was assigned quarters in the special-duty room on the first floor next to the captain's office and dayroom. On occasion, some of the older sergeants who lived off post slept there, too. Gradually, I got to know these sergeants, and they encouraged me to persevere as a bugler until other vacancies occurred. They also encouraged me to consider a career in the army. Listening to them, I began to realize that here might be the chance for the exotic, adventurous life I had dreamed of as a boy lost in the stories of Horatio Alger. Visions of advancement in rank and of life in the tropics led me on. The old-timer sergeants who had stayed on in the Philippines after the Spanish-American War all felt there were great opportunities available if a man was willing to work hard and had a few lucky breaks along the way. My desire to make the grade became an obsession; I knew that somehow, someway, I would succeed.

Cuartel de España was located within the walled city of Manila and housed the regiment headquarters, the band, and the 1st Battalion. The 2d and 3d battalions were located approximately three kilometers from regiment headquarters at Estada Mejor, which was closer to the downtown area.

Bugle practice was held three to five times a week. On those occasions, I drilled with the company until 10:00 A.M. and then caught the army bus from Estada Mejor to regiment headquarters for practice until 11:00 A.M. Since we were located in the heart of Manila, I then had plenty of time to explore the city. I often walked down Dewey Boulevard (named after the famous American admiral), which at that time was a beautiful palm-lined street where many Americans lived; my dream soon grew to include enjoying life the way I imagined they did.

One of the benefits a bugler enjoyed was not having to walk post, a duty carrying certain risks in both war- and peacetime, for different reasons. The peacetime hazard came to my attention one midnight when I was on guard duty as bugler. The officer of the day, a 2d lieutenant, was inspecting the guard posts, one of which was a warehouse area enclosed by a wire fence with one gate. When the lieutenant collected the key to this gate, the sergeant of the guard warned him to call out before unlocking the gate because, the sergeant said, some of the guards walking post there were a little trigger happy.

Ignoring the sergeant's advice, the lieutenant unlocked the gate without announcing himself first—and found the guard, a private, asleep on post. In fact, the guard was so fast asleep and so far from trigger happy that the lieutenant was able to take his rifle back to the guardhouse, where, grinning from ear to ear, he showed the evidence to the sergeant.

In the meantime, the private woke up, discovered his rifle gone, and went to the sub-guardhouse, where he found it leaning against the building. He repossessed the rifle and returned to his post, where the lieutenant, the sergeant and the corporal of the guard, and the relief guard found him walking post, with his weapon, when they came along about fifteen minutes later expecting to find him asleep.

The dumbfounded lieutenant insisted that the private had been sleeping on post, but he had no proof. When he preferred charges—against the sergeant's advice—although everyone knew exactly what had happened, the court-martial board acquitted the private for lack of evidence.

Sometimes, life with the 31st Infantry included the unexpected. One afternoon while I was taking a nap, my bunk began to shake.

Thinking that one of my friends was having a bit of fun disturbing my pleasant dreams, I grumbled, "Knock it off!" and went back to sleep. When the shaking continued despite my objection, I opened my eyes expecting to catch the culprit. To my astonishment, the ceiling light over my bed was swaying and suddenly I realized we were having an earthquake. That surprise well and truly woke me, and I ran out to join the bucket brigade that was formed in case the quake should result in a fire. There was no fire, but the quake had registered 5.5 on the Richter scale, and the mess hall was—a mess, with broken dishes everywhere.

Excitement not caused by Mother Nature sometimes occurred as a result of the barracks' placement next to the Pasig River. A swinging, single-span bridge crossed the river from the edge of the post and was used as a shortcut into town. Unfortunately, this route led right through a pretty rough neighborhood, and when soldiers used it late at night, the local toughs would gang up on them. If those of us safely at home in the barracks heard a loud splash, we knew molesters or soldiers, or both, had been dumped over the side of the bridge.

Besides the human variety, the river offered local toughs of another kind: river rats as big as house cats that would stand on their hind legs and bare their teeth at us. We were allowed to shoot these four-legged thugs and sometimes did, even though such sport entailed cleaning our rifles afterwards.

I wrote home, enclosing pictures of Manila and explaining about the barbers, barracks boys, and KPs, and how little they cost us. With a great sense of pleasure, I told my family I soon would be getting my promotion. And I told my mother how much I was enjoying myself and that she should not worry about me. For one thing, I added, Sternberg General Hospital was one of the best such facilities in the Far East.

The reply came. Dad (as I had decided to call my father now that I was twenty-one years old) wrote that perhaps it would be better for me to do the work rather than to pay the natives. I could, he suggested, send the eight dollars home each month, and he would put it in the bank for me. Well, I thought, no thanks! I'd been that route before. Although had it been a matter of family need, I gladly would have made out an allotment.

Eight months after I arrived in the Philippines, I was promoted at last to private, first class. My monthly pay increased by nine dollars, and I was conscious more than ever of my good fortune. The economy at home in the States had not improved and the future was quite uncertain; even then, we heard talk about an ex–house painter in Germany.

CHAPTER 7

A Slow Slide Home

I had been in the Philippines a year when one morning, six of us were sent on a work detail to paint the roof of a barracks. We started painting, moving backwards to the peak from the front edge, which was about twenty feet above a tin awning that shaded the sidewalk ten feet below it. We had been painting for about two hours when by accident, I stepped back into some wet paint and began a very slow slide. My work buddy yelled frantically for the men on the sidewalk to get a ladder in place below me and a rope up to the men at the roof's peak so that they could drop it down for me to grab. Desperately trying to hold on to the roof, I would slide down about a foot, then stop. Paralyzed by the thought of the approaching inevitable conclusion to my sticky backwards slide, I was unable to utter a sound. As my inexorable descent continued, my life flashed before me in sudden review; could it be, I thought, that farm life and Eureka were not so bad as I had judged? Still slipping slowly, knowing a drop of at least thirty feet was coming, I tried to relax, thinking that if I relaxed, I might escape serious injury. I knew it was impossible to get the rope to me in time, and even if that were possible, I would have to let go of the roof to catch it. The ambulance arrived as I reached the edge. Then over I went, hitting the tin overhang. I bounced straight up—and dropped to the blacktop. The aid men were waiting.

I was taken to Sternberg General Hospital, and then the real ordeal began. The pain in my leg was intense, and I asked the medical officer for something to relieve it. He asked me very sarcastically if I couldn't stand a little pain. I let him know that I could stand as much as he could, maybe a hell of a lot more. He said I could be court-martialed for my remarks and called the corpsman to help him set my broken bones. After the first twist, I passed out.

When I came to, another medical officer, a major, was there with the captain who had worked on my leg. He asked if I felt any other pain, and I said, "Yes, my right hand." Looking down, I saw a small bone protruding from the back of my hand. With the captain's method of bone setting fresh in my mind, I told the major I didn't want that bone set the way my leg had been. He wanted an explanation, and I told him what had taken place. The captain was sent away, and the major took over. Mercifully, he gave me a shot of painkiller and set my wrist and forearm, which was broken as well.

X-rays now revealed my heel had been shattered, and a pin was inserted, with a weight on the end to hold it in place. This uncomfortable arrangement was maintained for six months. Instead of enjoying life in the tropics, I was to spend my last year of duty in the Philippine islands in the hospital, which, prophetically, I had described so glowingly to my mother.

One evening as a medical corpsman was making his rounds, he accidently bumped into the weight at the end of my bunk, and I felt one of the bones in my leg move. I told him, and he asked if it was giving me any pain. Although I certainly had felt the bump, afterwards there was no pain. The medic looked, and said he thought the leg was all right.

The next morning, before he went off duty, the medic asked me not to say anything to the doctor about what had happened because he was afraid he would lose his rating. I told him not to worry; I wouldn't say a word.

About a month later, my leg was x-rayed again. One bone was found to have healed with its ends overlapping. I told the doctor I had no idea when that could have happened, but I felt a sinking sensation in the pit of my stomach as I thought about that bumped weight. The doctor said he could rebreak and reset the bone. I thought it over, finally asking him whether I would limp if we left it the way it was. He said he didn't think so and that he was more concerned about my shattered heel. I decided I would prefer he left the leg as it was. From that time on, the medical corpsman took special care to see that I had everything I needed or wanted, he was so relieved not to have been reported.

I had been in the hospital about four months when a Philippine Scout was moved in next to me. About a week after that, I noticed some small bugs on my pillow. I mentioned these to the nurse, who looked—only to announce that I had head lice. I said, "If I have, I caught them in the hospital." The Philippine Scout and I were sharing a nightstand placed between our beds, and he had used my comb. The nurse checked and sure enough, he had lice. When they told me they would have to shave off my hair, I said to go ahead since I wouldn't be going anywhere for some time, but the scout gave them an argument. He was given a choice: have his hair shaved off or be court-martialed. He decided to cooperate. When the nurse called him "lousy" after that incident, he was always acutely embarrassed.

After I had lain there for about six months with the heavily weighted pin through my heel, my leg was put in a cast, a welcome relief from the other contraption, which was removed. My right arm had healed, and I now had the use of both hands.

Several weeks later, I longed to have the pin back. My leg itched like fury; this normal side effect of plaster casts was intensified by the heat and humidity. Because of the cast, there was no way to scratch. I asked if the casts were ever changed. The doctor seemed to weigh his answer before saying in a grave tone that he had seen some that had been on a year. Noticing I was almost in tears over this news, he grinned and said reassuringly that the casts were changed every six weeks. I almost counted the minutes until that first cast would come off. When it did, my leg was washed in alcohol and water before the second cast was put on. Momentarily at least, I had some relief from the intense itching.

By this time, I was walking around the second-floor ward on crutches. To pass the long hours, we had a few poker games on paydays, whenever one of the old-timer nurses was on duty since they tolerated the gambling as long as we kept our money out of sight. We used matchsticks for chips. I was saving nearly all of my monthly paychecks and some of my winnings.

After I had suffered through another two months of itching, the second cast was removed. Again, my leg was washed and x-rayed, and put in a new cast, the third, and last, one.

The corpsman, by now a friend, had made me a scratching device out of a long, thin piece of metal. I could stuff this down between the cast and my leg and jiggle it around to get some relief from the infernal itching. This last cast was on one month, and when it was removed, I began physiotherapy in order to regain the use of my ankle, stiff after six months of immobilization. My leg was emaciated, and there was no muscle left at all. I wondered whether I would limp the rest of my life.

The nurse in charge of my physiotherapy made me her special challenge. She must have been the strongest woman in the army! On the first morning, she took my heel in the crook of her arm, rested my foot on her outstretched forearm, and started to bend at the elbow. I bent right with her, going straight up in the air. She said, "That didn't hurt," and grinned. I said, "The hell it didn't!" She kept calling me a sissy. I told her I had saved $350 and would bet the full amount that if I used the same flexion method on her, she would scream uncle sooner than I would. She said an officer can't bet an enlisted man. Some excuse, I thought. She was to become one of my best friends.

Within a month, the strength began to return to my leg. Eventually, the time came when I could discard my crutches. Because I hadn't walked in over a year, I had to learn all over again. But being young and strong, I was soon getting around quite well with only the help of a cane.

Captain Warshowsky, the company commander, had been in to see me several times while I was at Sternberg. He told me I was going back home on the *Migs*, a quartermaster supply ship that hauled supplies. I was being sent to Letterman General Hospital in San Francisco. He thought there was a good chance that I would be given a disability pension because the army had neglected to give us adequate protection while we were painting the roof.

I left the Philippines in 1937, one of twenty-six convalescent soldiers returning to the States on the *Migs*. The trip went smoothly until, on the third day out, we ran into a typhoon. The skipper took us two hundred kilometers off course, but we still encountered a good part of that storm. Almost everyone on board was sick, soldiers and crew alike. I was lucky; I never once got sick. We stopped at Hong Kong for supplies, and the chance to go ashore and stretch our legs was a welcome one.

Our next stop was Shanghai. This is a city that will remain in my memory as long as I live. Starvation and death stared at me from every corner as I walked along the streets. I desperately wanted to help, and I did buy food for a few people; but, when I contemplated the enormity of the task of trying to help the thousands of starving people, including men, women, children, babies, and the aged—I realized it was impossible for me to help. That was a devastating experience. I felt rent by the intractable suffering I witnessed. I had never seen such misery and desperation. Certainly, I myself had never experienced anything approaching real privation. In a few years, I would learn firsthand what it means to be desperately hungry, but in 1937 I was mercifully unaware of my future brush with starvation.

The *Migs* traveled north to the port of Chinwangtao. There, our four-day stay gave me the chance to go down to Tientsin where the 1st Battalion of the 15th Infantry was stationed. British and French troops were stationed there also, and a British soldier I met in one of the Tientsin bars invited me to his unit's mess for dinner. After being seated in the hall, I realized my host was standing behind me, and when I moved over and asked him to get a plate and squeeze in next to me, the other soldiers laughed, saying their customs were different from ours. When a guest was invited to their mess, the host forfeited both his meal and his rum! I felt extremely uncomfortable about that arrangement, but my newfound friend said not to worry, the mess sergeant would give him a sandwich later on.

I enjoyed several meals with soldiers assigned to the 15th Infantry. Most of these men liked that three-year assignment and were, or planned to be, professional soldiers. It would have been interesting to see the French camp, but I didn't receive an invitation.

Our soldiers' behaviour appeared to be more disciplined than that of their French and English counterparts, which was not surprising considering the fact that the 15th Infantry consisted of handpicked soldiers who had to have served three years before being assigned to that unit. The French and English services accepted raw recruits for the Tientsin assignment. Our men were better dressed, too, and even with the relatively few dollars they were drawing then, better paid.

Our next stop was Hawaii, where we had a three-day layover for loading and unloading supplies and cargo. We were given a three-day shore leave and the choice of staying in Honolulu or sleeping aboard ship. Since we had no duties to perform, most of us stayed in the city, where first-class-hotel rooms cost only five dollars a night. After shopping for gifts to send home, we spent our time taking sightseeing-bus tours. Honolulu was a good serviceman's city, and we were made welcome in the islands.

The next port was San Francisco. The day before we arrived there, I picked up a copy of *Life* magazine. Several pages of pictures looked very familiar. To my astonishment I was staring at the write-up of the fiftieth anniversary of my hometown, Eureka, South Dakota. Eureka once had been the largest primary wheat center in the United States—as a matter of fact, in the world—and this issue of *Life* featured an account of the sixteen saloons and forty-two grain elevators located there in its boom-town days. The pictures showed Eureka in 1892, and in 1937, when it had become just a small town of fifteen hundred people. That population figure remains constant to this year, 1987. I was delighted with my discovery, and everyone aboard the *Migs*, including the captain, had heard of Eureka, South Dakota, by the time we docked in San Francisco.

Upon our arrival, we twenty-six convalescents were taken to Letterman General Hospital. I was given a complete physical examination and was asked again if I wanted my leg rebroken and reset. I said no! I was still limping, and I stayed around the hospital for some two months before meeting with the Physical Review Board in order to establish my future status. Because my tour of duty was finished, I was offered a temporary medical disability paying approximately $7.50 a month. I refused this and requested that I be allowed to get back in the service within ninety days. The board agreed and it was so stated on my discharge.

CHAPTER 8

Second Tour at Fort Lincoln

In order to retain my reenlistment bonus while giving civilian life another shot, I decided to wait ninety days before reenlisting. One thing I knew: if I did reenlist, I wanted to advance in rank. The welcome mat was out now for service personnel in the States. The economy was a little better in 1938, too. But there was a war brewing in Europe, and I knew sooner or later I would be back in the service.

After my discharge from Letterman, I drew two hundred dollars; added to what I had saved, this gave me a total of six hundred dollars, enough to buy a new car, but such a purchase would have left me broke. I headed home, traveling by means of the less expensive—and to me more familiar—method: hitchhiking.

Eureka hadn't changed. The population remained static; so did the economy. Dad said the only work available was farm labor during harvest season. When he asked whether I intended to go back into the service, I told him if I did go back, I would make a career of it. I already had over five years in the service, but twenty-five more years seemed a long time. The army didn't offer a twenty-year retirement at that time.

My brother-in-law Gup Cirks and his wife, my sister Frances, came to visit from Iowa, and I returned to their farm with them to pick corn. Shortly after the corn was picked, trapping season opened for muskrat and mink. Remembering my early trapping ventures, I asked Gup if he would agree to split the profit down the middle if I stayed, and he agreed. We ran a trap line on his lake, which was well supplied with muskrat. The opening night of the season found us in his boat out on the lake looking in the shallows for the muskrat mounds we had earmarked for traps. In order to know exactly where to set our traps and not waste a minute's time, we had made a survey of these mounds prior to the season. Muskrat were in abundance; but so was competition from other trappers.

One minute after midnight, our first trap was set, and forty others belonging to us, also. We caught thirty muskrat that first night, and to our delight, three mink, worth thirty dollars a pelt. We skinned our catch and put the pelts on strong wire stretchers to dry.

Several days later, I noticed some unusually large mink tracks in the snow. I urged Gup, "Let's follow them. Chances are that mink's holed up in the drainage tile." The tile had been laid years ago to drain water into the lake. Gup was doubtful; but, the tracks were really enormous, and I was determined to track down that animal. Anticipating success, I asked Gup if I could keep all the money from the pelt. His answer was the usual, "Hell yes, Laddie."

After following the tracks for about half a mile, I noticed a small opening at the edge of the lake. It was one of the old drainage tiles, and the tracks led right into it. If the tile was plugged on the other end, I would have the mink I knew was in there sleeping or hiding. I set traps inside the opening, camouflaging them with grass and some cotton from the cottontails growing in the area. Then I plugged the opening with an old tin can held in place by a large rock.

The next day, Gup and I caught several muskrat and one large mink on our trap lines; Gup thought we had the mink I had been following the day before. I said, "The one I catch will make this one look like a midget," and reminded him that we had agreed to let me keep all the money. When we arrived at my trap, we noticed the chains had been pulled mightily. I got behind the opening and moved away from the front of the trap because a cornered mink will bite and fight. Gup was sure I had a jackrabbit. Getting a stick, I shoved the stone away. Out came the can with the mink's head inside! The rest of the animal was caught in one of the traps. Nearly twice as big as any of the others we had caught, this mink was the biggest one we had ever seen. We made good money that day—and, after all, we split it down the middle.

71

When the trapping season ended, I began thinking about the future. No doubt motivated by the trouble Hitler was stirring up in Europe, the army was taking in quite a few new recruits. It was just a matter of time before the United States would be involved in a war. Under the circumstances, I thought the best place for me was in the service. In case of a large military buildup, there would be the advantage that promotions would be given apace. Gup took me to the Fort Dodge, Iowa, recruiting station, where I told the recruiting sergeant I wanted to reenlist—if I could be reassigned to Fort Lincoln, North Dakota. He wasn't sure any vacancies existed there, so I paid for a call to K Company, my old outfit, and talked to my former boss, Captain Mickel. I asked if he remembered me and was pleased to hear him say, "How could I forget you with all the extra KPs I used to give you?" I asked if I could be reassigned to K Company and whether there were any chances for promotion. He answered yes! to both questions. (The recruiting sergeant and I met again about a year later, and I noticed with some satisfaction his surprise at my rank of buck sergeant.)

When I arrived at Fort Lincoln, the same sergeants and corporals were there who had been there when I was on my first enlistment. Two of them were due to retire within several months, and this would create vacancies. Because at this time the top rating for buglers was private, first class, and line soldiers could advance to the grade of 1st sergeant, I asked to be assigned as a line soldier.

I also put in for a correspondence course, the *Ten Series*. This could be taken, with a company commander's recommendation, through the Department of the Army. Upon completion of the course, I would receive a commission in the reserves as a 2d lieutenant.

All the men in my company (we had about one hundred men to a company then) were informed there would be a written and an oral test for the two vacancies that would be available when the two sergeants retired. For the next several months, I stayed close to the post and studied at every opportunity. One of the company platoon sergeants, Sgt. Frank Smythe, held a reserve commission (he had been a 1st lieutenant during World War I) and he helped me greatly with my *Ten Series*. Whenever he could, he would put me in charge of a squad, an assignment that actually called for the rank of a corporal. He gave me many breaks and I was determined not to let him down in class or on the field.

Just before the tests were to be given, my company was sent to qualify on the firing range. I recalled the trouble I'd had with the rifle before. In the Philippines, my weapon had been a .45 automatic pistol and I had qualified there with that. Although I hadn't yet fired a 30-caliber rifle while at Fort Lincoln, I made up my mind I was going to earn an expert rating and draw that extra five dollars a month. When I told Sergeant Smythe about the trouble I'd had in the past, he gave me some dry-run instruction. He assured me my first shot would be a bull's eye; and it was. I made expert rifleman.

The notice went up that the written tests for promotion would be given. There were three tests: one for private, first class; one for corporal; and one for buck sergeant. My platoon sergeant advised me to take the test for sergeant. He was sure I could pass it and probably would get a better score than some of the old-timer corporals who had been in since World War I. Most of those corporals wouldn't study; they believed the oral exams and field exercises would tell it all. I decided to go for broke.

The day we took the test, Sergeant Smythe said he didn't want me to use an eraser: my first answer to a question should stand. I was the only private taking the sergeant test. Sixteen men out of the one hundred in the company took the exam. I didn't get much sleep that night; my answers to the map-reading questions worried me, and the test results were to be posted on the bulletin board the following day.

The next morning, we were called into the dayroom and given back our papers. A short time later, Captain Mickel and the 1st sergeant entered. Captain Mickel said he could see some of us had done a lot of studying, but that he didn't know why some others had even bothered to take the test. In his estimation, he added, there were still rewards for soldiers who tried to get ahead in the service. He announced I had written the best test; however, since I was a private, I would be promoted only to corporal, with an automatic promotion to sergeant when the next promotion came up. He had tried to convince the commanding officer at post headquarters to promote me to sergeant but had been told to wait, because we were going to get an

73

increase in company personnel and that most likely would mean several more vacancies for sergeants. In high feather, I called home, and Dad told me I had made a wise career choice. I knew that meant he was proud of me.

Like my first tour of duty at Fort Lincoln, my second one consisted of not only army discipline and close-order drill, but also field maneuvers starting with squad and moving on to platoon and battalion battle tactics. On the parade ground for close-order drill, I was given a squad first, and next, a platoon. A few days later out on maneuvers, I was given a platoon. There were field exercises such as map reading, locating correct ground position, and issuing orders to squad leaders, all closely observed by the post commander and company officers. Again, I was lucky. The lessons I had studied in the *Ten Series*, and the tutoring from my friend Sergeant Smythe, really helped me. Two months after I made corporal, we got additional ratings in the company; one was that of buck sergeant. I made the grade, and that was the proudest day of my life. I was the youngest sergeant in the 4th Infantry.

Elated though I was, this time there was a problem. There were corporals in my platoon who had been in World War I, and they resented my promotion over them. The post commander and most of the company commanders believed in tying promotions to the results of the oral and written tests and field exercises, not to seniority and time in grade, a time-honored system allowing men promotions whether they were qualified or not.

Under the circumstances, living with these corporals wasn't easy for me. I sensed their resentment and could understand it, too. Some of those men were old enough to be my father. In their eyes, I was young and green and hadn't put in my time. For my part, I felt I had earned my promotion fairly; the opportunity was there for anyone who wanted to take advantage of it. The army had provided methods for advancement other than seniority and recognized and rewarded the men who followed through. It was a difficult situation. Once again Sergeant Smythe was helpful. One night at the NCO club, he happened to overhear a conversation about my promotion, and he joined in with a few words of his own. This cleared the air; after that I had no more trouble.

Up to this time during my second tour at Fort Lincoln, I don't believe I had more than one date. To my surprise, one evening I received a call from a sergeant's daughter congratulating me on my promotion. Since she had been so thoughtful, I invited her on a date to the post theater; she accepted. On Saturday night, I showed up to meet her for the date dressed in civilian clothes. I think the sergeant was a little disappointed I wasn't in uniform. However, this didn't seem to make any difference to his daughter, who turned out to be a very attractive girl. We enjoyed the movie and afterwards went to the NCO club for a sandwich and beer. Her father was there, and he kept one eye on me all evening. I took her home fairly early and was all set to kiss her goodnight, when I had a second thought and turned around in time to see her father walk up behind us. I looked him straight in the eye, bid him goodnight, and marched on down the sidewalk. His daughter and I had made a date to go out on the town the following weekend.

She was good company and liked nightlife as well as I did. We began steady dating, but the good times certainly cut into my savings. Much as I liked her, as time went by I began to feel it might be well to think the relationship over carefully before things got out of hand—and before I went through my whole bank account. I put in for a thirty-day leave.

The leave was granted, and I hitchhiked to Iowa to spend part of it with Gup and Frances. Becoming a farmer again for a short time and reminiscing with Gup about our trapping venture made a welcome break from army routine, and it gave me time to think over the situation with the sergeant's daughter. I wrote to her a few times and received some letters from her—and one from a corporal friend who passed along the information that no sooner had I left Fort Lincoln than she began dating. I quit writing and so did she.

My next stop was Minneapolis to visit my sister Ann, who had recently married. Since Gup and Frances also had planned to visit her, we drove there together, a departure for me from my usual method of thumbing, which by now was second nature to me.

Ann and her husband, Vern Jorgensen, were doing fairly well for that period of continuing economic depression, when times generally were difficult for young couples starting out in married life. The subject of marriage hovered in the back of my mind, and I found myself more observant than usual of the nuances of my sisters' married lives, and of the attendant responsibilities. I was fairly certain I wasn't ready for such a step myself.

I had chosen military life, liked it, and understood the discipline necessary to it. I didn't mind the constraints of regimentation; on the contrary, the orderliness of it appealed to me. My willingness to adjust to such a life must have been a source of surprise to my father, considering my early rebellious attitude toward the discipline he had felt necessary, certainly where I was concerned.

The army seemed to me to offer a chance to prove my independence, and there was opportunity within its structure to advance or mark time, whichever a soldier decided. The military life was a challenge I had assumed that I neither wished to give up nor wanted to share. Marriage was a constraint I wasn't ready for.

Thirty days of doing nothing save visiting and sleeping was more than enough, and I was glad to get back on duty at Fort Lincoln. About two weeks after my return, the sergeant's daughter called; she had heard I was back and wondered why she hadn't heard from me. I explained I was busy with the second lesson of the *Ten Series* and was trying my best to get a commission. She suggested we meet, and I agreed because it seemed best to try to resolve the relationship in some mutually satisfactory way. She wanted to know the real reason I hadn't called, and I admitted I had heard she was dating during my absence. After some discussion, we agreed that even though we cared for each other, neither of us was ready to settle down. Since our backgrounds were so different and the times were so unsettled, we decided it was best to continue as friends, dating occasionally but not exclusively. Eventually we simply stopped seeing each other, perhaps more to her parents' disappointment than to ours.

The army was changing rapidly in matters of dress and drill. The old britches, leggings, and campaign hats were discarded; the new issue was a nice-looking, well-styled, two-tone uniform of trousers, blouse, dress cap, and overseas cap. The squad was enlarged, and the drill simplified; the older, more complicated drill was now used only for show occasions.

The change was difficult for some of the older sergeants, and for one in particular who had become a good friend of mine. Sergeant Zaperdino had given me my basic training and had seen to it that I learned all that was necessary in order to become a good soldier. He was a man who sincerely cared about the army and the men assigned to him, but the newly rewritten regulations were very hard for him to learn because he had enlisted prior to 1917 and had had no formal education. We worked together on the new regulations and the changes in drills. Whenever he became disgusted, I would remind him of how hard he had been on me during my basic training. He always replied, "But I made a damn good soldier out of you!" I had to admit he had, and I threatened to use the same rough tactics on him. It wasn't long before he was out on the parade ground drilling his platoon according to the new regulations. We both felt good about that.

The army may have been changing in the latter part of 1938, but so were things in Europe. There was a great deal of talk about Hitler now, and most of us in the service thought that sooner or later we would be involved in a war.

I was still on the second lesson of my correspondence course, and since there was no time limit, my studying was done when the mood hit me. I had my own writing desk, several wall lockers, two straight-back chairs, and an easy chair scrounged from a friendly quartermaster sergeant, and my quarters were very comfortable for both studying and relaxing. The radio provided pleasant listening. There was church on Sundays; there were plenty of movies; and, I had money for evenings out. But still something was missing. I was in a rut. Finally, the company commander asked if I was in love or had lost my best friend. He suggested it might be a good idea for me to take a few days off and relax. I took his advice and went home to Eureka.

This time I wore my uniform, and if it had been up to my father and grandfather, I would have slept in it. To see the pride in my father's eyes was a wonderful surprise for me. Our past differences still made a barrier between us, but I was aware of Dad's approval. This was the best he could do; displays of affection between fathers and sons were not encouraged by the strictures of the paternal discipline customary to our region. I told Dad my goal was to get a commission; and, in his own way, he was proud of me, as were my mother and grandfather.

My later work as a recruiting officer had an early beginning in Eureka on this trip. When I returned to Fort Lincoln ready to resume my soldiering career with renewed enthusiasm, two young men I knew who had been in the Civilian Conservation Corps, Garret Zenk and Bob Martel, decided to return with me as enlistees. The army had started calling in quite a few of its reserve officers, and if war broke out, many of the fellows who had been in the CCC would be among the first called up. My work on the post at the time was with the new recruits as an instructor and I enjoyed this.

An event was about to take place now that would change the direction of my life. While making the rounds of the nightclubs on an evening out in Bismarck, I was introduced to a Bertha and an Adeline Hieb. We found we were third cousins, and as a newly discovered member of the family, I was given an invitation to the Third House Dance being given the following weekend in the large hallway of the new state capitol building, where both Bertha and Adeline were employed. Employees of the legislature threw a dance at the end of the legislative session and called it the Third House Dance. Employees at the capitol and at the state-owned Bank of North Dakota were also invited. This sounded like fun, and I was happy to accept—with the understanding that they were not to introduce me to any of the girls there as a sergeant from Fort Lincoln, because I was a little gun shy about the bad attitude toward servicemen still evident in Bismarck.

The following Saturday, I dressed in my best civilian clothes, picked up my cousins, and we went off to the dance. The evening was to be a very special one indeed.

The band was good, and I really was enjoying myself for the first time since I had stopped seeing the sergeant's daughter. During one of the dances, I suddenly noticed an exceptionally beautiful young woman. As my partner and I circled the dance floor, I found myself watching for this petite beauty. Her features were finely chiseled and delicate, and she had soft dark hair and eyes, and a lovely smile; there was a shining quality to her expression that appealed to me. She was

78

special! and I knew immediately that she would be very important to me. I asked Adeline to introduce me if she knew her, which she did. And Elaine Marr became part of my life.

Dancing together, we exchanged information about each other. When Elaine told me she was from New England, I assumed she meant the New England states and was somewhat disheartened since that area seemed very far away. I even wondered if her family there might not take her away from the Midwest. She worked at the Bank of North Dakota in Bismarck and was sharing an apartment with three other young women; Madeleine Newman, Ethel Rosenow, and Hazel Fixen, all of whom remain our good friends to this day. Because I was afraid Elaine might not want to see me again if she knew, I didn't want to admit I was a soldier; I told her I was a rancher's son from Montana—a step up from the orphan status manufactured during my early travels.

I was elated when she agreed to see me again; however, she was reluctant to give me her telephone number. Her friend Madeleine happened to overhear us discussing this and later in the evening gave me the number. The four friends were generally very protective of each other, but in this case I think even Madeleine sensed the unusual quality of this first meeting between Elaine and me. I knew from the first moment I saw her that we would marry someday.

The next day I called Elaine, admitted I had lied about my occupation, and invited her to Fort Lincoln. She agreed to come, provided she could bring Madeleine. We had several drinks at the NCO club that afternoon with Madeleine and a corporal friend and spent more time getting acquainted.

It was welcome news that the New England Elaine had mentioned was the small farming community of New England, North Dakota, where her parents were farmers. Our backgrounds were similar in many ways, and as we talked I realized how much we had in common. My feeling of the evening before was still there: I had fallen in love. After we had dated for a few weeks, there was an understanding between us that someday, when we could afford it, we would get married.

As our discussions about marriage became more serious, we began to consider whether our financial situation was adequate to the demands of beginning married life. In addition to my salary, if we lived off post there would be subsistence and quarters allowances, which would bring my wages to about ninety dollars a month. My tending bar at the NCO club would bring in a bit more, and then there were the winnings from an occasional poker game. (Elaine said she could always tell when I had won at poker because I would show up to see her in a cab. If I came on foot, she knew I had lost.)

Elaine's income was about eighty dollars a month. With both of us working, we could count on a monthly income of about two hundred dollars a month, which seemed fairly adequate for that time. However, we discovered that if she married, Elaine could lose her job. That was very discouraging news. The risk was not justified; good jobs were too hard to find.

Meanwhile, there was war in Europe, and it was spreading; Hitler's power madness was increasing; and it was only a matter of time before the United States became involved. I began thinking once again about the Philippines. It would be possible to save money there, but a short discharge as a sergeant would mean starting over as a private in the islands. Travel in grade still wasn't allowed. I hadn't discussed this with Elaine yet because there had been rumors that all battalion posts were going to be closed down and integrated into other regiments and divisions. The 4th Infantry consisted of three battalions: our battalion at Fort Lincoln; one located in Missoula, Montana; and one in Spokane, Washington. These battalions were to be moved to one location at Fort Lewis, Washington.

Of course, by increasing our complement of new recruits, our consolidation into one regiment would result in the need for additional rank, at least that was our hope. Also, the reserve officers who were serving on active duty as sergeants were hoping to get called to active duty as officers. Instead, for a number of years the army would keep calling the ROTC officers. It wasn't until late 1940 that this situation changed.

CHAPTER 9

Back to the Philippines

The idea of going back to the Philippines continued to preoccupy me, and finally I discussed it with Elaine. We knew Fort Lincoln would be closed down in the next three or four months, and I would be transferred, along with the men from the other two battalions, to Fort Lewis, Washington. Elaine felt she couldn't give up her job and follow me to Fort Lewis because, given the current political climate, we didn't know how long I would be stationed there. On the other hand, if I were to take a short discharge, I was positive I could get my sergeant's rank back without difficulty; and, a tour of duty in the Philippines would offer the chance to save some money. If everything went according to plan, we could be married in a few years, and the chances were excellent that I would get my commission before returning to the States. I wasn't quite ready to decide, but either way, since it took time for a short-discharge application to be approved, I would be going to Fort Lewis.

Servicemen now were being treated like war heroes in Bismarck. With Fort Lincoln closing, the business people began to realize the impact we had on the city's economy. To be welcome anywhere in town, even in uniform, was a nice change!

The orders finally came to move to Fort Lewis by troop train. The day I said good-bye to Elaine was one of the saddest days of my life. I was very much in love with her. Luckily, it never entered my mind that it would be six long years before I would see her again.

While I was at Fort Lewis, not a week went by without my writing to her, and she was very faithful about answering. Plans for our future together gave me the incentive to continue working toward my commission. By this time, I was almost positive I would take a short discharge and go back to the Philippines. There would be a better chance for advancement and more time to complete the *Ten Series*. My planning was to be in vain; it was 1939, and world events were taking place that would disrupt many personal plans for a long, long time.

At Fort Lewis we were quartered in old World War I barracks. Dwight Eisenhower was attached to our outfit as a lieutenant colonel in charge of plans and training. There would be rapid advancement in his career during the next few years. Promotions come quickly in time of war; unfortunately, it takes a war to give servicemen a break as far as advancement is concerned.

My assignment at Fort Lewis was to instruct and drill recruits, and an unexpected opportunity to switch services came my way at this time. The area used for close-order drill was next to an air force company, and I was approached one day by that company's 1st sergeant and the company commander, who suggested I put in for a transfer to their outfit with the promise of becoming staff sergeant the same day I transferred. This was a tempting offer; however, after discussing it with my old platoon sergeant, Frank Smythe, I decided to stay with the army. All my training had been in the army infantry, and the army was expanding and offered the same advantages as the air force. Besides, I had put quite a bit of time and effort into the *Ten Series* and still felt it was my best bet for advancement. I have wondered sometimes what direction my life would have taken if I had made that change.

Maneuvers were held almost every day. The equipment shortage was so severe, we were using trucks with the word "tank" written on their sides. Even such large field support pieces as the artillery howitzers had to be improvised. The government was trying to get us the proper equipment, but the services had been neglected for so long, we were in need of everything.

The idea of returning to the Philippines was on my mind almost daily now. One especially cold rainy day, we were out on the lake rehearsing scrambling up the side of a ship with full packs and complete battle dress. I was climbing up a cargo net draped over the side of an improvised ship with a soggy pack pulling on my shoulders and rain running off my helmet, and I finally decided I had had enough of Fort Lewis. As I remembered it, the tropical climate of the Philippine islands seemed like it would be an immense improvement over my present conditions. That night I wrote to Elaine and told her I was putting in for a short discharge and would complete my tour of duty in the Philippines. With any luck, I added, I would be back in the States before we got into war.

Men returning from the Philippines said the U.S. Army there was increasing in strength and ratings were much easier to get than they had been in the past. When I put in for my short discharge, one of the sergeants remarked that I would probably never get my rank back, but that was a risk I was prepared to take. I had done it once; I could do it again.

I left the 4th Infantry with what was called a "saltwater warrant," which meant I could wear my stripes until reaching my assigned company in the Philippines; it was the same as acting sergeant with the pay of a private. My duties aboard ship—the USAT *U. S. Grant*, the same ship I had taken to my first overseas tour—involved giving calisthenics every morning to a company of men; the rest of the day, I was free to do as I wished. I spent some of my free time gambling and my luck was still holding. I wasn't getting rich, but I made enough money to buy a new civilian wardrobe when I reached the Philippines. We made the same stops that we had before: Hawaii and Guam. Honolulu hadn't grown much, but I noticed there were more army, navy, air, and marine personnel around than there had been the last time I was there. I wrote to Elaine from Hawaii: I really missed her, but two years wasn't a lifetime; and I was going to knuckle down to it and study and finish my *Ten Series* as soon as possible. Love is a great inspiration.

I spent four days sightseeing in Honolulu. With no duties except the morning calisthenics, I made the most of all the shore leave I could get and spent it in the company of two sergeants who took me in tow and showed me around.

Enroute to Guam, we had a number of lifeboat drills and practice blackouts. The daily news was filled with Hitler's takeover of one Balkan country after another, and our eventual involvement in the war became a major subject for conjecture.

We had a day-and-a-half layover at Guam; the marines still had only one company of men stationed there. The ship left on schedule, and we arrived in the Philippines without encountering any problems. Manila was as beautiful as I remembered it; and, I was back with the 31st Infantry, in Manila on the island of Luzon—and in quarantine again!

This time, I stayed in quarantine; going over the fence for a night on the town wasn't worth the risk. On our second day there, after being issued new tropical uniforms and gear, we had a close-order drill for which I was acting platoon sergeant. Some of the 1st sergeants and company commanders turned out to watch us, and one of them happened to be my old 1st sergeant who had been with K Company when I was in the Philippines from 1935 to 1937. He told the company commander that I had soldiered in his outfit as a bugler. He congratulated me on having made sergeant in the States and wanted to know how it had happened; so, I told him about taking the written test and having the best score in the company and said that my goal was to finish my correspondence course and get a commission.

That afternoon, the sergeant called me to say his company commander would like to have me in his outfit. I had spent some time trying to find out which company would give me the best chance for a quick promotion, and this was certainly the break I was looking for. I didn't even ask if I would receive a promotion; I knew if Captain Warshowsky was still around, which he was, my worries about getting back my stripes were over. I requested K Company and was given the assignment.

When I arrived at K Company, I discovered a former corporal who had been in my outfit, and in my platoon, in the States was also there; but, he was now Sergeant Hoffman, and I was a private again. In my estimation Hoffman had made a poor corporal, and it wasn't likely that being a sergeant would make much of an improvement. It looked like trouble ahead. In my mind, those three hoped-for stripes receded a bit; but, I was determined to dig in and work hard. I was made acting corporal on my arrival and received my corporal's stripes about three months later.

One night while I was pulling a Charge of Quarters, the 1st sergeant and Hoffman came in, both of them drunk and noisy. They were drinking buddies and as a general rule shared off-base quarters with some local women with whom they were living. That night for some reason, they returned to the base. I tried to quiet them down and talk them into going back to their off-base housing or using the special-duty room, where a few extra beds were kept for emergency use. They said they both outranked me and would do as they damn well pleased. The racket woke up a couple of other sergeants who wanted to know what the hell was going on. I explained the circumstances and said I was placing both men under arrest of quarters until morning. We finally got them quieted down and in bed to sleep it off.

The next morning I got them up and asked if they remembered what had happened. Neither of them did, so I refreshed their memories and finished by telling them they were still under arrest of quarters. Sergeant Hoffman asked if I had logged them in that way, and I said, "No, but I should have." I knew he had done everything possible to keep me from getting my third stripe, and I confronted him with this knowledge. He denied it, of course. The 1st sergeant never said a word; he knew he was on walking on eggs. Had the circumstances been reversed, it was pretty obvious by noon I would have been a private. I said I would forget the incident, but that from now on I wanted a fair chance to make the grade if I could. I didn't want any help, but I didn't want any unnecessary obstacles either. Nothing was entered about the episode on my Charge of Quarters report. They were bound to mess up again; it was only a matter of time.

I was staying close to the barracks, studying, and writing to Elaine once, sometimes twice, a week. I had completed half the *Ten Series* by now and was doing a lot of cramming. Captain Warshowsky was helpful and encouraged me to continue.

I was now one of the three acting platoon sergeants. The other two were excellent soldiers; and, they had more time in than I did. It was going to be an uphill climb to win those three stripes. Sergeant Hoffman was openly hostile and told me I would never get his recommendation. I told him I didn't need it, and it might be *his* stripes I would be wearing. We left it at that.

At this time, we were doing combat exercises in the mornings and taking ten-mile hikes in the evenings. The wear and tear was beginning to show on some of the sergeants who were living with women off post. Finally, one morning, Hoffman showed up drunk. The company commander, who happened to be there early, saw what was going on. He gave Hoffman a chance to resign or take a court-martial, and Hoffman resigned, stepping down to private. Although I didn't get his stripes, I made sergeant three months later. Hoffman was acting corporal in my platoon for a short time. We had come full circle.

As acting 1st sergeant, I was placed in charge of all new recruits. A great number of these were coming in from the States at this time, and I had my work cut out for me. We were still attached to the 31st Infantry and were living in tents near Fort McKinley in the Manila area. Gen. Jonathan Wainwright frequently paused during his horseback rides to watch the recruits go through their close-order and rifle drills. He was always complimentary to me, and he seemed to enjoy listening to the conversations of the soldiers in the ranks.

The Filipino civilians were being mobilized at this time under the direction and command of Gen. Douglas MacArthur. Because of the shortage of officers, sergeants who could pass the entrance exams for Officer Candidate School (OCS) were being selected from the ranks. Orders came that I was being relieved at McKinley and would be attending OCS in Manila. I was almost ready to complete my *Ten Series*, but was sent to OCS anyway. There, I completed the courses without any problems and was given the permanent rank of master sergeant with a promise of a 2d lieutenant's rank in an emergency. If I wished, I could still complete the correspondence course, which might make it easier to get a regular army commission.

The war talk continued, and the news was bleak. Wives and children of servicemen were ordered to return to the States. Other civilians were asked to leave on a voluntary basis; anyone staying would remain at his or her own risk. There were a number of suicides among young recruits who had recently arrived from the States and were afraid war might break out before they could return home. Tragically, these eighteen- and nineteen-year olds simply couldn't come to grips with the idea of fighting in a war.

Espionage now became a problem. The memory of one incident in particular has stayed with me. Two brothers of German descent had immigrated to Mexico and from there to the United States, where they volunteered for duty in the army, eventually reaching the Philippines. They were working in our headquarters as secret agents for the German government. One of them was at the battalion level, and the other at the regimental. Headquarters was aware they were enemy agents and used them to feed misinformation to the Germans. It was risky: there was always the chance that real information might go out, and they were watched very closely. Returning from church one Sunday and still thinking about the post chaplain's sermon on the recent suicides, I decided to stop at K Company to pick up a few personal belongings and check the mail. A muffled shot came from the direction of I Company; soldiers suddenly appeared from everywhere. One of the men who had been passing information to the Germans had committed suicide. Holding a picture album against his abdomen, he had fired a .45 automatic pistol into it. The album muffled the shot, but this also had been an attempt to destroy its contents. The man was rushed to Sternberg Hospital but died the following day. What was left of the album contained enough evidence to convict him had he lived. His brother was placed under arrest immediately.

The day after this incident I was sent to the island of Negros, in the central Philippines, to train the islanders, the Visayans. I was assigned to the 1st Battalion, 71st Infantry, 71st Division, Philippine Army, with five other Americans: Lt. Col. Donald Bonnett; Lieutenants Sea, Speckard, and Porter; and Sergeant Brumback.

CHAPTER 10

Training Visayan Soldiers on Negros

With the exception of a few key officers, the troops being trained on Negros were all civilians from Negros itself or other small islands of the central Philippines. The battalion commander, Capt. Guillermo Nakar, and most of his staff were graduates of the Philippine Army Academy. The other officers were from the reserves and the majority of these had ROTC training. The officers were used to commands given in English, and they responded well to oral instruction provided we remembered to speak slowly and repeat what we said several times.

The recruits, however, had had very little schooling—some could hardly write their names well enough to sign the payroll—and most of their instruction was accomplished by means of demonstration. These men were especially adept at bayonet drill and had a natural skill with knives and knifelike weapons. Most of them spoke Visayan, the dialect of the central islands.

All in all, this was a very fine group of men. Our job was to turn them into top-notch soldiers. According to the news and ever more alarming rumors, we were running out of time.

Each week, Captain Nakar would outline what he expected of us. In general, we were to teach military discipline, manual of arms, close-order drill, hand and arm signals, bayonet drill, and sanitation. As long as the assigned work was completed by the end of each week, we were given a free hand. Originally, Colonel Bonnett and Lieutenants Sea, Speckard, and Porter were to help the Philippine Army

Academy officers organize headquarters, but that help wasn't needed and the American officers simply held the weekend inspections.

Right after we set up camp, for the benefit of the other companies I had one company dig some latrines exemplifying proper sanitation procedure. The first weekend inspection included my pride and joy: those latrines I had designed. They were clean as a whistle and had not even a trace of odor; however, there was an odor coming from somewhere outside. The mystery was solved when I discovered that in order to keep the latrines clean for inspection, the men had been using the area behind them. I had to explain that really, they had done a terrific construction job, but they were also to use these facilities; otherwise, within one week's time we would have to move our camp.

One day shortly after we arrived on Negros, a chauffeur-driven car pulled up close to where I was instructing a company in bayonet drill, and an older, obviously American, woman got out, introduced herself as Mrs. Harbour, and said she would like to talk with me. She explained that she had heard about the American officers on Negros who were acting as instructors for the Visayan soldiers. She asked how many we were and what our food situation was. I told her there were five of us in camp (Colonel Bonnett was at regiment headquarters), and that although we had been on the island for two weeks, the American rations we had been promised had not materialized; we were eating with the Philippine officers but did not like the Filipino food.

Explaining that her husband was a logging superintendent for the Insular Lumber Company and she lived alone with her Siamese cats in a large house in the small company-built compound for executives and foreign employees about five kilometers from our camp, she said she would be delighted to have the five of us stay with her. The compound, she said, was quite lovely and consisted of twenty homes built around a nine-hole golf course. She had plenty of room in her house, she added, and would welcome having someone besides the other compound residents to talk to.

As wonderful as this offer sounded to me, I wasn't sure I could afford an arrangement that included living accommodations, breakfast, dinner, and even a box lunch. Mrs. Harbour asked if thirty pesos (fifteen dollars) a month would be too expensive. Astonished, I quickly said no, but I wondered how she could afford to house and feed five of us for such a minimal amount of money. She told me not to worry about that and said we could move in that very evening if this was agreeable. I went back to camp with the good news. The three lieutenants and Sergeant Brumback were as delighted as I was with the unexpected change in our living arrangements.

When the five of us arrived at our new quarters, we found a welcome party waiting. Mrs. Harbour had invited some of her neighbors over to meet us, including a woman from Holland, several Canadians, and a retired British army colonel whose exaggerated BBC accent was extremely hard for us to understand. This man, the father of one of the lumber company executives, had his own private zoo in the compound, and his animal collection included an eighteen-foot-long python, indigenous monkeys, and a few of the small native wildcats and chickens.

Later, after the neighbors left, our new landlady showed us through the house. Three beds had been set up on the sleeping porch where the lieutenants were to be quartered. Sergeant Brumback and I were to share a bedroom with twin beds and its own bathroom. There were also the master suite and a small room belonging to the two houseboys, the only live-in members of Mrs. Harbour's staff.

Lieutenant Porter took exception to the arrangements because the three officers would have to share the upstairs hall bathroom. He said a more satisfactory arrangement would be to have the houseboys and sergeants sharing the sleeping porch so that the officers could use the two bedrooms and private bath. Lieutenants Sea and Speckard, both of whom outranked Porter, assured Mrs. Harbour that her arrangements were quite satisfactory. The disgruntled lieutenant was told he was under no obligation to stay, but rank conscious though he was, he was no fool. He stayed.

From the start, Mrs. Harbour treated me like a son and, maybe because we were both from the Midwest, we became good friends. My out-of-the-ordinary landlady was from Iowa, had been a school teacher, and was now about sixty years old. Her husband was from North Carolina. Since her only child, a daughter, now lived in the States, and Mr. Harbour came home only for weekends, during which he spent most of his time playing golf, she was delighted to find that I shared her enthusiasm for playing cards. Her favorite pastime was playing honeymoon bridge, which she taught me. We played for drinks, with the result that I drank about thirty dollars' worth of her beer and hard liquor each month. I enjoyed these evenings, perhaps as much for the opportunity to talk about my family, and Elaine, and about how I happened to join the army, as for the opportunity to indulge my love for cards.

Mrs. Harbour seemed to enjoy listening, and I soon found myself relating experiences that I never could have shared with my family, such as my having run the gambling games in the dayroom at Fort Lincoln with the blessings of the 1st sergeant, who received half the take. I even became quite friendly with the Siamese cats, who would lie in front of the door, sleek, well fed, and growling. These pleasant hours made a welcome contrast to the increasingly tense atmosphere at work.

It was now October 1941, and the rumors of imminent war grew stronger by the day. That the United States soon would be at war, not only with Germany, but also with Japan, seemed an incontrovertible fact.

My own sailing orders were for 20 December, and I only hoped I would be out of the Philippines before the start of hostilities. If I was not to be that lucky, then I hoped that I would outlive this war everyone believed we would win in six months because, I reminded myself with youthful optimism, I would have my commission and could return home a hero. One of the first lessons the army teaches its soldiers is never underestimate the enemy, and I should have known better. We all should have known better.

Not long after we had moved to Mrs. Harbour's, an invitation arrived at headquarters for the American advisory staff to visit one of the island's large family-owned sugar plantations from which, before the war in Europe intervened, sugar had been shipped to all parts of the world. Colonel Bonnett came over from regiment to tell us that he felt only the officers should accept the invitation and that Sergeant Brumback and I should decline. Mrs. Harbour, who was instrumental in getting us the invitation, pointed out that the wording of it included all of us. She told the colonel that, especially in view of the fact that Sergeant Brumback and I were to be commissioned, we should be allowed to accept, and she added further persuasion by remarking, "If they can't go, none of us will." Reluctantly, Bonnett conceded, but he was a West Point graduate of the old school and, while he liked the enlisted men—especially the NCOs—and often said we were the backbone of the American army, he didn't believe officers should fraternize with enlisted personnel. It was quite obvious he thought Sergeant Brumback and I would cramp his style on this occasion.

When we arrived at the plantation, I was very pleasantly surprised. The house was a beautiful fifteen-room casa-hacienda with a veranda completely encircling it. There was even an outdoor swimming pool. The owners were two very handsome brothers in their early thirties. They were mestizos: part Caucasian, part Chinese, part Filipino. Their two sisters were lovely, slender girls with cream-color complexions and elegant features. They had attended school in Germany and spoke English, German, Visayan, and Tagalog. When the older one discovered I spoke German, she spent the greater part of the evening with me, much to the annoyance of all the officers.

At Colonel Bonnett's insistence, Brumback and I were wearing civilian clothes, but this certainly worked to our advantage where the girls were concerned. On the way home, Lieutenant Sea remarked that if he had known how the evening was going to turn out, he would have joined Bonnett in insisting that we remain at home. Mrs. Harbour laughed and said, "It proves one thing, bars and eagles don't mean everything." Lieutenant Sea and I went over to the hacienda several times a week after that to visit the young women—chaperones were always present.

My busy social life notwithstanding, I also finished my correspondence course during my stay on Negros and forwarded the completed work through the 31st Infantry headquarters. In doing so, I set off a series of difficulties that would plague me later each time I received one of my various commissions and several serial numbers.

Late in November, orders came to move the regiment from Negros to Luzon. My orders to return to the States on 20 December still stood and I looked forward to this with increasing happiness. I could hardly wait to see Elaine again, take her home to meet the family, and show her my hometown. Here in this tropical region, it was difficult to remember that it was winter back there. The cold and snow of the Dakota prairies seemed very distant indeed, and the carefree times of so long ago when I spent the winter holidays ice skating were in stark contrast to the preparation for war that now was my daily life.

We were well aware the Japanese were a threat to our forces in the Far East. Until they were stopped by MacArthur sometime in August of 1941, Japanese naval ships came into Manila Bay and their sailors debarked to take pictures of our military installations. All war plans, including the Orange Plan, were practiced many times in peacetime.

The regiment was picked up by two tramp steamers the army had confiscated and converted into troopships. We landed in Manila Harbor and were taken to a bivouac area near Camp O'Donnell, about nine kilometers from Clark Air Force Base. We set up camp and began to dig in against the event of a Japanese air strike.

At last, on 4 December 1941, Colonel Bonnett pinned 2d lieutenant bars on my shirt. I was given the serial number of 0888099. I had been doing the work of an officer for years; the big difference now was the pay.

The area where we were bivouacked was ideal for maneuvers, and the men still needed the training. We covered the same training I had received over the past nine years, and I was trying now to pass it on to this newly formed army of civilians. The men were a far cry from combat-ready, but they were willing to learn. I came to respect and love them for their loyalty to the United States. Their situation was similar now to that of many American soldiers who were far from home. Many of them were married and had children. Moved from Negros to a strange island where different dialects were spoken, they were homesick and lonely. The increasingly warlike climate and my own thoughts of returning home heightened my perception of their position.

Out on maneuvers one day, my men and I spotted some planes in the distance dropping what appeared to be parachutists. We volunteered to search the area in question. I checked a map for the approximate location where the drop had been made and moved my platoon out in two trucks. Two kilometers from the drop area, I deployed men on each side of the road and sent scouts out ahead. We came upon some civilians who gave us the information that a supply drop had been made to some soldiers in the area. I took a squad of men, continued to advance, and encountered American troops on maneuvers who confirmed that supplies had been parachuted down to them. Relieved that we had not found enemy troops, we returned to our outfit. But the expectation of an enemy invasion had become part of our daily lives.

The latest news was that Hitler was overrunning Europe and encountering very little resistance. Although the United States had the largest fleet in the world and was beginning to supply England with the armaments she needed to hold him off, it seemed that everything was going Hitler's way. He would have to be stopped. At the same time, rumors about the Japanese war machine grew more ominous by the day.

CHAPTER 11

The Inevitable:
7–8 December 1941

Lieutenants Sea and Speckard and I had been working long hours, putting in extra time with some of the company officers. At last we decided a little time off was in order. Colonel Bonnett agreed and gave us two-day passes. On the morning of 7 December, we caught a ride on one of the trucks that made daily supply runs to Manila.

Arriving in the city, we checked into the Manila Hotel and went to the cocktail lounge for drinks. Manila was jam-packed with soldiers. It was now after midnight, or Monday, 8 December. In Hawaii, it was Sunday morning, 7 December, 1941.

Suddenly, all over the city sirens began wailing, and from truck-mounted loud speakers blared the announcement that the Japanese had attacked Pearl Harbor. Other loud speakers broadcast the information to military personnel that all leaves and passes were cancelled and they should report back to their units immediately. The civilian population seemed to take the news in stride; all of Manila had been expecting a Japanese attack, though not a sneak one on Pearl Harbor.

The three of us managed to find a ride to Clark Field where we called in to our bivouac area requesting that a jeep be sent to pick us up. We arrived back in camp in the early morning hours of 8 December, changed quickly into fatigues, and alerted our troops to be ready to move at a moment's notice. The entire regiment was now on alert. We were to repulse any landing the Japanese might try to make.

All the men were keyed up, and the atmosphere in camp was almost palpably tense. Would the Japanese land in the Philippines?

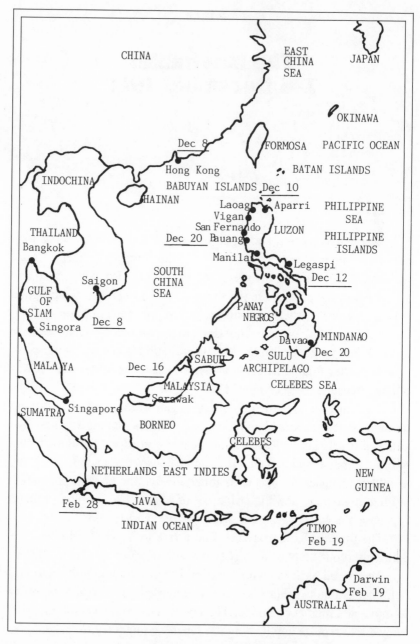

First Japanese Attacks, Far East,
December 1941–February 1942

96

Could we repel a Japanese invasion? These were the questions on every soldier's mind. Imaginations ran wild; every one of us tried to envision what this war meant and would mean, and whether or not we would ever return to our homes. The big question in my mind was, will I still be able to leave for the States on 20 December? In only a few hours, that question would be answered.

At noon while some of us were on our way to the officers' mess, we heard planes in the distance. One of the officers walking next to me said, "They aren't going to catch *us* sleeping like they did Pearl Harbor." At that very moment the air raid alert sounded. Above the sirens' shriek, we could hear the planes and identify them by the distinctive drone-and-fade-out sound of their motors. They were Japanese. We ran for the bomb shelters. While I ran, I said good-bye to my trip home.

Approximately sixty Japanese planes were involved in the raid that day. Their mission was to destroy the American air bases at Clark and Nichols fields, as well as the army installations at Forts Stotsenburg and McKinley. They came very close to accomplishing this. We were caught unprepared. In view of the fact that we already knew about the attack on Pearl Harbor, such total unpreparedness seems incredible and inexcusable.

The destruction at Clark Field was appalling. Many of the soldiers who were killed or horribly wounded had been caught in the mess halls and never had a chance. Only a very few planes were salvaged; parked on the field and in hangars, they too had no chance of escape. The conditions everywhere on the base were indescribable.

We learned that a Filipino sergeant working as an undercover agent for the Japanese had been caught guiding enemy planes to ammunition dumps by means of a mirror. He had confessed and was tried and shot that afternoon, but even swift retribution could not undo the damage he had made possible.

The regimental briefing on 9 December included more detailed information about the damage to our navy at Pearl Harbor and the bombing of Clark and McKinley fields. We were told of the imminence of enemy landings in the Batan and Babuyan islands, the most northerly of the Philippine Archipelago land masses. If the Japanese agreed, Manila was to be declared an open city. All military personnel would

97

be moved out; the city would not be defended. In this way, it was hoped that the Pearl of the Orient, as Manila was called in recognition of its beauty, would be saved from destruction.

For the next few days, we held squad, platoon, company, and battalion field exercises during the hours of daylight and listened to the news from the States that came over the shortwave radio sets at night. Most of these broadcasts reiterated assurances that help would arrive in time to save the Philippines.

Meanwhile, Japanese broadcasts informed us of the opposite and reported the occupation of islands north of Luzon, assuring us that we could not win the war and advising us to surrender the remaining islands unconditionally and immediately. These enemy broadcasts included promises that as prisoners of war we would be well treated by the Japanese Imperial Forces. According to this barrage of propaganda, no intelligent American soldier could possibly believe help was on the way when his country's forces were tied up fighting on two fronts (after Pearl Harbor, we were also at war with Germany) and its Pacific fleet was immobilized.

Privately, I desperately wanted to believe that help was coming and we would stop the Japanese and end the war in six months. More realistically, however, I came to the conclusion that MacArthur knew—and had known as long ago as 1935—that our position in the Philippines was untenable and that he would simply play for time, making the Japanese utilize a great number of soldiers in order to take, and afterwards to hold, the islands.

PART THREE

FROM THE DEATH MARCH TO THE JUNGLES

CHAPTER 12

From Manila to Bauang

On 15 December 1941, the 1st Battalion, 71st Infantry, Philippine Army, under the command of Captain Nakar, was ordered to take up a defensive position near the city of Bauang, in the province of La Union. I was assigned by Nakar to A Company as an advisor. We were given a half-moon-shaped sector on a ridge overlooking the south edge of Bauang, the Coast Highway, and the Lingayen Gulf. Behind us, a vertical cliff dropped 150 feet to a wooded area below.

B Company was to the south on our left flank. To the north on our right flank we tied in with a battalion from the Philippine Army's 11th Infantry. The 71st Infantry was now attached to the 11th Division, Philippine Army, which was commanded by Gen. William E. Brougher.

Our lines were very thin and were strung north to San Fernando. The area from Aparri to the north and as far south as San Fernando was manned by civilian volunteers with perhaps only a week of training.

Company A was ordered to dig in. Most of the men dug only foxholes, not deep trenches. I knew they would have to dig in much deeper for adequate shelter from the heavy shelling we could expect. Lieutenant Pilar, who was company commander, and I inspected the company's line of defense and called the NCOs and platoon leaders together for a conference. I asked one officer charged with a platoon how long he thought he could hold his position if the Japanese made a naval landing in the Lingayan Gulf and used their big guns on us. He replied that the shallow foxholes were a mistake and he would make the necessary changes. I told the group there was a 99 percent chance of a landing in the gulf, and the Japanese ships surely would give their landing troops plenty of overhead fire support. Deeper trenches were absolutely essential. This was explained to the men on the line, and we sent some of them into Bauang to confiscate as many burlap sacks as they could find to strengthen the walls of the trenches. The rest of the men started digging to reinforce the front, sides, and rear of their trenches for more complete protection against the expected naval bombardment.

During this time, nightly staff meetings were being held at battalion headquarters. We knew a landing was imminent. On 20 December the regimental and battalion commanders made an inspection of our line. This was the day I should have been aboard ship, on my way home. Most of my personal belongings—letters, pictures, and army records—already had been sent ahead in preparation for my departure. I was never to see them again. The irony of that situation and the futility of carefully planning for the future were things I would reflect on often in time to come. At the moment the present, with its absolute certainty of invasion and the necessity for intense preparation to repulse it, had my total concentration.

Company A was complimented on the excellent fortification job we had done. Lieutenant Pilar and I were told we would be the holding company in the event of a withdrawal; we were not to fall back until we received word from battalion headquarters, located to the south of us on our left flank.

The dawn of 21 December revealed a gulf filled with Japanese ships. A landing had not yet begun; apparently the plan was to take us without firing a shot. Later, we heard the Japanese were in contact with our division headquarters and wanted an unconditional surrender. The answer was, of course, no. And then the bombardment began.

Under heavy shelling, we watched the enemy soldiers climb down cargo nets into small landing craft. Wave after wave of Japanese soldiers came ashore. A few Stokes mortars were our only heavy-weapon support. These knocked out several of the landing craft, but the enemy guns were zeroing in on the mortars, and we had to switch positions. While the Japanese troops were landing at Bauang, their previously landed bicycle troops were coming down almost unopposed from the

Bauang and the Lingayen Gulf

north to join up with this landing force. There was no word from either our right or left flanks. I made a reconnaissance south and found none of our troops. I then told Lieutenant Pilar to make radio or telephone contact with battalion headquarters to report the bicycle troops. I decided to check to the north for our right flank because we had heard no gunfire from that direction either. I knew it was quite possible the right flank troops, who came from the 11th Infantry and had had only a few weeks training, had pulled out without notifying us.

While Pilar tried to contact headquarters, I took a runner and started north to follow our trench line. The heavy bombardment had caused quite a few casualties along the line. We reached the locale of our right flank under heavy enemy sniping. Like the .22-caliber rifle, the Japanese rifle had a very distinctive sound when fired. We ran into

103

a Filipino clad in civilian clothes who said he was a soldier from up north. When I asked him what he was doing dressed as a civilian, he said his officer had told him to change clothing. Then he had been captured by the Japanese who believed he really was a civilian and were using him as a guide. He knew our group was on the ridge and wanted to join us. He had no weapon. I wanted to question him further, but just then there wasn't time.

My runner was shouting that he had spotted several Japanese soldiers coming up the trail. We let them get fairly close and threw a hand grenade. All hell broke loose. A machine gun rattled and bullets whistled everywhere while we ran for a trench across an area covered with *cogon*, a coarse tall grass used in the Philippines for thatching. I was carrying only a .45 pistol and a few hand grenades and decided it would be a good idea to carry an automatic weapon whenever possible thereafter.

Heavy gunfire was coming from every direction except the rear. Crawling under the cross fire, in and out of the trenches, and through the tall cogon, I reached the extreme right flank, where I left word with the officer in charge to watch the flank closely and not to let the enemy in behind us. I told him I had not been able to make contact with the companies to our left or right and that I thought they might have pulled out. The officer told me his platoon also had been strafed and bombed heavily by enemy planes and had taken considerable shelling from the ships in the gulf.

My runner, the civilian-soldier, and I worked our way along the line and back to Company A headquarters. By now, the company had lost about thirty men and had some wounded. Our orders were to remain in the holding position so that the rest of the battalion, which had suffered very heavy casualties, could withdraw. However, we were receiving no messages and did not know whether or not the withdrawal had been accomplished. We were on our own and could only guess what the rest of the battalion was doing or how long we should continue holding before making our own withdrawal.

There was no possibility of fighting our way out to the front or flanks; any withdrawal would have to be to the rear and down the cliff. I estimated that we were opposed by nearly a battalion of enemy troops, and I knew our supplies were almost exhausted.

I asked Lieutenant Pilar to put his executive officer in charge so that he and I could reconnoiter the rear of our position again. We left the radio with company headquarters and took two runners. I borrowed an automatic rifle and took a few more hand grenades, and we began to move back into the cogon toward the edge of the cliff. We had covered about a hundred yards when we heard movement in front of us. Thinking it might be caused by some stray soldiers from our right flank, we called out. Machine-gun fire replied. The Japanese were expecting us to withdraw and had circled around to block the edge of the cliff, our only line of escape. The four of us spread out, and I opened up with the automatic weapon. The two runners and Lieutenant Pilar started moving forward, yelling at the top of their lungs and throwing hand grenades. The machine gun was silenced. We reached the edge of the cliff, made a cursory visual survey, and decided our men could drop down it, using the shrubs and small trees protruding from the side to break their fall.

We returned to company headquarters to find that the firing had died down somewhat. We passed along the word to withdraw to the edge of the cliff. We would leave some of the automatic-weapons men behind to cover our retreat; they were to follow us a few minutes later. At this point, Pilar asked me to take charge of the company. He didn't want the responsibility for a withdrawal from position without permission from battalion headquarters. His concern was understandable; his orders were to hold the position at all cost. I assumed responsibility for the withdrawal. But there wasn't any choice: our supplies were almost gone, and we were completely outnumbered.

We tried raising the 1st Battalion by radio for nearly four hours and received no response. Its men either had been captured or had made a safe withdrawal. A decision had to be made, and there was only the one option: to go over the cliff. I decided to start the withdrawal.

With the understanding that everyone was to reassemble in the wooded area below, we began the descent, hanging on to any shrubs and trees we could grab to keep from dropping or sliding too fast. Very shortly, the Japanese arrived at the edge of the cliff. They decided not to follow us, but they dropped hand grenades over the edge. Luckily, we were well under cover by then. Perhaps the enemy soldiers had a time schedule to meet and therefore decided not to risk pursuit. Anyway, they had taken their objective: the ridge overlooking Bauang and the Lingayen Gulf.

CHAPTER 13

The Back Road to Bataan

We were near Bauang. Of the company's original 120 men we had 60 left, including the wounded we were carrying. As we withdrew to the south, Japanese reconnaissance planes flew overhead. It was almost sundown. We infiltrated across the open ground toward the mountains, a squad at a time, until dark; I wanted to reach Baguio by the next day.

During one of the stops we made to rest and care for the wounded, I realized I was very thirsty and pulled out my canteen, only to discover it was empty—except for a Japanese rifle bullet that rattled around inside.

As night settled in, the civilian-soldier we had adopted was proving very useful; he knew all the back trails through the mountains to Baguio. Occasionally, we would come across civilians who had information about the route the Japanese were taking. From their reports, it appeared that the enemy was staying close to the Coast Highway.

Sometime close to midnight, we reached the town of Trinidad. We were now not too far from Baguio. Our forward point was challenged in English; he answered in Visayan, knowing that if the challenger was part of our regiment, he would acknowledge in Visayan, which he did. Quite by accident, we had found part of our regiment and our commander, Captain Nakar, who was very happy to see us. He explained that his communications equipment had been knocked out, and he had tried to get messengers through to us, but these had been either killed or captured. Our maintenance of the holding position had succeeded in

Escape Route, Bauang to Bataan

108

giving his group enough time for an orderly withdrawal, and he was pleased with the timing of our own withdrawal and very relieved to find that we had made it out. Some of the others had not been so fortunate. Lieutenant Porter and a number of the Filipino enlisted men covering Nakar's withdrawal had been killed. Porter had stayed in position until he ran out of ammunition. The battalion had suffered a 50 percent loss of manpower in wounded or killed in action.

We had had nothing to eat since early morning, and by the time some of the Trinidad residents cooked enough food for all of us, we were ravenous. I did not like rice—yet—and I ate fried eggs and strips of bacon graciously provided me in deference to my then-uneducated taste. While we ate, our hosts gave us various bits of information, such as that there were no Japanese in Baguio, and that some of the local miners together with a few Filipino soldiers had dynamited the narrow mountain paths that led there.

Captain Nakar thought he could find a radio transmitter in Baguio and try to contact our regiment or division headquarters for further orders. We all agreed that Bataan would be the natural place for a last stand, which would call for the Orange Plan.

War Plan Orange had been devised by military planners, including Gen. Jonathan Wainwright, as early as 1921–22. The plan had been based on the premise that Japan would initiate an attack against the Philippine islands, and it called for an orderly withdrawal onto the Bataan Peninsula, where a defensive position was to be held until reinforcements could arrive from the United States. This maneuver had been practiced many times by the 31st Infantry, U.S. Army, and many of us were familiar with it. The Orange Plan presupposed the existence of entrenchments and fortifications built by a civilian labor force; in fact, neither fortification nor labor force materialized. This work could have been done in the period between 8 December 1941 and 7 January 1942, with the eighty thousand inhabitants of Bataan digging the trench lines and fortifications that the plan called for. But it wasn't. Also unknown to us, as long as a year before the Japanese attack on Pearl Harbor military planners were aware that it would take considerably more time than the six months allowed for in the Orange Plan for the necessary aid to arrive to relieve the forces on Bataan. Thousands of unsuspecting soldiers were entering the maw of Bataan—from which many would not return.

According to the rumors we were hearing from the civilians, a large number of American troopships was on the way to the Philippines. I didn't believe this but said nothing. It was good for morale to believe help was coming. We set up listening posts and outposts so that we could get some rest before leaving for Baguio the following morning. We were all bone-weary. It had been one hell of a miserable day; and we knew there were more to come. We managed to get five hours of rest, and after an early breakfast, we moved out in single column on the back road to Baguio.

A few kilometers from Baguio, we encountered some more civilians and questioned them about the possible presence there of Japanese troops. Baguio was the home of the civilian-soldier who had joined us at Bauang, and since he knew the city well, he volunteered to go with these people to see whether any Japanese had arrived there that day. This man could be trusted, and he spoke several of the dialects used in Baguio, which was a great help to us. In about three hours, he returned with the information that the Japanese were still moving down the coast and encountering very little resistance. They were being harassed a bit from the hillsides by small bands of Filipino soldiers, and we felt certain these were from our regiment and the 26th Cavalry.

When we arrived in Baguio, we found a radio transmitter but were unable to make contact with our regiment. At last, Captain Nakar succeeded in contacting Col. John Horan, the senior ranking officer in northern Luzon, who informed him all troops had been ordered to Bataan. Horan also told Nakar that all roads were closed and, if possible, we were to use the back trails. Many years later when reading Colonel Horan's diary, I discovered he had done everything possible in his effort to contact and inform the troops who had been cut off in the north of Luzon.

The following extract is from Colonel Horan's personal diary:

> After my previous rebuff from USAFFE (United States Army Forces Far East) about being "unduly perturbed" and not knowing the enemy situation, I decided to hold fast until I could notify USAFFE by the

still active Bureau of Posts radio service. Same was done on the evening of the 22nd. Our code books had been destroyed and any message would have to be sent in the clear. So I tried to send a garbled message I thought any intelligence officer would understand, to wit: "My right hand in a vice, my left hand OK, my nose in a funnel, my bowels concentrated, my rear wide open, my left hand OK, request orders!" I thought they would interpret this as meaning that "The Naguilion Road is closed, the Kenyon Road is blocked, all troops are concentrated at Baguio, the Mountain Trail to Bontoc is open for retreat to the north or we could go east over the mountains to the Cagayan Valley." I believe I also asked for trucks at Imugan.

Someone evidently did understand as late in the evening of the 23rd I received word; "Save your command. Use mountain trails," by Bureau of Posts radio.

I immediately contacted Col. Bonnett and advised him to take his troops by motor to Bokod (Bangao) and thence by the old Spanish Trail over the mountains via Pampangand and Pingkian to Aritao, thence over Belete [sic] Pass to San Jose, Cabanatuan, and Bataan. After the war I learned that the old Spanish Trail dirt motor logging road was blocked by landslides, that he had sent all his transportation over a cliff, went on by foot and got transportation at Aritao from Colonel Townsend and got thru to Bataan.

Our battalion followed the mountain trails to Birac. We avoided Rosario, staying east of it because civilians said the Japanese had sent patrols there but then had gone back to the coast and Highway 3 to continue their push south. With this information came more rumors about the anticipated arrival of American reinforcements to save the islands—and us.

On Christmas Day, Captain Nakar made arrangements with some of the political leaders of Rosario to hide our wounded in barrios in the surrounding countryside. These men were to hide out in the hills until they were able to travel; then they were to form guerrilla units and harass the enemy in any ways they could.

Captain Nakar held officers call the following morning; he had received a message from Colonel Bonnett ordering him to proceed to Bataan if possible. Bonnett was near Aritao, almost due east of our position, with remnants of the 12th Infantry, and the 2d and 3d battalions of the 71st Infantry, Philippine Army. He was waiting for trucks to take them to Bataan.

Captain Nakar suggested we break into small units and head south to the Bataan Peninsula. I was familiar with some parts of the area having been on peacetime maneuvers there, and thought that, with a decent map to help me, I could negotiate the countryside alone. Captain Nakar gave us overlay maps of northern and central Luzon, and I returned with mine to A Company to discuss our next move with the company commander, Lieutenant Pilar. I offered to go to Bataan with him, but warned that since I was an American, my presence could create a problem for him if we were captured. His answer was, "We are Visayans and ourselves strangers on this island. I would be happy to have you with me." Limited as my knowledge was, he and his men were even more unfamiliar with the region, and I believe he felt I would be an asset. Certainly I was happy to be with them and not alone on that trip.

Our route would take us across the Japanese lines, which ran from north to south on Highway 3. It was understood that if we could not get through as a unit, we would each make our own way to a rendezvous near Baguio, which the Japanese had not yet occupied, or if that wasn't feasible, to an alternate rendezvous in the Cagayan Valley. Our orders were to avoid the enemy. We bid each other good-bye and good luck and broke up into small units for our march to Bataan. I was not in Lieutenant Pilar's group, and I did not see him again.

On 27 December, my group left the bivouac area near Rosario. Our maps were fairly accurate, and we expected to pick up guides as we moved south along the mountain trails to Bataan, a distance of some 125 miles. By making a forced march we hoped to arrive there by 2 January and, we also hoped, ahead of the Japanese, whose progress along Highway 3 had been slowed by harassment by the still-active guerrilla troops. The first day, we covered nearly 30 miles by walking until midnight. On the second day, we planned to reach a small barrio near Rosales, again by marching far into the night because the Japanese were infiltrating the area with motorized troops.

The civilians we met along the way were very kind, feeding us and allowing us to sleep in their barrios. We traveled light, with no supplies other than our weapons, ammunition, canteens, and shovels. Wisely, we made a point of always asking barrio residents if they could spare any food, and as a result, they were more than willing to share with us whatever they had. Although the Japanese were treating the Filipinos with kid gloves, because they had encountered more opposition to their occupation than they had expected and did not want unnecessarily to antagonize the island's population, their troops—forty-three thousand to forty-four thousand strong—were landed on Luzon with little or no food supplies. These men immediately began to live off the land. This was a serious strategic error on the part of the Japanese high command. Their troops scavenged and commandeered at will with little regard for the needs of the people and caused great resentment. Soon, the Filipinos simply resorted to hiding their stocks of food, including chickens, rice, and pigs.

We were on schedule in our movement toward Bataan. Occasionally, we came across some of our own units. Friendly civilians kept us well informed about enemy locations and activity, and as we made our way to the rugged coastal mountain range, we managed to dodge several Japanese patrols without being detected. Crossing the Agno River to the north toward Tarlac, which was occupied by Japanese troops, we went into the Zambales Mountains to the west and headed south in a direct line for the Bataan Peninsula. The terrain was extremely rough, but helped by our indispensable civilian guides, we managed to make our way without mishap.

On the fourth day, we were near Botolan, and we began to encounter many more of our soldiers heading for Bataan. Some of these joined us. The food shortage was beginning to be a problem, but we were told that if we could make it onto the peninsula, we would find ample food and ammunition there. The inadequate supplies of those items became apparent after our arrival. But by then, it was too late. One enormously frustrating aspect of this tragic situation was that after Manila had been declared an open city, huge amounts of food and

113

weapons were left there on the docks. The result perhaps of a lack of transportation or of poor planning, these abandoned supplies could have taken care of all our needs for quite some time.

Capt. Donald D. Blackburn of the 11th Division did manage to get into Manila just ahead of the Japanese and brought a truckload of much-needed telephone line and other related equipment into Bataan. This helped the communication between units immensely and in many instances also eliminated the use of messengers. Later, Captain Blackburn was to escape from the Death March and help organize the USAFIP–NL (United States Army Forces in Philippines–Northern Luzon). He was placed in command of the 11th Infantry Regiment, USAFIP–NL.

The Japanese were in control of Highway 3 from the north, to just beyond Olongapo, and to the east, to Aritao, effectively cutting off part of the peninsula. This meant we would have to cross their lines at least once, maybe twice. Our guide had taken other groups through and was confident he could get us onto Bataan. He suggested we cross the enemy lines around San Marcelino, afterwards staying in the mountains to cross again somewhere east of Olongapo, an area in which there were now quite a number of Japanese. Not only did we manage in this way to get to Bataan; we got there without firing a shot.

The Japanese time schedule for taking over the Philippines was not being met as planned. General Homma's plan had allowed a total of six weeks for the conquest of the islands. Instead, this was to take the Japanese Imperial Forces nearly six months and three times the expected number of men.

CHAPTER 14

The Battle for Bataan

The Luzon province of Bataan consists of a peninsula approximately thirty miles long, with an average width of fifteen miles. Located due west of and across the bay from Manila, its principal city is Balanga. To the northwest is Subic Bay (the United States Naval Base, Olongapo, is on Subic Bay). Two miles off the peninsula's southernmost point is the island fortress of Corregidor.

Steep mountains run from the north to the south of Bataan. In 1941, there were few roads other than the two highways: one that ran north and south parallel to the east coast on Manila Bay, and one that cut across the mountains and connected the north-south road with Bagac and Moron on the west coast. There were no railways. In 1939, Bataan's civilian population had numbered 85,538.

Hundreds of American and Filipino troops made their way onto the peninsula during the final days of 1941. Tanks and various other vehicles and equipment streamed in by way of Highway 3 and the two Calumpit bridges—one rail and one vehicular—that spanned the wide, deep, and unfordable, Pampanga River.

At dawn on New Year's Day 1942, after the last of the tanks used in the delaying action at Baliuang came across just minutes ahead of the Japanese troops, these bridges were blown up by order of Col. Harry Skerry, who was following orders issued by General Wainwright, effectively closing off this access to Bataan. Although Japanese planes flew over the strung-out lines of slow-moving troops and equipment, there was little bombing or strafing, and it has occurred to me that the Japanese purposely may have allowed us to get

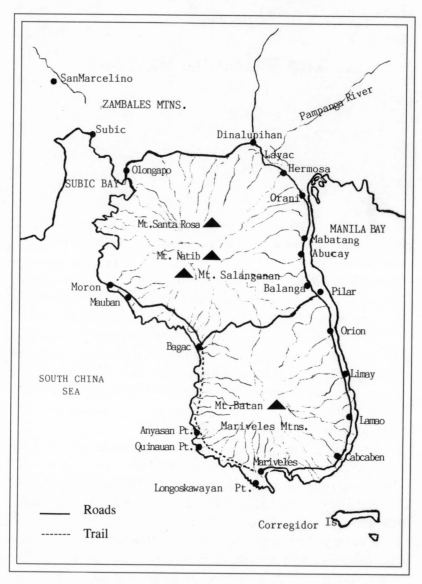

The Bataan Peninsula

onto the peninsula in order that all our troops could be bottled up there. Possibly, the enemy hoped to alleviate in this way any worry that small guerrilla groups would attack their rear and their supply routes.

The delaying action and orderly withdrawal from northern Luzon by remnants of the 71st, 11th, 21st, and 91st divisions, Philippine Army, and the fighting 26th Cavalry Regiment, played a major role in establishing our defense positions on Bataan and also enabled many of us who had been caught behind enemy lines to reach that peninsula. The Philippine Scouts of the 26th Cavalry, with remnants of the 11th, 21st, and 71st divisions, were the last to enter. The 26th Cavalry's Philippine Scouts and the remaining men of the 71st Division took over the roadblock line from the Culo River near the Layac junction and formed the defense from Hermosa to the woods of Dinalupihan.

The Japanese were advancing from the Lingayen Gulf, Vigan, and Aparri in the north, and from Mauban and Atimonan in the south. They intended to split the forces of General MacArthur, who had started to consolidate his lines on Bataan before abandoning Manila on 2 January and withdrawing to the peninsula. During MacArthur's withdrawal the Culo Bridge was blown up by Captain Chanca's 91st Engineer Battalion, closing off access into Bataan from Manila.

MacArthur's first line of defense, the Moron-Abucay line, was manned by the 1st Division, Philippine Army, remnants of the 26th Cavalry, and the United States Army's 31st, 41st, and 57th Infantry regiments. This line extended from Moron on the west coast, east across Mount Silanganan and Mount Natib to Abucay on the east coast of Manila Bay. Our troops were facing overpowering numbers of crack Japanese troops, but held this line of defense long enough to give us time to establish the second line of defense before we were forced to withdraw.

I Corps on the west side, consisting of the 91st, 1st, and 11th divisions, with remnants of the 71st Division and 26th Cavalry, was commanded by Gen. Jonathan Wainwright. II Corps defended the eastern half of the peninsula with the 41st, 21st, 51st, and 31st divisions, and was commanded by Gen. George M. Parker.

Upon being forced to withdraw to the second line of defense, the men of the 31st Infantry and the Philippine Scouts' 45th and 57th regiments placed barbed wire next to the road along their withdrawal route. This wire was connected to the Balanga electricity plant. When some eighty to ninety truckloads of pursuing Japanese troops were within the entrapment, the Philippine Scouts' 88th Field Artillery unleashed its fire power and set off the electric charge. As the Japanese jumped from their trucks and fell against the barbed wire, they were electrocuted. Very few of them survived. This allowed time to establish a well–dug-in, and well-fortified, main line of resistance, or MLR, which was known as the Pilar-Bagac line.

Although this was the only time our troops charged the barbed wire, which was strung routinely in front of our positions and was connected by concertinas, or large rolls of loose barbed wire decorated with tin cans, that one incident resulted in great insecurity for the Japanese. Thereafter, they could never be sure whether any of our wire emplacements were electrically charged, and they were very cautious when encountering these.

The Japanese paid a heavy price for their every forward step. Their losses were so great, we counted our withdrawal a victory for our USAFFE troops. It was a loss of face for the Japanese Imperial Forces they never forgot.

My men and I located the remnants of the 71st Infantry Regiment, 71st Division, commanded by Gen. Clyde Selleck and consisting of Visayan troops. I reported to Colonel Bonnett and inquired whether Captain Nakar or any of his men from the 1st Battalion had arrived in Bataan. He said a few soldiers had reported to the 71st Regiment, but he thought Nakar was caught behind enemy lines.

I was assigned the job as liaison officer between companies, battalions, and regiment, which meant a great deal of foot travel to check positions and report back through channels to the regiment.

Our first few days on Bataan were spent digging in, and the men of Company A knew that the order "Dig in!" meant digging more than a foxhole. They knew that well-fortified entrenchments were needed to protect them from the heavy enemy artillery fire and air attacks.

The American and Filipino troops numbered seventy-eight thousand, approximately. There were twelve thousand Americans (including noncombatant soldiers, sailors, and marines), and sixty-six thousand Filipinos. There were also twenty-six thousand civilians who, seeking safety, followed this army that was equipped with about a month's supply of rations and ammunition.

Immediately upon our arrival on Bataan, all troops were put on limited rations. Rumors abounded that reinforcements and supplies were on the way; but, in the meantime we were ordered to conserve our ammunition and cut down to one meal a day. Sometimes we were given breakfast and supper! but usually we had just one meal at noon. I ate monkey meat for the first time and thought it excellent; my extreme hunger overcame any initial repugnance. We were all grateful for anything that was edible.

The Japanese were using heavy artillery but were causing little damage because we were so well dug in. The battle was for time and employed the World War I tactics of entrenched warfare. During this period, the enemy gave us some good-old-American radio entertainment in the form of band recordings played over loud speakers situated on their trench line. Some of our soldiers would shout over to request particular songs, which on occasion would be played. Following each number, the Japanese would invite us to surrender, telling us we would be treated according to the rules of the Geneva Convention, and that it would be only a matter of months before we would be sent home.

Sometimes the Japanese would use English-speaking soldiers who posed as American soldiers in order to get into our trenches and kill some of our troops. After the first such incident, we set up volunteer listening posts at night in front of our outposts and waited for them to try this again. The listening posts in our area carried automatic rifles, hand grenades, and bolos; many of these volunteers were Igorots, and their weapon is the bolo. The Japanese couldn't trick these Igorot soldiers, who would bring back the evidence in the mornings, and it wasn't pleasant viewing. As a further deterrent, remains were left for the Japanese to see.

We began receiving heavier enemy fire. But, considering the artillery pounding we were taking, our losses were still low. There were as many men killed in the rear echelons as there were up in the front lines. Soldiers did get careless sometimes and would wander too far from their entrenchments or foxholes. Those who strayed were the ones who were caught by artillery fire or by the enemy planes that were bombing and strafing the area. Men at the rear were especially prone to carelessness because they knew there were soldiers in front, and they relied too much on this protection.

During lulls in the battle for Bataan, my thoughts turned often homeward, to my childhood, and to my mother and father, and brothers and sisters. I didn't have to ask myself whether they were praying for my safety; I knew they were. I tried to remember some of the Bible verses I had studied in Sunday school. Not a day went by that I didn't think of Elaine. I assumed that after I had reported to Colonel Bonnett, commanding officer of the 71st Infantry Regiment or rather, what was left of that regiment on Bataan, she and my family had been notified that I was alive.

We were receiving no news about the war in Europe, only rumors, and these were so obviously unreliable that when someone said, "I heard . . . ," I simply walked away. No one knew facts.

I had contracted dengue fever and a mild case of diarrhea, and I was losing weight. Colonel Bonnett, who had received a promotion and was now a full colonel, sent me back to the field hospital. After a week, I felt better and returned to my outfit.

Even though we were outnumbered and outgunned by a force that included superior air and naval power, our losses hadn't increased a great deal. Time went by quickly as the action increased. Only a few of our planes were left, and we were receiving heavy bombardment from both air and ground. Nonetheless, the troops held fast through the bombings and artillery poundings, and despite many enemy attempts to penetrate our lines, we wouldn't give an inch. Although I myself had ceased to believe help was coming, most of the men still thought the rumored supplies of food and ammunition would arrive—and in time to enable us to turn back the Japanese forces.

I ran into Captains Sea and Speckard at our regimental command post and congratulated them on their promotions. We exchanged the news of what had happened to each of us since our last meeting. They looked very run down. Both of them had spent considerable amounts of time in the hospital with malaria and dysentery. Captain Sea was thin and haggard, a shadow of the man he had been on Negros, but he had retained his very erect military bearing. Captain Speckard, a former football player for the University of Kentucky, also showed the effects of his bouts with malaria—and with such a severe case of dysentery that he had been forced to use a burlap sack for trousers: he explained that was a lot easier than trying to get his pants down in time. Throughout Bataan, the use of these makeshift burlap trousers was very common among those suffering from severe dysentery.

While they had been in the hospital, Speckard and Sea had heard rumors of guerrilla activities in the mountain provinces and the adjoining Cagayan Valley. We discussed this, and I felt it was very possible that these guerrillas were none other than Captain Nakar and the remnants of the 1st Battalion.

Before we parted, Captain Sea said he was going to recommend me for promotion. I thanked him and said I hoped we would all make it out of Bataan's malaria-infested jungles alive. About a week later, I was told to report to Captain Sea at the regimental forward command post. When I arrived I asked him, "What new job do you have for me?" He said, "None, but congratulations on your promotion." Then he pinned his old 1st lieutenant bar on my shirt. He showed me the order, dated 9 March 1942, serial number 0890454; however, the serial number I had received when I made 2d lieutenant was 0888099. I told him about the discrepancy, and he said he would try to get it straightened out. The mix-up in numbers and lost papers caused a great deal of confusion for many of us later on. The mass of paperwork generated by an army, and especially an army at war, is staggering. Paperwork must continue even under battle conditions, and a certain number of mix-ups, including lost papers, is inevitable.

Two of the battles on Bataan most costly for the Japanese became known as the Battles of the Pockets and Points. About two thousand Japanese troops managed to get to the rear of our line by using landing craft. They landed during the night at three different points: Anyasan, Quinauan, and Longoskawayan.

These men were trapped behind our lines until, in an attempt to save their starving fellows, about one thousand Japanese troops made a banzai attack at a weak spot in the center of the 1st Division's line and finally managed to break through at night. Because of the confusion during the break-through, the enemy troops never reached the three points but became separated and were trapped in two different pockets directly behind our lines. These two pockets were immediately enveloped by our forces.

The Igorots took a heavy toll of the enemy and prevented the reinforcement of the Big Pocket, as well as of the Small Pocket. The Battles of the Pockets and Points lasted about twenty days before all the Japanese were annihilated. It ended 16 February 1942.

By this time, we considered ourselves lucky if we received one meal a day. The supplies were almost gone. Most of the men on the defense lines were in dangerously weakened condition due to attacks of malaria and dysentery, both terrible killers in this war. Too sick and too weak to man the defense lines, nearly half of the troops were in hospitals. The makeshift burlap sarong became a common sight even in the front lines.

On 31 March, we were hit by large-gun bombardments from Japanese warships in combination with ground-based artillery bombardments and air strikes. We knew this was the big push. The unrelenting artillery bombardment, dwindling supplies of food and ammunition, constant hunger, and devastating illnesses were taking their toll and gradually sapping what physical and emotional reserves we had left. Hope of relief was replaced by grim determination to hold out, and finally, by terrible weariness as we faced the inevitable. There was to be no last-minute rescue. We had done what we were supposed to do: hold on as long as possible. And then we could no longer do that. Waves of Japanese shock troops poured through our crumbling defenses. The Japanese had overrun the entire Bataan Peninsula.

By 8 April our line already had been penetrated. I was on the right flank of the 1st Division, which was commanded by Brig. Gen. Fidel Segundo. There was no choice other than to surrender. Under a white flag of truce, I surrendered with one Philippine captain and approximately one battalion of Philippine troops. We were told to follow the trail east towards Orion. There was news of other groups surrendering and a rumor that General King soon would follow suit.

On the trail leading to Orion, we weren't guarded; but, along the route on our right and left flanks, there were Japanese troops looking for pockets of our men overlooked when our defense line was overrun. Occasionally, these search parties would stop us and ask the captain where we were going. He would explain that we had been told to go to Orion. "Okay, okay" was the standard response.

Although up to this time the Japanese had treated the captured men fairly well, already the idea of escaping was in my mind. I had been placed in charge of about forty soldiers from the Philippine Army, most of whom were from the island of Negros. Rumors were circulating that we would be interned at Camp O'Donnell, about ninety miles north of our present location. In view of the physical condition of the men, a march of that length was brutally inhumane. Weakened by my frequent battles with malaria and dysentery, I seriously doubted my own chances of surviving that march. Also, because I was an American, I knew if I were to be caught alone, I would be bayoneted or shot. So far, the Japanese had not noticed me among my group of Filipinos. I was about the same height as they were and had a good tan; I blended in easily. Actually, when I was discovered on 9 April, to my astonishment nothing happened to me.

On 9 April 1942, Gen. Edward P. King officially surrendered all troops on Bataan to the Japanese Imperial Forces under the command of General Homma. Ironically, it was the day on which Lee had surrendered to Grant at Appomatox. On that day in 1865, Lee had said, "Then there is nothing to do but to go and see General Grant, and I would rather die a thousand deaths." On this day in 1942, King's feelings must have been very similar. Further loss of life did not seem justified. There were seventy-five thousand men, twelve thousand of them American, involved in King's surrender: the greatest capitulation in U.S. military history.

Remnants of the army escaped to Corregidor, where General Wainwright had assumed command after General MacArthur was ordered to Australia to take charge of all Allied forces in the Far East.

General Wainwright was now in command of all forces in the Philippines. Gen. William F. Sharp was in command of the island of Mindanao and the Visayan, or central, group of islands.

CHAPTER 15

The Death March and a Bold Escape

Two days had passed since our surrender. The date was 10 April. Early that morning, we were given water for our canteens and a few scoops of rice containing a suggestion of fish. Day one of the Death March had begun. Our unit would be one of the first to leave the Bataan Peninsula. The Japanese had taken our names, ranks, and serial numbers but had not pressed us for any further information.

I said good-bye to my friends Captains Sea and Speckard. This was to be the last time I would see them. After the war, I learned they had been put on a prison ship bound for Japan. The ship was sunk by an American destroyer. Although some prisoners did survive the sinking, my two friends were lost.

That first day, many of the Philippine Army soldiers were unable to continue marching. Malaria and dysentery had taken their predictable tolls. The Japanese wasted no ammunition on these unfortunate men but used their bayonets and sabers to cut them down as they staggered and fell out of line. Realizing those who fell out would be killed, the stronger men tried to help their comrades by holding them up and literally walking for them; some devised litters to carry those too weak to walk at all. To see these brave, half-starved, sick men struggling to survive was heartrending.

Witnessing the brutal behaviour of the Japanese soldiers, I became more and more convinced I had nothing to lose by attempting to escape at the first opportunity. The thought was on my mind all that first day. I remembered the rumors we had heard of guerrilla activity in the

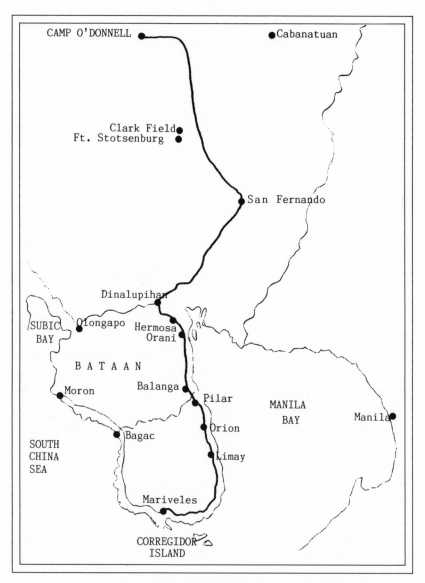

Death March Route, Mariveles to Camp O'Donnell

Cagayan Valley and adjoining mountain provinces. Not knowing whom to trust, however, I kept this information to myself and quietly began to watch our guards, waiting for an opportunity to escape and, I hoped, eventually join those guerrillas.

As we passed by, civilians along our way gave us the V-for-victory sign and tried to hand us bananas, papayas, and other foods whenever the guards, who were spaced quite far apart on both sides of us, weren't watching.

On the second day, my malaria and dysentery flared up. I realized I would have to attempt an escape before I became any weaker. Soldiers everywhere along the seemingly endless line continued to stagger and fall, like their fallen comrades of day one. And as they had done on the first day, the Japanese continued to bayonet those who fell out. Near me, an officer of about fifty years of age staggered and fell. And was bayoneted. I believe he was Colonel Bonnett, who anyway did not survive the march.

During a five-minute-rest period, I decided to tell my group of forty men about my plan to escape. This was not difficult to accomplish since the Japanese didn't understand English, and I was allowed to walk up and down our part of the line in order to check my men. Their reaction to my news surprised me. One man spoke for all: "We thought, sir, you would never ask us."

I had observed that whenever we came to an area overgrown with cogon, the guard on that side of us would move over to avoid this grass, which was usually four to five feet high and always rather sharp. The guard's action would leave one flank open. I suggested my men should observe the guard's behaviour closely and told them the best time for an escape would be just before sundown at some place where cogon to the left had caused the guard on that side to switch over to the right. We decided to discuss the plan further at the next rest period, which would come when the guards, not the prisoners, needed it.

At the next stop, we agreed to escape at the next opportunity. I was to give the signal. After that, it was to be every man for himself. We would rendezvous in the Cagayan Valley or in its adjoining mountain provinces. We likely would be separated after our escape, and several rendezvous points were necessary if we were to meet up again on our way to join the guerrilla force. While they traveled, the men were to leave word at barrios, informing the tenientes about their next destinations. If possible, they were to procure weapons from the barrio residents. And, they were each to say a prayer that we would all survive.

In the meantime, I had decided I would rather die of a bullet in my back than of a bayonet or saber thrust when I staggered to the side of the road. For one thing, I had no head covering to shield me from the unrelenting sun. I knew that heat exhaustion—a certainty in those tropical conditions—added to my malaria and dysentery would finish me before another two days had passed. I prayed the Lord would spare me somehow, and that I could be of some use were my escape to be successful. Then I settled down to watch for our chance.

Near sundown on this second day, while we were walking next to some cogon-infested underbrush, the guard as usual moved to the right behind my unit. Things happened very fast then. I shouted and we all fled into the tall grass, where we spread out quickly. Years seemed to pass in slow motion. Then the first shot was fired, and one of the guards sprayed the cogon with automatic-weapon fire. I heard some of my men scream when they were hit. The confusion and noise were nightmarish.

Other men saw what had happened. There was no time now for them to join our escape, but they yelled out encouragement to us and hollered to add to the confusion. I was shouting at my men that they should not bunch up, but they were frightened and inexperienced and did not realize they were more likely to draw fire and be hit if they stayed in groups.

Two men escaped with me: Enrique, an Ilocano from the area near Jones in Isabela Province; and Emilio, a Visayan from the island of Negros. Following my plan to skirt the Zambales Mountains and use the same route out of Bataan that we had taken in, we walked and stumbled northwest through the night into the jungles and rugged Mariveles Mountains. The stench of death from unburied bodies filled the air.

Of the forty men who attempted the escape, I never knew which ones had succeeded and which ones had been killed or recaptured. Although Enrique, Emilio, and I did meet some other men who had escaped from the Death March, we never encountered a single other soldier from our unit.

CHAPTER 16

Missing in Action

T he first night we walked straight through until daybreak the next day. Occasionally, we could hear Japanese patrols searching the area. Fatigue finally forced us to find cover, and we rested for about five hours. It was noon when we left our hiding place. We walked until nightfall and managed to avoid the Japanese soldiers whose voices we could hear all day in the distance. We had had no food since our escape, and I cautioned Enrique and Emilio to limit each drink from their canteens to one swallow only. I feared the water in the streams was contaminated by the dead bodies, and I had no idea when we would be able to refill our canteens from a safe water source.

On the third day, we met a civilian. Weak from hunger and needing information, we had to gamble that this man was loyal to the Phil-American cause, and we identified ourselves as Death March escapees in need of assistance. We were fortunate. He took us to his home, where we first ate our fill of the rice, chicken, eggs, and vegetables his family cooked for us and then slept. The kindness of these sympathetic people, and others like them we met along our way, is something I will never forget. I am sure they helped many Phil-American soldiers—and at considerable risk to themselves.

Early the next day, the fourth since our escape, the man led us across the main highway leading from Olongapo to Manila. The good Lord was still with us. As we made this hazardous crossing, we saw only a few Japanese trucks in the distance, and we were able to slip undetected into the underbrush on the other side, where we said good-bye to our guide. He too had heard rumors of guerrilla activity in the

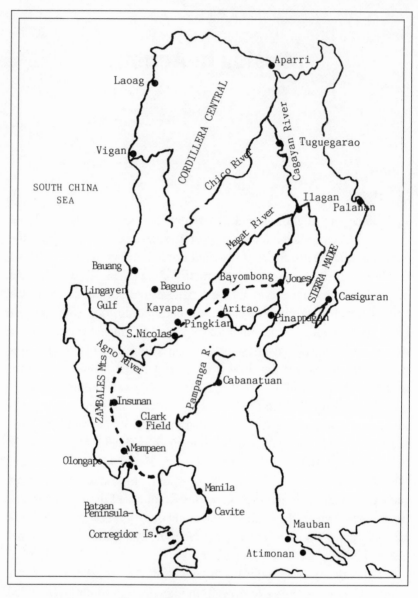

Escape Route, Bataan to Jones

mountain provinces and Cagayan Valley, and he assured us we would be able to find horses and another guide in the Mampaen area so that we could make our way to the guerrilla headquarters. We thanked him for all his help and quickly set out, hoping to reach the outskirts of Mampaen by nightfall. Just after dark, we arrived at a small barrio near that township, where we were fed and given horses and a guide who was to head us towards Insunan, a municipality north of Mampaen near the Zambales Mountains.

Since we were now on horseback, we could afford to lose some sleep, and we decided to make a forced march, traveling both at night and by day. I wanted to put as much distance as possible between us and the Bataan Peninsula.

We reached a barrio in the vicinity of Insunan on the morning of the fifth day. We rested there until noon, then left with fresh horses and a new guide furnished by the teniente. The forced marches continued until the evening of the seventh day, when we reached a barrio near San Nicolas. Here the barrio teniente supplied me with a map, a compass, and a semiautomatic .45-caliber pistol. He also gave me a boiled guava bark tea to drink, the local folk remedy for dysentery.

While in this area near Insunan, I heard that Lt. Col. Everett Warner and Major Nakar had established a guerrilla unit headquarters near the municipality of Jones. At this time, that area was not yet occupied by the Japanese, who had moved north only as far as Aritao, from where they sent patrols west to Kayapa but not toward Jones. According to my informant, these patrols had been ambushed several times both by guerrilla bands and by civilians.

Two days of trail riding in the Caraballo Mountains brought us to Bayombong, where we picked up a truck driver from one of Colonel Warner's outposts. We arrived in Jones late that night. It had been nine days since our escape.

It was here, on 19 April 1942, that I first met Lieutenant Colonel Warner and a Captain Minton. They were planning to leave for Casiguran on the east coast, where they were to be picked up by a destroyer and taken to Australia. Warner, a former officer in the 26th Cavalry, was now the commanding officer of the 14th Infantry. He intended to turn his command over to Nakar, who presently held the

Casiguran and Coastal Area, Aurora Province

rank of lieutenant colonel. I declined Warner and Minton's offer to accompany them and said I preferred taking my chances on land, not water. The following morning, I learned they had left for Casiguran during the night.

I met with the mayor of Jones and requested a guide to Lieutenant Colonel Nakar's headquarters. While I was there, a Visayan soldier from Negros showed up, recognized me, and volunteered to take Enrique, Emilio and myself there the next day. Very relieved to have finally located Nakar, I accepted gladly. A chance to recover from the fatigue of the journey with a good night's rest was very welcome; and, most welcome of all: a shower, a real shower, thanks to the kindness of the mayor, who opened his home to me. I must have used up a bar of soap in that shower. Dressed in my freshly laundered clothes, which some of the local women had washed and ironed, I felt like a new man. And I surely smelled newer.

Feeling considerably more socially acceptable, I was looking forward to dining and spending the night as the guest of a Señor Villanueva, a Spanish businessman who was one of the area's largest landholders. Echague Cigars, which were marketed worldwide, were manufactured by him, and he was a friend of the mayor, who had introduced us.

Assuming dinner would be served at seven, I presented myself at Villanueva's comfortable hacienda that evening at six o'clock. Built around a small court, the main house was surrounded by the ubiquitous veranda, or covered porch, which was equipped with easy chairs, lounges, and a large dining table. Great palm leaves attached to bamboo poles served the double purpose of keeping the veranda's occupants cool while chasing away the hordes of flies. A houseboy pulled a rope secured to the free ends of the poles, causing the palms to swish back and forth. Four or five other houseboys waited to serve the guests.

Although my host spoke little English, we managed to make conversation by speaking a combination of Ilocano dialect, which Señor Villaneuva spoke fluently and I was in the process of learning, and Tagalog, which I spoke fairly well and he understood.

Villanueva explained some of the customs of the plantation. The day started at five in the morning when he and his foreman rode around the plantation on horses to check the laborers. Because of the heat, they would return to the house at noon, eat a light lunch, and take a siesta until about half past five in the evening. Then they would ride out again.

Explaining why I had not been offered a drink, he told me it was the custom not to drink until the sun went down, and that the main meal was not served until midnight. That night when the sun went down, out came the bottles. The bar was lavishly stocked, and after the second drink, we were conversing in two dialects, Ilocano and Tagalog; and three languages, English, Spanish, and German. We were getting along well; but I was also getting very hungry. The intense feast-or-famine existence I had experienced over such a short period of time was beginning to tell on me. Finally at midnight, our host, who by now was feeling no pain, seated us. His guests were the mayor of Jones; a Señor Rodriquez; several other Spanish friends, and myself. There were no women present. Villanueva was a widower with a ten-year-old son; his wife, who had been a beautiful, well-educated Filipina, had died several years before.

That dinner was one of the best I have ever eaten. There were at least six different meat courses; many varieties of vegetables and fruit; rice; and the native sweet potato, *camote*. I still could not eat rice with any enjoyment. However, there was more than enough of everything else. The contrast between the starvation rations of less than two weeks ago and this sumptuous fare was almost too bizarre to contemplate. Mindful of how quickly things could change, I appreciated this meal even more and thanked my host for it with great sincerity.

My bedroom was another surprise. The bed was covered with at least fifteen large pillows. They looked very comfortable but ended up on the floor to make room on the bed for me. Some years later when I was on my way to the mountain provinces and was a guest in the home of another Spaniard, I again found my bed bedecked with pillows and decided this must be customary in Spanish homes; certainly the extravagant late dinners were.

The next morning, I was up at five. I felt as though I could have slept several more hours, but I could smell coffee. Señor Villanueva was up, hangover and all; and I wanted to be ready to report to Nakar's headquarters as soon as possible that day. After a breakfast of eggs and coffee, I thanked my host again for his gracious hospitality, and I told him I would do what I could should he ever need any help from me in the future. I also suggested that, to forestall any reprisals, it might be best if the Japanese didn't discover he had entertained an American officer. He thanked me and gave me some quinine, and a prescription medicine for dysentery. The guava bark mixture that teniente had given me on my way from Bataan to Jones had certainly helped. I was regaining strength and health.

Villanueva extended an invitation to stay with him any time I was in the Jones area, and I left for the mayor's office to meet my guides. They would be taking Enrique, Emilio, and me to Nakar's guerrilla headquarters located along the east side of the Cagayan River in the small barrio of Qumalabaza, near Jones. To the east of these barrios along the Cagayan River is Ilongot headhunter country and dense jungle as far as the Pacific Coast. It was here I was to make my home for the next two and a half years.

CHAPTER 17

The 14th Infantry Regiment,
Philippine Army

Our guide offered to take us to Lieutenant Colonel Nakar's headquarters at Qumalabaza by bangkâ or along the jungle trails, whichever we preferred. I decided it would be best to take the trails that ran along the east side of the Cagayan River. I wanted to familiarize myself with the area and also get to know the barrio tenientes in the region before the Japanese occupied the valley. According to our guide, the people of the area were loyal to the Phil-American troops, and when we passed through the various barrios on our way, the residents we met did seem friendly; many of them said they would be willing to make any sacrifice necessary to help us against our common enemy: the Japanese Imperial Forces.

One barrio teniente in particular impressed me: Teniente Reyes of Dabubu, who was on his way to Jones when we met up with him. He struck me as a man who could be trusted. I felt an instant kinship with this wiry, bow-legged man wearing the usual shorts, and strapped-on bolo. The grey crew-cut hair and bent posture, which at first disguised his taller-than-average height, gave me the impression that Reyes might be well past middle age, but how much past was impossible to determine.

I believe the feeling of instant kinship was mutual. He seemed to take a special liking to me, possibly because I made the effort to converse with him in his own dialect, Ilocano. He was very pleased with my gift of cigars from the supply I had received from Señor Villanueva, too! During my long stay in the jungle, I came to know and admire

Reyes, and I valued his friendship enormously. There would be many times in the future when just seeing him would bring tears to my eyes: the combined effect of relief and pleasure that he was there and a quite uninvited pity that overwhelmed me when I saw him bent under the load of supplies he brought with him on his shoulders, smiling face above and barefooted bowed legs below.

The trail on the east side of the river was very easy to follow, and we reached headquarters before noon. Colonel Nakar greeted me with a big smile that was reflected in his eyes, and I was welcomed warmly by those of his officers and enlisted men whom I knew from Negros. We all shook hands and exchanged congratulations on our good fortune in being back together again. It felt good to be back in their company; and, I was now once again part of a recognized organization; the 14th Infantry Regiment, Philippine Army.

Nakar inquired about Colonel Bonnett, General Selleck (the 71st Division commander), Captain Sea, and Captain Speckard. I gave him what information I had, including the news of what I believed had been Colonel Bonnett's fate on the Death March. He also inquired about General Brougher, the commanding officer of the 11th Division to which our regiment had been attached at the Lingayan Gulf in December. There was little I could tell him other than that I supposed he was in a Japanese prisoner-of-war camp somewhere.

I described my meeting with Colonel Warner and Captain Minton in Jones and told him of their offer to take me with them to Casiguran and then on to Australia. Nakar said he had sent messengers to intercept Warner; General Wainwright had directed him to get in touch with Warner to tell him to "Get the hell back" and stay with his command because there was no transportation available to take him to Australia. Later, we learned that Warner and his party had come back on their own when they weren't picked up at Casiguran. Under the amnesty, he and Minton turned themselves in to the Japanese at Ilagan. Warner was put through a very rough interrogation, but he did not divulge any information.

As ranking officer, Colonel Nakar officially became commanding officer of the 14th Infantry. He also became the owner of Colonel

137

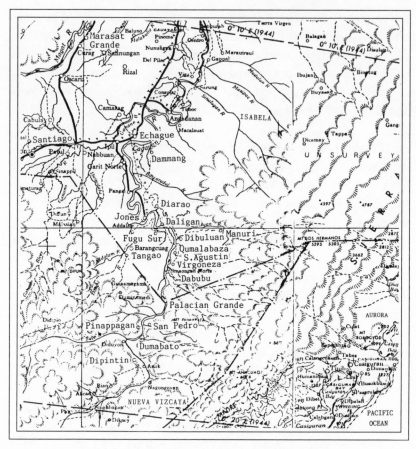

Location Area, 14th Infantry, Philippine Army

Warner's cavalry horse, a nuisance at the time, but later to be appreciated in an unexpected way. (I didn't mind soldiering under Nakar. He was a gutsy little man with a friendly, easy-going manner, but he could become very stern when orders were not followed. I am sure he had dreams of commanding a division someday.)

During our first discussion, I explained the dilemma of my promotions: that I had nothing in writing; no orders; and two officer serial numbers, 0888099 as a 2d Lieutenant, and 0890454 as a 1st lieutenant. Nakar had a Lieutenant Cabañero radio Corregidor for verification.

There, they had no record of me as an officer but wanted more information. All the information I could give them was that I had taken the *Ten Series* tests and had forwarded the last test paper back to the Department of the Army just prior to the war, when I was still a master sergeant. I mentioned that Nakar had been present when Colonel Bonnett pinned the gold bars on my shirt in December 1941. The reply came back from General Wainwright's headquarters that my promotion to 2d lieutenant would be recognized effective 9 March 1942—with a new serial number attached: 0890424. Nakar asked if I wanted to pursue the matter further, and I told him, "No, I think I am fortunate to have *anything* verified and in writing!"

Nakar appointed me assistant S–3 in charge of plans and training. The regiment consisted of 65 officers and approximately 960 enlisted men, now also including Enrique and Emilio.

In the latter part of April—perhaps it was the first part of May—Capt. Harry Roberts (fictitious name), SC (Signal Corps), reported to Colonel Nakar with a request to be assigned to our unit. The request was transmitted to General Wainwright's headquarters and was granted. Roberts was assigned as commanding officer, Headquarters Battalion, 14th Infantry, Philippine Army. He brought with him a Cpl. Harold Koopmann, who was a soldier from the air-warning unit in the area of Aparri Roberts had commanded prior to the war. Another soldier from this unit, a Private Luigio (fictitious name), was brought to us later by a 1st Lieutenant Hendricks, who then continued on to rejoin another guerrilla organization in central Luzon. Roberts's two enlisted men lacked combat experience and needed training in combat infantry tactics. They had a hard time fitting in with us, and I, for one, wasn't impressed with their general attitude. Notations from Colonel Horan's diary echoed my own concerns about these two air-warning men:

> At Natunin I found native guides to take the American airwarning service men over the mountains to . . . Isabela (Major Warner's outfit) by way of the native trails via the Dalalu Rest House, the Opul Rest House, down to Jones. Except for Arneo, Brazelton, and Pennington, they were all a pain in the neck, too lazy to hike the mts as couriers, too many drunks and too

139

much eyeing native girls, unforgivable among the Igorots. That is the last I ever heard of them. If they ever joined . . . they probably became part of Volkmann's [Volckmann] troops in 1945.

On 6 May 1942, we heard of the fall of Corregidor and Gen. Jonathan Wainwright's surrender to General Homma. As Nakar had received no further instructions from Wainwright, he dispersed his regiment in view of the scarcity of food, medicine, and ammunition. Each officer not needed at the regiment command post, which was to remain intact at a new location, was given a list of the men under him. These men were to report secretly to their officers at least once a week or as often as the situation required—or allowed. The officers were instructed to set up relay contact stations and submit intelligence information, S–2, back to regimental headquarters no less often than once a week, more if the situation demanded. Both officers and enlisted men were to mingle and live with the general population in the provinces of Nueva Vizcaya and Isabela. Enrique was among the more than nine hundred men who were dispersed at this time. Emilio stayed with the regiment command group.

On 13 May, the regimental staff, with ten officers and eighty enlisted men, was moved south via the Cagayan River to the barrio of Dumabato near Pinappagan, Nueva Vizcaya. The move was completed on 15 May 1942. The radio transmitter and receiver were to be set up about five kilometers from regimental headquarters on the west side of the river at Dipintin. However, we needed additional parts for both the transmitter and the receiver before we could contact MacArthur's headquarters in Australia. Captain Roberts contributed to this effort when he and Lieutenant Cabañero, helped by Sergeants Labrojo and Domingo, took the responsibility for getting the transmitter and receiver in order and set up to make radio contact with General Headquarters, Southwest Pacific, Australia.

Colonel Nakar thought this would be a good time to acquaint Captain Roberts with our sector. He decided to send him to Ilagan to meet Major Enriques, who was the officer in charge there and second in command to Nakar. (Enriques also commanded one of the battalions of

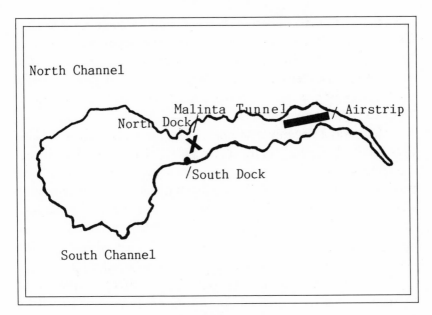

North Channel

Malinta Tunnel — Airstrip
North Dock

South Dock

South Channel

Corregidor Island

the 14th Infantry. He was a graduate of the Philippine Army Academy and was a very courageous officer. Subsequently after the capture of Nakar, Enriques would surrender to the Japanese and begin working as a double agent, giving them misinformation regarding the guerrilla forces. When the Japanese eventually found out that he was acting as a double agent, he was taken to Fort Santiago, tried, and executed.)

Roberts also was to obtain parts for our transmitter, if possible. I was to accompany him only as far as Jones, and if spare parts were available in Jones, I was to return with them to headquarters without delay.

We left Pinappagan, traveling by bangkâ north on the Cagayan River. It was an exhilarating way to travel. We negotiated several rapids, and the two oarsmen handled the craft like professionals. I made sure I had a good grip on the bangkâ's sides and put my trust in their skill. There was no doubt this wasn't the first time they had taken the rapids in such fashion.

On the way to Jones, we made a number of stops in the barrios in order to give Captain Roberts a chance to meet the barrio tenientes. On one of these stops, we had lunch with Teniente Reyes in his barrio of Dabubu, one of the few barrios in the Pinappagan area east of the Cagayan River. The teniente remembered me and said again if I ever needed help, he was ready to provide it for me and for any other loyal American or Philippine soldier.

There was a sincerity in this man's face and an honesty in the kind eyes that made me feel his friendliness was genuine and would be unchanging as long as its object was deserving. Jolly as the teniente was—and even the wrinkles in his long thin face seemed to have been etched by smiles and good humor—there was nothing superficial about him. He was the kind of man who made you feel somehow better, easier, more secure, just by his appearance. As I felt when I first met him, I sensed instinctively this was a man who could be relied upon.

Unaware at the time how important Reyes's offer to help would be to me and my men, I thanked him for it, and Roberts and I left for Jones.

On our arrival in that municipality, Roberts and I called on the mayor, who said he was sure he could find the spare parts needed for the radio transmitter. While Roberts and the mayor discussed the transmitter, I went to call on my friend, Señor Villanueva.

He was happy to see me but was very distressed over the news of Corregidor's fall and General Wainwright's surrender. We discussed the various situations that might arise in the area due to the surrender, and I expressed my determination never again to surrender under any circumstances. I was sure the Japanese would enter the Cagayan Valley in force after they finished celebrating their victories at Bataan and Corregidor. If this happened, I told Villanueva, I planned to evade them by staying in the jungles, which I thought would be possible provided friendly civilians supplied me with food and medicines. He immediately offered his help, should I need it, and I thanked him for his generous offer and his concern for my welfare.

In turn, Villanueva wanted to know whether I would permit him to fly the Spanish flag when and if the Japanese entered Jones; through his interpreter, he explained that he was still a Spanish citizen. He was very relieved when I said flying his flag would seem to be a sensible precaution. My understanding in this matter cemented our already-firm friendship. Later events were to prove I was fortunate in meeting and developing a friendship with Señor Villanueva. His aid sustained me many times during the Japanese occupation, which he and his workers survived unharmed, thanks in part to that flag.

Villanueva graciously extended an invitation to Captain Roberts and me to stay with him that evening, and I accepted with alacrity, remembering my last visit. I was positive Roberts would enjoy the treat, too. I hurried back to the mayor's house and found that Roberts had located some of the needed transmitter and radio parts, which I was to take back to headquarters the next day. I told the captain we had been invited out for the evening and suggested he eat something before we left for the hacienda. He said he didn't want to spoil his appetite because he had heard what a wonderful host Villanueva was and what a marvelous banquet he set for his guests. In between bites of a banana, I explained that the food was every bit as good as he had been told, but none of it would appear until midnight. He didn't believe me.

We arrived at the hacienda, and Roberts was duly impressed. It was as luxurious as I had remembered. Our host and his other guests discussed the crops raised in that area, of which tobacco was the most important and the best paying. Señor Rodriques, again one of the guests, told us about the various aspects of tobacco farming and described some of the problems that beset a plantation as large as Villanueva's.

The sun was sinking in the west when I told Roberts to watch for the drinks. From then on, the houseboys were kept busy filling the glasses, and by about ten o'clock Roberts was complaining about being hungry. Not too sympathetic and a bit smug in the comfort of my predinner snack of bananas, I said, "But I warned you we wouldn't eat until midnight!" He managed to control his impatience and expressed the opinion later that the dinner was well worth the long wait. It certainly was that; it was a ten-course meal I will never forget.

Roberts agreed with me that the Spanish citizens should be allowed to fly their country's flag when and if the Japanese occupied Jones. He felt as I did: that these Spaniards could be trusted and would be of help to us if we needed it.

After a good night's rest, an early breakfast, and showers that were pure luxury—and might be our last for quite a while—Roberts and I went our separate ways. The soliders who had accompanied us were sent back to Pinappagan by bangkâ; Roberts went north to Ilagan; and I began the trip back to headquarters on foot, visiting all the barrios on both sides of the Cagayan River and making plans for the future.

Late the following night, I arrived back at Pinappagan and reported to Colonel Nakar. With the spare parts I had brought, although we still couldn't transmit, we could at least fix our shortwave radio and stay abreast of the news broadcast by radio station KGEI, San Francisco. After the radio was in operation, we would listen from time to time to Tokyo Rose, especially to the music she played. Her programs were very entertaining. On several occasions, she spoke directly to the guerrilla forces, telling us to surrender and saying we would be well treated by the Japanese Imperial Army; it was clear that the Japanese knew we would be a thorn in their side throughout the occupation. I recalled the treatment of the prisoners on the Death March! My resolve not to take her up on that offer was strengthened.

As Plans and Training officer, I discussed my ideas with Colonel Nakar. If the Japanese were to occupy the area, I suggested we split the regimental staff into small units. In groups of seven to ten men, we would be able to survive, foraging enough food from the jungle to keep us going until the island was retaken by the American forces. He agreed. I related what I had witnessed on the Bataan Death March and told him I would never surrender. When he said he too would never be taken alive, I knew he meant that.

CHAPTER 18

An Oasis, Two Raids, and an Ambush

Several days after my return from Jones, Colonel Nakar sent word that he wished to see me again. I reported to him and he asked how I was feeling. I said, "Fine, why?" He explained that he wanted me to lead a small, ten-man, reconnaissance combat patrol through some unexplored territory to Bayombong. According to my map, the distance from Pinappagan to Bayombong was about forty-five kilometers. My primary mission would be to check the area for alternate locations for future regiment command posts; to gather intelligence information regarding enemy movements and strength; and to raid any small Japanese garrisons or outposts and ambush any convoys—if we could do so without endangering the lives of civilians. I had passed Bayombong on my way to Jones, and I knew there were some excellent locations for ambushes.

I selected my men—2d Lt. Gervacio Reyes, Master Sergeant Valdez, two other sergeants, and six privates, including a medic—and advised them it was going to be guerrilla warfare from now on. We began gathering enough supplies, including medical supplies, to get us to Bayombong.

We left our jungle headquarters and headed due west. We made sure to keep within calling distance of each other inside the dense jungle since we didn't know if the Ilongot headhunters occupied any portion of the west side of the Cagayan River, as they did the east side.

Our first day out was all jungle traveling and slow. In many places we had to cut our way through the undergrowth with the bolos that

145

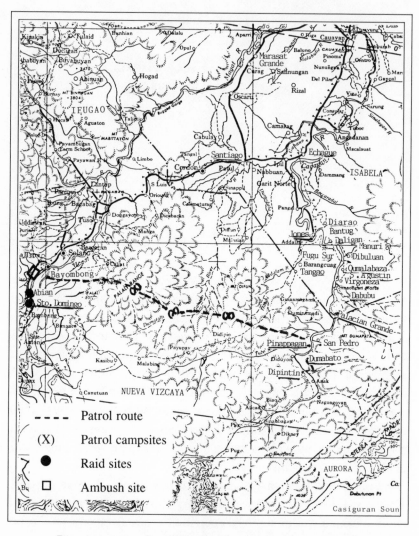

*Pinappagan to Bayombong, Reconnaissance Combat
Patrol Mission*

were part of our equipment. At the end of the day, we had gone only about six and a half kilometers. Reading our maps, we knew we should reach a valley by noon the next day, and the way looked easier from there.

That evening when we set up camp, we surrounded the site with strands of rattan strung with mess kits and eating utensils to rattle a warning if any wildcat, python, or headhunter attempted to enter. Another precaution we took involved embedding sharp pieces of bamboo in the ground with the thin sharp edge sticking up to injure the feet of anyone coming into camp. The headhunters went barefooted, and the Japanese wore canvas shoes that could be pierced easily. Sentries were posted two to each two-hour shift. We were taking no chances. Large rocks within the campsite provided extra protection, and with all our other precautions, we each felt secure enough to get a good night's rest.

Early the next morning, we again headed due west. We hoped to cover at least fifteen kilometers, or more than double our first day's progress. Before noon, we had worked our way across a small ridge to emerge at the edge, where we found ourselves gazing out over the vast expanse of one of the most beautiful valleys any of us had ever seen. There wasn't a human being or even a shack in sight, and we climbed down to explore this unexpected paradise.

The entire valley seemed to be completely untouched by civilization. There were small streams running through it, and high wooded mountains covered with junglelike vegetation rose on all sides. Nestled midway between Pinappagan and Bayombong, the place was an oasis of peace in a world at war; I had never encountered such absolute tranquility. Wild dove and chickens abounded—and snakes, of course—but there was no evidence, even beside the streams, of larger or more dangerous forms of wildlife. Altogether, this valley would make an ideal alternate campsite for the regimental command post or, I thought to myself, for one group's hidden camp should we be forced to disperse into small units.

Reluctantly, we climbed back out and continued our journey, covering seventeen kilometers by nightfall. We estimated that we had two more days of walking before we would reach the highway into Bayombong.

147

That night, we found a rock shelter, cut the surrounding grass, as we always did in case there were snakes in the immediate vicinity, and set up camp. During these nightly stopovers, I was learning from my men a few of the tricks useful in the improvisation of traps and snares for jungle wildlife. In exchange, I shared with them some of the tricks I had learned during my boyhood trapping days.

On the third morning, I studied the map and saw we soon should reach a sizable wooded area. I remembered the Bayombong region was enclosed by hills and small mountains, and that the vegetation consisted of extremely large pine trees rather than dense jungle growth, which would be a great relief after the two previous days of hacking our way through jungled terrain.

We packed up and set out. Soon, we were climbing the relatively easy slopes, making our way without difficulty through the pine forests. About noon, we stopped to rest under an enormous tree in the bark of which we found a deeply carved Spanish name with an early-seventeenth-century date. One of my men carved my name and the year, 1942, under the earlier carvings. Lieutenant Reyes and some of the other men added their names. I wondered, how many years would pass before another traveler saw our handiwork and added his name? Someday, I would like to see that tree again.

That evening, we set up camp, taking the usual safety precautions; and also as usual, after breakfast the next morning, we carefully cleaned the campsite to remove all traces of habitation, a procedure we considered vital to our continuing safety.

A three-hour hike brought us at last to the highway, which we were able to observe from a concealed position on an overhanging cliff. A straight drop of about 150 feet below us there was an ideal spot for an ambush where the road narrowed to one lane to circumvent the cliff. Spotting a man approaching this spot, we practiced our ambush without alerting him to our presence. Then I sent one of my Ilocano-speaking men to talk with him. My man was to say he had been in the army and was going home to Vigan, but that he wanted to stay clear of the Japanese until he got home. With no weapon or other military equipment, he indeed did look like a civilian.

From our vantage point above the road, we watched the two men meet. The real civilian began drawing in the dirt, giving our man directions. To those of us watching and waiting the conversation seemed endless, but in not much more than an hour's time, our man returned with the information that a Japanese patrol had been in Bayombong but hadn't stayed. There were about seven Japanese soldiers guarding a supply of confiscated rice in the barrio of Abian, south of Bayombong, and about four more guarding the same type of supplies in the barrio of Santo Domingo, about five kilometers west of Abian.

Lieutenant Reyes and I talked it over and decided a surprise raid on these two garrisons would be possible. We then could return the stolen rice to the barrios' residents, who were feeling the pinch of the Japanese method of food gathering. According to this man from Bayombong, the barrio people were fed up and angry with the Japanese for their heavy-handed confiscation of supplies, and many of them were planning to form guerrilla bands, raid the Japanese at night, and return to being mere farmers and businessmen during daylight hours.

This was encouraging information and made us believe the Filipinos had faith that even if it took a year or two, the Americans would return. With this kind of faith and loyalty behind us, I knew we would win the war no matter how many years it took, and I hoped these particular villagers would live to see the Americans retake the islands.

We had a group discussion about the idea of raiding the Japanese-guarded supplies. Everyone thought it was an excellent idea, and some of the men volunteered to go into the two barrios to reconnoiter. It seemed reasonable to assume security measures weren't very stringent if only seven men were guarding one supply dump, and only four, the other.

We had been gone from our headquarters four days and already had gathered some intelligence information; now we were anxious to make these surprise raids. If they were successful, we could gather supplies for our own use and, in a gesture of goodwill, distribute the rest to civilians, on whom we would have to depend during the Japanese occupation.

We devised a plan whereby we would hit both supply dumps simultaneously by splitting into two combat teams. Lieutenant Reyes, who had an automatic weapon, would take two sergeants and two privates, and they would raid Santo Domingo. I would take Sergeant Valdez and the remaining three men; we would raid Abian. My group also had an automatic weapon, usually carried by Valdez. I offered to carry it on our raid if he didn't want to. He smiled at my offer, saying he'd rather keep it with him. Remembering my experience during the Lingayen Gulf invasion, I understood how he felt. Not for the first—or last—time, I wished my group had more than one BAR.

That night, we bivouacked together close to the barrio of Abian. The following day, Sergeant Valdez and a sergeant from Lieutenant Reyes's combat team volunteered to go into the two barrios in civilian clothes to gather what information they could, and to familiarize themselves with the general surroundings. Since I wanted us to make our raids the next day during the guards' evening mealtime, I wanted the two sergeants to observe very carefully the situation at that time of day. They were to tell both Japanese guards and curious civilians they had been caught in the Manila area when the war broke out but at first had been afraid to go home until it was over. I also cautioned them both to be extremely diplomatic and to make the kind of flattering comments the Japanese liked to hear.

The two men left, and Lieutenant Reyes and his remaining three men went to bivouac on the outskirts of Santo Domingo. The sergeant from his group who had volunteered to reconnoiter that barrio was to report back to me and then rejoin Reyes.

Valdez entered the barrio of Abian. Following instructions, he told the people he was on his way home to Vigan, and he talked to the Japanese soldiers, telling them the same thing and adding that he thought it had been very kind of the Japanese officers to allow him to go home after the fall of Corregidor. He said he was sure the Philippine people would get better treatment from the Japanese than they had gotten from the Americans. Flattered into showing hospitality, the Japanese invited him to stay for the evening meal. He found they all ate at the same time and were very careless about where they put their weapons. On his return, he told me he could have wiped out all seven guards after supper with one hand grenade. I told him he would get his chance the next day.

The sergeant from Reyes's group reported similar conditions at

Santo Domingo and said he felt there would be no problems there, either. I gave him the information Valdez had obtained, agreed that we would have no problems, and sent him back to his unit with my prayers and good wishes. After the raid, we would rendezvous at a point between Abian and Santo Domingo and not far from the highway to Bayombong.

The following evening, each man was given one hand grenade, and each one checked his weapon and supply of ammunition. In the event that we were separated, I reminded the men of our rendezvous location.

About the time the Japanese were having their supper, my group entered Abian. We walked in pairs with Valdez in the lead. He had done an excellent job reconnoitering the area and now led us straight to the supply dump. Soundlessly, we took positions behind some buildings close to the hut the Japanese were using. The guards were sitting outside; however, we counted only six of them; one apparently was still inside.

Although the Japanese didn't see us, some of the barrio people began to look out from their grass huts, aware that something was about to happen when they saw we were armed. Fortunately, no one sounded the alarm. We waited a few minutes. Then I gave the word to open up and fire one volley. The six Japanese went down, and the volley brought the seventh to the front door of the building. A hand grenade finished him. In the distance we could hear gunfire from Santo Domingo.

Within fifteen minutes, all the people of the barrio had gathered around us. While Valdez interpreted, I announced that we would redistribute the rice except for what we would need in order to get back to our headquarters. To prevent reprisals against the barrio because of our attack, I told the residents to tell the Japanese a guerrilla band from the mountain provinces had entered the barrio and taken all the rice. I said to hide their own rice well and reminded them to be sure to blame everything on the guerrillas. When they heard the Japanese in the barrio of Santo Domingo also had been raided, the people cheered loudly.

The barrio teniente of Abian told us the Japanese might be sending a patrol into the barrio within a few days. I said, "I hope so, and if they continue north, we will be ready for them." In answer to my question, were these usually foot or truck patrols? the teniente said they used a truck and the soldiers were generally packed into it like sardines. I said, "Good. Send them north. Tell them that's the direction we've taken, and that we're all drunk and celebrating our victory!"

Later that night, we met Lieutenant Reyes at the rendezvous area. His raid had been successful, too, and he had distributed the rescued rice and some of the captured Japanese weapons and ammunition to the Santo Domingans, who had told him they wanted to fight the Japanese at any chance they could get.

The next day we moved out, bound for the previously selected ambush site on the outskirts of Bayombong. This time, we took the highway and reached our destination by noon. Along the way, we had encountered some of that city's people who had heard about the raids, and we told them we were returning to the mountain provinces in order to be consistent with the story for enemy ears we had left behind at Abian and Santo Domingo.

That evening after supper, we discussed our plans. We decided to wait no longer than three days. If the expected Japanese patrol hadn't arrived by then, we would mine the pass, alert the people of Bayombong, and head back to our headquarters near Pinappagan.

The next morning, we picked positions overlooking the highway. In case the Japanese should have men on foot patrolling the flank and point of a truck, two men were placed along the road below the narrow pass. I gave them Japanese weapons, which fired with a very distinctive sound, on the premise that if the Japanese heard shots from these, they would assume their own troops were doing the firing.

Around noon, we saw a cloud of dust in the distance. Using field glasses, we determined it was the truckload of Japanese soldiers for which we had been waiting. Quickly, we moved into position. Ten to fifteen minutes later, the truck pulled up a short distance from us, and three soldiers jumped out. My guess had been right: men on foot were to be used as flank and point. I immediately put an additional soldier facing downhill to our rear. I had a lot of confidence in the two rear-flank men who were already in position, but I wanted this added protection because there were about fourteen soldiers in the truck, which now continued on its way toward Bayombong.

Waiting until the truck was directly below us, we dropped eight hand grenades and followed this barrage with rifle and automatic-weapon fire. The truck went over the side of the cliff, blew up, and burned. We went after it. At the same time, we heard shots from American-made rifles below us and to our rear. Evidently our three rear-flank men didn't trust the Japanese weapons they had been issued. With the explosion of the truck, the detonation of the hand grenades, and the rifle fire, there was so much noise that it didn't really matter what weapons they used, and besides, the job was done. Looking over the edge of the cliff, we could see nothing moving: only the burning truck and dead Japanese soldiers. In the meantime, people from Bayombong began coming up the highway. They had heard about the raids at the two supply dumps. Their elation over that news, and now over the evidence of our ambush, was ample demonstration of the great resentment they felt toward the Japanese. We probably could have recruited the whole city for our guerrilla force.

We were invited to a celebration in the city that night. During that lengthy generous meal, I stressed that, when the Japanese arrived in response to the raids and ambush, the mayor should tell them we had forced his townspeople to feed us at gunpoint and, if need be, tell them an American officer had been in charge. I hoped, if he did this, no harm would come to Bayombong. Later, I was to hear that six people were executed as a result of our actions. Not understanding the Filipino psyche, the Japanese were using this not unusual wartime method of retaliation to turn the civilian population against us.

I have great admiration for the Filipino people; there were many other instances in which they proved their bravery and loyalty under great duress. One such instance concerned a Philippine civilian under interrogation by Japanese soldiers who claimed he was a farmer during the day but at night was ambushing Japanese soldiers. In his case, this wasn't true, but all manner of torture was used to force a confession from him. He was hung up by the heels for nearly a day, but still he refused to confess to what he said was a lie and steadfastly continued to deny he was a guerrilla fighter. Incensed by the suffering they had caused him after he had repeatedly told them the truth, he vowed if they turned him loose, he *would* become active in central Luzon with the various guerrilla forces. The Japanese admired such bravery, and they let the man go. Later, I learned he did indeed join the guerrillas and was very active against the enemy at every opportunity.

CHAPTER 19

Pinappagan Routine:
The Usual and the Unusual

The day after the ambush of the Japanese patrol, we started back to our headquarters. On the way, I marked some of our campsites on my map for future reference, unaware at the time I did it that this map eventually would cause great confusion for a number of Japanese patrols when they spent many fruitless days searching these areas for me.

We arrived back at our headquarters during the first week of June to find Colonel Nakar anxiously awaiting the report on our mission. I showed him our route on the map and gave him the information we had received from the various people we had met. I described our two raids on the rice supply dumps and the ambush at the pass near Bayombong. He was very happy with the patrol's success. I also told him I was nearly positive the Japanese knew me by name, and that my life wouldn't be worth a plugged nickel if I went in to surrender!

When I asked if MacArthur's headquarters in Australia had been contacted yet, Nakar said, "No, but I expect Captain Roberts back any day." He was still waiting for Roberts to bring the additional parts needed to get the transmitter working. Several days later Roberts showed up, and we started transmitting on 16 June.

After making numerous attempts to raise a station, we finally made contact with what we hoped was a friendly station in Australia. We were given call letters and told to transmit our messages in any code or language. Not knowing for sure whether we had contacted friends or the Japanese, we decided to verify their identity, and our own, by asking for the time and relaying a message asking for the name of Captain Roberts's wife, identifying the captain only by his army serial number. We then would request that the word "Mabuhay!" (Hooray, long live!) be used by the news commentator, William Winter, of radio station KGEI, San Francisco. These prearranged signals would assure us that we were in fact communicating with our side.

The transmitter was operating on a daily schedule, but it was not until the latter part of June that we contacted GHQSWPA (General Headquarters Southwest Pacific Area) at Darwin, Australia. A few days later, we heard Mabuhay mentioned three times just prior to the end of William Winter's news commentary giving us verification that we were reaching headquarters. A shout went up from the men in camp that evening, and morale was high.

On 29 June, Nakar received the following message:

> Lt. Col. Nakar:
> The courageous and splendid resistance maintained by you and your command fills me with pride and satisfaction stop It will be my privilege to see that you and your officers and men are properly rewarded at the appropriate time stop
> My affection and best wishes
>
> MacArthur

On 14 July, a message from General MacArthur was received directing that all Philippine Army troops under Colonel Nakar's command be inducted into the Army of the United States. This same message spelled out the pay and allowances for private through full colonel. Nakar now sent this message to MacArthur:

> To: General MacArthur   15 July 1942
> From: VCJC
> Officers of Fourteenth Inf PA accepted commission in USA and EM [enlisted men] of this regiment all enlisted in USA as of July fourteenth comma nineteen hundred forty-two stop Acceptance and provisional papers are kept in record and will be forwarded to that hqs as soon as practicable stop Request information

if we retain designation as Fourteenth Inf Army US query.
Signed Nakar

Wilson

Nakar perhaps had fallen prey to his ambition to win a promotion to the rank of full colonel. He was trying mightily to impress MacArthur's headquarters with his zeal in gathering—and relaying—intelligence concerning enemy troop movements. He was transmitting other information as well that he obtained from several patrols. He informed GHQSWPA, Australia, of the severe maltreatment suffered by the internees in the Japanese prison camps, especially by those civilians interned at the University of Santo Tomas in Manila, and of the huge number of deaths occurring daily at both Cabanatuan (east of Tarlac) and Camp O'Donnell due to the prisoners' lack of food and medications.

This daily transmittal of information, however, was endangering our position and, if it continued, very likely could result in the capture or disbandment of the 14th Infantry. Captain Roberts and Lieutenant Cabañero, the two signal officers, warned Nakar to cut down on the frequency of his messages to Australia, reminding him that otherwise, the Japanese were bound to intercept one of them. Unfortunately, Nakar did not heed the warning.

In the meantime, the Japanese were patrolling the Pinappagan area by air, dropping leaflets to Nakar telling him to obey Wainwright's order to surrender. When I discovered that Nakar was considering obeying that order, I discussed the situation with Roberts, and we decided to try to dissuade the colonel from such an action. We told him, and we believed this to be the truth, that Wainwright was under duress when he made the order. At the time, we didn't know that Colonel Horan had finally obeyed Wainwright's order, and our argument succeeded because Nakar reasoned if Colonel Horan, the ranking officer, hadn't surrendered, then he didn't have to surrender his regiment.

Although Wainwright had given the order and this properly should have been obeyed, some of the top officers justifiably decided to disregard it and continue fighting the enemy as guerrillas. Nakar never

157

again mentioned the subject; however, he was a good soldier with a strong sense of responsibility, and his disregard of the order bothered him. Some time later, we received word that after being contacted by Colonel Galbraith, the liaison officer who was carrying an official surrender order from General Wainwright, Colonel Horan had surrendered on 14 May.

The days were fairly quiet for a time and seemed to slip by uneventfully. Then one day while I was listening to some of the records Tokyo Rose was playing, trying at the same time to analyze and read between the lines of her accompanying news broadcast, an urgent message came from a Mrs. Domingo asking me to come at once to the agricultural school in Pinappagan. Mr. and Mrs. Domingo ran this school, and I had met them on several occasions. This couple also did missionary work and had been trying very hard to make Christians of the six or seven Ilongot students who attended the school.

According to the story Mrs. Domingo told me when I went to see her on this unusually hot and humid day, the young Ilongot students had decided to have a race with the carabaos they had just watered. In that heat, the exertion of a race would have killed the animals, but Mr. Domingo had caught the boys in time to stop them. He had given the Ilongots a good dressing down, intending to let the matter stop there. Other students had been present.

Later that afternoon, the Ilongot students had invited Mr. Domingo to go with them to hunt for snails and to fish on the other side of the Cagayan, where many small creeks run through the dense jungle to empty into that river. He had accepted the invitation and had gone with the boys. It was about five o'clock in the evening when Mrs. Domingo had called me because her husband had not returned. She was terribly worried and afraid that the Ilongot students may have been plotting some revenge for their—to them severe—loss of face in having been reprimanded in front of the other students.

I tried to be reassuring in order to calm her worries and said I would take a patrol across the river to make a thorough search. Mrs. Domingo said that some of the other students could tell me where the impromptu hunting party had crossed the river, and she added the information that Mr. Domingo had been wearing hip boots. Hoping that an attitude of optimism on my part would lessen her fears, I maintained my own composure, but actually I was very concerned that those fears were justified. I knew the Ilongots were considered treacherous and that they were not easily civilized—or Christianized.

I took Sgt. Benjamin Dolatre and five other men, and we crossed the river. We found the party's tracks almost immediately and followed them, paying special attention to the ones left when the group had gathered snails along a small creek. The Ilongots had bare feet, and we also could see the imprints of Mr. Domingo's boots. We had walked only a few hundred yards farther when, just where the thick of the jungle began, one of my men called out. Dolatre and I ran to where he was pointing. Horrified, we saw a human hand. About a hundred feet farther on, we found the head. It was horrible. Mr. Domingo's body lay about ten feet beyond his severed head.

We improvised a litter of bamboo and rattan, covered the remains as best we could, and took our tragic burden back across the river. We advised Mrs. Domingo not to look under the makeshift covering. We told her it had been a quick death, which Dolatre and I both knew was not true. Mr. Domingo must have fought hard for his life. This was a lesson about the Ilongot headhunters I never forgot. I was to live among them for three years, but I had learned that day never to relax my vigilance while in their jungles.

Late in July, I was ordered by Colonel Nakar to confiscate a printing press owned by a Chinese man living in Santiago, Isabela. I chose Sergeant Dolatre and Corporal Koopmann to accompany me on this mission. It took us several days to reach one of the several barrios of Santiago. There we learned that the man who owned the press had moved all his belongings, including the press, to the town of Marasat Grande, about fifteen miles north of Santiago. As we were entering that town, we heard a band playing. Thinking that perhaps the townspeople knew of our approach and wanted to entertain us on our arrival, we stopped someone and asked why the band was playing. I was very glad we inquired before going any farther, because we were told the welcome was for a seven-man Japanese patrol that had just come from Ilagan and would be stationed in Marasat Grande.

We made a quick about-face; and three days later, I reported this information to Colonel Nakar. Eight days later I was back in Marasat Grande with a combat patrol of twenty men. Our surprise attack during lunch hour took no more than ten minutes; the Japanese patrol never had a chance.

After this raid, we instructed the people to give us a five-hour start before reporting the attack to the Japanese and then, for their own safety, to inform the Japanese that they were reporting it immediately.

Before we left, we acquired a cart and carabao and called on the Chinese man, who was very cooperative. He gave us the press and told us a bakery in Santiago was wrapping its bread in manila paper, which also could be used as newsprint. On our way back to Pinappagan we requested and received the paper from the owner of the bakery.

By the early part of August, Lt. Benjamin Perdido, Jr., one of our staff officers, was printing the newspaper *Spirit of Bataan* and signing it "Matanglawin" (Hawk's Eye). Thousands of these papers were distributed by our officers and enlisted men throughout northern and central Luzon giving the news we received via radio from the States and also whatever we wanted the civilian population to know in order to help build morale. If we constituted a thorn in the side of the Japanese, the *Spirit of Bataan* drove the thorn deeper; civilians caught reading it were severely punished, even executed.

On 2 August 1942, Nakar received a message signed by the order of General MacArthur promoting some of the officers. Roberts was promoted to major, and I got my old grade back as 1st lieutenant with the same serial number that was last assigned to me.

The transmitter was operating nearly twenty-four hours a day now, and Major Roberts and I were certain it was just a matter of time before the Japanese came in force to Jones and on to Pinappagan. Roberts was positive the Japanese had intercepted some of our messages by now. He begged Nakar to limit his time on the transmitter, but Nakar continued to transmit daily. Camouflaging our headquarters so it couldn't be seen from the air by enemy planes was about the only precaution we could take.

Finally word came via our reconnaissance patrol that the Japanese were sending small truck-mounted patrols down the Cagayan Valley south from Ilagan to Echague. I suggested we send out a combat group to mount an ambush. I volunteered my services, but this time another officer was sent instead. He wiped out a small patrol evidently headed for Jones, which was just a few kilometers south of Echague. This information, as usual, was passed on to headquarters in Australia.

In the meantime, there had been many instances of ambushes and raids against the Japanese in the mountain provinces. Through our radio contact with GHQSWPA, we were aware of other guerrilla organizations operating in northern Luzon, including a large guerrilla force commanded by a Major Praeger, who was an American, and another commanded by Capt. Walter Cushing, also an American, that operated from various headquarters in the mountain provinces. Cushing's groups were feeding intelligence information to Praeger, who had a transmitter and was in contact with GHQSWPA.

Colonel Nakar now requested permission from MacArthur's headquarters to organize a full division of guerrillas and station them throughout the island. He did not receive a reply, at least not from Australia. The next day, however, a reply of sorts arrived in the form of several Japanese reconnaissance planes that came flying in low and close to our encampment. For several days after that unwelcome visit, Nakar stayed off the air.

Our civilian-clad outposts, officially spies, meanwhile had reported that a battalion of crack Japanese troops had arrived at Jones by way of Bayombong, and that Japanese patrols now controlled the highway from Aparri south to Jones.

Realizing the Japanese knew we were in the area and alarmed by the probability of reprisals against the barrios in our vicinity that had been supplying us with food, we called a meeting of the local tenientes, advising them that if they were questioned, they must tell the Japanese they had supplied us under threat of death. We said they should also report that we were living hidden somewhere in the jungle; they did not know exactly where, but we had been observed crossing the Cagayan River to the east, where the jungle was at its thickest. (Most of the civilians in Pinappagan of course knew that our regimental command post was located on the west side of the river in Dipintin, and that the remainder of our regimental group was at Dumabato, an alternate command post where our records were kept and maintained.)

161

Reports soon came in that the Japanese were sending a twelve-man patrol around to the barrios outskirting Jones. We decided not to launch a surprise raid at this time. The patrol's activity was apparently limited to entering the barrios to collect a few pigs and chickens, and some rice, fruit, and vegetables. Since the Japanese consistently retaliated by killing civilians whenever we ambushed a patrol or raided them, we felt a raid now would be unwise. The worsening mood of the Japanese in Jones was only too evident. When the tenientes began to complain to the Japanese commander there about the depletion of barrio food supplies, all they got were beatings.

This Japanese major, who would dog my steps trying to capture me or get me to surrender for the next two and a half years, called all the barrio tenientes and the mayor of Pinappagan into Jones and interrogated them individually. They told him the story we had suggested. The major did not believe we were east of the river. He knew better but didn't tell the mayor and tenientes that some of our messages had been intercepted and our transmitter's location, which was close to our headquarters, almost pinpointed. Dismissing them, he simply said anyone who continued to give us supplies would be shot. The major added that from now on, they would have to turn over one-third of their rice crop to the Japanese forces in Jones and furnish them with fish, chicken, and pigs. This was considerably more than we had ever asked, and we knew the Japanese were guaranteeing that the people of the area would feel great antagonism toward their heavy-handed, brutal conquerors.

The Japanese next questioned the barrios' residents very closely about an incident that involved five Japanese civilians and Colonel Warner. Warner's men had captured the five civilians, and according to what Nakar told me, Warner was drunk at the time and shot them. Nakar told me Warner was a heavy drinker and difficult to deal with when he had been drinking.

This had happened before Warner left for Casiguran and before I joined the 14th Infantry. The Japanese now admitted one of the civilians was in fact a Japanese army officer, in other words, a spy. The teniente of Qumalabaza told the Japanese major the guerrillas shot all of these civilians while they were trying to escape. This story apparently was accepted as the truth. Sometime after I joined Nakar, this same teniente told me that the five Japanese, who were trying to escape after being captured, really had been shot by Warner.

About two weeks after Jones was occupied, we were informed by our S-2 agents that the Japanese were moving two full companies into the Pinappagan area. Nakar immediately took the risk of contacting Australia to give them this information. GHQSWPA replied that we were to discontinue all raids because of the reprisals the Japanese were taking against the civilian population and were to use the transmitter only for vital intelligence such as the concentration of enemy troops, location of ammunition dumps, and placement of airfields. If necessary, we were to break into small units and continue to exist in this manner until General MacArthur returned to the islands.

Our last message, on 17 August 1942, was in acknowledgment of these instructions. We radioed: "We will discontinue sending messages until 27 or 28 August 1942." We then dismantled our transmitter, put it inside a galvanized tank, and buried it at the edge of the jungle near the barrio of Dumabato.

Since the Imperial Japanese Forces had failed to induce Colonel Nakar to surrender, they now resorted to an all-out mopping-up operation against Nakar's troops and the remnants of Major Praeger's forces, which were now mostly dispersed throughout the mountain provinces. Captain Cushing, officially under Horan's command, was one of the most sought.

In view of this, Colonel Nakar decided to move headquarters battalion, under the command of Major Roberts, about eight kilometers into the jungle west of the Pinappagan area. Capt. Arturo L. Dingcong, commanding officer of headquarters company, made a reconnaissance of the area and picked a campsite quite some distance off the main trail next to a dry creek bed. The following day, Nakar ordered us to move to our new location.

Headquarters battalion consisted of forty enlisted men, including two Americans, Corporal Koopmann and Private Luigio; and three officers, Major Roberts, Captain Dingcong, and myself. Ten of the enlisted men were assigned to me.

We left the Pinappagan headquarters area with enough rations to last us a week, and we took the horse Colonel Warner had left with

Colonel Nakar when he left for Casiguran. Some days after our move, we were very hungry for the taste of meat; we decided to butcher the horse. We ate our fill and agreed that horsemeat tasted good compared to some of the food we had eaten thus far during our stay in the jungle.

I was instructing my men daily in map reading and combat training. I cautioned them always to carry their weapons and not discard them as some of the soldiers had when we first met the enemy in December 1941. The men were eager to learn and showed promise of being good soldiers, but time was again an element; there never seemed to be enough of it.

I was worried about the possibility that someone in Pinappagan would betray our location. There was a civilian in that village who knew exactly where we were. I distrusted this man and was very concerned. I mentioned my feeling to Captain Dingcong, but he felt I was unduly alarmed and that the man could be trusted. I resolved to stay alert in case my instincts were right; and I advised my men to do the same.

Before we moved our headquarters into the jungle, Colonel Nakar had given instructions that in the event of a surprise raid, it would be "every man for himself," with rendezvous at various points. My rendezvous areas were either of the two barrios on the east side of the Cagayan River, Dumabato or San Pedro.

If the Japanese were occupying our two rendezvous areas, we were to reassemble in the jungle at the edge of Dabubu. I told my men about Teniente Reyes's promise to help me or any of my men if we needed help, and that I felt sure he could be trusted. The men, who for the most part were Visayans, were glad to know of someone who could help them if the need arose. We would need Reyes's help sooner than any of us expected.

On one of my visits to Pinappagan, I received news of Colonel Nakar's move to the north to relocate the regimental headquarters; and, I learned that the Japanese were on their way to Pinappagan.

CHAPTER 20

The Japanese Raid Our Camp

The Japanese moved into Pinappagan in force. Their patrols began a determined search for us in the outlying barrios, and with each failure to track us down, their treatment of the barrio tenientes and their families became more severe. Each instance of Japanese brutality increased the danger that our location would be disclosed, and my concern grew that sooner or later, reacting to fear or hoping to gain more by currying favor with the enemy, someone would tell where we were. I was convinced that our discovery was imminent, and I had been sleeping at night fully clothed, even wearing my pistol belt with several hand grenades attached to it.

Suddenly just before daybreak one morning, Japanese soldiers swarmed over our campsite. They had overpowered our outposts before even one warning shot could be fired. Now the rest of us were completely penned. Just as I feared would happen, the enemy had finally gotten to the right man in Pinappagan.

Everything happened in a few seconds. As the Japanese soldiers closed in on our camp, their voices seemed to come from everywhere. Panic added to the ensuing confusion. In their haste to escape, those of our men not captured on the spot sought to evade entrapment by running down the nearby dry creek bed. Desperation is not the best mother of invention: that creek bed was an approach route. I knew the Japanese were sure to have it well covered.

Spotting Captain Dingcong, I yelled to him that he should head into the jungle; then I took my own advice and jumped across into the thicket about two hundred feet from camp. I crawled under a tangle of lianas and low-growing vegetation where I lay, quiet and—I hoped well enough—hidden for the next several hours.

Two of our men who were too sick to run had been captured. I could hear and see the Japanese soldiers demanding information, in English, from Villanobles and Mayoga about the whereabouts of Colonel Nakar and "the two American officers" (Major Roberts and myself). When Villanobles and Mayoga refused or were too confused to answer, they were tortured. One of the two had his eyes burned; then he was killed. The other was bayoneted and buried alive. To lie there helpless and unable to go to their aid was a horrible experience. Without an automatic weapon, it was hopeless for me to try to rescue the two men.

The Japanese rummaged through our supplies and records and searched the jungle around the camp. Then I heard someone chopping his way toward my hiding place. I looked up to see a Japanese soldier with thick-rimmed glasses peering in my direction. I almost stopped breathing. He never would take me alive, I decided; I would use my .45 on him and then throw a hand grenade into the camp. That soldier stood there for what seemed like hours; then he turned and left. I had done a lot of praying: the prayers had been answered.

Towards evening, the Japanese left the camp, or what remained of it. I waited for a long time, as motionless as possible, trying to determine whether they had all gone, or if some of them had been left behind. I knew I couldn't risk staying where I was much longer; a patrol might decide to search the area again. Moving carefully, listening for any sounds of movement, I began working my way through the jungle toward Pinappagan and our rendezvous areas on the east side of the river. My progress was slow and difficult because the jungle in this area was almost impenetrable without the aid of a bolo, and for my safety, it was vital that I make no noise. Eventually, I came to a creek and I followed this until dark, keeping just inside the bordering jungle wherever possible.

That night, I sat with my back against the trunk of a banyan tree, which the Filipinos call a "walking tree" because, with the profusion of roots that grow from its branches down to the ground to root and become new trunks, this member of the fig family spreads almost indefinitely: one tree can appear to be a whole thicket.

I crawled between two of the larger roots and made a camouflage covering of leaves and twigs to hide myself from view. I had no way of knowing whether I had strayed into headhunter territory, and I tried desperately to stay awake, listening to the jungle's night sounds, ready with my hand grenades and pistol. Toward morning, however, I must have dozed.

Suddenly, I was aware that something seemed to be moving through the shadows in front of me. Shadows often seem to hold some mystery or threat; they can be unnerving; dangers can hide in them ready to leap out. Apprehensively, I reached for a stick I had been carrying the day before; raising it slowly, I brought it down with all the force I could muster. Nothing happened! At daybreak, I found nothing more threatening than a small plant, now squashed by the force of my blow. I was alone in the jungle. I realized then that my imagination had magnified everything around me into something to be feared and attacked.

With difficulty, I continued to follow the creek as it twisted and turned on its tortuous way through the jungle, and I stayed near it always to avoid getting lost and wandering in circles. I knew eventually it would empty into the Cagayan River, which was almost due east of our campsite. My only food that day was bamboo roots, which I peeled and chewed. That evening, I sought out another "walking tree" and sheltered in its roots.

Hungry and exhausted from the struggle to push my way through the dense undergrowth, I was still following the creek the next day when the subdued late morning murmur of the jungle was pierced by the shrillness of a rooster's crow. Startled, I quickly moved back into the protection of the jungle to avoid being seen by anyone who might be drawing water from the creek. The familiar sound meant I was near an area where I might obtain food and information, and I dropped down and began crawling in the direction of the crowing rooster.

In about fifteen minutes, I came to a small clearing with a bamboo hut in the center; a Japanese flag hung next to the hut's entrance. Everything was still. I couldn't tell whether there were Japanese occupying the hut; perhaps, I thought, its owner had been forced to fly the enemy's flag. I crawled out a little farther to locate the sun's position. It seemed to be nearly noon: siesta time.

I waited about an hour, straining to hear any slight sound that might tell me if the hut's occupant was friend or foe.

At last, a man appeared. To my relief, he was a Filipino, and I recognized him as someone I had seen before in Pinappagan. He turned in my direction, and I hissed at him in the Filipino equivalent of an American whistle. The unexpected sound drew his attention, and he saw me waving at him. Luck was with me. The man's name was Juan—and he was pro-American.

Juan told me the Japanese had forced him to fly their flag, threatening torture for him and his family if he refused, and that they had become ruthless in their treatment of the people in the outlying barrios of Pinappagan. Juan and many others were aware of the guerrilla forces hiding in the area and were sympathetic and willing to help whenever that was possible, but in order to survive, they had to appear obedient to the enemy's orders. These people were in a precarious position and their conflicts were severe: they were forced to supply food for the Japanese; they wanted to help the guerrilla fighters; and they had somehow to save enough food to feed their own families.

The Japanese had confiscated a large portion of Juan's rice supply, some of his chickens, and his pig; but when I told him I hadn't eaten in two days, he went to the house and returned with a bowl of fish and rice. That day I finally acquired a taste for rice!

While I was eating, Juan related what he knew of the Japanese raid on our camp. Quite a number of our soldiers had been captured, including Captain Dingcong who had been tortured but refused to reveal any information. Major Roberts, Corporal Koopman, and Private Luigio had escaped. The Japanese were still searching the jungles for the four Americans—I was the fourth. In their continuing search, the Japanese patrolled the edge of the jungle three times a night, and the area's residents were supposed to report any guerrilla troops they saw during the daylight hours, an order ignored by most of them.

Feeling better for having eaten, I questioned Juan about the exact movements of the Japanese patrols and the possibility of getting a guide to help me find the trails back to my rendezvous areas. My intentions were to cross the Cagayan River the following night after I had rested, and to head north to the barrio of Dumabato. According to Juan, the Japanese hated the jungle and, if at all possible, avoided going into it—especially at night. He was sure I would be safe where I was for at least one night. He offered to go into Pinappagan the next day to find a guide and see if there was any more news of Colonel Nakar and Major Roberts.

With Juan's help I built a small lean-to about one hundred yards back from the creek where the jungle was very thick. By evening, my refuge was well camouflaged, I had been well fed, and I was reasonably comfortable with a mat provided by Juan to sleep on. When we parted at sunset, we shook hands; I told him my trust was now in the Lord—and in him. He said he would never betray me, and I believed him. We had to trust each other. He had placed himself in danger by helping me, and if I were captured, the Japanese might suspect him of having done so; on the other hand, I might tell them he had helped me if I thought he had betrayed me.

Exhausted from the events of the last few days, I tried to rest but found myself waking often. I was learning to sleep lightly and vigilantly, forming a habit that would last for the next three years. Around midnight, I heard the voices of a Japanese patrol—and the voice of my new-found friend. The patrol went by again just before daybreak.

A whistle early the next morning brought me to the edge of the jungle; it was Juan—with breakfast. He had brought his wife along and when he introduced us, she began to cry. Dismayed, I asked why she was crying, and Juan answered saying, "She feels sorry for you, fighting for us and being so far from home." Her concern seemed genuine, and I was touched by it. I assured her I would be all right. It looked as though it was going to be a long war, I said, but as long as good Christian people like themselves were willing to help, I was sure I would live to go home when it ended.

As promised, Juan was going into Pinappagan for information and to one of its outlying barrios to find me a guide. I was very well aware that my presence jeopardized the safety of all those who helped me, and I told him I did not want to cause problems for anyone, including himself.

That day was a long one; I could only wait, trust Juan and hope he hadn't encountered any difficulty. In the afternoon, his wife brought me more fish and rice and apologized because it was all they had to offer me. I said it was very good, and the compliment seemed to please her. For the first time since Juan had introduced us, I saw her smile.

In the evening, Juan returned with the news that, although they had been assured that the Americans could never survive in the jungle, and even if they did, sooner or later the Ilongot headhunters would get them, the Japanese had not given up their search. Several of the barrio's families had been beaten severely because the Japanese suspected them of aiding us. Among those beaten were the teniente and his family. This teniente was Juan's brother-in-law and the man who was to be my guide. After their beatings, he and his family had been released with a warning that should they help us in any way, they would be executed. In view of this warning, Juan explained, his brother-in-law wanted to wait one more day, in order to allow things to quiet down before he attempted to take me across the river to the Dumabato trail.

I still had my hand grenades and quite a few rounds for my .45, but after spending several days in the jungle without a bolo, I didn't want to attempt any more jungle trails without one. A bolo was essential if I was to make any headway, and when Juan brought me a supper of more fish and rice, I asked him if he could spare one. He said he had quite a few of them, and he gave me one that could be strapped to my canteen belt.

That night, after the Japanese patrol went by, Juan and I left my hideout. I was about his height, and in the *callugong*, or native hat, he gave me, I looked like a Filipino. We crossed several rice fields and finally reached the teniente's house, which was within one hundred feet of the river trail. The trail itself ran along about twelve feet above the river with cogon covering the steep banks down to the water's edge.

The teniente agreed to take me across the river, but not until morning when the Japanese would have finished their night patrol. He felt it would be too dangerous to try crossing at night when sounds

170

along the river carried quite far. Daytime would be safer since there were usually no patrols after daybreak.

Juan asked his brother-in-law if he could hide me for the night. The teniente was reluctant, but he finally suggested I might bed down in his bangkâ, which he and his son had pulled into the tall cogon along the river below the trail. I asked him if his son could stand guard while I got some rest. He refused to allow this and reminded me that he and all his family had been beaten because the Japanese suspected them of helping guerrillas. Should his son be caught with me, he added, his whole family would be executed. He did promise to take me across the Cagayan River and show me the path that led to Dumabato. Under the circumstances, I was lucky he agreed to do that much.

After midnight, when the Japanese patrol had passed, Juan and I went down to the bangkâ. I thanked him for everything he and his wife had done for me, and we said good-bye, parting in the hope that some-day, when the Americans had retaken the islands, we would meet again. After the Americans had landed on Leyte, I did see Juan and his wife once more just before I left the Manuri-Dabubu area to join Colonel Roberts.

I climbed into the bangkâ, pulled cogon grass over me for a camouflage, and settled down with my .45 beside me in case the Japanese searched the banks along the river trail and found me during their next patrol.

In spite of trying to stay awake, I dozed off, only to be awakened by a noise near the bangkâ. It sounded as if someone was crawling toward me through the grass. Immediately, I thought of the Japanese patrols. The moon was full, and I peered through my cogon covering and tried to locate the source of the noise, which kept coming closer. Then there was a thump against the boat that almost stopped my heart when I spotted its source in the moonlight: three of the largest crocodiles I had ever seen. They were huge; and I didn't know what to do about three such reptiles big enough to jolt what now struck me as a very frail craft. I hoped and prayed they were headed for the river and that their meeting with the bangkâ was both accidental and temporary. Finally, I took my bolo and tapped it against the side of the bangkâ. The crocodiles slithered off, and I heard them enter the water. Not long after that

I heard the Japanese patrol. About six soldiers passed by on the trail above me, talking and not even glancing in my direction. After the patrol passed, I dozed off again.

The next thing I knew, someone was shaking my shoulder. Startled, I jumped up with the pistol ready in my hand. Then I heard a man's voice say, "Sir, I am the teniente. My son and I are here to take you across the river." It was just before daybreak, and I asked if the Japanese had finished their patrolling. The teniente said he was positive they had, and that they wouldn't be back until sometime that afternoon, when they would return to collect the food unwillingly supplied by his barrio's farmers, and which he and his son must gather up as soon as they returned from taking me across the river. Both men were very nervous and obviously wanted to get me on my way as quickly as possible. Considering all they had suffered at the hands of the Japanese, I could understand their anxiety, but nonetheless it worried me.

We shoved the bangkâ into the river and rowed to the east side. There, we pulled the bangkâ into the cogon and found a small path almost completely overgrown with underbrush and very difficult to follow. The teniente said it was about five kilometers to Dumabato. When I asked him about Japanese patrols there, he said one had been sent earlier, but he was positive there were none there now. We headed down the path.

I was lagging behind somewhat when ahead of me, a sound off the path alerted me to a development I had been expecting ever since we had crossed the river. Surmising my erstwhile guides had said their unofficial good-byes, I raced back to the bangkâ. I wasn't about to be left wandering alone in headhunter country while I searched for the main trail to Dumabato.

When the teniente and his son brushed aside the cogon hiding their bangkâ, they were mighty surprised to find me sitting in it with my .45 pointed straight at them. I reminded the teniente he had promised to take me to the main trail. If he didn't do this, I said, I would surrender to the Japanese and tell them he had been hiding not only me, but also some of my men.

The bluff worked. Fifteen minutes later we had reached the Dumabato trail. When I thanked him, he asked if I really would have turned them in to the Japanese. I admitted I couldn't have done that after all the help his brother-in-law Juan had given me, and I said I would remember all of them in my prayers—which I did.

Progress along the narrow, tangled trail was slow, and many times I had to cut my way through the undergrowth with the bolo Juan had given me. After about two hours, I came to a small open area where a horse was staked out to graze. Crossing to the other side of this clearing, I hid just inside the jungle. Except for the horse, there wasn't another sign of barrio life. I needed rest—and time to decide what to do. Sooner or later, someone would come to water the horse; but I was afraid if I were to show myself, whoever that was would have the daylights scared out of him: with my long, unkempt beard, I looked like a wild man.

While I rested, something seemed wrong to me. Then I realized the jungle had become very quiet. I had frightened off the small animals and birds; the horse had stopped grazing, and its ears were pricked in my direction. I sat very still, and before long the familiar jungle sounds returned; the horse snorted, and I could hear it tearing the grass as it resumed grazing.

Around noon, I heard someone coming up the path whistling. A boy about fifteen years old appeared at the edge of the clearing. When he began to untie the horse's rope, I moved onto the path in order to stop him from running down it should he become frightened when I spoke to him. I started to say *babaonen a lalaki* (boy). I had intended to ask, in Ilocano, if there were any Japanese in the barrio of Dumabato, but I never got beyond the first word. At the sound of my voice— and his first sight of me—he took off straight into the jungle. My effort at being friendly had only succeeded in frightening him. I caught the horse, staked it out again, and started walking in the direction of the barrio.

After a few minutes, I reached a large open patch of sandy beach. I could see a small creek with a wide path leading down to the water between two embankments. I had reached one of Dumabato's watering spots, and I knew that before long someone was bound to come with a carabao-drawn water sled containing numerous jars to be filled with the day's supply of water.

Choosing a place where I would have a clear view of the path, I sat down to wait and listen. I was aware of the usual jungle sounds, but I heard no voices coming from the barrio. I wondered if the quiet was due to it being siesta time, or whether there were Japanese soldiers in the barrio, a presence guaranteed to have an oppressive effect on the inhabitants.

About an hour later, I heard someone coming down the path singing, and along came a water sled with the singer, a young girl, astride the carabao's back. Jumping from her perch, the girl guided the sled down between the embankments and into the creek, where she turned the sled around. She waited a few minutes and, when the water had cleared, began filling her jars, singing all the while. The sound was such a happy one, it made me think perhaps there were no Japanese in Dumabato. Encouraged by that thought, I decided to take the chance of crossing the open beach after the girl left so that I could crawl up the embankment and wait there for the next sled, which I intended to stop by jumping down in front of the carabao after the water jars had been filled.

As the girl's sled disappeared down the path, I ran across the sand and hid in some brush on top of the embankment. In a few minutes, I heard another sled approaching. This time the driver was a boy about fourteen years old. He passed my hiding place, swung his sled around, and filled his jars. When he was finished, he jumped back on his carabao. I let him get about halfway up the path, then I jumped down in front of him with the pistol in my hand. I asked him if he spoke English. Terrified, he shook his head, and I switched to Ilocano, asking, "Adu idiay Hapon barrio?" (Are there Japanese in the barrio?) Again, he shook his head. I jumped up behind him, poked my pistol into the small of his back, and told him, in English, that if he was lying, I would have to kill him. He seemed to understand that. He was trembling and crying, and I was sorry to have frightened him; but I couldn't take chances. If there were any Japanese around I had to know.

As we entered Dumabato, an elderly man saw us. I asked him the same question, "Adu idiay Hapon barrio?" He answered, "Saan, apo." (No, sir.) By the time I had holstered my pistol, we had attracted a group of villagers. I climbed down from the carabao and asked one of the younger men to tell the boy I was sorry I had frightened him. The man said the boy could speak English. I asked him why he had said he couldn't, and the boy said he was so scared, he forgot all his English. Everyone laughed, and I said if I had been in his place, I would have been scared, too.

Forming a Guerrilla Force

The news of my arrival in Dumabato spread quickly, and the welcome I received was warm and friendly. That first evening, I was the guest of honor at a feast in the barrio. There was plenty to eat, and I savored every bite, remembering how hungry I had been during the past days. I enjoyed the many exchanges of toasts made with the local *basi*, a potent rice wine.

I was relieved to hear the news that some of the ten Visayan soldiers assigned to me had also escaped the raid on our camp and had joined Lieutenant Reyes and his five men in the vicinity of Dumabato. Lieutenant Reyes had been ordered by Colonel Nakar to stay in Pinappagan as an S-2 agent to gather intelligence regarding Japanese troop movements, numbers, and supply dumps. After our camp was raided, he had moved his men east toward Dumabato, where my men had found him. The Dumabatans were supplying the combined total of thirteen men with food.

Dumabato was a poor barrio, and I appreciated the efforts made by its people. I thanked the teniente and told him we would all be leaving the area in a few days after we had rested. Fourteen extra people to feed put quite an added burden on the barrio, but when I told the teniente we would need about a four days' supply of rice and meat to help us reach the destination I had in mind, he generously agreed to do what he could for us. He asked where we were going; but I thought it best if no one knew since the Japanese already had been in the village about a week prior to the arrival of Lieutenant Reyes and his men, and

I assumed they would be back again to look for us. By now, I was only too familiar with their methods of extracting information, and I wasn't taking any chances.

The day after my arrival in Dumabato, the teniente, who brought some of his men to carry our supplies, led me to the temporary, extremely well camouflaged camp Lieutenant Reyes and his group had set up. It was good to be reunited with these men. They were excited and happy to see me because they thought Major Roberts and I had been either captured or killed in the raid. They were anxious for news of the other men who had been there. I told them about the deaths of Villanobles and Mayoga, and what Juan had told me of Captain Dingcong's capture and torture. They had had no word of either Colonel Nakar or Major Roberts.

We thanked the teniente and his men for the supplies and wished them a safe journey back to their barrio, which was about an hour's walk from our campsite. They left, promising to return in two days with the food we would need for our coming journey. That evening, Lieutenant Reyes, Sergeant Valdez, Sergeant Dolatre, and I discussed our situation. While we talked, my initial impression of Reyes was confirmed. Nakar's S–2 lieutenant was not only handsome and quite patrician looking; he was highly intelligent and possessed an abundance of energy. I soon learned that, as Valdez would also prove to be, Reyes was a man quick and eager to volunteer whenever such an opportunity presented itself.

Reyes asked if he and his men could join my group. I agreed; and the fourteen of us now became my responsibility as senior officer. We couldn't continue to stay in the vicinity of Dumabato; our presence brought both danger and hardship.

I suggested we head north toward Jones, Isabela, keeping to the east side of the river. There were quite a number of barrios near Jones: Dabubu, Virgoneza, Qumalabaza, Palacian Grande, and Manuri, all bordering the jungles of Ilongot headhunter country. I had met and made friends with some of those barrios' tenientes, and now I thought about how they had told me, if I ever needed help, they would take care of me and any men I brought with me. In particular, I was thinking of Teniente

177

Reyes of Dabubu. In the Jones area, we would be perhaps uncomfortably close to about five thousand Japanese, but the jungle was large, and if the headhunters could survive in it, so could we.

The various barrios could supply us with some of our food, but much of it would have to come from the jungle. At least there were plenty of monkeys, which some of us had eaten before, in Bataan, and could eat again.

We talked a little about our projected need to trap wildlife for food. The snaring and trapping would present no problems for the men, who were for the most part already proficient in these skills, but the preparation necessary to prepare a catch for the cooking pot was another matter altogether. The question was, who would take care of this repugnant chore? The men did not even know how to go about doing it because, with the exception of wild pigs, the Filipinos rarely eat jungle animals and birds, and the preparations are anyway left to the women.

Once again—and not for the last time—I was thankful for my boyhood trapping experiences and the skill I had developed in the process of becoming a part-time fur trader. I told the three worried men that I would skin and gut all the birds and animals we caught, and that promise seemed to make them feel better about the prospect of living in large measure off the jungle.

That issue settled, we decided where we would rendezvous in case the group became separated during the journey north. Dabubu, Virgoneza, and Qumalabaza were the three barrios I chose for that purpose; Lieutenant Reyes and the two sergeants were to instruct the men that in the event we were separated, they should head for one of those places and tell the teniente there that I had said they should hide in the nearby jungle until I arrived in the area.

Two days later when the teniente did not arrive as promised with more supplies, we had to ration our remaining food to last until he did show up. I suspected the Japanese had sent a patrol to the east bank of the river to search for us. We decided to change our campsite in case anyone in Dumabato had been coerced into revealing our present location. Removing, as much as possible, every trace of our occupation, we cleaned up the camp and moved two kilometers to another excellent site, covering our trail as well as we could.

Sergeant Valdez volunteered to go to the edge of Dumabato to scout the situation. I told him to take one soldier with him and, in the event something went wrong and one of them was captured, one who could be trusted implicitly. He picked his man, one of those I had trained on Negros, and made a good choice. I cautioned that they should stay off the trail whenever possible and said I would expect them back the following day.

After Valdez and his man left, we put out listening posts to give us warning of any Japanese who might come upon our location while we were waiting for the two men to return. Should the area be searched during this time, I planned to move us again, to one of our new rendezvous to the north, and I warned the men that they should sleep fully equipped. If we were to be raided, I stressed, they must be sure to take their weapons, ammunition, and especially their bolos, with them. My own experience in the jungle without a bolo had made me acutely aware of how necessary that useful piece of equipment is to anyone who has to travel in jungle terrain: survival could depend on it.

By noon the next day, Sergeant Valdez and his man still hadn't returned, and I was getting ready to move camp, fearing something might have gone wrong. I said a silent prayer for them, and about an hour later, they walked into camp.

Valdez said that upon their arrival at the edge of Dumabato, they discovered a patrol of ten Japanese was in the barrio. They had waited until the patrol left the following morning and then had entered the barrio to see what had happened.

The Japanese had accused the teniente of supplying food to the two American officers, Major Roberts and Lieutenant Hieb, and the teniente had replied that was impossible; he didn't have enough to feed his own people because the Japanese forced him to turn over all the barrio's rice and meat to them. He had been slapped around for that remark and was very angry.

Valdez had suggested that in spite of how he felt, he should flatter the Japanese and act as if he agreed voluntarily to their demands. There was nothing to be gained by opposing them openly, he had told the teniente, adding, "Our day will come, and then we will be the soldiers telling them what to do." Valdez said the Japanese actually had gotten very few supplies because the people were beginning to hide whatever food they had.

The teniente had promised Valdez he would be at our camp the following morning. Since he didn't know the campsite had been changed, two of our men were sent to intercept him and show him the way.

About ten o'clock the next morning, our two men brought the teniente back to the camp with the promised supplies, and a few extra bolos, for which I was very thankful. The teniente's cheek was bruised, and I asked if the Japanese had given him the water treatment. (This method of torture involved forcing the prisoner to drink water until he was at bursting point, then he was subjected to severe kicks or other blows to his abdomen.) He replied, "No, but I like water." Everyone laughed. He was a brave man. He wanted to know why I had moved the camp, and I told him we had been caught once and I never wanted that to happen again.

We thanked the teniente for the supplies, and Lieutenant Reyes made out a receipt for them, which he refused to take. He said he owed his country and the Americans that much, Then he warned me quite seriously not to wash my neck too often, saying the headhunters, who preferred Christian, especially white, heads, would think it a great honor to get an American head as a trophy. I told him I would let my hair grow even longer. I asked the Lord to bless him and all the people in his barrio. And I told him that someday he and his people would hear about us again. We shook hands and said our good-byes.

After the teniente's group left, we finished our preparations for the journey through the jungle in the direction of Palacian Grande. Lieutenant Reyes and the two sergeants divided the supplies and distributed a portion to each of the men. We cleared camp and headed north with Sergeant Valdez carrying the compass that belonged to one of the enlisted men. Two men were out in front as points; we carried their equipment, except for their rifles and, of course, their bolos, while they cut the trail for us.

Because the work of hacking through the underbrush was so tiring, when the going was especially slow the points had to be changed as often as every half hour. And the going was indeed slow: it took us three hours to cover two kilometers. Fortunately in our case, that tropical jungle growth grows back so quickly to cover any path chopped through it, I knew our trail, cleared so laboriously, would be invisible again within a very few days.

By five that night, we were exhausted and ready to make camp. We found a spot close to a creek. Our evening meal included snails, which we boiled, sucked from the shells, and ate accompanied by rice. Listening posts were positioned for the night.

I was more worried about headhunters than about the Japanese; we were on the fringe of Ilongot territory. The men already had been warned to be on the lookout for any sign of headhunters. Now I cautioned them against firing their rifles because, although the bow-and-arrow-armed Ilongots are deathly afraid of firearms, the sharp sound of gunfire carries for miles in the jungle and the risk of alerting the Japanese to our presence was too great.

The following morning, we ate a breakfast of rice and dried fish, took a compass reading, and headed straight north. We might have made better time had we followed the river, but not only is the Cagayan a very winding waterway, I assumed it was being used by the Japanese as a transportation route. Having walked it many times, I knew on the west side of the river there was a well-used trail leading from Jones to Pinappagan that we must avoid, too. There was no trail on the east side of the Cagayan River from San Pedro north to Palacian Grande.

We covered little more than one and a half kilometers that day. Our every step had to be hacked out and chopped clear. At that rate, even though we made free use of the snails we found everywhere along the way, I knew our supply of rice would run out long before we reached our destination. The many chattering monkeys that followed and seemed to scold us for invading their territory made tempting prospects for the cooking pot, but while they could chase after us with great ease, we couldn't follow them quickly enough even to attempt snaring one: the jungle was too thick and our time too precious. We had no choice other than to cut back our meals to one a day.

The season for heavy rainfall was approaching, and on our third day the sky started to cloud over. I hoped we would reach Palacian Grande, the next barrio to the north, in another few days: our rice

181

supply was at the critical stage, and now we probably faced weather problems as well.

All along the way, occasionally we would have to move farther into the jungle in order to skirt a barrio that might contain Japanese soldiers. Once, when we passed San Pedro, we had been close enough to hear men shouting in Japanese. We knew the search for us was intense, and we were constantly wary lest we walk into the net of soldiers, which according to the grapevine was spread through the area in the hope of capturing what the Japanese mistakenly thought were thirty of us. Now, during this day, we heard some enemy soldiers going upriver in what sounded like four bangkâs. Otherwise, the day was uneventful. As we had the previous day, we covered only about a kilometer and a half.

We stopped to bivouac at a small stream, where we found the usual plentiful supply of snails to eke out the nearly exhausted rice supply that now stretched to a mere handful each. I had formed the habit of praying nightly for the safety of my men, my family, Elaine, and myself. This night, I prayed for the strength somehow to get my men safely to our destination. I knew if I were to be caught by the Japanese, I would be shot at once. Certainly, I had not changed my decision never to surrender. I had made up my *starrköpfig* (stubborn) mind I would see this war out to the point of our victory no matter how long I had to stay in the jungle, and in the meantime, I intended to nip at the enemy's heels whenever an opportunity presented itself.

On the fourth day, it began to drizzle rain, and Lieutenant Reyes said this could be the beginning of the monsoon, or rainy season. I only hoped we would reach Dabubu before we were caught in some typhoon.

That night, we were forced by the rain to build lean-tos, and we gathered palm leaves in order to cover the wet ground. We also made three of the ingenious kind of bamboo bed used by the Filipinos, who split six-foot lengths of thick bamboo down the middle to make poles and then tie and loop thin strands of rattan crossways from pole to pole, spacing the strands about two inches apart, until a mat has been woven. The size of these temporary beds depends on the number of people to be accommodated; each of ours was made to hold four of us, and we placed all three about four inches above our ground covering of leaves. In spite of the rain, we kept warm and dry, and I assigned only one-hour shifts to the men on listening-post duty in order to allow them respite from the weather.

By the following morning, the rain had stopped, and we made an inventory of our supplies—only to find they would not last through the day. We hadn't seen any monkeys the day before, but now we decided that if we saw one today, we would shoot it—even if the sound of the shot did carry. It seemed a matter of necessity if not survival.

We discussed the situation. The journey was taking longer than we had expected. I knew we could make better time by following the river, but this was dangerous. We could risk traveling near it only if we took extra precautions to avoid being seen by the Japanese transporting supplies along the river by bangkâ or by backpack along the trail on the river's west side.

I asked for a man to volunteer to disguise himself as a G-string–clad headhunter. I knew the Japanese wouldn't cross the river to investigate a lone Ilongot. This volunteer was to be our point, and if he saw any Japanese, he would have plenty of time to warn us. There were several volunteers, and Sergeant Valdez chose the soldier he thought best for the job. This man was given a little rice and a piece of dried fish, which he put in a small bag made of leaves and tied to his G-string. We wished him luck, and he moved out ahead of us; we followed a few minutes later.

Around noon, we heard the sound made by banging two pieces of bamboo together. This was the prearranged signal from our disguised point. We hid behind an outcropping of rocks just at the river's edge, and in a few minutes, we heard some Japanese coming upriver.

If, when the bangkâs came into view, we saw they were carrying supplies, my men were to open fire at my command. We waited another five minutes. When the bangkâs rounded the bend, we saw there were only two of them, with four men in each paddling upstream and not making much progress. I told Reyes and his men to take the first boat; my group would take the second one.

When I gave the signal, we fired; it was over in a few minutes. Several soldiers jumped over the bangkâs' sides, but we shot them when they hit the river; all eight men were killed. Valdez swam out to the lead bangkâ and pulled it to shore. We lifted out the dead Japanese, hauled the bangkâ into the jungle, and camouflaged it with underbrush. There was more rice in it than we could carry, so we put the excess in a sack we tied in a tree and left for the next wayfarer.

It was difficult to leave that rice there. In all likelihood, a time would come when we would need it ourselves, but a decision had to be made: we could take the extra rice or the Japanese weapons and ammunition. We decided on the weapons. Some of the men took the canvas shoes the soldiers had been wearing. The bodies were covered with rocks and hidden in the underbrush. In a short time, there would be no trace of what had happened. Nothing lasts long in the jungle.

Covering our tracks, we entered the water and walked downstream to meet our point. He had pulled the other bangkâ ashore. It contained a few chickens and some dried meat, which we added to our store of supplies. Then we disposed of the boat and its bodies. My Visayan soldier—and pseudoheadhunter—had done a good job.

We were loaded down with the enemy rifles and supplies, and as pleased as we were with the success of our ambush, we found our progress considerably slowed. I was caught between knowing that we needed the weapons, ammunition, and supplies, and realizing that we would have to travel faster in order to avoid the Japanese and beat the monsoon to our destination. Finally, I suggested we make a litter to carry our load, thus freeing more hands for the work of clearing the trail. A couple of the men made the litter, and Valdez improvised a harness with some of the rope we had taken from the bangkâs. I thought regretfully of the sack of rice now far behind us in the tree, or, I wondered, was it perhaps by now in some headhunter's cooking pot?

That evening, we had a real feast. I warned the men we were getting close to the barrios, and every man was cautioned to be on the alert. The Japanese could have patrols in any one of these villages. We divided the supplies among us, and should we be raided, each of us was to take only his own weapons, throwing the Japanese ones into the jungle because they would make too much to carry.

When we broke camp on the sixth day, it was raining again. We cleaned up the campsite and set out for what was to be one of the most miserable days I have ever spent. We were drenched by rain the entire day, and the tangled jungle was thicker than ever and seemed to have a life of its own in resisting our bolos. I had become quite proficient with the bolo; that day I had plenty of practice.

We kept going north. I had hoped that by evening we would have reached the edge of the jungle at the barrio of Palacian Grande, but as it turned out, we had to make too many rest stops and fell considerably short of that goal. I had no idea how far we had walked and crawled by the time we made camp that night. We built our shelters for protection from the nonstop rain and boosted our morale with a hearty meal. Glancing around our circle as we enjoyed that repast while the rain poured down the sides of our small lean-to, I realized that, weary and fatigued as we were from the misery of the day's trek, there was a growing sense of kinship within the group. For my part, I was very aware that this was a special group of men. I had given most of them their basic training on Negros, and their faith and trust in me called for the best I could give of myself in return. The shared adversity of the past few weeks was drawing us closer and closer together. We took strength from each other and from our sense of duty toward our common cause: victory over the Japanese invaders and freedom for these islands.

Before leaving camp on the seventh day out from Dumabato, we made a special effort in cleaning up and camouflaging the area. I was certain this was the day that we would arrive at the barrio of Palacian Grande, and I wanted every man to be especially alert. The rain was still very heavy and masked the normal jungle sounds, but about noon one of the men thought he heard a dog barking. I asked Valdez if men from the barrio could possibly be hunting wild boar, and he said, "No, sir. The dogs couldn't track in this kind of weather."

I knew we had to be getting fairly close to our destination if there were dogs around. We decided to send scouts to the edge of the barrio to determine whether there were any Japanese in the area. Valdez and one of the other men volunteered to go. They took the necessary supplies and said they would be back in the morning. After they left, as a precaution in case the Japanese captured them and forced them to talk, the rest of us moved our campsite about five hundred yards.

On his return, Valdez told us he had talked to a villager and discovered there were over one hundred Japanese in Palacian Grande because "Major Roberts, Lieutenant Hieb, and some of their men had ambushed two supply bangkâs." He had asked, who was feeding the patrol? and had been told the people of the barrio were. His informant had remarked that he "wished to hell the Japanese would leave!" I asked Valdez if, as well as patrolling inside the barrio's confines, the Japanese patrolled its edges. He said that during periods of heavy rainfall the villagers had to patrol for the Japanese. I prayed for rain the next day.

The following morning it was still raining, and after an ample breakfast, we started in the direction of Palacian Grande. When we stopped at noon for our rice and dried fish, we could hear dogs barking again and roosters crowing. We decided to go to the edge of the jungle to reconnoiter from a safe distance. To the east of us, we spotted the patrolling villagers wandering around the barrio's perimeter and knew the rain-hating Japanese must trust these men. The wind was blowing harder now, and the rain was heavier than ever. We returned to our camp and spent part of the evening making raincoats from large palm leaves.

Just before dark, a typhoon hit with eighty-mile-an-hour winds and seemingly solid sheets of rain. For our purposes, the weather couldn't have been better! Now our movement through Palacian Grande would be that much more difficult to detect; in small groups we would blend with the locals, who all looked alike in their callu-gongs and palm-leaf raincoats. Our voluminous raincoats would be hiding the weapons and supplies concealed beneath them.

We gathered for one last briefing in the morning before leaving the protection of our campsite. Food was distributed, and I made sure every man understood the procedure to be followed.

Moving out at ten-minute intervals, we would infiltrate through Palacian Grande in groups of three to four men. Sergeant Valdez would take the first group; I would take the last, including a man who spoke Ilocano in case we should be stopped by a civilian patrol. We would regroup on the north side of the barrio just inside the jungle on the trail leading to Dabubu. Most of us were familiar with the trails on both sides of the river from here to Jones, which was the municipality for all the barrios in the area.

According to the information Valdez had received during his scouting expedition into Palacian Grande, there were no Japanese soldiers in Dabubu. This was good news because it was in the area around Dabubu that I now planned to maintain my guerrilla force until the Americans returned—however long that might take. I had selected this locale because of its isolated situation near dense jungle and head-hunter country, and also on the basis of my acquaintance with Reyes, its teniente, whom I had first met when I was on my way to join Colonel Nakar after my escape from the Bataan Death March. Reyes had offered then to help me, and any men with me, if the need ever arose, and now I was going to put my trust in that offer. Survival in the dense jungle of headhunter country would be a daily challenge and a test of endurance for all of us, but the alternative of surrendering to the enemy was completely unacceptable. If Reyes and the people of his barrio could help us with a few supplies, I knew we could meet the test; if not, we would die trying.

After the briefing, Valdez moved out with his men; ten minutes later Lieutenant Reyes's group left; then Sergeant Dolatre took his three men; and finally, my group was moving. We hadn't gone more than a few hundred yards when a voice behind us called, "Halt!" I turned with my .45 drawn, and a man, one of the two who had stopped us, said in English, "Lieutenant Hieb, I will lead you to your men."

Fearing a trick, I told him and his companion to move out in front of us and warned them that if they led us to the Japanese, in that instant they would both be dead. They said they understood. Twenty minutes later, we were reunited with our other three groups, which also had been led safely through Palacian Grande by our two unexpected guides.

I asked the two men how they had known I was the American in charge of the group, and they said they had guessed I would be, not Major Roberts, because they knew I was familiar with the area. They said there were Japanese soldiers everywhere in the Pinappagan area, all looking for Major Roberts: they thought it was his group who had ambushed the two supply bangkâs. Those soldiers were to raise hell looking for Roberts for quite some time, but, I discovered later, because he had only a few men with him and therefore was able to move from place to place much faster than we could, the Japanese couldn't catch him.

I thanked our guides and told them we were going northeast into Ilongot country. They wished us luck and apologized that they couldn't help us with supplies because theirs had been depleted by the Japanese.

Dabubu was only a few kilometers from where we regrouped on the trail. Sergeant Valdez went ahead with two Ilocano-speaking soldiers to contact Teniente Reyes to tell him small groups of us would be showing up at different intervals, and that I would be with the last of these.

CHAPTER 22

My Guerrilla Force Grows

My group arrived at the barrio near midnight, and I went straight to Teniente Reyes's hut to find him waiting for me. In the meantime, his son Juan had taken my men out to the edge of the jungle to wait for my arrival. Juan, who spoke excellent English, had been one of my soldiers under Colonel Nakar's command. When that unit was dispersed after Wainwright's surrender on Corregidor, he had returned to Dabubu to live with his family until such time as he would be recalled to his unit.

In his broken English, Teniente Reyes told me that a Lt. Pedro Vea and about thirty more men were also hiding in the nearby jungle. Among this group were four of my men, including Emilio, who had managed to reach Dabubu after the raid at Pinappagan. That group added to my present one would make a sizable number of extra mouths to feed. When added to the burden of furnishing the supplies the Japanese demanded, this would be quite an undertaking for the barrio. Reyes said he would help for as long as he could, provided the Japanese didn't take too much from his villagers.

We shared some of his homemade basi while we discussed the situation, and I expressed my gratitude for whatever help the barrio had given Vea and whatever help he could give us. When Juan returned, the three of us set out to rejoin my men, carrying with us a sack of rice and the dry fish and meat that the teniente had given me. We collected my men at the jungle's edge and took a trail that led into that wilderness for an hour and a half; then we left the path, continuing on for another hour. It was almost three in the morning, and still raining, when we reached Lieutenant Vea's campsite.

It was well camouflaged, but to my surprise we walked right in without being challenged, an indication there were no listening posts out. That lack of precaution worried me, and this was something that would have to be rectified if we were to be successful in evading the Japanese.

Wishing them Godspeed, I thanked Teniente Reyes and Juan again for all their help, and they prepared to return immediately to Dabubu. Between the supplies we had brought with us and those already at the campsite, our needs were assured for about a week, by which time the teniente promised to return with more supplies.

Lieutenant Vea and his men had made an excellent choice of campsite, which was inside a rock cave. But even so, as soon as possible I wanted to discuss the necessity for listening posts and other security measures with the lieutenant. I had Sergeant Valdez set up a four-man listening post for that night, and the rest of us turned in for a much-needed rest. Exhausted from the arduous trek through the jungle, we were grateful to have shelter in the cave from the incessant rain.

The following morning, Lieutenant Reyes, Lieutenant Vea, and I assessed our situation. Including Corporal Koopmann, the American from Major Roberts's air-warning unit, there were forty-three enlisted men, most of them Visayan soldiers I had been training on Negros before the Japanese invasion. We three officers made a total of forty-six men in camp. The enlisted men would look to us for food, clothing, medicines, shelter—and direction; we were responsible for their welfare and safety. As the senior officer, I was in charge of and responsible for us all—and the first thing on my mind at the moment was security.

I asked Vea if he thought we had encountered any problems escaping from the Japanese raid on our camp near Pinappagan. He replied instantly, "Plenty!" Then I told him, "My thirteen men and I could have wiped out your entire camp early this morning if we had been the enemy." He looked puzzled and said, "But sir, we trust the barrio teniente. You said he could be trusted."

"I trusted the people of Pinappagan too, and look what happened to us," I reminded him, trying to control my impatience. "Considering that experience, I don't think it's too much to expect of a soldier to ask him to pull a one-hour listening shift at night, especially when the lives of others depend on it."

Vea agreed. Then I asked how many local people he thought knew our location. He said, "Two, Teniente Reyes and his son. I don't think anyone else in the barrio knows there are any guerrilla forces in the jungle."

I was sure that considerably more than two people knew we were in the area. The teniente and Juan were not our only source of supply; all the Dabubuans were contributing, and they would know there were quite a number of us from the amount of supplies that were needed. I also knew that many of these people were in fact the teniente's relatives; while he felt they could be trusted for that reason, I did not share his confidence. No matter how loyal people were, I well knew the Japanese had all-too-effective methods of extracting information. Although the people of the barrio were sympathetic to our cause and willing to help us, alternate campsites of which no one was aware, not even Juan and the teniente, were necessary for our protection.

Lieutenant Vea then informed us that he and his men had been assigned as S–2 agents in the barrios of the municipality of Jones by Colonel Nakar when the regiment command post was moved from the Pinappagan area. I asked if he knew where Nakar had established his new command post. He thought it was somewhere in the jungle east of Jones. He stated he had not been contacted by anyone from Nakar's command post.

When the Japanese started to patrol the barrios of Jones on a daily basis, he had decided to contact Teniente Reyes of Dabubu, who he knew was a loyal Phil-American. Reyes had informed Vea that he was already hiding four of "Hieb's Visayan soldiers" who had escaped the Japanese raid on Pinappagan. Vea then had asked if the teniente could supply him and his men. Reyes had said he would do his utmost to supply any guerrilla forces in the area.

I asked Vea how many Visayan soldiers he had brought into camp with him. He said, "Twenty." Those, with the four who were already there, and the eight we brought, made a total of thirty-two Visayan men. The remainder of the enlisted men consisted of one American,

191

two Tagalogs, and eight Ilocanos. Vea also informed me that there were many more Visayans still hiding out in the barrios near Jones.

After lunch, Lieutenant Reyes assembled the men, and I reviewed the problems that confronted us, stressing the bad times certain to befall those men who elected to stay with our group. The Japanese still offered amnesty to anyone who surrendered voluntarily, and if any of them wanted to surrender, I said, they would have my permission and my best wishes for their safety. Those who stayed would face extreme hardship. Undoubtedly, the days ahead would be filled with misery, hunger, illness, and, possibly, death. We could not expect the barrio to support us indefinitely. I reiterated my early assertion that we would have to learn to live off the jungle as the headhunters did, and at the same time, defend ourselves against those headhunters.

We would have to be on the alert and ready to move instantly to avoid another situation like that at our camp near Pinappagan. I added that the only time we would ambush the Japanese would be when they came into the jungle, and even then, we would do so only if we could lead them deep into Ilongot territory, away from our source of supplies in order not to endanger the villagers. In general, I warned, there would be no firing of weapons except in a real emergency.

The Ilongot jungle would be our home for the next six months, a year, two years, three years—or however long it took for the Americans to return to the islands. I knew they would return, I told the men, and I would wait it out until they did and would not surrender under any circumstances. Deep in my heart, I added, I knew someday we would be on the offensive, and we would be the victors. I asked if any of them, knowing the dangers and tribulations that lay ahead for those who stayed, wanted to surrender. All of the Visayans I had trained on Negros shouted, "No!" The rest of the men agreed with them. I asked again, and again the answer was a unanimous and resounding "No!"

Next, I explained my plan for alternate campsites and outlined the security precautions we would use for the duration of our jungle stay. From now on, I said, we would station listening posts day and night, and our campsites would be changed frequently. Alternate camps would be set up in advance in case we had to move in a hurry.

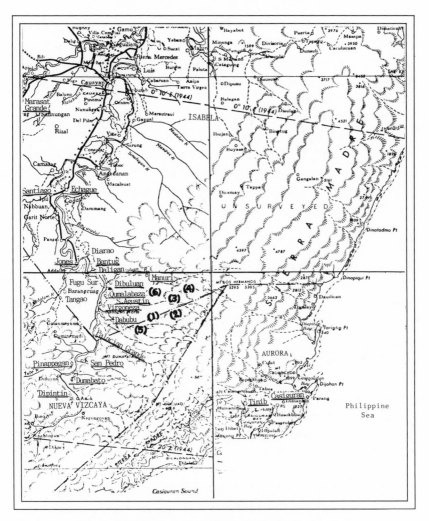

Guerrilla Campsites, Manuri—Dabubu Region

193

Our lives depended on our ability to move out on a moment's notice. Safe places for regrouping were essential, and, if we were to remain effective as a fighting unit until the Americans returned, reliable supply sources. We had to prepare for what could be a very long stay in the jungles of Luzon.

The alternate campsite plan was one I had been formulating since before the raid at Pinappagan. This, our present campsite, would be considered Campsite One, and Sergeant Valdez would be placed in charge of a group of soldiers who would help to locate alternate sites.

The rain continued to pour down for the next five days before the weather finally began to clear and intermittent showers were broken by lengthening spells of sunshine. Along with the better weather came Teniente Reyes and his son Juan. Our listening posts were on the job; we received word of their arrival about fifteen minutes before they entered the camp, and they were impressed with the efficiency of the warning system and thought it was a very good idea. We were happy to see the two sacks of rice, and the dried fish and meat, they had brought with them.

We had begun to adjust to our jungle existence. If we rationed our food, there would be enough rice now to last for about two and a half weeks. We could hunt for snails and fish in the many creeks that intersected the jungle, and there was a wide variety of wild fowl and animals available, including wild chickens, doves, other birds, monkeys, wildcats, rats, bats, pythons and other varieties of snake, and a million different kinds of ants. The best tasting of all this wildlife was wild pig, which I thought was better than the American domestic pig. The Filipino soldiers were skilled at making traps and snares, and I added a few of my own inventions to the collected know-how. If we could overcome our natural aversion to eating some of the stranger creatures, I knew we would manage somehow to survive.

I updated Juan, explaining what I had told the men, and he said when the day came that we needed him, he would be ready to join our unit. I thanked him; then I asked him how many people in the barrio knew our location. He said only his father and he knew where we were; however, he reminded me, the rest of the barrio people were all relatives of theirs and were helping them supply us. They knew that having helped us, they could expect great abuse from the Japanese if we were discovered. He understood, however, when I explained that only he and his father were to know our exact location, adding that maybe not even they would know in the event that things got rough and the Japanese entered the jungle to search for us.

Juan brought us news of other comrades from Pinappagan. He had heard that Judge Cataline Valbuine, who had done some intelligence work for the regiment when we were in the Pinappagan area, and two of our soldiers had been bayoneted and killed when the Japanese were moving prisoners from Pinappagan to Jones. Captain Dingcong had managed to escape by diving into the Cagayan River. (Later we heard he had joined Major Roberts.) The Japanese had tortured some of the people from the barrio of Palacian Grande after we passed through but were unsuccessful in getting any information from them. Now they were moving three hundred soldiers to the vicinity of Pinappagan with orders to keep looking for Nakar, Roberts, and Hieb. I more or less knew the vicinity where Colonel Nakar was in hiding and, through information Teniente Reyes had received from loyal Filipinos, that Roberts was hiding out with some of his men in the jungle west of Pinappagan.

Friendly and smiling like his father, the highly intelligent younger Reyes was extremely quick and able. Also like his father, he was taller than average and of slender build. A handsome man whose courage was somewhat rash from time to time due to a youthful nonrecognition of personal danger, Juan was to play an important part in our on-going fight to survive. A strong bond of friendship and mutual respect grew between Juan and myself, and his sense of humor, which he got from his father, would lighten many a gloomy moment for my men and me.

A few days after Teniente Reyes and Juan's supply run out to our camp, it finally stopped raining altogether. While the weather held was the time to find some other likely locations for our alternate campsites. Lieutenant Vea had reconnoitered the area from our present camp to the end of the Dabubu trail, about an hour's walking distance. Now we could explore beyond this point, beginning at the trail's end. Carrying enough food to last us for a day and a half and using the compass, Sergeant Valdez and I set out with a group of men to search the area; we

195

planned to return the following day. In my absence, Lieutenant Reyes was in charge of the camp with Dolatre acting as 1st sergeant.

Forty minutes after leaving camp, we reached the trail, where we turned east for about a kilometer until we came to the large stream where the trail ended. Valdez and I synchronized our watches, and we all pulled off our shoes, entered the water, and began walking north, upstream. I could see I was slowing the men down, and I told Valdez I was not used to going barefooted. He smiled and said he could see that, but it was better that we take our time so I wouldn't cut my feet and really slow us down. About every half hour, we took a break and checked the terrain on both sides of the stream in case we ever had occasion to cross it at any of these resting points.

There was dense jungle on both sides of us, but eventually we found a huge rock next to the stream with a banyan tree nearby. This would serve us as a shelter while we ate and rested with our backs protected by the rock, from which we had a few meters of uninterrupted view up- and downstream. As we sat down, I mentioned that I had a feeling we were being watched. My feeling was shared by everyone. We ate our lunch and rested for about an hour, all the while conscious of the uneasy feeling that we weren't alone. We had penetrated headhunter country, and our disquieting suspicion that a hostile presence was watching us persisted.

Valdez suggested we leave the large stream and follow one of the smaller ones in our search for a campsite. We took this good advice and branched off at the first creek we came to, just a few meters from where we had our lunch. The going was somewhat harder now, since this creek was narrow with patches of underbrush growing over it. I found myself wishing I owned a spare pair of combat boots so I could be wearing one pair; but, if the war lasted any length of time, I would need the boots I was carrying, and I resigned myself to going barefooted.

After walking for about an hour, we discovered a large cave ideal for a campsite. In addition to the main opening, there were two others, one of which faced the stream and was concealed by a large banyan tree.

We gathered some of the area's abundant supply of wood and damp leaves in order to build smoky fires inside the cave's three entrances. All of the men were very good at starting a fire by pounding two rocks together and blowing the resulting spark onto a small pile of wood slivers, but Valdez was the expert; he could do this as quickly as striking a match.

Soon bats began leaving the cave by the hundreds, and we kept the fires—and smoke—going all night long, driving out a veritable horde of insects, snakes, and small animals. The next morning, Valdez had the men fashion brooms and rakes in order to clean it out. We knew the bats would not be back if the smoke lingered for some time, and to assure this, we found a large log that we pulled into the cave and set afire to continue smoldering long after we left. We now had Campsite Two, our first alternate campsite.

After lunch we started back, reaching our original campsite at about half past three that afternoon. The minute we walked in, I sensed something was wrong. Lieutenant Vea met us with the news that Corporal Koopmann had surrendered himself to the Japanese.

The corporal had been on duty manning a listening post with another soldier, and when it had been his turn to stay awake, he had waited until the other man was asleep; then, leaving his rifle behind, together with a note saying he was going in to surrender, he left. His note said we were not to worry: he would not give our position away to the enemy but would say he had gotten lost in the jungle after the raid at Pinappagan, found his way out finally, and decided to surrender.

Vea said Reyes had gone into Dabubu for news of Koopmann. As a precaution in the event that Koopmann, despite all good intentions, had been forced to give away our position, I sent Vea off to post listening guards, three to a post every quarter kilometer, all the way to Dabubu, where he was to join Lieutenant Reyes. We had no intention of being taken by surprise.

After I had attended to the business of our security, I tried to bandage my feet, which were bleeding from the hike. One of the men found some guava leaves and suggested I tie them to the soles of my feet to stop the bleeding and prevent infection. I did this, and by morning, my feet looked 90 percent better. I was amazed. I decided for the next few days to use guava leaves as a cushion inside my socks whenever I wore my boots, and within those few days, my feet healed completely.

197

While waiting for word from Vea or Reyes, I sent several men to resupply the listening posts with rice and dried fish. These men went as far as the edge of the barrio but saw neither the lieutenants nor any sign of Japanese activity in the barrio. It was not until two days later that Vea and Reyes finally returned with the news that Koopmann had been executed by the Japanese. For quite some time, I was unable to verify this. Most of the Filipinos I talked to after we came out of the jungles during the landing of American troops on Leyte thought he had been killed after he was taken from Jones, supposedly headed for a prison camp.

Upon Reyes and Vea's return, I decided to move our campsite. Reyes and Valdez were in favor of this, but Vea did a little grumbling. I asked him if he had forgotten the raid on Pinappagan. There was little he could say, except "No, sir."

CHAPTER 23

Hunger, Headhunters, and Illness

We broke up into three sections for the move: Lieutenant Reyes and his men were in the first; the second one was headed by Lieutenant Vea and included Sergeant Valdez; I brought up the rear with Sergeant Dolatre. To complete my group, I asked for volunteers because I would be going barefooted again once we reached the stream, and I knew I would slow everyone down; as usual, all the Visayan soldiers volunteered.

Early the next morning, we packed all our supplies and cleaned up the camp. The groups prepared to leave at twenty-minute intervals. Each group was to walk in the stream after reaching the main trail so that there wouldn't be any tracks. In a few days, the underbrush would cover our path to the main trail. Reyes led out, and he and his men were to be responsible for putting Campsite Two in livable order; Lieutenant Vea and his men would help with this work when they arrived. Valdez was to locate four good areas to use as listening posts.

Twenty minutes after Vea's group left, Dolatre and I followed with our men. When we got to the stream, I took off my boots. A couple of the soldiers brought some leaves and helped me wrap them around my feet to protect them from the sharp rocks in the stream. For about twenty minutes, this worked well, but then I needed new leaves. For the trip's entire duration, every twenty minutes we would have to stop, and new leaves would have to be found and wrapped around my feet. Our progress was slow, but we did finally arrive at Campsite Two.

The smouldering log had done its job of ridding the cave of the spiders, insects, and bats, and the men who had preceded us into camp had been busy. The cave was beginning to look quite livable. This location actually was better, and had better shelter, than Campsite One. Even Vea, who had grumbled so about moving, thought we would be safer here than at the other camp. The site was large enough to accommodate all our supplies and men. In places, the cave had a ceiling ten feet high; in others, the ceiling dropped to four feet. Our four-man bamboo beds were placed in the areas with less headroom, leaving the higher-ceilinged spaces for walking and standing.

Valdez arrived back with his outpost team; they had found four likely locations surrounding the camp where three-man listening posts could be stationed, one hour on and two hour's off, in twenty-four-hour shifts. His team had built shelters for the outposts, making these as comfortable as possible but still allowing clear views in every direction. He mapped the locations on the ground, and the following morning I inspected them; I was not surprised to find that he had picked excellent sites.

Just before dark, we sent out our first three-man listening-post detail with enough rations for twenty-four hours and instructions to watch for Ilongots; according to my standing orders, the men were not to fire at the headhunters, except in a life-threatening emergency. The Ilongots are smaller in stature than the other Philippine people, and I knew—and had told my men—that any one of us armed with a bayonet or bolo could best an Ilongot in hand-to-hand combat. No one disagreed with my assessment.

We continued the strict rationing of food, and we practiced an unwavering policy of share-and-share-alike with all wildlife catches. When, for example, a wild chicken was snared, it was divided into forty-five pieces, and we each enjoyed our small slice.

One day, we saw the tracks of a wild pig. With great enthusiasm the men began digging pits and making cages, baiting these with wild roots: all, alas, to no avail. The wild pigs continually evaded us, while visions of a porcine feast increased our persistence. These unsuccessful efforts with traps and snares were not without benefits, however; they served to occupy the men.

Our luck with game of any kind was intermittent. We snared several wild doves, always carefully dividing each one into forty-five tiny pieces. We hunted for snails; and, we tried to catch some fish, but with little luck. The food supply in the streams was so abundant that nothing we used as bait would tempt those satiated fish. Already, our supplies were running very low; each man now received less than half a handful of rice per meal.

I sent Lieutenant Reyes and two other men into Dabubu, of course to glean what information they could, but mainly to gather supplies. Anything, I suggested, would do: even year-old corn, which the Filipinos normally fed to their hogs. The idea of eating corn was repugnant to my men, but I had no such cultural problem and tried to convince them it would be good. We could boil it all night, I said, and it would be edible if we could get it soft enough.

Reyes and his two men returned two days later with only a few supplies; the Japanese were patrolling the area daily and confiscating much of the barrio's food. The Dabubuans were feeling the pinch. They did bring back dry fish, half a sack of rice, and one full sack of shelled corn.

We boiled some of the corn all night and until noon the next day. This was to be our first, but not our last, meal of corn soup. To me, it actually tasted good and the other men were hungry enough that they ate it. I had to admit it would have tasted better with a little salt, but this was a truly precious commodity—so precious in fact that certain of the men became salt snitchers. They would manage to find small amounts of salt on supply runs into the barrios, but rather than share this with the rest of us, they would hide and keep it for their own use. For most of our three years in the jungle, we all suffered from a critical shortage of this vitally important mineral. In the heat and humidity, our bodies were rapidly depleted of whatever traces of salt were supplied naturally in our diet; additional supplies were virtually unobtainable because the Japanese controlled the salt mines.

It was raining still, although not as heavily as when we had first arrived at our new camp. Occasionally now, we would have a day or two of cloudy, but dry, weather, and these rain-free days would bring us visitors: monkeys that watched our activities from the safety of their treetop playground, seeming to regard us as sources of both amusement and alarm. A vanguard of one or two of these monkeys would appear first to jabber and point at us, especially at me. My long beard apparently interested them, and no doubt they were curious about me because I looked different than the other men.

After a while, the monkey, or one of them if there were two, would leave, to return about twenty minutes later accompanied by a group of as many as forty cohorts, all chattering and making a great ruckus. Obviously, they felt we were intruding into their territory, and they were not about to let the intrusion go unnoticed. They screeched and screamed and cavorted crazily in the trees, providing us with a source of constant amusement. After visiting us every day during a whole week of dry weather, the group seemed to accept our presence in its domain. Watching each other became a pleasant pastime for both men and monkeys.

Our supplies continued to dwindle, and one day Valdez, always ready to volunteer for any job, volunteered to set snares in the trees to catch one of the monkeys. The following day when our noisy visitors showed up as usual, he was ready for them, and after several failures, he finally snared one. The outraged monkey fought and scolded—to no avail—as Valdez pulled it down from the tree. The rest of the troupe fled.

One of the Visayan soldiers killed the struggling animal with his bolo. The problem, however, was that someone would have to skin the catch. Since I had promised I would be the official skinner, I took the dead monkey into the jungle where I skinned and gutted it, throwing what could not be eaten into a hole one of the soldiers dug, which afterwards was filled in. When I had cut the meat, including the liver, into small pieces, Valdez and I washed all the portions in one of the nearby creeks and brought them back to camp. The men looked at the meat and decided that, after all, they might as well try some of it. Those of us who had eaten monkey before on Bataan said we thought it had a sweet flavor and tasted better than carabao, but the others were very dubious. Our cook prepared some of it for the evening meal; to the men's great surprise, all of them found they liked it. Unfortunately, our monkey's companions didn't come back the next day.

By now, we knew we were capable of surviving in the jungle and that we could manage, if we had to, without help from the people of Dabubu. We had augmented our diet by watching the monkeys to see what they ate and then trying that foodstuff ourselves. Some of the berries, fruits, and leaves eaten with much enthusiasm by our friends in the trees proved to be rather too sour for our tastes, but nothing eaten by the monkeys was in any way harmful to us. Another source of food was the plentiful palm core, or *ubog*, which we peeled and ate like sugar cane. Perhaps not as appetizing as the ubog and certain of the fruits and berries, the lizards, rats, and snakes could provide nourishment, too.

My own adjustment had progressed even to the point where I was becoming used to going barefooted and did so regularly. The soles of my feet now looked almost as tough as my men's. It really had not taken long for me to adjust to jungle life. Without a doubt, my upbringing in the farm country of the American Midwest had helped me. I had learned there to understand the land around me, and although this land of jungles was in strange contrast to that of my home, the habits I had developed there were enabling me to survive here.

Since Corporal Koopmann had surrendered, I was the group's only American, but my officers spoke English, and most of the enlisted men spoke it too in varying degrees of fluency. I spoke a little Visayan and some Ilocano. Among us we had managed to work around the language barrier so that it now caused few problems.

I felt extremely fortunate to have ended up, quite by accident, with two such officers as Lieutenants Reyes and Vea, and my respect for Sergeant Valdez grew by the day, too. I was growing to depend on the absolute professionalism of this former career 26th Cavalry Scout, and his unmistakable, in-built military bearing, made all the more impressive by his comparatively great height, continued to amaze me throughout the months ahead. He was well versed in military tactics, which was a great help to me in my effort to perfect our various ambush-and-escape techniques, and he carried out orders without question and to the letter. He, like Lieutenant Reyes, was also a born volunteer.

Sergeant Dolatre was also a fortunate adjunct to our group. He was well-educated, intelligent, and quick, as well as being likable and easy going.

One day not long after our monkey dinner, I took Valdez and a few other men on a day hike east from our camp in order to search out another campsite, which subsequently was to become Campsite Three. We investigated an area that we hadn't been through before and located a suitable camping spot. Our day hike turned into an overnight outing when we decided to bivouac there until the next day. At regular intervals all through the night, the surrounding jungle would become uncannily quiet, and we would have an eerie sense of some invisible, stealthy movement around the camp's edges. I had spent enough time in the jungle by then to have learned the difference in its many sounds. The sounds, however, were not as worrisome as their absence: silence is the first indication of danger in the jungle; as Sergeant Valdez said, "Worry when you don't hear anything!"

That night, each time the jungle became suddenly silent, I would ask Valdez if he was asleep, and he would answer no; he was as uneasy as I. Our listening post said he thought he had heard some movement near him. We all knew that the night's stillness indicated the probable nearby presence of headhunters, who undoubtedly would have known we were there and would investigate our incursion into their territory.

The next morning, we carefully searched the camp's perimeter and found footprints that led away to the east of the site.

I told Valdez that, even though there were headhunters in the area, in a few days I would send some men back to clean and prepare this spot for Campsite Three. Sooner or later, I said, we would have to show our strength to the Ilongots so that they would not feel inclined to bother us and would accept the fact of our presence, unwelcome as it might be, because we would be sharing their jungle home for quite some time.

On our return to Campsite Two, Lieutenant Reyes and three of the Ilocano soldiers volunteered to go to Dabubu for supplies and news. On his last trip there, the lieutenant had told the teniente we had moved our camp after Corporal Koopmann's surrender, but he didn't tell him where and said only that from now on, we would contact him so that no one from Dabubu would have to come into the jungle.

No sooner had the four men left than I began to feel extremely weak and very ill. I knew I was having an attack of malaria. Valdez quickly sent a runner with a message for the lieutenant that he should ask Teniente Reyes for a supply of whatever medication his people used in treating malaria.

My symptoms had come on rapidly and without advance warning. The first sign had been an attack of severe shaking; this was followed by high fever and intermittent delirium, which came and went all night long. The next morning, Valdez told me during the night I had prayed for the safety of the men, and I had talked about my mother and my family. He was curious, he said, about the girl I called Elaine. I explained that Elaine was the girl back home to whom I was engaged, but of course he had guessed that much from my delirious conversation. I asked Valdez to explain my feverish ramblings to the men, and when he did, they thanked me for including them in my prayers. This episode brought us all closer together and gave the men reassuring proof that, even when I was ill, I had their well-being at heart.

The following day, Lieutenant Reyes and his men returned with the distressing news that Colonel Nakar and some of his men had been captured in a cave near the barrio of Manuri. I surely feared for their safety. Reyes also reported that he had heard there were thousands of Japanese in the area looking for Major Roberts and *Captain* Hieb. Evidently, the Japanese had given me a promotion; I told the men they were trying to use a little psychology on me. It would take more than a boost in rank to get me to consider surrendering; everything I heard worked to strengthen my resolve to continue evading such an end.

According to Reyes, the Japanese were abusing the barrio tenientes, threatening their lives because, supposedly, they were feeding the guerrilla fighters. None of the tenientes knew exactly where we were, and they couldn't give the Japanese any information, even had they wanted to. But the knowledge of these instances of abuse and threat reinforced our resolve to remain alert.

Our friends, Teniente Reyes and his son Juan, still were forced to give the Japanese supplies whenever they came to Dabubu, and consequently, they had little food to spare. The lieutenant and his men had brought back a little rice and more corn, which we boiled all night and ate as before. I grew to like this mushlike soup, but I don't think my soldiers ever learned to enjoy eating it.

One night while one of the listening posts was keeping the fire going under the boiling corn, he spotted a large animal creeping toward the pot. Raising his bolo high, the man brought it down hard and killed the would-be marauder. The noise the dying animal made woke everyone in the camp. At first, we thought the creature was an extremely large rat, but on closer inspection we found it was a small wildcat.

"Good!" I said. "We'll have wildcat for dinner tomorrow." The rest of the men did not share my enthusiasm, and they all looked ill at the mere thought of such a dinner. Remembering their reactions to other unusual items of food, I ignored this one and simply remarked that I would skin and clean the cat first thing in the morning.

Shortly after dawn, Valdez made me a skinning frame by pounding two bamboo poles into the ground and tying a strong crossbar between them with pieces of rattan. I stretched and tied the wildcat's hind legs to the crossbar, and then, as an old hand at this thanks to my former trapping days, I was ready to skin the cat. Valdez stayed to watch.

First, I made cuts down both sides of the hind legs and straight across from one to the other. Then, I cut all around the tail. Using my fingers, I pulled down on the hide, and before long, I had it off all four legs and the body. Next, I cut off the head and tail, which last item I was about to throw away, when Valdez stopped me and said he would like to skin it. While he was working on the tail, I gutted the wildcat and cut the carcass into small pieces. In the meantime, one of the other men had dug a hole in order to bury the entrails. Finally, I washed all the meat with great care to remove every trace of hair and delivered the cleaned pieces to the cook.

That night, we ate wildcat. I had suggested to the men that they simply imagine they were eating pork or steak, but to their surprise, in spite of their initial qualms, they liked their wildcat dinner. In fact, they thought the dish so tasty, from then on they were on the lookout for wildcat tracks near which to set snares.

During the next few days, we also caught more wild chickens and a few doves. The cook mixed this meat with the now-ubiquitous corn to make an excellent soup.

CHAPTER 24

Suspicion and Surprise

About a week after Lieutenant Reyes had been to Dabubu, we heard shouting in the direction of the trail. There was no way to tell whether the voices were those of friends or a Japanese patrol. Reyes took five men with him intending to sneak up on the intruders from behind; Valdez and I took ten men and approached from the front. Everyone double-checked his weapon and ammunition. If we found Japanese soldiers, Valdez, our men, and I would lead them east into the jungle where we would waylay them. Should any return, Reyes was to ambush them. Vea and his men were to guard our supplies and, if necessary, move them back to Campsite One.

Reyes's and my groups left immediately. I didn't think the voices were Japanese, but they could belong to Philippine Sakdalistas, soldiers who had betrayed their government and were trained and organized into constabulary battalions and companies by the Japanese. This organization's official name was the Bureau of Constabulary, or BC.

About an hour later, a runner from Lieutenant Reyes came to tell us the shouting had come from Juan, the teniente's son, and that he, his men, the teniente, and Juan would meet us somewhere on the trail. My men and I followed the runner back to the trail, and in a short time, we ran into Lieutenant Reyes.

Juan and his father had been searching all over the jungle for us to tell us there was an American captain, a doctor, who wanted to join us. There were also reports of two other American officers in the area, he said. One was a Lieutenant Colonel Warner, and the other, a lieutenant colonel who had been instructed by General Wainwright to find the

207

guerrilla units commanded by Major Roberts and Lieutenant Hieb and ask them to accept the amnesty and go in to surrender. Juan had told the captain he was sure there were guerrilla forces in the area, because someone had been stealing food from the barrio, and had offered to take a small search party into the jungle.

I immediately felt the report of the two other American officers in the area was erroneous, and that the supposed other, unnamed, lieutenant colonel might actually be the same officer who was purportedly a captain and a medical officer. Juan reported that the American captain did seem to have some medical supplies with him, which supported his story of being a doctor. I told Juan that Valdez and I, and two other men, would come to the edge of the jungle that night to lead the captain out to our camp, but Juan was to say we would not be there until the following day, thus insuring us against a possible entrapment. Juan was not to tell the captain that I was in charge of the group.

We sent one man back to Campsite Two to tell Vea the latest developments. Except for the four of us, the rest of the men would return to Campsite One with Lieutenant Reyes to clean it up. Valdez and I, together with our two men, would try to get a few supplies and proceed to the edge of the jungle where we would meet the captain, who would be told to spend the night at the edge of the jungle for his own protection—and for that of the barrio people, who had sworn they were not helping any guerrilla forces.

We waited until dark, watching the trail, and eventually, the captain appeared accompanied by one of Teniente Reyes's relatives. I had Valdez ask the villager if there were any Hapon in the barrio; the man said no. Hearing that, I stepped out and introduced myself to Captain Mark, as he called himself, and the teniente's relation left us.

The captain looked run down, but his combat boots and uniform didn't look as though he had been hiding out in the jungle. I wasn't sure why he was here, and I was suspicious about the whole situation.

To buy time while I thought it over, and to lend credence to Juan's story that we were stealing from the villagers, I told Valdez to go into the barrio and steal some corn, rice, and anything else he could find. Valdez left with one man. The rest of us waited. About an hour later,

Valdez came back with some dried fish, meat, rice, shelled corn, and, to my amazement, even a cooking pot. He had remembered we had no cooking pot at Campsite One. Keeping a straight face, I said, "Good thinking," and let it go at that. Later, I told Valdez that I was very impressed with his impersonation of a thief.

In the meantime, Lieutenant Reyes had done his job well and was taking no chances: before we entered Campsite One, we were challenged twice.

I told the captain we would talk in the morning because I was recovering from an attack of malaria and still felt rather weak. He said that was fine, found a place to lie down, and was soon asleep. I still didn't know if I could trust him. I knew he was an American, but I suspected he was the liaison officer who had been sent out to contact Major Roberts and me. If he was the liaison officer, I was trapped between three alternatives, two of which were quite unpalatable: as a soldier, my duty was to obey orders, and Wainwright's were to surrender; on the other hand, I knew if I surrendered, I was a dead man; then, there was the higher order from MacArthur's headquarters that superceded Wainwright's order, which I still felt had been made under duress. I didn't get much sleep that night, and I prayed for guidance.

After breakfast the next morning, Captain Mark and I went downstream to talk. I asked him where he had been hiding out. He said in the mountain provinces with a pro-American Philippine family, and that while there, he had heard Colonel Nakar, Major Roberts, and Lieutenant Hieb were in the Jones area with a sizable guerrilla force. I told him I had heard Colonel Nakar had been captured. He said he had heard Colonel Nakar had surrendered to the Japanese under the amnesty agreement and that Roberts and Hieb were still hiding out with some men.

I thought it best at this point to tell Captain Mark, or whoever he was, that my men and I had made a pledge never to surrender and the only way the Japanese would take us would be dead. I said I had given every man an opportunity to surrender, but Lieutenant Reyes, Sergeant Valdez, Sergeant Dolatre and I would never surrender, and our men had made a pledge to stay with us.

I told him about Koopmann. I said the amnesty the Japanese were talking about didn't seem to apply to everyone because we later discovered that, after Koopmann surrendered, he was used for bayonet practice. And, I continued, we had heard Colonel Nakar had been betrayed by one of his own officers, Lieutenant del Rosario. We knew his camp had been raided by the Japanese and the Bureau of Constabulary, or BC, but we still didn't know what had happened to him. I told him I would hate like hell to think what they would do to me if I were to surrender, and to the soldiers with me, who were not from this island and were strangers on Luzon. We wouldn't have a chance should the Japanese ever have us in their hands.

Mark asked what we had been eating. I told him snails, monkey, wildcat, wild berries, and ubog. He asked if any of my men had beriberi. I said no, and that I would recognize the symptoms when I saw them. I told him we knew of a tree whose bark could be boiled to make a drink useful in treating malaria. Teniente Reyes and Juan had given us invaluable information about how to survive in the jungle by using leaves and barks for medicinal purposes, especially the bark of the duhat, guava, and bangbangsit trees. The leaves from the tamarind, alibangbang, and malungay we usually mixed with our corn-mush soup to add to its nutritional value. Mark finally commented that he had thought he was the doctor; however, we seemed to know how to take care of ourselves.

When I asked him how he had passed safely through the thousands of Japanese in the Jones area, he said a Spaniard by the name of Villanueva helped him get from the town of Santiago to Echague; then, bypassing Jones, he had come straight to the barrio of Dabubu, where we contacted him.

Trying to verify this story, I didn't mention that I knew Villanueva but asked if Villanueva was from Jones. Mark said yes, he was, and that he grew tobacco and sugar cane. The captain did seem to have the right answers. Finally, I asked if he thought he could hold out with us until the Americans retook the islands. He said he wasn't sure: he had been raised in the city, and he didn't know if he could rough it with the rest of us.

The only other question Mark asked was, who got away after we were raided at Pinappagan? I told him I had, together with the men he had met here at the camp. I don't think he bought all of my story; but then, I certainly wasn't buying all, or maybe any, of his.

I had the feeling he was trying to find out if we really could survive in the jungle, or if we were just stumbling from day to day. I think finally he knew we could take care of ourselves. My instinct still told me this man was the liaison officer sent from Wainwright, and I told him several times that we had been ordered by MacArthur not to surrender.

The days slipped by. Our monkey visitors returned, and we were lucky enough to snare another one. The captain—I still doubted he was a doctor—couldn't keep his piece of meat down; he went out in the jungle and vomited, which seemed to the rest of us a waste of food. Our palates and stomachs had adjusted to a strange variety of anything that might be edible.

The day following this incident, Mark came to talk to me. He said he felt he would be too much of a burden on us, and that it might be best if he surrendered. If he did, I told him, we would have to move our campsite. He asked if that was because I didn't trust him, and I explained that it wasn't a matter of trust; it was a necessary precaution. As a doctor, I said, he might have a chance to survive in a prisoner-of-war camp because medical officers were always needed. Once again, I told him we were not going to surrender; rather than do that, we would stay with our pledge to die. If the Japanese ever came in after us, we would draw them deeper into the jungle and continue ambushing them as long as we could. My thought in saying this was that if he did surrender to the Japanese and were to tell them anything, he could tell them that. However, I really felt that Mark was not so much going in to surrender as returning after his mission as Wainwright's emissary.

He left that afternoon. We wished him good luck, and one of the men took him to the trail. When our man returned, we left immediately for Campsite Two. As he was leaving, Captain Mark had heard me give the order to clean up the camp and be ready to move out in order to get a good distance between the campsite and us before darkness set in.

The next day, I told Vea to go to Campsite Three with as many men as he needed to make it livable. He was to reconnoiter the area around it for any sign of the Ilongots, and he was to look for signs of wildcats, snails, or any wildlife that might be edible. He was to return to Campsite Two in two days.

Our company clerk, Sgt. Enrique Dannug took this opportunity to bring the log book up to date. There were only a few empty pages remaining in the book I had started when we left Dumabato; so on his next trip to Dabubu, the sergeant found a notebook, and from that time on, we kept a proper log. Dannug was very bright, well educated, and an excellent administrator. He spoke Tagalog and Ilocano and had an exceptionally good command of English. Originally from the 11th Division, he had been with Lieutenant Vea when I first arrived at Campsite One with my men. Later, I promoted Dannug to 1st sergeant, replacing 1st Sergeant Dolatre, who was promoted to master sergeant.

The log wasn't kept in great detail, but it contained enough information to refresh the memory of names, events, places, enemy movements and strength, and all other information we had about the enemy and the civilian collaborators.

A few days after Captain Mark's departure, I made plans one day to go to Dabubu that afternoon with Valdez and four of the men for news and supplies. Just before we were to leave, Vea and his men arrived back from Campsite Three. He reported that they had found wild-pig tracks and many monkeys near the camp. There had also been human footprints around the site, which, because they were so small, he was sure must have been made by headhunters.

Late that afternoon, Valdez, the four men, and I left as planned for our previously selected meeting place on the edge of the barrio, timing our arrival there to coincide with dusk. As far as we could tell from our hiding place in the brush, there didn't seem to be any Japanese around. Watching the residents as they moved about the barrio, Valdez finally spotted a man he recognized. Calling out, he asked if there were any Hapon in the barrio. No, the man said, there were none. Then Valdez asked if he would find Juan and tell him we were waiting to see him. A short time later, Juan joined us. He said supplies were being gathered for us to take back to camp the next day; we certainly needed them.

Juan reported that Captain Mark had surrendered to the Japanese.

212

I hoped he was all right. I still had no way of knowing for certain who he was, but I believed then—and I still believe—that he was Wainwright's staff officer posing as a medical officer in order to investigate our situation and our intentions in regard to surrendering. He hadn't tried very hard to convince me and my men to surrender after I told him about the message we had received from MacArthur's headquarters encouraging our resistance.

After the war, I tried to find out exactly who Captain Mark was. I believe he could have been Lt. Col. Ted Kalakuka, one of two American officers sent by Wainwright into northern Luzon to contact the guerrilla forces fighting there; both officers carried Wainwright's order to surrender. Kalakuka was not seen again, and he was reported to have died as a Japanese prisoner.

At some point, we learned that the other officer was indeed Colonel Warner, who was sent out on a similar mission by the Japanese after his surrender to them.

When I asked if there was any news of Colonel Nakar, Juan said it was rumored that the Japanese had killed him.

The following morning when Juan, his father, and his uncle Jose showed up with our supplies, they also brought more news. They had heard that Capt. Walter Cushing was looking for Major Roberts: he had information he wanted to forward immediately to General MacArthur's headquarters in Australia, and he thought Roberts still had the transmitter, which had been dismantled when Nakar dispersed his command.

At this time, Cushing was in the area after making his way from Abra through northeastern Luzon in an effort to contact the various guerrilla bands, especially those formed by the remnants of the 14th Infantry, including my group. Earlier, he had been in contact with Major Praeger at Kabugao, Apayao, where the only other radio transmitter was located. Cushing often disguised himself as a priest, and his mestizo bloodlines had equipped him with a short stature and a dark complexion, making it easy for him to pass as a Filipino. His ability to speak fluently most of the Philippine dialects, as well as Spanish, also helped him move about for the most part undetected, and unsuspected, by the Japanese, who were desperate to catch him because his guerrilla organization had caused them so many casualties, especially on the Il-ocos coast of Luzon.

The Reyeses had a written message for me. It was from Roberts. I recognized his handwriting, and when we had been together in Pinap-pagan, he had taught me the single and double transposition code in which the message was written. The message read:

> Am happy to hear you are safe. Am upriver with un-captured remnants CP [command post]. You can trust our contact here, but suggest that you stay where you are unless your safety is jeopardized. If so, our con-tact could arrange guide to our location. Report loca-tion and strength.
>
> Good Luck!
> Roberts

I asked Juan if anyone was waiting for a reply; he said the messen-ger would be back in a few weeks. Although I recognized both the handwriting and the code, I worried about the possibility that Roberts might have been captured by the Japanese and forced to write the mes-sage. I asked if Juan had heard anything about Roberts being captured. When he said no, I said I would have an answer in a few days and would send it by runner. We thanked him for the supplies and started back to camp.

Bad news awaited us on our return. Emilio was sick with beriberi. At thirty-five years old, he was somewhat older than the other soldiers and was careworn from hard work. He had left a wife and several chil-dren on Negros when the 71st Infantry was ordered to Luzon, and he al-ways worried a great deal about how his family was faring without him.

I went straight to where he lay and asked him how he felt. He said, "Not sick, but very, very weak." When I pressed down on the skin of his forearm, my fingers left indentations. I agreed: it was beriberi. We just weren't getting the right kind of food or enough of it, and there didn't seem to be much we could do about this situation. I was afraid the strain of our living conditions was beginning to tell on all of us. We were all in weakened physical condition due to our poor diet; thus, we were more susceptible to the various jungle ailments. We had so little reserve strength or resistance left, what medicine we did have was not always effective.

That evening, after reading Major Roberts's message to the men, I led them in a prayer for Emilio's recovery, and from this time on, it seemed only natural to have nightly prayers. I had been given a Bible and a prayer book by a minister in Pinappagan, and I found myself thumbing through them for the comfort they gave me. I carried them with me throughout the war, and they are still with me.

The men seemed to draw strength from these evening prayers. I certainly did. We were all grateful for the moments of peace they brought to our hearts at the end of each hard day.

A few days after our return from Dabubu, I forwarded my answer to the message I had received from Roberts. Teniente Reyes was to give it to the messenger Roberts was to send.

> To: Commanding Officer
> Thanks for your message. We were very happy to hear from you and that you are still evading the Japanese. The people here have been very good in giving us some supplies. Although sometimes we exist only on what we can forage out of the jungle. At present I have forty-two enlisted men and two officers. If you have any orders for me or would like to join me, please let me know. I would prefer not to move at this time if OK with you.
>
> > Good Luck,
> > Hieb

The author's great-grandfather
Jacob Hieb (1832–1926)

Left, the author's grandmother
Katharina, and *right,* grandfather
George Hieb.

George Hieb's farm, Eureka, South Dakota, circa
1915. *Left to right*: The barn, the first house, the
original soddy, the second house with its groves of
trees. The cabbage patch shows in the foreground.

Wedding picture of author's father, John J.
Hieb, 28 January 1908

Wedding picture of author's mother, Eva
Bauer Hieb, 28 January 1908

Author's childhood home, Eureka, South Dakota

Left to right: the author's father, sister Ella, mother,
circa 1911.

George Hieb's farmhouse, circa 1923, with family group including, *third and fourth from left,* George and Katharina. *Left to right of front door* are the author's uncles Emil and Bill.

Above left, a header pulled by four horses; *right,* a header box pulled by two horses.

The 3d Battalion Band, Fort Lincoln, North Dakota, 1934. *Second row, first on right:* the author.

The 3d Battalion, 4th Infantry, Fort Lincoln, North Dakota, 1934. A 120-mile hike to Brush Lake. The horse-drawn field kitchens were identical to those used during the Civil War.

The USAT *U. S. Grant,* 1934

Pan American Airways System's *China Clipper*,
Manila Harbor, 1935

The author in front of the Customs
Building, Manila, 1935

Entrance to Manila's walled city, headquarters of the
31st Infantry, United States Army, 1935. *On right,*
the author.

Carameta-pony-drawn vehicles, downtown Manila,
circa 1935

The road to Baguio, Benguet Province, Luzon

Camp John Hay, Baguio, circa 1935

The golf course, Camp John Hay

The famous rice terraces near Baguio

Left to right: the author and his
brother-in-law Gup Cirks, Iowa, 1937.

An outrigged bangkâ, also rigged for sails, anchored
in Manila Bay

A carabao-drawn cart

A barrio on the Cagayan River

A simple bangkâ on the Pasig River

Jungle scene, Isabela Province

An Ilongot headhunter with trophies

Igorot women roasting dog

An Igorot town at Bontoc, Mountain Province

An Igorot group

Mail call, Bessang Pass, 1945. *On right,* the author.

Elaine Marr, 1945

The author on his return to the States, 1945

The author's wedding day, 13 November 1945. *Left to right:* the author and Lt. Col. John Patrick O'Day.

Elaine Marr Hieb and the author, Minneapolis, 1945

Elaine Marr Hieb, 1946

The author at his retirement
from the Army of the United
States, January 1957.

CHAPTER 25

Christmas, Death, and More Hunger

The second wartime Christmas came and went. In that tropical jungle where my men and I celebrated this day, there was little to remind me of the season, which I associated with snow, decorated trees, carols, and festive church services of thanksgiving. Thoughts and longings for our families and homes beset us all: homesickness was the order of the day. I wondered how many more Christmas Days I would spend in these foreign islands before my countrymen returned to liberate them.

All Dabubu had contributed food so that we could enjoy a Christmas feast, of sorts. For once, our portions were generous and our rice was snailless. We ate chicken in abundance; there was plenty of rice; and—an extra special treat—the barrio had sent along *lechon*, or pork. Our thanks to the Lord included special gratitude for the barrio's help; the Dabubuans had so little themselves; yet they shared so willingly with us.

Some days before Christmas, my runner had returned from taking my message for Roberts to Teniente Reyes. The man had brought back news of increasing guerrilla activities everywhere in the islands, but especially in the mountain provinces of Luzon. At the same time, the Japanese were claiming they had captured or killed all the guerrillas!

I wondered how the people in Dabubu were getting all this news. The runner said it was coming through Colonel Nakar's bamboo telegraph, a system that was operating much the same way as the old Pony Express had. When, at the dispersal of Colonel Nakar's 14th Infantry command, his nine hundred officers and enlisted men had melted into the general population, the enlistees, following Naker's orders, had continued to report regularly to their officers. To handle this, the officers had set up relay contact stations, also in accordance with our former commander's instructions. Now message centers had been set up in all the barrios and towns where the people were sympathetic to our cause, and information filtered through those of the tenientes and mayors who were loyal. This remarkable news network and spy system was working beautifully and covered the areas of Nueva Vizcaya, Nueva Ecija, Isabela, Cagayan, and some of the mountain provinces. In all these places, small bands of guerrillas continued to exist, many of them consisting of former members of the 14th Infantry who sometimes sent us information. (These were the groups that Captain Cushing was trying to contact.)

The Japanese were reducing the number of troops stationed in the Jones and Pinappagan areas. As their soldiers left, they took with them most of the food belonging to the surrounding barrios. The men and I wanted to go into Jones to ambush some of the Japanese in retaliation for the atrocities they had committed in the area, and to gather supplies. However, those of the tenientes who were friendly thought the Japanese were leaving altogether, and they were afraid if we raided Jones, they might decide to stay in force. We postponed any raids or ambushes, but we knew our day would come. Rumors were both constant and consistent that the Americans were on the offensive and were on their way back to the islands. I believed this and so did my men.

The days seemed to drag. Even survival in the jungle can become tedious. As a pastime, I would watch the armies of ants that were always present. Their apparent intelligence intrigued me, and I was impressed by the perseverance they displayed as they conducted their various maneuvers and wars, in which victory did not depend necessarily on greater size: even a colony of small ants sometimes would win in battle against an army of large ones.

I was often lonely, for while the men respected me, and, especially between the Visayans and me, we had some sense of mutual trust, I was not one of them and anyway, my position as commander of our group did not allow the development of a peer-type relationship. Language was also somewhat of an isolating factor—and age! In general, the men regarded me as being practically an old man. At twenty-eight, I was much older than they were and was made still older-seeming by the responsibility and authority I bore.

They did ask me many questions about life in the States, which they somehow envisioned as uniformly sumptuous for Americans who were all rich. I told them about my childhood and about farm life and its many hardships, but much that I described was so foreign to the Filipino way of life, I found they really could not conceive of such ways as some of ours. The story of my hitchhiking adventures must have seemed almost a fairy tale with its trains that traveled countrywide: there were few railways in the Philippines then. Most incomprehensible of all, however, was the fact of my running away from home. In the islands, families are very close knit, and at that time certainly, the young people stayed in the barrios where they were born and raised, or at the most, when they married, formed a new barrio close by. Some barrios, Dabubu among them, were populated entirely by members of one family.

I spent a lot of time daydreaming, and a lot remembering my childhood and my various run-ins with my father. Perhaps as a result of conversations with my men in which they explained the great importance of education in their culture—no matter how remote the barrio, every home invariably had on display the college diploma of at least one family member—I frequently played the game of What If with myself: what if I had finished my own education?

To break the stupifying monotony of the long, hot, humid days, I instructed the men in both guerrilla tactics and offensive warfare. Sergeant Valdez made a bamboo box that we filled with sand and used for war games. Turning the box into a replica of our own area's terrain, we improvised tactics, plotted attacks and traced their various outcomes, and practiced ambush-and-retreat techniques. The men were enthusiastic and looked forward to our daily sandbox-school sessions. Many a heated discussion was produced as we debated the advantages or disadvantages of the various situations we devised for our mock encounters with the enemy.

We were well into January of 1943 now. The Dabubuans could not help us anymore with even small amounts of rice; corn was all they could spare. What rice we still had, we gave to Emilio. When any man was sick, the others, without being asked, would give a portion of their own rations to be added to his.

But Emilio grew weaker, his condition continued to deteriorate, and the rice, ubog, and natural folk remedies didn't seem to help him. He was dying. One day, he asked Valdez to tell his family that his last thoughts had been for their well-being. The following morning, he was dead; he had died in his sleep.

The loss of Emilio upset me profoundly. I grieved as I remembered how we had escaped the Death March together and shared all the events and tribulations of the next twelve months. From Negros to Bataan to Dabubu, all the mutual experiences had formed a close bond between us in spite of our differences of nationality, background, language, and rank. Perhaps most of all, the months since Pinappagan had strengthened a comradeship born while Emilio, Enrique, and I worked our way north from Bataan to eventually rejoin the 14th Infantry and Colonel Nakar; with Enrique's departure after the Pinappagan raid, Emilio and I were each other's only link to that terrible time, which we had managed to survive. And I grieved doubly over the frustration of a death so unnecessary and avoidable in time of peace—or in time of war had we only had regular access to proper food. Our jungle existence was beginning to take its toll.

I sent a runner into Dabubu to notify Teniente Reyes that Emilio had died, and Reyes sent back a fine-looking chicken as a burial offering. Astonished, I questioned Lieutenant Reyes about the chicken. He explained that it was their custom always to place offerings on graves. Obviously deep-rooted and dating from very early times, this custom was now Christianized: Teniente Reyes's chicken was an offering to the Lord, and as such, it was not to be touched. Certainly, it was not to be eaten.

Well, if that was their custom, I told Reyes, I would honor it. He thanked me and said he knew I would understand. Sadly, we buried our comrade. Sergeant Valdez was especially sorrowful: he and Emilio had been like brothers. I said the words of prayer, praying also for the

219

family whose well-being had been the dead man's constant—and final—concern. Valdez placed the chicken on the grave.

None of the other men would ever know what torment that chicken caused me. I lay awake that night and all I could think of was the chicken: the perfectly edible, plump chicken that now was lying atop Emilio's grave, where it would quickly rot and where it was totally useless in the midst of forty-four nearly starving men. All night long I fought the temptation to go out myself to eat the chicken, ants and all.

It was sometime after this that Teniente Reyes told me about a Dabubu man who had died because a dead man had "bumped" him from the grave. According to this story, the man had offended the dead man while the latter was still alive; so, the deceased got revenge by bumping his offender and thus causing him to sicken and die. (To myself, I guessed the cause might have been appendicitis.) I knew already that the Ilocanos believed in ghosts, and when the teniente told me his bumped-by-a-ghost story, I was very glad I had not given in to temptation about the chicken. I would not have knowingly belittled these people's beliefs for anything in the world.

By the early part of 1943, about 99 percent of our food was coming from the jungle. We had begun snacking on such things as beetles, which we chewed raw after snapping off their heads. On several occasions we ate rats and, even worse, bats. Most of the men didn't know what they were eating: Lieutenant Reyes, Sergeant Valdez, the cook, and I were the only ones who knew. Valdez and I did most of the trapping. We dug pits and placed sharp-edged bamboo stakes at the bottoms so that if we caught a wild pig we would hear it squeal when it encountered the stakes. Sharp bamboo stakes were also placed around our campsite to alert us if any intruder were to get near our hideout. In spite of all our efforts, our rations were skimpy. Hunger nagged at us, and I worried about the lack of nutritional value in much of what we did eat.

For a long time now, I had been unable to think of much else other than food. The hungrier I was, the more I thought of my grandfather's laden dinner table and the seemingly endless procession of food that emerged from my grandmother's kitchen accompanied by great puffs of delicious-smelling steam. And the more I thought of those summer-time farm dinners, the hungrier I got. My memories of and longings for "cheese buttons," and "pigs in the blanket," roast beef, and coco-nut pie were so vivid, I could taste these dishes, while my saliva ran and my stomach growled and groaned and cramped. I would shut my eyes and see before me mountains of chow mein; tub-size pitchers of milk; I spent hours planning my first meal when I should at last arrive back in the States: chow mein, shrimp cocktail, and milk. I was not alone in this preoccupation. I could hear the men talking to each other about food, and while our dishes were not the same, our hunger was.

I redoubled my efforts continually to invent new tactical exercises for us to practice in our sandbox theater. The replenishment of our drinking water supply, which I insisted must come directly from a source because I feared the pollution that I knew the Ilongots caused, occupied a certain number of men for a certain amount of time each day. Everyone of us bathed daily in nearby creeks and streams, which were so plentiful in the area we couldn't walk twenty feet without run-ning into one. But busy as I tried to keep us, there were still too many hours in which to think—and dream—of food.

One morning when I went down to the stream to take a bath, I no-ticed my skin had a yellow tinge. Several days later, I noticed that when I pressed down on my forearm with my thumb, it left an indenta-tion. I thought I might have beriberi and perhaps jaundice, as well. When I mentioned this to Reyes, Vea, and Valdez, they thought it looked like beriberi. We desperately needed to supplement what we were eating; otherwise, we would all become ill, and others of us might die as Emilio had.

CHAPTER 26

We Steal for Vengeance

The fear of betrayal was a fear we all lived with, and at about this time, we received the news that an informer by the name of Hernandez, helped by his two sons and some of his neighbors in the barrio of Fugu Sur, had betrayed Captain Cushing to the Japanese. The information had come from several sources, and there were several different versions of what had happened to Cushing. We relied on the information given us by Enrique, who had been living in the barrio of Tangao ever since Nakar had dispersed the men of the 14th Infantry. Later, we would learn Cushing actually had been killed, and Teniente Reyes and Juan would confirm this. At the time, we knew only that he had been turned in by Hernandez and the others.

I asked Valdez, by now well and truly my right-hand man, if he thought the men would volunteer to cross the river to raid Fugu Sur. He himself volunteered instantly and said he wouldn't have to ask for volunteers. The whole camp was ready to raid the barrio for its food supply in retaliation for the betrayal of Cushing.

Valdez was right: the whole camp was ready to go. We felt five men could do the job, and he chose four to accompany him. The plan was to get Juan Reyes to take the raiding party across the river by bangkâ under cover of darkness and point out the Hernandezes' hut. We did not know the identity of the other informers; so, it seemed best to restrict the raid and not risk frightening people unnecessarily.

After Juan helped Valdez locate the hut, he was to return to the bangkâ and hide there until the raid was over; I stressed to Valdez that I didn't want to get the Reyes family or their barrio involved. If there were Japanese soldiers in Fugu Sur, his group was to raid another west-side barrio that was pro-Japanese. Obviously, we did not want to raid any of the barrios that had supported us. On the other hand, if we didn't get some proper food, I was afraid the rest of the men would get beriberi. I worried that we might become so weak we wouldn't be able to travel if the Japanese or the BC came looking for us.

The men left carrying rifles, hand grenades, and Valdez's BAR. After two anxious days of waiting on my part, they returned to camp carrying two sacks of rice, and some dried meat, vegetables, papayas, and camotes. The rest of the men and I were overjoyed to see these re-plenishments, and I hoped they would last us a couple of weeks if we rationed them very strictly. We never had had to resort to stealing be-fore, but now our health depended on getting the right kind of food. It was too late for Emilio, but the rest of us could still be helped.

Valdez reported on the raid. He had done an excellent job. The day that his group reached Dabubu, they had found Juan and told him their plan. Valdez said all the men in the barrio would have volun-teered to go along with him because the Japanese had stopped confis-cating the food supplies from Fugu Sur after Cushing had been betrayed, and the people in Dabubu were very angry about this. Many of the people on the west side of the river had plentiful food supplies because they were pro-Japanese and collaborated with the enemy.

After Juan had learned there were no Japanese or BC in the target barrio, his uncle Jose decided to go with him and the raiding party, and Juan and Jose took the party across the river and pointed out Hernan-dez's hut. After that Valdez sent the two back to wait at the bangkâ so that they wouldn't be seen and possibly recognized by any villagers.

Dogs began barking, and candles were seen to be lit in a few of the huts. The men surrounded the Hernandez home. Valdez called to Hernandez to come out, telling him they were a patrol of BC. When Hernandez and his two sons appeared, Valdez and his group closed in and surrounded them. Valdez threatened to shoot all three men in-stantly should they make one false move: they were so frightened, they couldn't speak. Holding the father and one son hostage, Valdez now sent the other son to collect all the supplies he could—and to do it in a hurry. Valdez remarked that the barrio was surrounded and if the young Hernandez, or anyone else, tried any tricks, it would be burned to the ground and every man would be shot. In about forty-five minutes the son was back; he and several men with him had brought all the supplies they could carry.

Valdez told the Hernandezes this food was only a partial payment for their betrayal of Cushing. When the three men started to deny their complicity, the sergeant said he had plenty of proof and knew exactly who had been involved. He advised them not to disclose anything about the raid to the Japanese or BC and said they should get back in their hut and stay there.

Taking care to shield themselves from the villagers' view, Juan and Jose came out from their hiding place in the cogon, loaded the large bangkâ, while Valdez's men stood guard, and pushed it into the river. They headed downstream because Valdez was sure the people in the barrio were watching to see which way they would go. Once they had rounded a bend in the river and were out of sight of the barrio, they pulled the bangkâ onto the east riverbank and unloaded it. Juan, Jose, and one of the soldiers carried the bangkâ; Valdez and the other men carried the supplies to our meeting place at the edge of the jungle near Dabubu.

Juan had offered to return the next day to help carry the supplies to our campsite, and the next morning he showed up with the news that everyone in the barrio had heard of the raid and approved of it. Valdez's ruse of going downstream had worked. The people of Dabubu had already heard from Fugu Sur that the raiding party was seen heading north toward Jones, where according to the rumor another raid was to be staged.

Our men were pleased with their success and enjoyed the rumor crediting them with planning more raids. In all likelihood, the previous night's raid would bring the Japanese back to the Jones area, but to some extent we had avenged Cushing's betrayal, and the fresh supplies would enable us to get our strength back so that we could continue to exist in the jungle.

About three weeks after the raid, word came from Juan that a Japanese patrol consisting of one officer, twenty enlisted men, and twenty BC had entered the jungle to search for us. Thus far, the search was concentrated in the vicinity of a trail leading from Diarao or Bantug, both barrios north of Jones. But, I told the men, we should expect patrols to be sent to all the barrios on the east side of the river; once again we reviewed our ambush-and-retreat plans.

I had not left the campsite since my latest bout of illness, but after we received this news, Sergeant Dolatre went into Dabubu to ask Juan to meet me the following morning at the end of the trail. I was feeling quite a bit better, as were the rest of the men: the direct result of having had rice and vegetables to eat for about three weeks. My symptoms of beriberi and jaundice had disappeared, and I felt stronger. Fortunately, I had been in excellent health prior to the war, and the reserve strength left me from that time was helping me to recover now. I was exercising daily in order to keep that strength up: I knew it would continue to be tested.

Reyes, Valdez, my runner, and I were waiting on the trail the next day. When Dolatre and Juan came, we found Teniente Reyes had accompanied them. We discussed the probable Japanese procedure for flushing us out of the jungle. I surmised that from their starting point opposite Jones—either at Diarao or Bantug—they would work south, coming down the east side of the river. They probably would enter the barrios closest to the jungle and question the residents about guerrilla forces hiding farther to the east. The villages could be in for a bad time. The frustration of their thus-far-unsuccessful search undoubtedly had served to whet the Japanese soldiers' appetites for cruelty.

My plan was that while the Japanese were working their way south toward our area, we would be moving north and still farther east. I asked Teniente Reyes if he thought we could work our way north through the jungle until we were opposite Jones. He said he and Juan had hunted that entire area for wild pig and knew it well. Juan said if necessary, he could lead us to the coast across the Sierra Madre mountain range. I had decided to ambush the patrol some distance northeast of our campsites. I thought it would be better if Juan remained in Dabubu, but his father said it was all right for him to go with us, which, of course, he wanted to do. I didn't want to put the Reyes family in a precarious situation should the Japanese enter Dabubu and inquire after the whereabouts of family members. The teniente said he would tell the people that Juan had gone for rice to Santiago, where the family had relatives.

I said we should prepare to move out immediately. Juan wanted to go back with his father to get his rifle; but I told him we had an extra one at the camp and there was no need to get his. Earlier, I had been relieved to hear from Valdez that Juan and his uncle Jose both had rifles that they had taken along on the retaliatory raid several weeks ago. According to Juan and Jose, many of the soldiers who had been dispersed from Nakar's command still had rifles and ammunition, which they kept well hidden. It was good to know that the Filipinos who were pro-American would be armed and ready to fight when the Americans came back to free the islands.

We said our good-byes to Teniente Reyes and took Juan with us to Campsite Two. When we got there, Juan said he had figured the camp was somewhere in this vicinity. I was glad to welcome Juan to our camp. He had proven to be trustworthy and loyal, and in the days to come, he would be an invaluable addition to our group.

CHAPTER 27

Protective Ambush:
We Strike First

That night after supper, we reviewed our plans for the coming encounter with the enemy. It was to our advantage that we knew the Japanese were coming after us, and I wanted to keep that advantage as long as possible, in order to meet them on our terms, and in our territory—the jungle. The men were ready; we had practiced our ambush-and-retreat tactics many times. We were prepared; now we had to find the right location—our choice, not theirs—and get accurate information on the size of the patrol and when to expect it.

We left camp the next day after dividing the food and ammunition among us. Juan and one of the other men acted as our two-man point. I divided the rest of us into groups of fifteen: the first group, under Lieutenant Reyes; the second, under Lieutenant Vea with Sergeant Valdez; and the third group, under myself with Sergeant Dolatre. If we were ambushed, we would rendezvous at Campsite Two.

With Juan in the lead, we moved out in single file and followed the stream in a northerly direction; occasionally, Juan would head us in an easterly direction until we ran into another stream going northwest. This crisscross progress continued all morning, with a ten minute break every hour.

We stopped at noon, and I moved forward to talk with Juan. He was eating wild berries, as we all had been since finding them about midmorning. The chronic shortage of food kept us on the lookout for anything at all with which to safely supplement our diet. We had cut down to one meal a day, and if we ate sparingly, we were carrying enough rations to last us a few days.

Showing Juan where on the map our second campsite was, I asked him to help me locate our present position because there were no distinguishing landmarks in the area to aid me in pinpointing our location. He pointed to a trail some distance northeast of Dabubu and said soon we would be crossing this path leading to the barrio of Virgoneza. Since he had relatives in that barrio, he volunteered to inquire there about Japanese patrols in the area. This offered an excellent chance to update our information about enemy movement and numbers, and when we reached the Virgoneza trail about a half hour after our midday break, Juan and Corporal Nueves, who also spoke Ilocano, left for the barrio while the rest of us took cover and waited for them to return. The two men intended to hide their weapons before entering Virgoneza, and Juan was to tell his relatives they were on their way to Santiago, incidentally getting as much information for us as possible. Juan was proving to be quite an asset; as a jungle guide, he was invaluable.

About sundown, Juan and the corporal came back bringing a little rice that Juan's relations had given them, and which they generously shared with the rest of us. Juan had learned that the Japanese had been combing the jungle around several barrios north of Dibuluan, itself north of Virgoneza. A combat patrol, which included BC, were expected to arrive in Manuri, northwest of our present location, at any time. Juan said Manuri's teniente was an old man, "tough as they come," who had fought with Gen. Emilio Aguinaldo against the Americans during the Philippine Insurrection of 1899–1901. Like Aguinaldo, however, the teniente was now avidly pro-American, and he hated both the Japanese and the Philippine people who had joined them. Under the impression that he still hated the Americans, the Japanese had left him pretty much alone. All in all, Manuri sounded like a promising place near which to stage our ambush.

(General Aguinaldo, who had become a national hero for fighting against the Spanish and who had actually allied himself with the United States at the onset of the Spanish-American War—until the

Spanish were defeated—was used, against his will, by the Japanese after their invasion of the Philippines in 1942.)

Planning to start early the next morning in order to reach Manuri by noon, we found shelter off the trail in some heavy undergrowth surrounding a group of large banyan trees. The listening posts were sent out with instructions that, if any Japanese were to pass by on the trail, they should be allowed to continue so that we could then ambush them to their rear and flanks.

The night was uneventful, however, and the normal jungle noises kept us company and were uninterrupted by the suspicious silences I had learned to be wary of. It was now habitual for me to sleep lightly; either sudden silence or unusual sound would wake me instantly. We had all learned much since the Pinappagan raid, and we had good reason to be proud of our abilities to adapt and meet the challenges of survival.

In the morning when we reached the outskirts of Manuri, Juan and Corporal Nueves went in alone to talk with the teniente. Should there be any Japanese in the barrio, they were to return immediately to where we were hidden on the trail. Otherwise, they once again were to pretend to be on their way to Santiago, and as discreetly as possible, gather the additional information we needed about the Japanese combat patrol.

In the meantime, I left Valdez in charge of the waiting men, and Reyes, Vea, and I reconnoitered the area by going northeast about one kilometer to the end of the trail, where we entered a stream and continued walking east into the jungle. As we were going upstream, I noticed large rocks on both sides that would provide excellent cover and protection for an ambush. One rock was about fifty feet to the north of the stream and provided a good view of the terrain for a short distance; the other was about two hundred feet upstream on the south side. I decided this was where we would set up our attack. Upstream on the south side, Reyes would man the area of that rock. Vea would take his position at the rock on the north side. We also selected one of several well-concealed positions farther upstream from Reyes's position where two of his men would be posted. I cautioned Reyes to instruct his two men not to fire on the enemy point until they heard our groups open fire.

My group would split into two small units: one under the

command of Sergeant Valdez, whom I intended to borrow from Vea, replacing him with Sergeant Dolatre; the other, under my command. We would be farther downstream from Reyes and Vea's positions in order to leave enough distance between the patrol's point and the last man in the main column so that Valdez and I would be able to catch the whole column in a good cross fire, inflicting the maximum number of casualties. The BAR would stay with Valdez, who knew how to handle it. Reyes and Vea were not to open fire until they heard Valdez and me fire, and they were to tell their men to pick off as many of the enemy as they could, but to be careful not to expose themselves unnecessarily; I didn't want any casualties. I thought it unlikely the Japanese would deploy into the jungle; they would either advance or retreat or— my guess—it would be a rout. If the ambush were to be unsuccessful, or were something unforeseen to happen that separated us, our rendezvous would be Campsite Two.

The three of us went over the plan carefully, and I asked if Reyes or Vea had any questions about any aspect of it, which they had not. We returned to our men and explained the procedure in detail, using hand-drawn sketches of the area. Our sandbox instructions were paying off.

Reyes picked the two men for the next day's point position and gave them their additional instructions. I showed Valdez my sketch with the two locations we would occupy, and an alternate position in case the Japanese patrol was spread out farther than we anticipated. We would have to be back far enough from our forward ambush-men so that the last Japanese soldier would pass us before we opened up with cross fire.

By now it was getting close to sundown and Juan and Nueves still hadn't come back. Thinking something might have gone wrong, I was preparing to move us to another location when the outposts halted two men: Juan and Nueves. They reported there were no Japanese in Manuri now, but the villagers were expecting them to arrive the following day, or the next day after that. The barrio teniente had said he thought the patrol might consist of about twenty BC, fifteen Japanese soldiers, one Japanese officer, and one BC officer. Some of the numbers I had been getting from various sources conflicted, but thirty-five men with two officers seemed like a fairly accurate estimate.

230

The barrio teniente, whose name was Leaño, had told Juan the Japanese were claiming to have killed guerrilla forces every time they entered the jungle. However, no one had ever heard any shots being fired at those times, and people felt they simply were trying to save face, something they seemed to do frequently; face to them was almost more important than life itself. The Japanese soldiers were known to hate the jungle and to avoid going into it; this was to our advantage since we had been living in it and knew how to move through jungle terrain.

I asked Juan and Nueves if Teniente Leaño knew there were guerrilla forces in the Jones area, and Juan said the teniente knew "Captain" Hieb and some Visayan soldiers were around somewhere in the area. Leaño didn't think Major Roberts and his men, still somewhere in the Pinappagan area, were being harassed as much as they had been during the latter part of 1942 and early part of 1943.

While they were in Manuri, the two men had picked up the information that Colonel Nakar really had been shot by the Japanese. I felt very sad and hoped against hope that it wasn't true; however, I knew the information seemed too accurate to be merely another rumor. According to what they had been told, Nakar had been captured in a cave near Manuri on 29 September 1942, after one of his own officers, Lieutenant del Rosario, had betrayed him. I had known Nakar for a long time, and I knew how much country and honor meant to him. He had told me more than once that he would rather die than swear allegiance to the Japanese. He was a professional soldier in every way; his family had good reason to be proud of him.

Juan and Nueves had been told that a few days after Nakar's capture, the Japanese had found the 14th Infantry's records. This meant the Japanese now had a list of every officer and enlisted man in that unit and knew the locations of all our rendezvous areas. Furthermore, they had copies of the intelligence information that had been forwarded to General MacArthur's Australian headquarters.

Along with this windfall, the Japanese were in possession of some maps, one of which Leaño described as showing several Xs marked between Pinappagan and Bayombong. This information gave me a moment of amusement. I knew exactly what that map was: I had carried it on the reconnaisance mission undertaken before Nakar had disbursed us—the same mission that saw our raids at Abian and Santo Domingo and our ambush on the Bayombong highway. The Xs marked our campsites during that excursion, and in case of future need, I also had marked that lovely, peaceful valley we had discovered.

The Japanese, however, thought the Xs marked current campsites. Expecting to hit the jackpot and capture both myself and Major Roberts, who they thought was hiding in that area too, they had sent patrols to all the spots marked X. Several patrols had gotten lost, wandering for weeks and losing men to various jungle-induced illnesses and accidents. After that frustrating experience, Teniente Leaño had told Juan, the enemy troops were pulled from the Pinappagan area, which was patrolled only occasionally now.

After their report, Juan and Nueves were briefed on the ambush plans, and they were as eager to put them into action as the rest of us. Nueves reported to Lieutenant Reyes for more instruction, and Juan asked to be part of my group. Juan knew I trusted him and he proved many times that this trust was well founded. He had the makings of a good soldier. Quick, intelligent, and well liked by the other men, he was a very courageous young man with an innate self-confidence that sometimes led him to take risks guaranteed to make a more experienced soldier blanche. His ability to find his way through the jungle was amazing. He knew the Ilongots' territory as well as they did, and he could tell some hair-raising stories about these fearsome headhunters.

That evening Juan told us about a time when he and his father had gone into the jungle and had wandered far into Ilongot territory. Their dogs alerted them to the presence of three Ilongot headhunters armed with bows and arrows. They knew the Ilongots wanted their heads as trophies in order to prove their bravery. Thinking quickly, Juan's father told the Ilongots if they were to kill them, his three dogs would tear them apart. For a long few moments, it was a stand-off. The headhunters finally left, and Juan and his father retreated back to the trail leading to their barrio.

In turn, I told Juan and my men about trapping skunk in my childhood. First I had to describe the skunk and tell them about its distinctive odor: there are no skunks in the Philippines. Then I described how the skunks would build their nests in the small culverts on the country roads of the Dakotas, and how I had figured out a way to catch them without the use of a trap by using a fifteen-foot flexible steel cable with three short prongs on one end and a crank handle on the other end. I would insert the the pronged end into the culvert, and if a connection was made, the skunk would eject its pungent offensive—and oily—secretion. Then, by using the crank, I could lock the prongs in the animal's fur, pull it out, and shoot it with my .22 rifle.

Early the next morning, we cleaned up thoroughly before leaving the campsite and carefully covered our tracks when we left the trail to reach our chosen battle position. As soon as we reached the ambush area, the men began digging in. They understood what had to be done. Each unit had a few hand grenades, and everyone double-checked his weapon and ammunition supply. When everyone was in position, I gave further orders to the men to get all weapons, food, ammunition, and hand grenades from the dead enemy soldiers. I reminded them to be very cautious about approaching a fallen enemy soldier and assuming he was dead—he might be faking. Then I posted security to the front of our position, and we settled down to wait. But, no Japanese came that day.

For supper, we ate a little cold rice, more berries, and some dried meat. Our food supply was getting low—again. Security was doubled for the night; but still no Japanese came. None of us got much rest and the waiting made the hours seem to drag. The next morning brought more waiting.

Finally, we heard the sound of a dog barking in the distance and knew this meant the patrol was hunting for us, using as its point some-one from Manuri who owned a tracking dog. I asked Juan if he was sure the barrio teniente was pro-American. He said, "I'd bank my life on it." So I immediately sent Juan with a message to Valdez, Vea, and Reyes to watch for the Manurian with the tracking dog who was leading the enemy point. Reyes's two-man point was not to fire at this man, and they were to let the enemy get past all our units. If he was pro-American, I was sure that guide would know what to do when he heard us open up on the patrol's main body.

About thirty minutes after Juan returned from delivering the message, we saw the dog, the Japanese point, and the guide approach. We let them pass. Juan identified the guide as Teniente Leaño. There was a rope around the dog's neck to keep him from running off if he got the scent of a wild pig. I was certain the teniente knew exactly where we were—and what was going to happen in the next few minutes.

The BC contingent came into view with the Japanese soldiers following close behind. When the last Japanese passed, Valdez made a clean sweep down the column with the BAR. Seven of the Japanese dropped. Vea and Reyes took care of the BC. There were fifteen BC dead, eight Japanese, and one BC officer; no wounded or prisoners were taken. The remaining Japanese and BC fled in a westerly direction toward the barrio of Manuri. It was a rout.

The Japanese point had been boloed by Leaño who had also cut out his tongue, which he later boiled and ate, following an ancient belief that eating the tongue of an enemy would make a man strong and brave. Juan was right: the teniente may have been old, but he was as tough as they come. My first impression, which time strengthened, was that this was no man to have as an enemy.

Teniente Leaño told us he thought about eleven Japanese got away, and then he asked why we hadn't fired at him. I said Juan had told me he was loyal to the Philippine government and pro-American. He said he had known there was an American with the ambush party because he had seen my narrow footprints: Filipino feet are quite wide. I said after I had spent another two years in the jungles, he wouldn't be able to tell the difference.

I told Leaño we would contact him in the near future, and in the meantime, he could tell the Japanese he had been lucky to get away alive. If they asked him whether an American was with the ambush group, he could tell them there was: some of the men who got away may have heard me shouting orders in English. He and his hunting dog would take a different route home so he wouldn't arrive back in Manuri before the Japanese who had escaped the ambush.

Before he left, the teniente said if there was anything we ever needed—and they had it in the barrio—he would share it with us gladly. This meant that, if the Japanese accepted his story, we would

234

have another source of supply. Leaño was highly respected in the area, and he knew which tenientes could be trusted in the barrios on both the east and west sides of the river: a fact of great future importance to us.

Apparently I had passed muster with the fierce little man, as he had with me, and I realized that the whole time we talked, he had been sizing me up. He had just about x-rayed my character with eyes whose steady intensity belied the incredibly sun-worn, wrinkled, round face framed, like Teniente Reyes's, by crew-cut grey hair. Unlike Reyes, Leaño did not smile much. He had a stern, though not unkind, look about him, which was further emphasized by his very erect posture and straight legs. He looked the staunch and sturdy friend that indeed he proved to be.

After Leaño left, we stripped the dead of all the food they were carrying and took their rifles, hand grenades, and ammunition. The men also took what articles of clothing they needed, and I finally acquired another pair of combat boots; then we buried the bodies.

The men's morale was high after the successful encounter, and they were confident we could rout the Japanese again. Only our two point men were disappointed: they had never gotten to fire a shot.

Now Juan led us deeper into the jungle to the east. For an hour or so, we followed a stream flowing southwest until we came to a likely hideout in the form of a rock cave, where we stopped. The listening posts were set up for the night, and then, for a change, we all had a good supper, which added to our elation over the day's work. I called a meeting and gave out the promotions earned that day by various men who had carried out their duties as soldiers in exemplary fashion.

Juan was promoted to corporal, and after he was sworn in, he was officially in the 14th Infantry, Army of the United States. I made several other promotions recommended by the two lieutenants and the three sergeants. Master Sergeant Valdez and Master Sergeant Dolatre were as high as they could go in their enlisted grade. I asked them if they wanted a direct field commission, but they both declined, saying they were satisfied with their present grades.

I was very pleased with the site we had chosen for our camp that evening, and I asked Juan how far it was from here to Campsite Two. He said that by the route he would take, it would be about a three-hour hike. In view of that proximity, I asked the officers and noncoms what they thought of the rock cave as a location for Campsite Four. They agreed with me that it would be ideal because it was far enough off the trails to the three barrios, Manuri, Virgoneza, and Dabubu; and it was deep enough into the jungle and Ilongot territory to make it relatively safe from Japanese incursions for some time. After our return to Campsite Two, a squad of men could be sent back to make it livable.

With four good campsites, we ought to be able to continue evading the enemy for the time being; however, after today's ambush, we could be certain the Japanese would be out looking for us again in the very near future.

Juan would have to stay with us at Campsite Two for about a week before going home since the people of his barrio thought he had gone to Santiago for supplies. I asked if he wanted to go into the barrio to let his parents know he was all right, but he was sure they already knew he was safe through word from Teniente Leaño. News travels fast in the barrios. It also becomes exaggerated; I figured by the time news of our ambush reached Dabubu, the number of casualties probably would have grown in the telling to one hundred.

CHAPTER 28

Making Plans

The next morning we headed back following different streams and always going in a south-by-west direction. The men were to watch for any landmarks—trees, streams, large rocks—that would enable them to find their way back to the cave. We made good progress and reached Campsite Two in about two and a half hours. There was a small cave near the site in which we stored the rifles and hand grenades—not the ammunition—camouflaging the entrance afterwards. We had been running low on ammunition, but the BC in the patrol we had just ambushed had been carrying American weapons, and we had replenished our supply by taking theirs.

Our first task when we returned to the campsite was to clean our rifles, using small bamboo stakes for cleaning rods. Most of my men wore their shoes without socks, and so we made our cleaning patches from little pieces of socks taken from the dead Japanese soldiers.

The day after our return, I asked Juan if he thought he could get into Dabubu without being detected. We needed news and supplies; especially, we needed salt. Aside from its usefulness as a flavor enhancer, salt was crucial to our physical well-being, and although we had taken small amounts from the dead soldiers, there was a shortage of salt throughout the whole province of Isabela, and I was very concerned that we would suffer severely from its lack.

Juan was sure he could make the trip without any problem and said he would return the next day—with supplies if he was lucky. I spent a sleepless night waiting for whatever news and supplies he would bring. I was hoping to get another message from Major

Roberts; otherwise, I would have no way of knowing whether he had received my reply to his first message.

As I did always, I prayed that night for the safety of my men. And I prayed for everyone back home, wondering how they were, and what was happening to them. Were my brothers Harry and Max in the service somewhere? Were they all right? It had been a long time since Elaine and I had made plans to marry. Was she still waiting for me? My mother must have been terribly worried. I wished there were some way of letting her know I was alive. I didn't want her to be burdened with anguish and anxiety because of me. I knew that after our dispersal from Nakar's command, I was probably listed as missing-in-action. It was a restless, miserable night.

Around noon the next day, we heard Juan being challenged by our outpost, and we were all there to greet him when he entered the camp loaded down with food, including two big baskets of camotes and papaya, and a sack of rice carried atop his head. His father and uncle, he said, were at our old meeting place with more supplies. They asked that we pick up the supplies quickly because the teniente didn't know just when the Japanese might show up, and they had to return at once to the barrio.

Four men hurried to the rendezvous point to get the supplies and thank the teniente. There were three more sacks of rice, some dried fish, and more camotes and papaya. I asked Juan where in the world they had gotten all that food, and he explained that Teniente Leaño had some of his men bring it to his father's home for us. It was more food than we had seen in a long time. It was an unbelievable abundance.

While in Dabubu, Juan learned that the Japanese officer who was with the raiding party had returned to Manuri with several men before Teniente Leaño had and had reported that he was sure the teniente had been killed in the ambush. He had been very surprised when Leaño and his dog showed up. The officer also had told the people of the barrio that many of the guerrilla fighters had been killed, but that "the American, Captain Hieb," had gotten away. He had never once mentioned his own casualties. When he left Manuri at noon the next day, he had a total of nine men, including himself. I concluded there must have been two more Japanese wounded, or dead by now, left in the jungle. Before leaving, the officer had thanked Teniente Leaño for his help. Leaño had said anytime he could help the Japanese army, he would be happy to do so. He had probably already boiled and eaten the tongue of the soldier he had killed the day before when he said that. In effect, he was now working as a double agent. He was a courageous man.

That Japanese officer and his men had returned to Jones, but others would be back after us. I was hoping they would think we were headed farther north, or across the Sierra Madres toward the east coast and the Pacific Ocean in the area of Palanan. Perhaps they would assume we would backtrack to the south, to Casiguran or Tinib, which were also on the east coast. In the meantime, we would just have to wait to see what happened.

I decided to have a meeting with all the officers and NCOs to discuss what our strategy would be when the Japanese did come after us again. Once again, they had lost face, and their code of honor would not permit them to accept or forget this. Next time, they would come after us with a much larger force, and I was sure that rather than use the trails, they would use the streams, as we had been doing. It was essential that we have a plan and be ready for them.

We began to formulate our strategy. In order to move faster, we would break up into small units. We would allow the enemy force to come into the jungle as far as four kilometers from the barrio where it started; then our first unit would strike, using our ambush-and-retreat tactic in an effort to draw the remaining men deeper into the jungle in an easterly direction.

We had a total of forty-five officers and enlisted men, including Cpl. Juan Reyes and myself. If we broke into three groups of fifteen men each, this would give us a good striking force of combat units and allow enough men in each unit for flank protection. After our first contact patrol hit the Japanese, the second group, in place and waiting about one kilometer away, would ambush the force's remnants and then would pull out through the third combat unit. We would keep a three-man unit on each flank of the engaging units after the first strike. Our password would be "Lillian" because the Japanese could not pronounce the letter *L*: their pronunciation of it sounded like *R*; so, if one of them were to give this password, it would sound like "Rirrian."

We went over this plan, drawing streams and ambush areas in our sandbox. We kept going over and over this ambush mission for about a week, until I was satisfied that everyone was familiar with the strategy.

The next step was to try actual field maneuvers. We divided into two groups; some of the men acted as the Japanese attack force, and the remainder of them, as our ambush units. Everytime the attack force used a three-prong frontal attack, the ambush units surprised it. The mock Japanese attack force couldn't outflank us. We practiced these tactics all day, and the NCOs and officers in charge executed them flawlessly. I had confidence in the men and officers, and they had confidence in themselves now. The success of our latest ambush was a source of pride to one and all, and we were eager for an opportunity to implement our new plan.

Juan had gone into Dabubu again for news about the Japanese and when he returned, he again had supplies—but no salt. The people in the Jones area were sending supplies to Teniente Leaño, who shared them with Teniente Reyes, who, as he had been doing for over a year, helped us.

Juan's news included the information that the Japanese officer who had led the patrol we had ambushed was no longer in Jones; he had been transferred. However, the feared Japanese Kempeitei, or secret police, together with the Philippine Sakdalistas, or BC, were on their way to Jones to reinforce the garrison there. I doubted that at this point they would find anyone willing to cooperate with their efforts to get information; the Filipinos had access to the same news we were receiving: the Americans were on their way back to the Philippines. Most of the barrio tenientes wanted the guerrillas to keep ambushing and leading the Japanese deeper into the jungles. We did not intend to disappoint them. We were on full alert, and in return, the barrio people were doing everything they could to supply us with food and other necessities.

Juan also informed us that some of the officers and enlisted men who had been dispersed by Colonel Nakar before the raid on Pinappagan now wanted to join us. They had married local girls and were

240

living in the Jones area, changing their names to protect the villagers and themselves. These officers, Lt. Benjamin Aviles, Lt. Enrique Cruz, and Lt. Leonardo Galima, and some of their men had been helping to gather intelligence information. I asked Juan to tell the barrio tenientes to inform the three lieutenants that because of the shortage of food, and the burdens we were already putting on Dabubu and Manuri, I felt it best to have any other men join me at some later date. I asked that the three lieutenants keep giving us any intelligence information they had—such as enemy strength and movements in our area, and fifth column activities—and to pass this request on to those NCOs and enlisted men they knew were loyal to our cause.

About a week and a half after our ambush of the Japanese patrol, Juan moved back to Dabubu. He would have preferred to stay with us, but he was more valuable to me in the barrio where he could gather as much reliable news as possible. He planned to pay Teniente Leaño a visit because the teniente went to Jones about once a week and usually came back with quite a bit of information. Whenever Juan had news of any importance, such as the Japanese movements in our area and the enemy strength in Jones, he was to report back to me. He promised to bring additional supplies out whenever he had news to report.

Our present supplies would last us about a month if we went back to restricting our rations. The men were still trying to catch wild pigs, and they renewed their efforts when we spotted some tracks about a kilometer from our camp. The barrio men normally used dogs to track wild pig and deer but, since the occupation, the Japanese, knowing guerrillas were in them somewhere, would not allow anyone to go into the jungles to hunt. I now told the men, if they spotted a wild pig, shoot it. This gave them added incentive, and they were all on the lookout for that elusive pig. We snared a few wild chickens and some dove, but the wild pig continued to elude us, and although I saw a few deer tracks during my stay in that area of the jungle, I never saw a deer. So far, there hadn't been any sign of monkeys in this area.

About every other day we would review the ambush plans, and we were ready to implement them immediately if the Japanese gave the invitation. Each combat unit had a small sack of rice in reserve to be used for combat missions only; each man had a rifle, a good supply of ammunition thanks to our latest ambush, and a hand grenade, bolo, canteen, cup, and web belt. We still had only the one BAR assigned to Sergeant Valdez. There was also a stored supply of ammunition for our use in Dabubu that had come from soldiers who had left it there before surrendering to the Japanese during the amnesty.

During this period, Valdez returned to Campsite Four with a group of men to clean it up and make it livable; we didn't know this yet, but we would be needing it soon.

While Valdez was gone, Juan brought news that Japanese reinforcements had arrived in Jones. This meant from now on the barrios would be patrolled almost daily, and it would be only a matter of time before the Japanese sent patrols into the jungle. We needed to know how many would be in these patrols, and from which barrios they would start their searches. Juan went back to Dabubu to gather more information for us.

If the Japanese were to make a simultaneous three-prong search-and-destroy mission from three different barrios, I would divide the men into three combat groups of approximately fifteen men each with an officer in charge of each. For planning purposes I chose the barrios of Manuri, Virgoneza, and Dabubu. The group under Reyes would take Manuri, the barrio farthest north; Vea's group would take the central barrio of Virgoneza; and my group would take Dabubu, the southernmost barrio.

I intended to use hit-and-run tactics again, and I drew the plan in our sandbox giving Manuri the designation X, Virgoneza, Y, and Dabubu, Z. We kept rehearsing both plans; both utilized the same tactics. I was counting on the facts that the Japanese didn't like jungle warfare and especially hated dealing with guerrilla tactics. The guerrilla forces already had taken a heavy toll of the Japanese Imperial Forces in the Philippines because of these attitudes, and before the war was over, the toll would be even greater.

Teniente Leaño sent word with Juan that there were about five thousand Japanese troops in Jones. They looked well trained, but he thought we could best them easily in ambush-and-retreat combat deep in the jungle. Juan said that in the jungle, if Japanese enlisted men became separated from their leaders, they invariably got lost. Then, if the Ilongots didn't get them, the wild animals did. There were, for example, many large python; and there was a variety of small poison-ous snake, one bite from which reportedly caused instant death. This kind was usually found on bamboo leaves where its protective green coloring made it almost invisible. However, it was not an aggressive snake and normally would not bite unless provoked.

When Juan brought supplies on his next trip, he also had un-equivocable confirmation that Colonel Nakar was indeed dead. In ad-dition to the information we had received previously, we now learned his betrayers included the mayor and the chief of police of Jones as well as Lieutenant del Rosario. He had been executed at Fort Santiago because he would not swear allegiance to the Japanese Imperial Forces. He had been told to bow to or salute the Rising Sun, and he had refused, spitting on the ground and saying he would never salute or bow to the Japanese flag. It was either then or soon after that the Japanese had shot him.

There was pride in the eyes of the Visayan soldiers when they heard this account. They had all been under his command when he was a captain on Negros, and they knew he was a man who had remained loyal to the Philippine government. Everyone agreed that his was a lesson in courage and bravery for all of us to try to emulate.

While he was in camp on this trip, I explained Plan Two to Juan, who immediately asked if he could go with our group. I said I had planned to put him in charge of one of my flank units, which pleased him.

Four days after he had brought us the information about Colonel Nakar, Juan was back again. He reported that the Japanese Kempeitei and the BC had been in all the barrios on the east side of the river. They had tortured some of the tenientes but had been unable to get any information because there was none to give. Teniente Reyes and his family had told the Japanese they were sure there were guerrilla forces in the jungle, but they couldn't possibly be supplying them because they were giving almost all their food to the Imperial Forces, barely had enough food themselves, and were now existing on year-old corn. The answer seemed to satisfy them.

Juan said half the population of Jones couldn't be trusted, and some of the people in the barrios on the west side of the river were fence sitters: there was no way to determine their loyalty. When I said I wanted the names—and definite proof of their disloyalty—of all those who had collaborated with the Japanese and were not loyal to the Phil-American cause, Juan supplied the names of the traitors in the Jones area. Sergeant Dannug logged these for future reference, adding them to a list that already included Captain Cushing's betrayers, the Hernandezes, and Nakar's.

Another week went by, and then one afternoon Juan showed up with a sack of rice, more camotes—and news: there were about one hundred Japanese headed toward Dabubu. He intended to go back and watch their arrival from the edge of the jungle. I asked him if some of the Japanese who had met him before on their trips into Dabubu might be with this company. He said he and his father had thought of this possibility before he left, and his father was to explain that Juan was out trying to buy rice for the barrio because its people were on corn rations and there were many sick.

While Juan was away spying on the enemy, we would move to Campsite Three, now the best location from which to move either north or south to get into position and implement our plan of drawing the troops deep into the jungle in their efforts to find and capture us.

When Juan came back to join us at Campsite Three late that night, he almost got shot. He had forgotten the password. He finally remembered to say "Lillian"—just in time. He reported that the hundred Japanese were in Dabubu, and they planned to enter the jungle in the morning. Quite uncharacteristically, they had given the villagers a little rice when they found out they had been eating corn. Juan said they would not use dogs or guides and hoped to take us by surprise—if we were still around, which they perhaps doubted. I was certain they didn't want guides along in case they took a heavy loss again: they couldn't afford another loss of face.

Because there was only one Japanese patrol group, we would use Plan One. Valdez and his flank unit would be the first to strike since he was carrying the BAR. I would catch the point and move farther back along the trail. Valdez, after his initial attack, would also move back and to my left inside the jungle. Juan would wait in place to the north, or right, of me. If Juan and his men didn't hear any enemy movement to their front or flank, they would withdraw in a straight line inside the jungle. We would continue to withdraw through the contact patrols of Lieutenant Reyes. Then Reyes would withdraw through Lieutenant Vea's position. We would continue this entrapping procedure as long as the Japanese fell for it. I told the men if the groups were separated, I would like to draw the Japanese to the foothills of the Sierra Madres, circling around to the rear of them at that point. If we did get separated, we would rendezvous at Campsite One or one of the other three campsites with which everyone was familiar. Juan asked me why I moved to Campsite Three after he had gone to the barrio. I said to give the men some practice, and also, if the Japanese had entered from the barrio north of Dabubu, it would have taken us longer to get into position from Campsite Two.

CHAPTER 29

A Plan-One Ambush

I gave the order for silence and Juan led out saying we could get into position before daybreak, which we did. I reminded everyone not to forget the password, Lillian, and I said that with the Lord's help and guidance, we would all meet again that evening.

We had waited only about an hour when we heard some of the enemy approaching. It sounded as though they were using about a squad of men for their point this time. Valdez let them pass, as I had hoped he would, and not too far behind their point squad was a column of about fifty men, two abreast and bunched up.

I moved my men back to give Valdez a better chance at the large column. We let the point get nearly opposite us; then Valdez opened up. My men tossed several hand grenades into the point group of eight men and opened up with rifle fire. I could hear rifle fire coming from Juan's direction. When Valdez opened up on them, the troops scattered to the north into the jungle, where Juan hit them. We could hear Japanese screaming from every direction. I shouted for a withdrawal. We covered the kilometer to Reyes's position in short order, shouting our password as we ran.

I stopped and told Reyes the Japanese might break up into smaller groups and to hit them and withdraw, being sure to use good cover for his men. I knew there were quite a number of casualties among the Japanese, which was exactly what I wanted because this would mean they would have to use some of their troops to carry the wounded back into Jones or Dabubu. Just when I was ready to fall back to Vea's position, Valdez and Juan showed up. I asked Valdez if he had done much damage to the large column, and he thought he had. Juan said his unit had killed at least four enemy soldiers. Valdez said he had wounded one of the men in the point squad and had bayoneted him before withdrawing to Reyes's position. I said I thought my group might have gotten most of the point with the two hand grenades. At any rate, we had inflicted heavy casualties; thus far, we had suffered none.

Now I moved my groups on to Vea's position, gave him all the information, and told him to watch for Reyes and his men when they pulled out through his position. I told him my group would head due east through the jungle for about a kilometer and then deploy. He was to tell Reyes about how far to the rear we would be.

We weren't hearing any gunfire and I decided that the Japanese were regrouping. I told Juan to lead us due east for about one kilometer. Juan really enjoyed guerrilla warfare, and he said, "Yes, sir," with a grin. We cut our way through the jungle for a short distance, then came to a small stream running in a northeasterly direction. We followed this for some time until we came to another stream, which emptied into the first one, and then took this in a southeasterly direction. We had just entered the second stream, when at last we heard gunfire, which went on for about ten minutes, then stopped. I said a silent prayer for Reyes and his men. Judging by the sound of the rifle fire, all three of his patrols had made contact with the enemy. We continued to follow the second stream for a short time, until I determined we were one kilometer east of Vea's position.

At the point where we stopped, there were several high areas on both sides of the stream. Juan took one on the north, Valdez took one directly to his right, and I took one farther upstream in order to catch the Japanese point. We all got into position. I had a good view of the line of approach. I waved to both Valdez and Juan. They could see me when I stood up on top of a large rock some of my group were using for cover. The rest of the men also had found cover offering excellent front views along the stream.

When Reyes arrived with his men about an hour and a half later, he said the Japanese had used a three-prong attack on him, but his men had heard the enemy soldiers thrashing around in the jungle long before their point appeared on the trail, so there was plenty of warning.

247

Reyes let the point get opposite him before his men threw hand grenades and opened fire. At about the same time, the flank contact opened fire as the enemy flank men were floundering through the jungle. Reyes said he and his men inflicted casualties, but he didn't know how many. None of his group was wounded or killed.

I said now he was to go upstream for about two kilometers, set up an ambush in that vicinity, and wait for us. He was to follow the largest stream, leaving footprints facing our direction when he reentered it.

In midafternoon we heard rifle fire and exploding hand grenades. The sounds lasted several minutes and then all was quiet. Now we had to wait for Vea and his men to pass through our lines and Reyes's.

Vea and all his men arrived with the information that the Japanese were using only two men as point now; Vea said his group had had to pull back in order to give his flank patrols a chance to ambush the main enemy column. I asked what had happened to the enemy point. Vea said as soon as his flank had opened up on the main body, his men killed the two point men.

I told Vea to head east, toward the mountain he could see from our position, and keep moving east until he had passed Reyes's position. Then he was to take a position about two kilometers to the rear of Reyes's position. I asked him to tell his men to try to get by on short rations, and to give Reyes the same information when he passed his position. As he moved out I asked him to say a prayer for us, and he said everyone was praying.

Sometime later we heard the Japanese coming upstream. What sounded like two men were chopping through the jungle on both flanks of the patrol. They were making enough noise to wake the dead. I spotted the two-man point, and a short distance behind that was the main body, consisting of twenty men with an officer to the rear and a noncommissioned officer at the head of the column. I waited for Valdez to open fire. When I heard the BAR, and a few exploding hand grenades that had been tossed in the direction of the enemy flank, I saw both point men drop, either dead or wounded. We attempted to shoot the officer, but he was well trained. He hit the ground faster than any of his soldiers. Juan had tossed several hand grenades in the direction of the Japanese soldiers on his flank, and then he had opened fire

248

on some who had deployed to his side of the stream. We spotted several of these floating face down in the stream. We didn't know if they were dead or faking, so we fired directly at them. If they weren't dead before, they were then. I yelled at Valdez and Juan to withdraw on the double.

We made good time. In about an hour Lieutenant Reyes's men challenged us to give the password. Reyes asked how the second ambush had gone, and I said we had no casualties, but the Japanese had at least eight dead, and I didn't know how many wounded. What was worrying me now, I added, was whether or not there was a support column to the rear of the one we had been ambushing all day. I asked Reyes to give up his position and move out with us. As we moved out, the men cut short and very thin bamboo stakes with needle-sharp ends. These were passed along to the rear guard, who inserted them at intervals in the stream and along its banks for the canvas-shod Japanese to step on.

It was nearly sundown when we reached Lieutenant Vea's position. There we broke into three groups. Reyes's group was to head southeast, circle back to the southwest, and make contact with the rest of us at one of the four campsites. Vea would go northeast, circling back to the northwest and returning to one of the campsites also. I would head straight east. From this point on, we were to engage the enemy only if we were fired upon. We were to walk until just before dark; then we would locate a well-protected spot and set up camp for the night. I wished everyone good luck, and we set off in our respective directions. I hoped we would all return safely to meet as planned in one of the campsites in a couple of days.

With Juan in the lead, my group headed east along a stream. We continued placing bamboo spears in the ground and stream behind us, hoping if some of the enemy soldiers stepped on these, the results would stop the patrol for the night. If the patrol reached the place where we had split up into our three groups, I doubted that it would split into three combat units at night. The Japanese were more likely to camp for the night and resume their search in the morning.

After walking about forty-five minutes, I spotted a protected area that would serve us as a camp for the night. My men were getting tired, and we all needed rest. Nine men were selected for listening post duty. If there was enemy movement during the night, we would break camp and follow the stream east, using Juan as our guide and keeping in close contact with each other and moving as fast as we could.

The next morning, we continued east along the stream until noon. We made camp, set up our ambush positions, and waited. We planned to wait and listen all day if necessary; if no Japanese appeared, we would circle away to the southwest. Just past noon, we heard shouting in the distance, coming from downstream. Some of my men smiled. I asked Valdez. "What's so funny?" He said the men were sure some of the Japanese had stepped on our sharp bamboo stakes. I was glad to hear that and told the men, "Good, now they'll return to the barrio. They'll figure we have set other traps for them. Tomorrow we'll start the return hike to one of our camps."

CHAPTER 30

A Sniper and an Important Decision

The respite that afternoon was welcome. Some of the men picked wild berries and brought ubog back to eat. We rested quietly, regaining our strength for the next day's push through the jungle.

Early the next morning, we were on our way: this time moving to the southwest. We had to cut our way through the undergrowth in many places. By noon, we reached a stream going west by south that Juan thought he recognized. We followed this for about an hour then stopped to rest and eat a bit of rice and dried fish. Juan said he knew exactly where we were, and I asked him if he thought we could reach one of our campsites before dark. He didn't think so; we would have to find a place to bivouac by evening. This meant another night out, and we were running very low on food; but if we couldn't make it to one of our permanent campsites by dark, rather than travel at night, I thought it wiser to stop until the next day. We would have to cross the main trail leading into Dabubu, and there might be footprints or other evidence of some kind to indicate whether the Japanese had returned to the barrio or were still out looking for us.

We walked until midafternoon. Eventually, we reached a place Juan said was about two kilometers from the main trail into Dabubu. I had been looking for another location to use for a fifth campsite and this spot was ideal; it was equidistant from Palacian Grande and Dabubu, which would give us access to another supply source. After looking it over, the men all agreed this was a good choice for Campsite Five. We stayed there for the rest of the day and for that night. The listening posts heard no unusual sounds, and we concluded the Japanese must have returned to Dabubu, or else they were wandering around lost in the jungle.

In the morning, we followed Juan upstream for about an hour and then cut back into the jungle. Cutting our way through the underbrush was very noisy work, and I called a halt to ask Juan if the jungle was this thick all the way to the main trail. He said we were very close to a side trail leading into the main one, and we could walk there in complete silence with plenty of distance between the men. In about ten minutes, we reached the side trail and began to make good time. As we neared the main trail, I called another halt and gave orders for the men to infiltrate across, two and three at a time, reassembling and taking cover on the north side.

Juan and his men went first, and as soon as they arrived at the main trail, a shot rang out. Everyone dropped to the ground and found cover. Certainly none of us had fired the shot, which anyway had come from a Japanese rifle. Our lead point fired an answering shot, and I said a silent prayer. We had made it this far without losing a man; I hoped everyone was all right still.

Valdez and I deployed our men on both sides of the trail. I told the sergeant I would take a runner and crawl to where I thought Juan was. If we found that the shot had been fired by a stray Japanese soldier, I would send the runner back with the details and further instructions. We had started in the direction of the shots when I heard a voice to my right whisper "Lillian." It was one of Juan's men. I asked him if any of our men had been hit, and he said he didn't think so; when the first shot rang out, he had seen Juan make a dive for cover, and he thought it was Juan who had fired the answering shot.

I yelled to Juan to give me the password so that I could locate his position. Just as he did this, there was another shot; this one had been aimed in our direction. I told my runner to scream as if hit the next time a shot was fired. I shouted again to Juan, telling him what we were going to do, and two more shots rang out. Although I couldn't see him, I was sure the sniper was in a tree. As instructed, my man was screaming, and another shot rang out. I was cussing in English; undoubtedly the sniper knew he hadn't hit me yet, but he sure as hell was going to keep trying. Then he threw a hand grenade that exploded just short of the two of us, and as he did, I spotted him in the tree.

I yelled to the rest of the men that I could see him and would pick him off. Using a rock as a rest for my rifle, I took aim and fired at the same time that he fired again in our direction. Reloading, I aimed, fired again—and hit him. I called out that I had hit him, but I didn't know if I had killed him: he hadn't dropped from the tree. I suspected he might be tied in it. Crawling up to Juan's position, I took another shot. There was no return fire; the man was either dead or too wounded to fire his rifle.

Juan's group moved forward in attack formation in case of an ambush. I sent my runner to Valdez with instructions for my men and his to circle to the northeast, cross the main trail, and work their way back west so that they would be in a direct line with Juan's men and myself. He was to send a runner to report to me when they were in position. I would stay with Juan and his men; and in the meantime, we would work our way as close to the sniper as possible. We would have to give the others at least an hour to reconnoiter the area and make contact with us.

About an hour later, Valdez's runner showed up with the message that there were no Japanese in the area. Cautiously, we approached the sniper. I had been right; he was tied in the tree with his rifle strapped to his arm. He was also dead. By now Valdez had joined us and volunteered to cut him down, after checking to see if he was booby-trapped. The man was covered with dried blood. Evidently, he had been wounded, and his comrades had tied him in the tree to wait for us to come back along the trail. I thought they were either crazy or cowardly to tie a fellow soldier to a tree and leave him. We buried the unfortunate man and moved out for Campsite One.

While we were walking along the trail, I told Juan to take a look at his trousers. Mistaking my meaning, he said he hadn't been afraid when the first shot was fired. I said that was why I wanted him to look. He looked down—and saw where a bullet had entered and then exited his pant leg. He laughed somewhat shakily. I told him to keep the trousers for a souvenir. He wanted to know why I had been able to spot the Japanese sniper in the tree when he couldn't see him. I said that was probably because I was color blind. He didn't know what I meant, so Sergeant Valdez explained it to him, including the interesting fact that in 1940 the armed services had discovered that people who were color blind could see through camouflage much easier and faster than people who weren't. Subsequently, the air force began to use color-blind service personnel as bombardiers.

Juan led out with his men for Campsite One. I told everyone to watch for shoe tracks. We reached the campsite in about an hour and a half. No one had been in the camp while we were gone.

Juan now asked if he could go that night to Dabubu for news. I thought it would be better if he waited until the following day, and he said he agreed with that, but he knew we needed supplies. I said I realized we did, but a dead soldier didn't need any and he might be dead if I let him go in. That convinced him. We ate what rice and dried meat remained, put out our listening posts, and settled down for the night, which was uneventful.

It was now the middle of June and the beginning of the monsoon season had brought a light rain. I had Valdez send two of his men to Campsite Two to look for our other men. If no one was there, they were to continue on to Campsite Three, and then Four, until they did make contact. Great care was to be taken to avoid any Japanese stragglers or Ilongot headhunters. They left carrying orders for Reyes and Vea to return at once to Campsite One with their men. Juan went into Dabubu to get the latest news and some supplies. If there were Japanese in the barrio, he would try to smuggle out enough food to last us a few days.

It was a long day of waiting for whatever news was in store for us. I kept the men busy fixing the rain shelters over the listening-post positions. At midafternoon, the two messengers, Reyes, Vea, and all their men showed up. I congratulated all of them on a job well done. Reyes asked me if it was true I had shot a Japanese sniper who had been tied in a tree. I said yes, but that he had been wounded beforehand and couldn't have survived another day. I told him about the dried blood we had found all over the man when we had cut him down. Reyes remarked that if his fellow soldiers had to tie him in a tree, he wouldn't call that brave, but rather barbarous, action on the part of his commanding officer.

Just before dark, Juan returned to the camp all smiles. The barrio had heard of our successful ambushes. I asked if any of the people had been abused because of them, and he said no. He brought back a sack of rice, some camotes, a few bananas, meat, and fish. Juan said the following day there would be more supplies sent by Teniente Leaño and some of his friends.

The cook outdid himself with plenty of everything for all of us. Good as it was, however, the men were still hopeful they would eventually be able to add wild pig to the menu, but Reyes and Vea told me they had checked our old boar pits, and they were still empty: lots of tracks, but still no luck.

After dinner I had Juan tell us about his trip to the barrio, and especially, the local account of our last ambush. He said about one hundred Japanese had come to Dabubu: about sixty of these entered the jungle looking for us. Not long after that, the villagers heard gunfire and hand-grenade explosions. Shortly after our first encounter, a Japanese soldier came out of the jungle to give an officer a written message; then twenty other men entered the jungle carrying stretchers. They returned carrying the wounded.

The Japanese told the villagers many of the guerrillas had been killed. At the very time that they were saying this, there was more rifle fire. Thirty more of their men went into the jungle with stretchers. Three hours later they returned with eight wounded. Again there was rifle fire.

In the meantime, they had left about seven men in the barrio to look after the wounded with the help of some of the barrio women; now these soldiers entered the jungle too. By this time it was past noon; much later five more wounded were brought out. There was more firing. This was our fourth contact. Late that night, five more wounded arrived.

The Japanese left the following morning after bringing in the last of their wounded; the villagers had been sure some of these would die before they reached Jones. Two of the soldiers had foot wounds obviously caused by bamboo spears. The Japanese said they had wounded some of the guerrilla fighters and told them to surrender, but all the answer they had gotten was more rifle fire, so they had had to kill all of them. I guessed that would be the same story they would tell their commanding officer in Jones in order to save face.

The patrol's commander had admitted that the "American captain got away," and he didn't know whether he was wounded or not. The Dabubuans had told him that the Ilongots used needlelike bamboo spears, pits, snares, and other devices against the barrio people; sooner or later, they assured the officer, the headhunters would get the American if he was still alive.

The teniente had counted thirty-one wounded Japanese and estimated approximately the same number had been killed. I had figured twenty-nine were killed, and I asked if anyone had counted the Japanese troops before they left for Jones. Juan said no one had, but he thought the barrio count of killed and wounded was pretty accurate.

I said I didn't believe we would be bothered by the Japanese during the monsoon season, but we could be sure from now on they would patrol all the barrios on a regular basis.

I asked Juan if he had shown his father the bullet holes in his trousers. He had, he said, and his father thought he was very brave—and very lucky. His mother had cried and said she was very happy we were all alive and well.

That night, some of the privates were promoted to private, first class, and Cpl. Juan Reyes was promoted to sergeant. I had 1st Sergeant Dannug enter all the promotions and the account of our successful ambush in the log. There had been only a few promotions in two years, and after our latest successes, the men who qualified were well and truly deserving.

It was raining heavily the next morning when Sgt. Juan Reyes, with five other men, and I left for the barrio; but, by the time we arrived at Dabubu, it was only misting. I hoped we might see Teniente Leaño, which was really my purpose in coming along.

Juan left his rifle and gear with us and went to bring his father to meet us at the edge of the jungle. When he arrived about fifteen minutes later, I asked Teniente Reyes if Teniente Leaño had come with supplies. He said no, not yet, but that they expected him momentarily. Next, I asked him if he knew his son was now a sergeant in the Army of the United States. He knew I had made Juan a corporal, but it was a surprise to him that Juan was now a sergeant. I could tell he was very proud of his son. Juan went back with his father to wait for Teniente Leaño—and to tell his mother the good news about his promotion.

Shortly after noon they returned with Leaño, bringing four sacks of rice, and baskets of camotes, vegetables, dried meat, and fish. I shook hands with Leaño and asked him who was helping with all the food he was giving us. He said some close friends and relatives had contributed. He wanted to know if it was true, as rumored, that we had killed one hundred Japanese. I said, "Saan apo (No, sir), teniente," but, I explained, we had killed or wounded at least sixty of the hundred men the Japanese had sent into the jungle to flush us out and capture, or kill, us.

The teniente had heard about the wounded Japanese sniper who had been tied in a tree. He asked, very seriously, if I had cut out his tongue and eaten it. I replied, just as seriously, that I hadn't thought of it at the time. I knew better than to laugh or even smile.

I explained we would do no more ambushing, unless the Japanese caught us unawares and raided us; then—and only then—we would ambush and fight them again. We planned to lie low for a while, I told him, because we were afraid the Japanese would retaliate against civilians; and, we would move from our present campsite to one deeper inside the jungle, and much farther off the main trails leading to the barrios.

When I had finished Leaño said he was going to Jones the following day to ask the Japanese for permission to go into the jungles with his dogs to hunt. He thought he could get permission because the Japanese had left his barrio with very little livestock, and if he did get it, he would enter the jungle on Tuesdays and Thursdays, weather permitting. So, if we heard the dogs, we would know it was he, and not the Japanese. I said we would be on the lookout for him.

While we were talking, Mrs. Reyes and her sister-in-law arrived bringing us warm rice and meat with gravy, which I poured over the rice and ate with a bamboo spoon that I made. After thanking the women, I told Mrs. Reyes I would send her son, Sergeant Reyes, back to her tomorrow so that he could gather more information for us. She smiled when I said sergeant. The teniente explained to her, in Ilocano, about the promotion. I thanked them for their support and asked if there had been any news about Major Roberts. Since they had heard nothing, they thought he was still safe.

As we said good-bye, I told Teniente Leaño I would like to come to Manuri to see him. I would stay at the edge of the jungle and send one of my men in to contact him. I intended to ask him about acting as a double agent. Juan had told me he could be trusted, and that he would give his life for his beliefs. The first time I met him, I had felt the strength of his character; however, I wanted the opportunity to talk with him again to be mighty certain. After the experience of the raid on our camp at Pinappagan, and knowing what had happened to Colonel Nakar and Captain Cushing, I was cautious about trusting anyone.

We returned to camp loaded down with the supplies from the two tenientes, and our meal that evening was of generous proportions, which the men appreciated. I knew there would not be many more like it for some time to come. After we had eaten, I called in all the officers and enlisted men for a meeting, including two-thirds of the men on listening-post duty.

Since we were entering the May-to-November monsoon season, I didn't think it likely the Japanese would come into the jungle during this time. We had attacked, harassed, and humiliated them; now it was time for us to pull back, retreat deep into the jungle, and remain as well hidden as possible. I told the assembled men I thought we should leave for Campsite Four in the morning. We would plan no more attacks on the Japanese unless they came after us again. If they did, Campsite Four was the best location from which to implement our plan to draw them east toward the mountains, and afterwards to split ourselves into three groups to pull them farther into the jungles to the east, north, and south. If we employed the tactics used by the Ilongot headhunters—sharp-edged spears, pits, and snares—we could confuse the enemy troops. They wouldn't know if they were tracking us or the Ilongots, and the jungle would be our ally.

The move would take us farther from our sources of supply; but if

Teniente Leaño in Manuri was the man I thought he was, he would continue to help us. The real test would be whether we could endure extended periods of time without outside supplies, subsisting solely on the jungle, as the headhunters did. We would be deep in Ilongot territory, and these people would be resentful of our intrusion into their lives. It would be a waiting period, filled with more hunger and uncertainty than ever before; but, if the Americans were on their way back, this wouldn't last forever, and we would endure somehow until they did return.

We were now nearing the end of June 1943; most likely we would be foraging all of our food from the jungle by October. If the supplies we had left were to last us a reasonable length of time, we must go on short rations very soon.

After I had presented the difficulties to be faced, I asked if there were any objections to my proposal. There were none: the men agreed to go along with whatever I had planned. They felt I had brought them this far, and they trusted my judgment.

I thanked them and told them what we had accomplished up to now had been because of their willingness to obey orders and work as a team. We were not alone in our struggle, I said, and I believed that God would not abandon us. We would live to see the American and Philippine soldiers retake the islands. After the evening prayers, the listening posts returned to duty, and everyone turned in for a good night's rest.

PART FOUR

A SURVIVAL TIME
OF WAITING

CHAPTER 31

Settling In at Campsite Four

Early the next morning, we cleaned up the camp in preparation for leaving it, and said our good-byes to Juan, who would be returning to Dabubu where he would stay to gather news and information for us. He knew the locations of Campsites Four and Five and could find us if there was anything of importance to report.

On our way to Campsite Four, we passed through Campsite Two to check the cave where our cache of weapons was hidden. Nothing had been disturbed. We piled more rock around the cave's entrance and camouflaged it thoroughly. I was sure no one except ourselves would ever locate it. After pausing for a quick meal of cold rice, we continued moving northeast through the jungle.

By early afternoon we had reached the campsite, and the day had turned cloudy and misty. I hoped we would have the camp in livable condition before the heavy rains began.

The first task was to clean out our cave before nightfall so that we would have dry sleeping quarters. The men made torches to burn the brush and smoke out the snakes, spiders, and bats that had moved in since our last occupation. Besides the main opening, which had a huge tree in front of it, there were the other three, smaller, entrances, all surrounded by some type of natural camouflage. Our listening posts would be able to remain inside because each of the four entrances allowed a complete view of the whole campsite, and since there were no overhead openings in the cave, we should all stay reasonably dry when the monsoon rains did begin.

After the brush was burned out, we swept the cave and set about making replacements for our bamboo beds, which we had destroyed before vacating the site so many months ago. Some beds were made to sleep one person, and others, three or four. We even had enough room in our five-hundred-square-foot quarters to hang up some of our supplies, and there was a space where bamboo shelves could be built to store others.

Just before dark, I had two men stand out in each of the areas that could be seen from just inside the four openings in order to locate any dead areas, or blind spots. We found one such spot between two of the smaller entrances, and I had Valdez mark the spot with a stake and put up sharp-tipped bamboo spears for the night. In the morning, we would dig pits in that area and line them with spears before camouflaging them.

The day had been long and tiring, and we decided to postpone our last big feast before we started short rations until the next evening, when the camp would be completely set up. The listening posts took up their positions at the entrances, and the rest of us dropped wearily to sleep. Nothing disturbed the usual nighttime jungle noises.

The next morning everyone was up early, ready to get the camp organized for a long stay. I had Dannug set up a duty roster, which included a three-man-listening-post team for each entrance; a detail to build and check traps, pits, and snares; a log-and-wood-burning detail; and a detail to dig the long, narrow trench for the latrine—and I reminded the men to be sure either to use the buddy system when using this at night, or to relieve themselves before dark. I couldn't help thinking that my Visayans had come a long way since their training days on Negros when I had had to explain so carefully the whys and wherefores of a camped army's latrine system.

We were busy the rest of the day gathering firewood, digging pits, setting traps and snares, and investigating the edible plant life in the area. Late in the afternoon we gathered to inspect the camp, make a tour of the traps and snares, and check out the safe entrances to the camp: spots where there were no needlelike bamboo spears.

We even had a kitchen just inside the cave near the main entrance, where the cooking could be done when it was raining. A small fire was to be kept burning there twenty-four hours a day. This was our most comfortable camp. The men had done a good job of making it livable and were eager to sample the big meal the cook prepared for us that night. Starting the next day, with the exception of anyone who was ill, we would be on half-rations.

One day, after we had been living in the camp for about two weeks, we heard dogs barking in the distance. I asked Dannug what day it was, and he told me it was Tuesday. Since it hadn't rained in two days, and it was a Tuesday, I concluded Teniente Leaño must be out hunting. Valdez said we could locate him easily simply by heading toward the sound of the barking; so, taking three men with us we followed the sound to the trail. The dogs were just ahead of us now, and we could hear voices on the trail behind us.

We stepped back into the protection of the jungle, and in a short time the teniente and another man passed by. Valdez called out, and Leaño turned around and came back down the trail with his companion. He told Valdez he knew I was with him: he had spotted my footprints on the trail; after all, my feet had not become indistinguishable from my men's. We shook hands, and he introduced the man with him as his friend and relative Jose.

The two dogs began barking furiously, and Leaño said they must have cornered a wild pig. We hurried toward the frantic yapping, and found the dogs taking turns nipping at a cornered boar. Almost shouting to be heard above the squealing and snarling, I asked the teniente if he wanted us to shoot the animal, and he said no, he was afraid the shot might be heard in the nearby barrios, and the Japanese were patrolling them daily. He said that he always killed wild pigs with his bolo. He gave an order to the dogs, and they renewed their attack, drawing the boar's attention away from Jose and Valdez, who already were holding their bolos in striking positions.

Teniente Leaño was an older man of sixty-odd years, but he moved in and with one blow nearly severed the boar's head. I recalled my first impression of him on that day when he boloed the Japanese soldier and then cut out his tongue. There was no doubt about it: he was tough.

At Leaño's invitation, Valdez gave the coup de grâce, and that was the end of the fight. The boar was a good-size one, and they proceeded to butcher it right there. As their reward, the dogs got parts of the intestines, and the rest of the meat was packed in the baskets Jose and the teniente carried on their shoulders. They gave us enough meat for one good meal and I knew we would all enjoy it.

Before Leaño left to return to Manuri, I asked if he had heard any news lately from the outside world. He said yes, that Señor Villanueva, who had a radio, had said the Americans were on their way back to retake the Philippines. There were still quite a few Japanese in Jones, and they patrolled the barrios religiously. Sometimes there were only four soldiers in a patrol, but they always demanded food. The villagers' stock reply was that they were running short of rice, but they could spare corn.

I thanked the teniente for the news and the fresh pork and told him I had remembered he had said he would hunt on Tuesdays and Thursdays; so, when we heard the dogs barking, we thought it might be he. He said he was glad we had come because we had brought him good luck. We shook hands and said good-bye.

The cook exceeded himself that evening trying to fix the pork to suit everyone, all the while getting unsolicited advice from the men, who were anticipating the special treat that would accompany their usual small portion of rice.

For the next two weeks, it rained steadily. About a month had passed since we had last seen Teniente Reyes or Juan. From what Teniente Leaño had told me, I was sure the Japanese were still patrolling the barrios at least every other day. I was wondering if they would also give Teniente Reyes permission to hunt wild pig. It was likely he would ask them now that they had allowed Leaño to hunt. If he did get permission, he and Juan would be entering the jungle with their dogs, and we would be seeing them again soon.

The heavy rain continued through the last two weeks of August, during which time we took to weaving baskets and making straw hats of various designs to break the monotony. Many of the hats were quite ingenious. I remember making one that looked like an Australian soldier's hat. One side of the brim turned up, and the other stuck out to the side; the top was creased down the center. I thought it looked pretty good, and I sported the result of my craftsmanship until it fell apart. As someone who had always enjoyed nice clothes and had taken special pride in a varied wardrobe, jungle living definitely limited my options. By the time this experience was over, I had firsthand knowledge of what threadbare really means.

Caught up in a competition of creativity with the other men, Dolatre got the idea of building a bamboo typewriter. He spent hours fashioning the various parts until his handiwork really began to resemble a typewriter. The keys were made from bamboo strips, which he had notched and labeled. He offered to teach me to type, painstakingly showing me the correct finger positions and patiently giving advice, while I did my best to be an apt pupil.

While working on one of these projects, I nearly lost my trigger finger when I got careless with my bolo. The cut went to the bone, and I worried about getting gangrene, but my soldiers came to the rescue with their knowledge of the plant life around us. They located a tree near the camp with leaves that had remarkable healing properties. They pulled the cut together and wrapped one of the leaves around it, using small strings of rattan to hold it in place. In about an hour the throbbing stopped, and a week later the cut was healed.

When the weather cleared a little, the men ventured out to set up new snares and traps and to dig new pits. Foraging groups went out for ubog, berries, snails, and any greens that might contain the vitamins our bodies needed.

Then, one morning as we were getting up, we heard dogs barking to the south of us, toward Dabubu, and I was sure they belonged to Teniente Reyes and Juan. I asked for volunteers to investigate, cautioning them to be on the alert in case an enemy patrol was out using a villager's dog to track us. Lieutenant Reyes said he would go, and he left with eight men and enough rations for a day. In the event they found a Japanese patrol, they were to ambush and pull it farther east into the jungle, using our hit-and-run tactic, and make contact with us again only when it was safe to do so.

About an hour after their departure, our listening post challenged someone entering the camp. The answer came back—"Lillian." It was Juan, who was as overjoyed to see us as we were to see him. He had brought us a little corn, and a few camotes, bananas, and greens in a knapsack. I was surprised to see bananas because most of those grown in the area were confiscated by the Japanese. Teniente Reyes had received permission from the Japanese to go hunting, and Juan had taken the opportunity to bring us some food. He said the Japanese had left Dabubu with only its carabao, one boar, one pig, a few chickens, and one rooster, and the villagers had to beg them not to take those. If he and his father caught a wild pig, they had promised to share it with the Japanese for allowing them to hunt.

There were four soldiers with a noncommissioned officer in the patrol that came through Dabubu regularly, and these five men had become very insistent in their demands for food. On their most recent visit, they accused the villagers of hiding their rice from the Japanese Imperial Forces. Juan said his father had denied this and told them he was happy the Japanese had liberated his people from the Americans. This seemed to placate the soldiers, and they left the barrio without further ado.

When I asked if there had been any word from or about Major Roberts, Juan said his father and he were sure the Japanese hadn't captured him, or any of his men either. They thought Roberts had one American corporal with him, a Philippine lieutenant, and two enlisted men. Occasionally, Juan added, a rumor circulated that both Major Roberts and "Captain" Hieb had died in the jungles.

The distant barking suddenly changed to frenzied yipping, and we knew the dogs had probably cornered a wild pig. I told Juan to tell his father to keep the Japanese happy by agreeing with them and giving them a share of the pig if necessary. Promising to be in touch if anything new developed, he left to join his father.

About three hours later, Lieutenant Reyes showed up with enough meat to allow each of us a small portion. He said Teniente Reyes had gotten a large boar, and since he was going to give some of the meat to the Japanese so that they would continue to let him hunt, he mentioned that he might poison those portions. Lieutenant Reyes said he told him not to because of the certain retaliation. The teniente said he knew; that it was only a thought; but, he could hardly wait for "our day to come," adding the information that there was still a large garrison of Japanese troops in Jones.

To get an enemy-strength report from the Filipinos was difficult. Whenever I tried to get a specific number, most of them would say, "Many, sir." Having spent one tour of duty in the Philippines from 1935 to 1937, and another from the latter part of 1939 to now, I had learned the word many could mean any number from one hundred to five thousand. I decided to ask Juan to get an accurate count the next time he came to camp.

CHAPTER 32

A Serious Shortage— and a Solution

We had to do something to improve our diet. We needed more than the few calories a day we were getting. October had arrived, and our rice supply had been gone for some time. All we had left was corn, and some of this we had been saving for an emergency. We were all watching ourselves very closely for any symptoms of beriberi. If we didn't get more rice and meat, we would all become ill.

Dengue fever was causing me problems, and I had had another bad bout of malaria. Dengue fever is disabling for a day, but the type of malaria I had would hang on for several days, each time leaving me very weak.

We tried fishing the streams, and sometimes we would catch a few fish, but after we divided these among forty-five men, the portions were just too skimpy to do us much good. On occasion, we caught bats and large jungle rats, which I skinned and cleaned, scrubbing the hell out of the meat before I cut it into pieces and threw it in with the corn to disguise it. At times even I would almost gag on the results, but to keep from starving to death we all had to try to forget what kind of meat was mixed in with our corn mush. Our listening post at the entrance to the campsite was responsible for boiling the corn. The mush itself wouldn't have been too bad, if we had had enough of it; and if we could have added salt. But, we had been without salt for a long time.

One morning, after eating nothing but snails and the small portion of mush that was supposed to satisfy our hunger for the entire day, I called the men together for a meeting. We desperately needed to replenish our supplies, and there were two possible ways of doing so.

It had occurred to me we could attempt to get a written message to Señor Villanueva, my Spanish friend, asking for quinine and food. Perhaps Teniente Leaño could contact him and offer to barter wild pig for rice—if the teniente agreed; but, carrying the message would itself involve some risk for him.

Or, I said, we could cross to the west side of the river and steal from those civilians who had been very friendly with the Japanese. These people had more food than those on the east, or our, side. However, I really wondered whether in our weakened condition we could move fast enough to stay clear of the enemy.

I asked the men to break into two groups and talk it out among themselves. After some discussion, the consensus was that contacting Señor Villanueva would present the least amount of danger.

The written message, however, presented two problems. First, we wanted to get it delivered with as little risk to Teniente Leaño as possible; second, it had to be written in such a way that Señor Villanueva would know it really was from me and was not a trap. After some thought, I wrote the following:

> Señor Villanueva
> Dear Compadre:
> My men and I are in desperate need of any kind of food supplies, mainly rice, greens, peas, and camotes. I had one man die of beriberi. However, not by Japanese gunfire as they claimed after the two trips into the jungles to wipe us out. I know you have a shortwave radio set. Could you give us some late news? Remember you once told me, when I gave you permission to fly the Spanish flag when the Japanese arrived in Jones, that if I ever needed help and it was possible, you would help me. You once asked me if I had a wife back in the States and I said no but I was engaged to a girl by the name of Elaine. I know now you will believe this message is from the undersigned.
> Harley Hieb

After carefully rewriting this message several times, I was satisfied Villanueva would have no doubts about its authorship.

Lieutenant Reyes and Lieutenant Vea were interested in how I happened to know Villanueva, so I explained his dilemma when the Japanese were coming into Jones, and how I had given him permission to fly his Spanish flag to protect himself. After hearing the story, the lieutenants agreed there was a good chance he would help us, if we could get the message through to him.

Now all we had to do was wait for Teniente Leaño to come into the jungle to hunt again. I decided we would wait a week, and if he hadn't come in by then, I would go to Manuri with Sergeant Valdez. The week dragged by slowly, with no sign of any hunters. At the end of it, Valdez and I left for the barrio, taking with us the two healthiest, strongest men in camp to carry back the corn I was optimistically hoping we would get from Leaño.

At the edge of Manuri, we stayed hidden just inside the jungle. A light rain was falling, and we built a small palm-leaf lean-to so that we could keep dry while we waited for a safe opportunity to contact someone in the barrio. Valdez was looking very tired, and I knew I was in such a weakened condition that any exertion at all exhausted me. Although the other two men seemed to be in good shape—at least compared to Valdez and myself—we were all grateful for the chance to rest and keep reasonably dry.

We waited there about an hour. Then we saw a man come out of his hut. Valdez went to talk to him, making a detour in order to approach from another direction so that our hiding place wouldn't be revealed. I heard him call out a greeting in Ilocano, *comusta* (hello), as he walked toward the man. Then I heard the word Hapon and wondered if this meant the Japanese had been in the barrio recently, or if they were still there.

At last, I saw the two head for one of the larger huts, and when the villager called out, Teniente Leaño appeared in the doorway. After a moment he came down the ladder and shook hands with Valdez. The other man left, and Leaño and Valdez talked together for a few minutes, after which Leaño went back inside. In a short while he came out

272

again, carrying a basket and wearing his palm-leaf raincoat. Now he and Valdez came in our direction.

I greeted Leaño with a handshake and a hug—and saw tears in his eyes. I quickly asked Valdez, "Is something wrong? Have the Japanese mistreated him or members of his barrio?" He answered, "No, he feels sorry for you; you look half-starved." (My appearance must have been shocking: my beard reached far down my chest; my hair was also very long; and, like all my men, I had lost a lot of weight— my arms and legs looked grotesque, they were so thin.)

The teniente said, "Here we are talking about how sick and hungry you look, and I forgot that my wife sent out food for you." He set the basket down. I gave thanks to the Lord, and to all the people of Manuri. Then while Leaño watched with approval, the four of us dug in and ate until there wasn't a crumb of rice, greens, or fish left.

I told Leaño about my plan to contact Señor Villaneuva, and he said, "Let's go to my house and I'll see what I can do for you." I asked him if that wouldn't be dangerous—the Japanese might make a surprise visit. He said the barrio knew an hour in advance, day or night, when any Japanese were approaching, and all the villagers had taken loyalty oaths and could be counted on not to break them. But, when he added an invitation for us to spend the night, I was really very reluctant to accept; I was extremely concerned about the possible danger to the barrio.

Leaño said he knew my concern was sincere, but I would be doing him an honor if we stayed the night in his home. In the meantime, Valdez and the other two men were looking at me hopefully, and so I agreed, by now pretty pleased with the idea myself. This would be the first time I had slept in a barrio since the raid at Pinappagan.

Leaño's hut was considerably larger than any of the other fifteen in the barrio. Like the others, his had a ladder from the ground up to the front entrance, and as I climbed up, the bamboo door slid open. I saw a young woman who I assumed must be my host's daughter, and I tried to hide my astonishment when he introduced her as his third wife!

As I entered the front room, I could hear voices coming from the next room, and the teniente called out, "Come in and meet the

American lieutenant and some of his men." This time, two young women appeared, and Leaño introduced us to his daughters, Rosa and Lucie, both of whom had been to school in Jones and spoke English.

Rosa then explained that she was married; her husband had been inducted into the service before the war, but she had had no news of him for a very long time. She didn't know whether he was alive or dead. I said someday, when the American forces retook the islands, they would find out for her. She was aware, because her father had told her, that the Visayans in our camp were from the island of Negros, and she thought perhaps her husband might also have been sent to another island. Since the heavy fighting had been on Luzon, I had my doubts about this possibility, but I didn't want to upset her by saying anything.

Hoping to encourage her I told her I was sure I was listed as missing-in-action, and my family was probably worried too, but that I knew I would return home; so, there was hope for her husband, also. She wanted to know if I was married, and I said, "No, but I'm engaged to a girl, Elaine, back home." I told her my parents, brothers, and sisters were all alive—at least they were up until the beginning of the war. While Rosa and I were talking, Lucie was interpreting our conversation for the teniente and his wife.

After a while, I asked Rosa and Lucie if there was a secluded spot where my men and I could bathe. Rosa said, "Yes, where all the women take their baths." The teniente said he would stand watch for us, and we headed down toward the river, where we walked a short distance to a bend, out of sight of the barrio. There we stripped and bathed, and afterwards washed our clothes as best we could, wrung them out, and put them back on wet. While we waited for them to dry on us, we sat down to talk with the teniente.

I asked Leaño if there was any more news about the American forces. He said there was some guerrilla activity in the mountain provinces, and I said I had meant General MacArthur and his forces. He said, "Yes, they're taking islands north of Australia, and they are on their way to retake the Philippines. The Japanese claim the Americans tried to retake some of the islands and failed, but the Philippine people don't believe that." The Japanese also claimed that in just one ambush, they had killed nearly all the guerrillas, and the rest, on a second one (this was in reference to our recent ambush). The teniente said he didn't believe any of this because he knew I still had all my men.

When our cut-offs were nearly dry, I suggested we return to his hut where we could discuss the purpose of my visit. While we had been gone, a number of neighbors had gathered to see the "American who could survive in the jungles." I was something of an oddity, and they were all very curious. I shook hands with everyone, thanking each one for his help. Some of them wanted to feel my beard to see if it was real. Very few Philippine men have beards; they pluck the hair from their faces with tweezers, leaving only a mustache. Very kindly, all the women had brought various foods with them, which they left with the teniente for us.

After they left, we went with Leaño into one of the hut's three rooms and sat down on the floor to talk. I explained our plan and asked the teniente how well he knew Señor Villanueva. I wanted to know if he thought the Spaniard could be trusted; I did not intend that any harm should come to Leaño—or anyone else—because of the message. He said, "Señor Villanueva can be trusted; I know he helped some of the officers who escaped from the Japanese when Colonel Nakar was captured."

The teniente said he would be happy to deliver the message. He explained that he would roll it in a cigar, and if he was stopped and questioned or was in any danger of being caught, he would light the cigar and—quite literally—smoke his way out of danger. I had not been wrong in my estimation of this remarkable man. He was brave, courageous, and inventive, and I had a great admiration for him. He was also a very intelligent man, and I felt that he would get my message delivered without taking any unnecessary risks.

I suggested that if Señor Villanueva went along with the plan, Leaño should tell people, including the Japanese, he was using the barter system: swapping wild pig for rice. The Japanese knew the barrio was nearly out of rice, and it would seem logical to them that the teniente would turn to bartering. Leaño thought the idea was a good one because the weather might clear soon, allowing him to take his dogs into the jungle again to hunt. I added that I hoped he would get

275

me as much up-to-date information as possible from Villaneuva about the American forces.

I then asked Leaño if he would act as a double agent, getting such intelligence information to us as enemy strength, location, movements, ammunition and supply dumps, and also verification of all pro-Japanese Filipino spies and collaborators. I told him if he had to tell the Japanese anything, he could volunteer the information that on one of his hunts in the jungle, he had come upon tracks made by about four guerrillas who seemingly had survived the attack on them, and these tracks had led toward the east. He agreed to the plan and we shook hands.

After we had finished our discussion, Leaño called to his daughters, and they brought us rice cakes and basi. Then it was dinnertime—and Mrs. Leaño had prepared a wonderful one. We had fried fresh fish, rice, greens, camotes, peas, fried bananas—and more basi. I ate so much, I was sure I had put on at least three pounds. We thanked Mrs. Leaño, telling her she would spoil us with such delicious food. Rosa acted as my interpreter, but I had the feeling the teniente's wife understood more English than she would acknowledge.

After dinner, I asked Rosa if they had a pair of scissors we could use so that one of the men could cut my hair. Rosa offered to cut it herself, saying she usually cut her father's hair. I agreed, with the proviso that her father give his permission. I knew that young Philippine women were closely protected by their families and followed a very strict set of rules in their contacts with men outside of their families. She smiled and said since she was married, she didn't need her father's permission, but she would ask if I preferred she do so. Her father laughed and said to go ahead and cut it, but only as far as the neck line. When I asked why, he said the Ilongots might see the white of my neck, and it might tempt them to use a bolo on me in order to acquire a prized white man's head. I said, "Okay, and while you're at it, please cut off ninety-nine percent of my beard."

Rosa worked on me for about an hour; there was a lot of hair to cut. When she had finished, she brought me a broken mirror and invited me to inspect her work. She had done an excellent job. Without all that hair on my head and face, I must have looked considerably younger; with a look of surprise, the teniente asked me how old I was. I said I was twenty-nine. He said he had thought I was at least fifty.

Next in line for haircuts were Valdez and the other two men. I noticed Rosa had kept the hair from my beard on a palm leaf. The rest of the hair, including that from the men with me, was in a separate pile. When I asked her why she had separated my beard from the rest of the hair, she blushed and said she wanted to keep it for a souvenir because it was brown and curly and so different. I said, "Thank you, Rosa, but you'd better be careful not to let the Japanese see it since they could become very suspicious." She said she would keep just a little.

Rosa and Lucie brought us more rice cakes—and another cup of basi each, which by this time I would have liked to refuse, but I knew it would be impolite. After we ate all the cakes we could possibly hold, the sisters cleaned up the room and brought us each a sleeping mat; and the family bid us goodnight.

The next morning, we were delighted to see that the sun was shining. Without the rain, the trip back to camp would be much easier. We had more rice, fish, and greens for breakfast, and there were plenty of supplies to take back to the men. The Manurians had gathered two large sacks of corn for us; and, there were camotes, peas, dried fish, and a small amount of rice, which Valdez and I carried in makeshift backpacks. The corn sacks were secured to two poles that the other two men carried over their shoulders; then we were ready to leave. The whole barrio turned out to see us off, and everyone apologized for not being able to give us more food. Teniente Leaño said he would try to deliver my message to Señor Villanueva before the end of the week.

We were back in camp by noon, and I immediately asked the cook to fix a big meal of greens, camotes, fish, and a little rice mixed in with our corn mush. He asked, "A *big* meal?" I said, "Yes, we may have some luck with a new source of supplies." I was feeling guilty about the three big meals the four of us had had while the rest of the men were eating corn mush and snails, and I wanted to share our good fortune with them as quickly as possible.

The men looked the four of us over very carefully, eyeing our haircuts, and especially my trimmed beard, and then asked jokingly if we had gone all the way to Jones for haircuts. Valdez said, "No, we had a couple of good-looking girls cut our hair, and they even trimmed the lieutenant's beard." I told the men on the next trip to the barrio I would try to get a pair of scissors, but no girls to do the haircutting. A loud groan went up, and everyone had a good laugh.

It rained nearly every day for about a week, and then there was another break in the weather. The sun came out, and the monkeys came back. The snares we had set for them were now too rain soaked and swollen to be effective; so, we pretended to ignore our visitors, thinking if we didn't pay too much attention, they would continue coming back on a daily basis, giving us ample opportunity to catch some of them. They kept up a steady stream of chatter, pointing at us all the while. A colony of at least thirty had gathered before evening.

Valdez and some of the men began making new snares, and that night they set out about eight. I was sure that because we hadn't bothered them, the monkeys would be back the following day, if it didn't rain.

The next morning we heard chattering and screaming; Valdez and his helpers had been up early and had snared three of the animals. The sergeant sharpened his knife and killed them, and I went to work as before, skinning, butchering, cutting the meat into small portions, then carefully washing these so there wouldn't be any hair left on them. Several of the men put some of the remains out as bait on snares for other game. The rest of the colony had long since disappeared.

We were ready for a feast. I told the cook to wash all the meat again, and I put my order in to have my portion well done. Then everybody else began to put in orders—most of them for well done also. We had been eating cold dried meat and fish for so long, we all thought a hot meal of cooked meat would do us good.

The next day, barking from the direction of Manuri alerted us that Leaño and his dogs had entered the jungle to hunt. I asked Valdez if he would like to go with me to see the teniente and watch the hunt. The two soldiers who had gone with us on our latest trip to the barrio also went along, and we took some monkey meat to give to Leaño.

We were getting close to the high-pitched, frantic yipping that told us the dogs were in hot pursuit of their quarry when we spotted the teniente. He said he was sure more than one pig was cornered, and when we caught up with the dogs, they were in a frenzy of excitement, leaping and nipping at a boar, a sow, and three small piglets. The sow was charging and fighting to protect her young ones. The teniente, Valdez, and the other two men closed in. Two dogs were circling and snapping at the boar, and the teniente was waiting for an opening. When he got his chance, he killed the boar with one blow. One of the other men got the sow; Valdez caught one of the piglets. Leaño said it was the largest number of pigs they had ever caught in one day. He was convinced we had brought him good luck again.

I asked if he had been able to get my message to Señor Villanueva. He said he had, but Villanueva had made him wait several hours for the answer. I asked if he had been worried about the delay, but he said no, that Villanueva was probably checking with his friend and neighbor, Señor Rodriquez, to see if he could help us also. Villanueva thought the barter system was an excellent idea because there was a great shortage of meat in the Jones area. However, even though I had given him other proof in my message, Villanueva wanted to verify my signature. (I remembered I had signed his guest book, using my hometown address.) At last, he told Leaño to come back in about a week with a couple of sleds for hauling supplies.

I suggested the teniente should keep some of the anticipated supply of rice for the people in his barrio, and I gave him the monkey meat. He wanted to give us two of the piglets, but we took only the one Valdez had caught. Leaño said he would give the sow and the boar to Villanueva, adding that the next time we heard the dogs barking, he would have supplies for us. There would also be more news about the war, but in the meantime, Villanueva had asked him to tell me that the Americans were definitely on their way back to the Philippines, and already they had taken some islands north of Australia.

On the way back to camp, I noticed Valdez clutching the pig he had caught as if he weren't ever going to let go of it; I asked him facetiously if he was going to share it with the rest of us. He grinned and said, "Maybe, sir." I said, "Okay, *maybe* we will share some of the supplies we're getting with you." It was good to have something to laugh about.

Three hours later we were back in camp, and Valdez and the cook butchered the little pig, which, of course, the sergeant shared with the rest of us.

CHAPTER 33

Christmas, and a Birthday Forgotten

It was almost the end of November 1943. I thought about Christmas being less than a month away. This would be my fourth Christmas away from the United States. Christmas 1941 in particular seemed like a very long time ago; we had been retreating onto Bataan from the disaster that had overtaken us after the Japanese landing at Lingayan Gulf. As I reviewed all that had transpired since then, I wondered how much longer we would have to wait in these jungles. The past year had been a rough one for all of us. We had learned what it was like to live on a starvation diet. Hunger had become a part of our lives. We even dreamed of food: the nightmare continued to be the hunger that was our daily reality.

Now added to my own dreams were the wonderful German dishes Mother used to make, especially my favorite, *halupsi*: a mouth-watering mixture of hamburger, potatoes, rice, and raisins wrapped in boiled cabbage leaves, covered with tomato sauce, and then baked until it was tender and flavored throughout with tangy juices. I tried to describe this dish to the others, but they were at a loss to understand my craving for something that sounded so peculiar to them. They at least were eating some of the foods familiar to them, albeit not nearly enough.

I remembered in vivid detail the early, hearty breakfasts with which our days began. There were pancakes the size of dinner plates topped with sweet, home-churned butter and syrup or currant jelly. These were accompanied by the quivery-soft fried eggs Mother made with the large brown eggs her prized Rhode Island Reds produced; big platters of highly seasoned sausage, which Dad cured in the smokehouse that stood near the back of our huge garden; and inch-thick slabs of homemade bread, with crisp, yellow-brown crusts, still warm from the oven of the large old-fashioned black stove that filled one corner of the kitchen. I recalled the pungent odor of the hams and the variety of sausages hanging from the rafters of Dad's smokehouse. And I saw the haunting vision of Mother's storage cellar with its dark, earth-smelling potato bin; large crockery jars of sauerkraut; other, sand-filled, crocks in which were concealed garden-fresh carrots and beets; and white shelves that lined the walls and held row upon row of sparkling jars standing in colorful array, all filled with every variety and combination of fruits and vegetables possible to grow in South Dakota. We were a well-fed family, and I knew if I had the chance to taste of that cornucopia once more, I would never again take for granted such abundance of food.

Once I was so desperately hungry and so obsessed by the thought of food, I actually thought of Mrs. Harbour's Siamese cats. As I remembered how they would lie in front of the door growling, they seemed to turn into wildcats. Suddenly, I imagined them boiling in our cooking pot. Another time, I even thought longingly of the huge river rats that had plagued the barracks in Manila, now so long ago.

Now that the rainy season was over, the jungle began to blossom, turning into a magnificent flower garden. In the midst of the worries of war and hunger, we were everywhere surrounded by wild orchids, and by many other wildflowers of every color known to nature. We were waiting to ask Juan which of these were edible. I didn't want us to try eating any until we knew for sure which might be poisonous.

The first week in December, Juan returned to camp, bringing a little corn. He said the people in his barrio were out of funds and couldn't buy rice, and most of the barrios were short of food. I asked him why his father hadn't been hunting. He said they were supposed to wait for renewed permission from the Japanese, but in desperation, they had come into the jungle that day to hunt without it. He brought the same news Teniente Leaño had: that the Americans were on their way back. I asked him if he knew how many Philippine soldiers in the Jones area had surrendered to the Japanese, and how many could be counted on to join us in order to form a fighting unit. I was positive many of the soldiers who had taken advantage of the amnesty were still loyal to the Phil-American cause and would be ready to join us when the time came. He thought there would be at least 125 enlisted men and 3 officers who could be trusted, and who would be ready to take up arms against the Japanese. He was also sure there were enough weapons hidden in the Jones area to supply all the trustworthy soldiers we could muster.

When the landing in the Philippines became imminent, I planned to reorganize, inducting as many loyal Philippine soldiers into the 14th Infantry as possible. There were other guerrilla forces in Cagayan Province and in some of the mountain provinces; we could either join one of these, or act as an independent strike force. I would have to wait until I heard from Major Roberts before proceeding further, but I wanted to be ready when the Americans landed.

I inquired if there was any news of Major Roberts and if Juan knew how large a garrison the Japanese maintained in the Pinappagan area. He had heard there was only a platoon of enemy troops there, maybe thirty or forty men. Major Roberts and the other American with him were still safe. He wasn't sure how many Filipinos were with the major; he had heard there were four or five Philippine soldiers and one officer, but perhaps no more than a total of seven or eight men. It occurred to me that Roberts's mobility was much greater than mine.

I told Juan about the message we had sent through Leaño to Señor Villanueva and of my hope that we would be getting supplies from him, which, I said, we would share with the people of Dabubu since they had treated us so kindly.

About an hour after Juan had come into camp, we heard Teniente Reyes's dogs in full chase, so we knew his barrio would enjoy some good eating that night. Juan said every barrio in the vicinity had heard the story of the hunt that had netted five wild pigs. Juan then left to join his father, saying he would return when there was more news or when they came to hunt again.

Another week went by, and then one day we heard sounds that told us another hunt was in progress. This time Leaño would be bringing in the supplies from Señor Villaneuva. Sergeant Valdez and I prepared to leave, taking ten men with us. Lieutenant Reyes wondered how much food I expected to get. I replied, "Hopefully, all the men can carry." We headed toward Manuri, hoping to cut across the teniente's trail; two of the men were out in front as point, just in case there were Japanese soldiers with him.

In about two hours we came to the trail, and about ten minutes later Leaño and his men appeared, all heavily laden. We stepped out of the jungle. The teniente remarked that we were beginning to move like headhunters. I said, *"Salamat po."* (Thank you, sir.) We shook hands and then examined the sacks they carried; there were seven of rice, and several of carabao meat, greens, camotes, and peas. My men were overjoyed; it would take all of us to carry the supplies back to camp.

Leaño said Villanueva thought the Japanese would soon pull all their troops out of Jones. Guerrilla activities were increasing in northern Luzon, and the Americans were taking island after island in a progression that led straight for the Philippines. Villanueva had said, when the Japanese officers were drunk (if they partook of his usual hospitality, this was a distinct possibility), they told the truth: they were on the defensive.

Villanueva had invited some of the officers to a fiesta when he had received the two wild pigs from Leaño and had told them he was swapping rice for meat. The officers had liked the meat and said, "Let Teniente Leaño hunt if he wants to barter with Señor Villanueva." This was the kind of news I had been waiting for.

We wished the teniente good luck with his hunting and sent many thanks to Villanueva. We were about halfway back to camp when the dogs' barking signaled a successful hunt; now there would be more meat to barter.

As we approached camp, the rest of the men came out to greet us, knowing we would have supplies. The cook began to prepare for a big fiesta of our own, and everyone pitched in to help. We had a wonderful meal that night. After we had finished, I told the others I felt we should share our good fortune with Teniente Reyes and explained that Dabubu was out of both rice and money.

Lieutenant Reyes and six men took three of the seven sacks of rice to Dabubu with a message from me that if the teniente caught any wild pigs, he might take some of whatever portion he had planned to give us to Manuri so that Teniente Leaño could trade it to Señor Villanueva for rice for Dabubu.

The lieutenant asked if he and his men could stay in the barrio overnight and return in the morning. They had been confined to the camp for some time, so I said it would be all right if they all behaved themselves and didn't make advances to any of the young women.

The sun came out the next morning, and the day was warm. The jungle could be very beautiful, and this day I found myself relaxing in the pleasant surroundings thinking of home and family. I wondered, was Elaine still waiting for me? Somehow, I felt she was, and that she was praying for my safe return, as I knew my family was. I dozed off for a bit, only to be shaken awake by Valdez. Lieutenant Reyes had returned to camp with supplies from Dabubu.

The lieutenant said Teniente Reyes had tears in his eyes when he was given the rice we had sent and sent us his heartfelt thanks for thinking of his villagers. The people in Dabubu knew of the bartering Teniente Leaño was doing, and they had already caught a couple of wild pigs and taken one over to Manuri. Leaño was going to Jones with the two pigs caught the day he had brought our most recent supplies; altogether there would be three wild pigs for bartering with Señors Villanueva and Rodriquez, who already had given us, and also the desperately needy people of Dabubu and Manuri, so much help.

Teniente Reyes had also told the lieutenant there were now many pigs in the jungle because they hadn't been hunted by the barrio people for almost two years. He and his men were going to continue to hunt, with or without consent from the Japanese, now that they knew they could barter the wild pigs for rice. There were very few domestic pigs left in the Jones area. Unfortunately, the rice supply was low everywhere; people refused to plant it because they knew the Japanese would only take it from them. This expressed the general attitude of the loyal Philippine people: they simply did not want to see food going to the Japanese.

Christmas Day 1943 arrived and we splurged with a big meal. With our hunger comfortably satisfied for a change, we were all resting quietly when the whole camp was aroused near midnight by voices shouting in the distance. Extinguishing our fire, the men quickly gathered all the food and weapons, and we immediately evacuated the camp, heading for Campsite Five.

With Valdez acting as guide, we were going to make a half-moon-shaped arc, traveling east by south, until we got to a point where we could move straight west to the campsite. The men were to maintain silence, and each man was to keep the man in front of him in sight. As we moved out a little after midnight, we could hear all kinds of racket—men yelling and dogs barking. Sometime before daybreak we reached Campsite Five, tired and—once again—hungry. The listening posts took up their positions, and the rest of us dropped to sleep in minutes.

I awoke with a start to find someone shaking me. It was one of the guards. He shook Valdez awake too, explaining we both had been gasping for breath and saying "No!" I told Valdez I had dreamed the Japanese had found us and had a bayonet at my throat. Valdez looked at me with astonishment and said he had had an identical dream. I knew from the expression on his face he was telling me the truth. I told him not to say anything about it to the other men because some of them were very superstitious. This was a disquieting experience and we both wondered what it meant.

It was noon the next day before everyone was rested enough to get the camp in shape. The cave had to be cleaned out and all our usual precautions taken; however, by evening we were settled in, and the cook served plenty of rice because everyone had worked so hard to get the work done. Five was our second-best camp. The listening posts had good cover, but they couldn't be in the main cave as they had been at Campsite Four.

The following morning I asked for four volunteers to go to Dabubu to see if they could discover who or what was responsible for all the noise we had heard two nights before. Lieutenant Reyes and three other men volunteered. I reminded them to stay off the main trail in case a Japanese patrol was out looking for us. While they were gone, there was nothing we could do but wait for whatever news they might bring back before deciding what action we should take next.

About midafternoon, we heard someone approaching the camp. It was Juan. The guards halted him, checking to see if anyone else was with him. He was alone; but, he reported that a Japanese patrol of ten men with a young officer in charge had been in Dabubu and had stayed several days. Probably the idea had been to catch us off guard during the Christmas holiday. I asked Juan whether the people of the barrio had been forced to give the patrol any food. He said the villagers had hidden what little rice they had and had offered the Japanese corn, which as usual they refused; not as usual, they had brought with them enough food to last several days.

Then I asked Juan the question we had all been asking ourselves: Who was it in the jungle with the dogs? He said it was Teniente Leaño and some of his men who had made all the noise. Instead of the Japanese patrol we had assumed it to be, it had been our friend trying to contact us. He wanted to give us rice cookies and other desserts, and some Christmas cards his two daughters had made to help us celebrate Christmas.

Juan had heard the ruckus too, and he knew we would probably move out thinking it was the Japanese. He had checked the other campsites trying to locate us to let us know what really had happened. When Teniente Leaño couldn't find us, he had gone on to Dabubu with rice for Teniente Reyes and with the things he had been trying to deliver to us. I was sure Lieutenant Reyes would be as relieved as I to discover what the commotion had been about, and that he would be returning soon.

Juan said after the patrol left Dabubu, he followed it and saw the Japanese cross to the west side of the river. Since it was not likely they would return, at least for a few days, he asked to stay in camp for the night to wait for Lieutenant Reyes to return. His parents were not expecting him back yet; they knew he would be checking all of the campsites in his effort to locate us.

Juan also told me his father had received permission from the Japanese to hunt wild pig once a week, provided he reported to them any signs of guerrillas in the jungle. This was the same condition placed on Leaño's pig hunting. Juan said his father still had some rice coming from Señor Villanueva, who had told Teniente Leaño he and Señor Rodriquez could use all the wild pig he could bring them; their arrangement was that they would deal only through Leaño.

Later in the day, we heard Lieutenant Reyes respond "Lillian" to the guard's challenge, and he entered the camp with our belated Christmas presents from Leaño and his daughters. He brought some of the delicious, traditional sweets the Filipinos make at Christmastime, and homemade Christmas cards addressed "To The Gallant Guerrilla Forces." That evening, in a considerably lighter mood than that of the previous evening, we repeated our Christmas dinner and Christmas services. I read passages from my prayer book; we sang Christmas carols; and our thoughts and prayers were for our homes and families so far away.

With the new year approaching, our conversation turned to the future, and Lieutenant Reyes asked me what my plans were for the time when the Americans landed on one of the Philippine islands. I said I would have to report to the ranking American or Philippine officer. At present, Major Roberts was the ranking officer, but there were rumors that a lieutenant colonel was in Mountain Province. I told the officers and men there were enough Philippine soldiers in northern Luzon to organize several regiments, possibly a division. If we were to use raiding parties on the Japanese garrisons like the one in Jones, they would be forced to pull in their patrols and concentrate their troops in one area, thus allowing us to move about more freely. All of the men were looking forward to the day when they could come out of the jungle.

In the days that followed, we could hear the sounds of hunting from the directions of both Dabubu and Manuri. Our interest was keen, for a successful hunt meant our own supplies would be replenished. Juan showed up in camp one day when a hunt was on and asked if anyone wanted to go along. Vea, Valdez, and a few of the men said they would like to go.

That evening our hunters returned to camp with a good-size portion of wild pig. Juan was pleased that the hunt had been so successful. They had gotten four pigs, but they were still trying to beat Teniente Leaño's record of five in one day. Today's hunt had yielded three large sows and a boar; Teniente Reyes planned to have Leaño trade two of the animals when he went to barter with Villanueva or Rodriquez for rice.

I said, "Fine, then we can celebrate my birthday." Juan asked how old I would be, and I said, "Thirty years old, and I have spent eleven of those years in the army." The men wanted to know if I intended to be a career soldier. I said that was my plan. They wanted to know if my girl friend would approve of my career choice, and I explained that Elaine knew I was a professional soldier, and that I was in the army when we first met.

After Juan left for Dabubu the next morning saying he would see us again when Teniente Leaño returned with the rice, the two officers, the NCOs, and I discussed moving back to Campsite Four. It was located midway between Dabubu and Manuri and was our best location in the event of a surprise attack or raid because of the four escape routes within the cave. If we moved during the first part of February, the underbrush would quickly grow back to cover any signs that we had ever occupied Campsite Five. Moving would also relieve us of a major source of irritation at this campsite: the enormous mosquitoes. At Campsite Four we could have a small fire burning at each entrance: smoke seemed to keep out the mosquitoes and other insects. All things considered, this move seemed wise, and we decided to accomplish it after the first of February.

It was now about the twentieth of January. My birthday had come and gone. In fact, I hadn't even thought about it until one day, Lieutenant Reyes said, "More than two weeks have passed since the wild-pig hunt. Shouldn't we be getting ready to celebrate your birthday with a big feast?" I told him it had completely slipped my mind. I hadn't even remembered New Year's Day. I had long ago concluded it might be better to forget about dates occasionally, thus making time seem to go faster. I changed the subject by telling him if we didn't hear from Juan soon, we would make a trip to Dabubu to gather what up-to-date information on the enemy there was.

CHAPTER 34

Among Other Things, a New Friend

The Japanese still had a large garrison of men in Jones. Sometimes we would see low-flying enemy planes with their Rising Sun insignia skimming over the nearly impenetrable jungle near our position. We knew we couldn't be spotted from the air, however, and these intruders gave us some diversion rather than any problem. I happened to be talking to Juan one day about the peculiar distinctive sound made by the motors of Japanese planes, when we heard one roar, fade away, and roar again. Juan remarked that his father said, from the sound of things, the Japanese must have run out of petrol and be using peanut oil. I laughed and said I hadn't realized the teniente had that kind of a sense of humor. On the contrary, Juan assured me, his father did, and in fact, he constantly poked fun at the enemy.

If the patrolling planes were not a problem, now that the monsoon was over, the nomadic headhunters were to be. During the dry season, they moved their campsites often, hunting at will throughout the jungle. I knew this would present a major worry for us, and I warned everyone that we would have to be on the lookout for Ilongots. No one, I said, was to leave our campsite alone; if the men went out to forage for food or check snares and traps, they should always go in groups of at least four.

Not long after I issued that order, fresh footprints were spotted along a nearby stream where a group of my men was attempting—unsuccessfully as usual—to fish. The men were positive the prints had been made by Ilongots because of their small size. When this alarming discovery was reported to me, I warned everyone to be especially alert at night and had several men put out more stakes and dig a few more pits. I surely hoped it wouldn't be too much longer before we could leave the jungle for good and start living like civilized beings again— not that the worries would be fewer necessarily, but they would be different and faced in more comfortable surroundings.

Juan showed up another day carrying a sack of rice and saying there were two more sacks and other supplies for us from Señors Villanueva and Rodriquez. In addition, he brought me the following message:

> Dear Hieb:
> You have been promoted to major by the Japanese. They have spread leaflets in the barrios asking you to come in and surrender. They say you cannot survive and will starve to death in the jungles The leaflets say they will feed you and let you play baseball and basketball. You are to come out of the jungle carrying a white flag. Señor Villanueva says not to surrender; the news is good. The Japanese are losing island after island. What they do not want is to be harassed by guerrilla units.
> Señor Rodriquez

I told Juan, when he thanked Villanueva and Rodriquez for us, he should also tell them they could rest assured the Japanese would never take me alive. I could just imagine what torture they had planned for me if they ever did capture me. I didn't want to die slowly and after days of torture; fast and fighting was the way to go. I knew why the Japanese wanted me alive, however; they thought I knew the whereabouts of Major Roberts, for one thing; and, of course, I myself represented a sizeable problem for them.

My men and I told Juan about the footprints by the stream, and he confirmed our guess that the Ilongots were on the prowl. He explained that before the war, the barrios occasionally had given the headhunters rice: in return, they had left the villagers unmolested and allowed them to hunt in the jungle if they didn't trespass beyond the trails. Now, however, there was no rice to spare, and none even to steal, which the Ilongots had been trying to do. Added to this provocation was the fact that the villagers were forced by necessity to hunt in what the Ilongots considered their own inviolable territory. Anger and hunger combined were undoubtedly bringing the headhunters to the point of outright warfare.

For a long time, I had been curious about why the trails going east led only so far into the jungle and then stopped, and I asked Juan if there was a reason for this. He said the ends of the eastbound trails were generally considered to be the boundary lines of the Ilongot territory. What happened, I wondered, if hunting dogs chased their quarry beyond the trails? Juan said that if the dogs had a wild pig cornered, the hunters went after it—and sometimes one of them would fall into a spear-lined Ilongot pit. This, he explained, was the headhunters' way of keeping villagers in line. If the trapped man was found by a young headhunter out to prove his manhood, his head became the Ilongot's trophy.

I was sure the Ilongots suspected that the barrios were supplying us with rice; their next step would be to try taking some of this from us. I had been certain this situation would arise sooner or later. Now that it had, we would have to continue taking extra precautions, even increasing the number of safety measures already in effect.

When the men went back with Juan to collect the rest of the supplies, they went in a larger group than usual, and I told them to be doubly alert for even the slightest indication that Ilongots were in the area. As he was leaving, I told Juan that if the Dabubuans wished, when they went hunting some of my men could go along for added protection. Juan was sure his father would appreciate that help.

Lieutenant Reyes and eight men left with Juan, promising to be careful and not to loiter. They returned at noon the next day with the other two sacks of rice, and the sacks of camotes, bananas, peas, greens, and dried fish. There were even bandages, aspirin, and a few quinine pills—and a surprise: Teniente Leaño's daughters had found out somehow that I had had a birthday and had sent along some cookies. I didn't feel right celebrating just my birthday; so, I told the cook we were going to have a big party and celebrate all our birthdays that night. It was a good birthday party in spite of the fact that ants had gotten into the rice cakes. (We ate them anyway, ants and all.)

As the first of February approached, the number of hunts increased, and there were always plenty of volunteers to act as guards and bring back the bounty. The men were careful to go in large groups and remain watchful for signs of headhunters.

Valdez went out with a group of seven men on one occasion, and when they returned he reported that they had come upon an Ilongot campsite. He said you could smell it before you could see it. The Ilongots never dug latrines. They just moved when the site got too dirty. The odor carried. Near their campsite, the men had been very careful where they stepped because there were traps all over the place.

Now it was time to get Campsite Four ready. Lieutenant Vea left with twelve men to get it cleaned up. They took along enough supplies to last them for a few days until we joined them. If Vea and his group were attacked by anyone, they were to use the rifles. I knew the Japanese wouldn't enter the jungle again except in large numbers, and at the moment, the Ilongots presented more of a danger to us anyway. Vea was to take all necessary precautions, day and night, for the protection of his men.

On the following day the rest of us cleaned up Campsite Five, covering the latrines and camouflaging the area. Then we packed all our supplies, weapons, and ammunition and left for Campsite Four. Everyone was in good spirits.

Lieutenant Vea had done an excellent job of cleaning up the camp, and I complimented him. He always responded to a compliment for a job well done by working even harder. He was a good officer, and he always carried out orders, even though he tended to be easygoing and casual, swinging his long arms and moving leisurely about his tasks.

That evening Vea reported with a grin that we had another soldier in the camp. It seemed that the big tree in front of our camp was now the daytime home of a large, pregnant monkey. I looked up in the tree but couldn't see anything. Vea said she probably would be back in the morning.

When Vea's group had reached Campsite Four, they checked the pits we had dug in the hope of catching wild pigs and found blood in one of them, and also more headhunter footprints. We all wondered if we had finally caught a wild pig or some other animal. Whatever it

293

was, the Ilongots had enjoyed it—unless it had been an Ilongot who had fallen in. Vea and his men had dug new pits, and we made the rounds of the camp to familiarize ourselves with these and with all the old ones, too.

Although we would have to cut back on food again—I didn't know how long our Spanish friends could continue to help us—we were all glad to be back at Campsite Four, and to give everyone something to look forward to, we could have one really good meal a week.

After a good night's rest, I woke early and walked out the cave's front entrance. The listening post was laughing, and hearing rustling above me, I looked up: there was the largest monkey I had ever seen in the Philippines. She was eyeing me and, like other monkeys before her, seemed especially fascinated by my beard and long hair. I talked to her, calling her *dalaga*, which means girl in the Tagalog dialect; the name stuck, and from then on, everyone called her Dalaga. If I waved at her or gestured, she would imitate me. Toward evening she would disappear, but she would always be back the next day. She was a source of endless amusement to us, and the men agreed not to harm her. Once in a while, she would drop some of the wild fruit she ate, which we had seen growing in the jungle but were not too sure about eating. Now that we had seen her eat this, a squad of men went out to look for more of it. They came back with a basketful; it was delicious. Dalaga didn't know it, but she was teaching us a few things about survival. There were other roots and berries she dropped that we searched for to add to our own diet. Sometimes we tried to coax her into giving us some of what she was eating. Sometimes she would!

It was not long before Dalaga knew her name, and she was a joy to all of us—most of the time, that is. One morning as I was coming out of the cave, I called to her. I had no sooner said her name than she defecated on my head. I looked up, and there she was grinning and jumping up and down and pointing at me. The men laughed all day about that. I went down to the stream and had a good bath.

As well as adding to our food supply, the wild-pig hunts helped to break the monotony for us. I decided to go along on the next one in the hope of gleaning some news. It was nearly the first of March 1944,

294

and we had been at Campsite Four for almost a month. I was getting anxious for news. It was difficult to make any kind of plans when we didn't know for sure what the situation was outside the local areas.

The men had been listening for the sounds of a hunt for a couple of days when Dolatre reported that he thought two hunts were in progress, one to the north, and one to the south of us. He and Vea said they would take a group and head toward the south hunt; Valdez and I took a group toward the north one. I hoped Teniente Leaño would have news from Jones.

We made contact with the teniente just as he and his men were closing in on two large pigs. I told Leaño we had moved to a different campsite, and also that there was evidence the headhunters were moving about the territory. He said there were seven or eight rifles in his barrio, and in the future, he and his group would carry a few when they went out hunting. The villagers were aware that the Ilongots knew we were getting supplies from them, and he warned us to continue moving in large groups.

There were supplies for us from Villanueva and Rodriquez in Dabubu, and, Leaño said, the Japanese had quit patrolling the barrios. He wondered, had I seen the leaflets making me a major and asking me to come in and surrender? I said I couldn't surrender now; I had a *magandá* (beautiful) dalaga in camp with me. He knew what the Tagalog words meant, and a very surprised look spread over his face until Sergeant Valdez explained about our pet monkey, adding the information that she had shat on my head. Leaño was still laughing when we left to go back to camp. He advised me to come to the barrio for another haircut and beard trim; then, he said, maybe the monkey wouldn't pick on me.

Later, Vea and Dolatre returned to camp with their group and reported that Juan had told them he had heard the Americans were taking a heavy toll of Japanese ships and planes.

Lieutenant Reyes had already left for Dabubu to pick up our supplies by the time I awoke the following morning. I wasn't feeling well, and I asked some of the men to stand guard while I bathed and went for a swim in the stream, hoping that would help me feel better. By the time I had finished, I knew another attack of malaria was coming on.

Although dengue fever was always present in our camp, most of the others seemed to be immune to malaria.

This was to be the worst attack during my stay in the islands. I was delirious for almost a week. When I came out of it, I was nothing but skin and bones. The men had caught a wild chicken and Sergeant Valdez had been feeding me the broth. I didn't remember any of this. Valdez said I had done a lot of praying while I was delirious, and the men had prayed for my recovery. I said the Lord must have answered their prayers, and I thanked the men for their concern.

The next day, Valdez asked if he and some of the other men could go to Manuri for any news. I said it would be all right as long as he took at least six men with him. I was moving about now and trying to regain some of my strength, but it would take several good meals before I could even think about resuming my daily exercising.

Late that afternoon, Sergeant Valdez returned with some supplies, including tobacco leaves and a large jar of what looked like colored water. He said the solution had been made from bark that contained quinine. I asked him if that was why he had wanted to go into the barrio. He said yes, they were all afraid if I had another attack like this latest one, I might not make it back to the States. The men's concern was evident, and I thanked them very much. We had become a very loyal group of men concerned about each other's welfare. A sense of mutual trust had grown out of our shared adversity.

Sergeant Valdez said Teniente Leaño had said for me to take a couple of swallows of the bitter drink before each meal. In about a week, I felt much better and had gained back some of the weight I had lost.

During my convalescence, my friend Dalaga was a welcome visitor and a pleasure to watch. She must have wondered what had happened to me, because the first time she saw me after my illness, she jumped up and down, making all kinds of gestures. She amused all of us for hours with her antics. One of the men remarked that if she weren't a girl, we could induct her into our unit. Dalaga stayed in our vicinity until she was about ready to give birth; after that we never saw her again.

From the news Valdez had brought back from Manuri it sounded as though the American forces were bypassing some of the Japanese-occupied islands. It might be just a matter of time before the enemy would have to concentrate its forces closer to the possible troop-landing areas of Luzon, which meant the Japanese would be moving out of the Jones and Echague areas altogether, withdrawing their soldiers to the coast. Teniente Leaño didn't think the Japanese had any troops left in Pinappagan. They were moving a lot of their men out of Jones at this time, but no one had any information about where they were being moved to. And there was still no word from Major Roberts.

CHAPTER 35

The Ilongots Raid Our Camp

Late one night, I was awakened by one of the listening posts. Everything was too quiet. The night noises had stopped. He suspected something, or someone, was out there. Quietly, I awakened all the others.

I had no sooner finished whispering my instructions to be on the alert than an arrow came whizzing through the main entrance of the cave. Valdez grabbed his BAR and opened fire. I gave orders for the listening posts to open fire and spray the area from right to left in front of them as far as they could see. There was a scream, and then all was quiet. I asked if anyone had been hurt by the arrow. One of the men said it had lodged in a sack of camotes.

We didn't get any more sleep that night and waited apprehensively until dawn to see what would happen next. Nothing happened. But at daybreak, we found two dead Ilongots, and a wounded one trapped in a pit, where he was pulling bamboo slivers out of his feet. This Ilongot was only a young boy, and he had a flesh wound where Valdez had caught him with the first burst of the BAR. The men wanted to kill him.

Recognizing an opportunity, I told them no, that we would take care of his wounds, heal, and feed him; then we would use him to make contact with his tribe. Maybe we would be able to reach an understanding with these Ilongots. The men were a little doubtful, but I thought it was worth a try.

The boy couldn't have been more than fourteen years old. He was about four-and-a-half-feet tall and had small wide feet with very widespread toes. His hair was long and black, and he wore a G-string and carried a bolo. We showed him the two Ilongots we had killed. His expression never changed until Valdez told him we were going to feed the dead bodies to the wild pigs. That scared him. He may have thought he would be next. He obviously understood enough Ilocano to get the message. When Valdez asked, how many men attacked us? he shook his head. Explaining that the headhunters couldn't count, Valdez drew pictures of men on the ground—first one, then two, three, four, five, six. When he got to ten, the boy nodded his head, pointed, crossed out two; then he pointed to himself and crossed out another. Apparently seven had gotten away. Perhaps some of those were wounded, but the boy didn't seem to understand anything further; so we couldn't find out any more.

About a week later after slowly gaining the boy's confidence, we asked him to communicate with his tribe. He was to say we had taken care of him, fed him, and made him well. Also, he was to assure his tribesmen we wouldn't harm them. Yells and calls back and forth in the Ilongot dialect went on for three days before they produced results. At last, an Ilongot man appeared at the edge of the camp. Although he probably wasn't more than thirty-five, he looked about seventy years old, partly because of his dark color: Ilongots are darker than other Filipinos. He was dressed in a G-string and carried a bolo. He understood some Ilocano, and he said he was the boy's father.

I had Valdez ask him why his tribe attacked us. He said they needed rice and camotes. Valdez asked him why they didn't grow their own. He replied that it wasn't their custom. In the past, he said, they had traded fish for rice and greens and, in turn, had allowed the Christians to hunt as far as the end of the trails. Now the Christians had no food to give them, and they were going beyond the trails to hunt wild pigs anyway.

I asked Valdez, "Who told them they owned the jungles?" The man answered that his father and his father's father had told them. Then I had Valdez show him the BAR, fire a quick burst, and announce in no uncertain terms, "We now control the jungles, and if you ever attack us or any of the Christians, we will hunt you down and kill all of you, including your women and children." I asked Valdez if the headhunter understood, and Valdez said he was sure he did.

299

We told the Ilongot we had very little rice, but if his people would bring us live fish, we would give them some rice and camotes and return his son. I emphasized that we wanted live fish; there was always the possibility dead ones might be poisoned. The man agreed, and Valdez told him to be back by Friday. Then the segeant said, "Hell, these headhunters don't have names for the days of the week." Taking a piece of rattan, he tied three knots in it and told the Ilongot, when the sun went down, he should cut off a knot; the next day when the sun went down, he should cut off the second knot; and he should return on the third day with the fish, adding that he could bring his companions if he wanted, and we would give him his son and the food.

Before the man left, he squatted on the ground and drew a picture of the sun on the horizon; he moved his finger from sunrise to sunset and then took his bolo and made a motion to cut the knot. Valdez nodded. I had Valdez ask him one more question: how many others had we hit when they raided our camp? The Ilongot drew a picture of two men and said they had both died. I told him we would have some tobacco for them if they brought enough fish. He said something to his son and left. Valdez remarked that he thought he could pick up their dialect in a short time because it probably consisted of no more than a hundred words.

Two days after this, Juan returned to camp with some information for us. The Japanese had sent out small patrols to all the barrios on the east side of the Cagayan the day after we fired on the headhunters. It wasn't possible that the shots had been heard in Jones, and this meant there definitely were informers in a nearby barrio, probably one on the west side of the river. Juan thought he knew who some of these turncoats were, but I wanted definite proof before we took any action against civilians.

He asked how many Ilongots we had killed. We told him two at the time, and two more who died later of wounds, according to the information given us by the boy's father. Juan decided to stay in camp overnight so that he could meet the Ilongots when they came with the fish. He knew a few words of Ilongot and was able to communicate with the young boy, who indicated he knew Juan, although Juan wasn't sure he knew him. Juan thought possibly the boy might have seen him during some prewar food-gathering trip to Dabubu.

300

I asked Juan what people had told the Japanese patrol about the rifle fire. He explained they had said it sounded like it came from beyond the trails, inside Ilongot territory. They had assured the Japanese some of the guerrillas must have been killed because the headhunters attack at night, and the guerrillas would have been taken by surprise. Where the guerrillas could have come from no one seemed to know. After all, hadn't the Japanese announced they had killed most of them? These answers had seemed to satisfy the Japanese; they were the same ones being given in all the barrios.

The following morning eight of the Ilongot men showed up, including the boy's father, with plenty of fish. They were dressed in G-strings and carried bolos; however, this time they had no bows and arrows with them. Evidently they wanted to come as friends so that they could get the boy back and arrange for future bartering.

Most of the fish they brought were still alive, and their method of fishing was obviously more successful than ours. Ilongots dive for their fish, and these they had caught with their bare hands; when liveness does not matter, they spear them.

We gave the group a quarter-sack of rice and a few camotes, including the one with the arrow in it. Juan asked if the camote was worth the loss of four men—and the near loss of their leader's son. (We had determined that the boy's father was their tribal leader.) The Ilongot men agreed it wasn't worth that price. I told the chief again, if any more attacks were made on guerrilla forces, we would wipe out all of them, leaving none alive. But, if they brought us fresh fish now and then, we would help them.

He promised there would be no more raids, and that after this, they would call out before entering the camp. I said that would be fine and extended my hand. He looked at it, and finally it must have dawned on him that I wanted to make an agreement. We shook hands. I patted the boy on the head and told him to go with his father. The boy wanted to know if he could have one of the rifles. I said, "No, you might think yourself a warrior and try to kill us." I told his father to spread the word among the tribes that we wanted to live in peace with them. As the group left, Juan told them "When our enemies are driven from the surrounding barrios, we will go back to planting rice

301

and there will be some for all the Ilongot tribes if you remain friendly."

The next morning, after reminding us that the Ilongots have a very short memory and we should not trust them, Juan left to go home. I asked him not to risk coming into the jungle alone unless it was an emergency. We could contact him in the barrio every week or so for news, or find him during a hunt. Conceivably, Juan could be in some danger from now on because the headhunters knew he was our friend. I had no intention of trusting the Ilongots; I knew they were treacherous, and I suspected they would want revenge for the whipping they had taken. I intended never to give them the chance for it. I told the men we would still travel in groups of six or more.

When the next hunt took place, Vea again volunteered to go. There was no problem getting enough men to go with him because they all enjoyed the chase. From the yipping and yapping, it sounded like half the barrio was out with its dogs. I remembered how, when my grandfather's dogs had cornered a rabbit, badger, or other wild animal, long before I could see it, I could hear by the changed sound of the barking that their prey was cornered.

Vea returned to camp with a message sent through Teniente Reyes from Teniente Leaño that there were supplies in Manuri for us from Señors Villanueva and Rodriquez, and that I was welcome to come along with my men when they came to collect them.

Valdez and six of the men accompanied me into Manuri the next morning. After checking to make sure there were no Japanese patrols in the area, we spent some time at the pleasant bathing spot near the barrio, swimming and washing our clothes before presenting ourselves at the teniente's hut.

During lunch with the Leaño family, I described the Ilongots' raid on our camp, and our arrangement with them to exchange rice for live fresh fish. The teniente was very interested in my account but advised me against trusting the Ilongots. I assured him I had no intention of letting my guard down where they were concerned.

After lunch, Rosa, Lucie, and Mrs. Leaño set up their impromptu barbershop, and we were all treated to haircuts, which in my case also included a beard trim. There certainly were times when I missed the

302

amenities of civilized life; and, I thought, for the rest of my life, I would really appreciate even such a simple thing as a haircut.

Our Spanish friends had told Teniente Leaño that the Japanese were concentrating more of their forces along the coast. They had bivouac areas near the larger cities, and at certain air strips such as the one at the provincial capital of Ilagan in Isabela. They were now patrolling north and south from Ilagan by truck. In unguarded moments, when they were drinking in social situations, for example at Señor Villanueva's, the Japanese officers admitted they had lost some islands in the South Pacific to MacArthur and were on the defensive; but, they still insisted they would win the war. At the same time, however, they looked worried!

They also asked probing questions concerning the whereabouts of Major Roberts and "Major" Hieb. They definitely knew I was in the area and reiterated the offer of amnesty for us if we would surrender; no doubt, they were fairly certain this would reach our ears. I said, "Teniente, you know how I feel about surrendering, especially now that the war has turned in our favor."

Our discussion turned to the profusion of hunting taking place since the opportunity to barter wild pig for rice had arisen, and Leaño said he had heard of Teniente Reyes's big kill of four pigs a few days ago. He was planning a hunt himself in a few days and asked if some of my men could meet him on the trail when they heard his dogs. Sergeant Valdez volunteered at once, as did the other men. I assured the teniente that anytime he needed men for anything, all he had to do was ask, and I would be pleased to grant any reasonable request.

As time for the evening meal approached, the teniente said he expected us to join his family, and also to be his overnight guests. I said we would be happy to stay; however, we didn't want to jeopardize the lives of his people. He assured me the village's excellent warning system was still proving to be most effective in giving advance warning of any approaching Japanese patrols—or outside informers.

The men and I were ready for a good meal, and the steady stream of neighbors bringing food had not gone unnoticed by any of us. Our host brought out some basi, and everyone enjoyed a few glasses of this strong rice wine. It was pleasant to relax and forget for a time the miserable conditions we had been living under for longer than any of us cared to remember. Rosa, Lucie, and Mrs. Leaño placed a feast before us, and we did justice to it, which pleased them very much. We ate as though we hadn't had food in a month; and then more basi followed the repast.

In the midst of friends, and in the comfort of having shared a civilized meal and a glass of wine, for some reason the song "Oh Johnny, Oh Johnny, How You Can Love" came to my mind from out of the past. I had enjoyed the big band renditions of this song and had danced to it before the war; now I began to hum the melody. Rosa and Lucie immediately wanted to know if I would teach them the words to a real American song; so, I sang it while they copied down the words. Then we all sang it together. In return, they taught me an Ilocano song I still remember. That evening stands out in my memory as a pleasant oasis of warmth and friendship during a time of deprivation and uncertainty.

The next morning, after thanking Teniente Leaño and his family for their hospitality, we returned to camp loaded down with supplies. I noticed on the hike back that I was gradually regaining my strength.

CHAPTER 36

We Add a New Danger to Our List

I had never had a problem with my teeth, but the evening after our return from Manuri I was tormented by a toothache that kept me awake all night. I even considered having one of the men pull the tooth, but the risk of infection worried me. The next day my entire jaw was sore and swollen, and I couldn't eat. Lieutenant Reyes took a look and said my teeth looked perfect except for the swelling where a wisdom tooth should be.

The second day I was still in misery and unable to eat. We could hear the sounds of Teniente Leaño's hunt beginning, and when Sergeant Valdez left with his men to join it, I asked him to find out from the teniente what was used to cure a toothache, especially of a wisdom tooth. The tooth throbbed all day, and I sat and waited for Valdez to return, hoping that Leaño knew of something that would relieve the pain.

When Valdez returned, he had some basi, which he and Leaño thought might ease the pain, and the teniente had suggested putting green tobacco leaves on the swollen area—which I did—and had said some people chewed betel nut, which they claimed kept them from getting toothaches. I tried this but thought more likely it would just slowly rot away my teeth. Placing the green tobacco leaves on the swollen area seemed to give me the most relief. I still couldn't eat, but a shot of the basi at night helped me get some sleep. After about a week, the wisdom tooth came through and the pain was gone. Now it was essential to regain my strength because a tough task lay ahead of us: preparing for the landing of the American forces. There would be plenty of planning and work to do.

The month of May was approaching. Early one morning someone called out near the camp. It was the Ilongots, with fresh fish—and plenty of them. We took stock of our rice supply and gave them a little of that and some corn, explaining that we were running short of rice ourselves. They asked for camotes and tobacco, which we gave them. They left, quite as pleased with their end of the bargain as we were later with our meal of fried fresh fish.

Lieutenant Reyes returned one day from assisting at one of the hunts with the news that the Japanese were pulling out of Jones by the hundreds. He said, "The rumor is there are no more enemy troops in the Pinappagan area." I said, "Major Roberts is probably living in one of the barrios there." I was wondering why we hadn't heard from him in almost two years. Surely if he had been captured or was dead, we would have heard the news or at least a rumor to that effect. I had a feeling it wouldn't be too long before we would be able to move about more freely in the barrios without endangering the lives of the inhabitants. We might possibly be able to make personal contact with Roberts.

I asked Sergeant Dannug for the log he had been keeping so that I could check the entries since the Pinappagan raid. I read through it from that date on. Dannug had made all the proper entries, covering all the events that had taken place, and the log made very interesting reading. If the plans I had been considering materialized, there would be more to add before we were done. I remarked to Dannug, "You know, this sounds like it would make one damn good book." He said the same thought had occurred to him. I told him when we came out of the jungle, I would give the log to someone I could trust. (Through a series of misfortunes, the log was lost, together with the lives of several civilians charged with its safekeeping.)

Rumors of guerrilla units in the mountain provinces and the central-plains area north of Manila persisted. Someone, I thought, would have to organize these guerrilla units into a fighting force, whether a battalion, regiment, or division. I knew there were approximately 150 men in the area who could be trusted, and who would join my group of 45 men, making us a very efficient fighting outfit. Some of these men were

306

former soldiers I had trained who had married Ilocano women and were living in the area; some were soldiers who had been imprisoned at Camp O'Donnell and then released after a few months. There were also soldiers who had been dispersed by Colonel Nakar at Pinappagan with instructions to set up message centers for the bamboo telegraph.

At a meeting with Lieutenants Reyes and Vea and the noncommissioned officers, I briefed them on part of the plan I had in mind for gathering the men. I told Lieutenant Vea to bring Juan back to camp with him the next time he went to Dabubu. To carry out my plans, I needed accurate information, and I hoped Juan would be able to get it for me. I was sure we could find enough weapons and ammunition to arm the soldiers we gathered. If not, we would use the Japanese weapons we had hidden; and, there was always the possibility of ambushing the enemy and collecting more of these. I wanted to organize a good fighting force, and we would get the weapons for it somehow.

During this period while we waited for the Americans to return, groups of Huks (Communists) and other bandits roamed the countryside, taking advantage of the uncertain situation to maraud and terrorize the general population for their own benefit. Many of the bandit groups called themselves guerrilla units and had self-appointed officers, from 1st lieutenants to majors. They robbed the barrios and at times actually attacked them, terrorizing the inhabitants. This lawless behavior and the unnecessary acts of terrorism were unforgivable, and I decided if I had the chance, I would see to it that these bandits were dealt a taste of their own methods. Above all, I wanted to make sure the fighting forces my men and I created did not mistreat the civilian population. The men we gathered would be fighting for the freedom of the Philippines from the Japanese Imperial Forces, and not for the purposes of personal greed and aggrandizement. After the harsh treatment the people had suffered under the Japanese, they deserved an honorable fighting force that maintained their national interests.

When the next hunt from Dabubu began, Vea left with a group of men to intercept the hunters. I asked him to get the latest news and to bring Juan back with him the following day. Valdez left at the same time with a group to join the hunt from Manuri. He returned four hours later, a bit disappointed that the hunt had flushed out only two

307

pigs. He had learned that there was only one company of Japanese, a little over one hundred men, left in Jones with some BC. The Japanese were definitely concentrating their forces in other locations. Villanueva and Rodriquez thought they now had large troop concentrations in the following areas: the Lingayan Gulf; the provincial capital of Ilocos Norte, the city of Laoag; and the provincial capital of Ilocos Sur, the city of Vigan. There were also the bandit groups calling themselves guerrilla forces, and of course the Huks, terrorizing the people in the barrios in and around Santiago and Echague.

Lieutenant Vea and his men returned to camp the next afternoon with Juan, a few supplies, and a small portion of wild pig. I asked Juan if he could get me the names of 14th Infantry soldiers by contacting Lieutenants Aviles, Cruz, and Galima, who I was sure had a list of soldiers absolutely loyal to the Phil-American cause. He said he knew he could get the names of at least 125 loyal men through these officers. As for weapons and ammunition, he felt there would be no problem, because every barrio had weapons hidden, and he knew most of the soldiers had hidden theirs. I told him we would wait a few days in order to give me time to form my plans; then I would like to have him accompany me on a trip to Manuri to consult Teniente Leaño.

We had Ilongot visitors again the following day, and they brought a good catch of live fish. They had heard the dogs barking the day before, and they figured we now had rice. We gave them a quarter-sack of this, a few camotes, and more tobacco leaves. I asked Juan to explain to them that our rice supply was low, and that, for the time being, we would not be able to trade as often as before.

Things had been fairly quiet around the camp, when one day— almost in our backyard—we heard the squeal of a wild pig. My first thought was that we had finally caught one in a pit. The noise seemed to be coming from near the spot where we usually took our baths, and we had a pit in that area. When we reached the scene of all the commotion, the pig was really squealing; but, it wasn't in the pit; instead, it was right behind the log where we usually sat after our baths, and the life was being squeezed out of it by a monstrous python. The pig was putting up a tremendous fight, but the python just kept wrapping itself tighter.

We shot the python, and boloed the boar. After stretching out the snake, which was reddish grey and patterned with a longitudinal ladder of broad dark stripes, I found a bamboo pole of about my height and measured its length. It was a little more than twenty feet long. Juan cut it open and chopped out the liver, which we all tasted along with a good-size portion of wild pig for our evening meal. Eating python's liver was supposed to give courage, according to Juan.

He said python are usually found near water, where they hide behind logs, foliage, or rocks, or hang from tree branches. They feed on small mammals, which they kill by coiling around them and squeezing until they suffocate. Pythons do not crush their prey. Some of the large kind found in the jungles of Luzon can kill and swallow goats and pigs. Only on rare occasions have they killed humans. However, Juan said the barrio had lost a number of unwary young men to pythons, which had caught them while they were out hunting. He cautioned us to go in groups of at least two men and to always carry a bolo for protection. He added that, after a kill, a python will wait up to a month before striking again—that is, if the prey is as large as a person or a wild boar.

I asked the men, how many times had we sat on that log? In all likelihood, that snake had been lying in wait for weeks behind the log we had been using as a bench by our swimming hole. From now on, we would have to watch trees, fallen logs, rocks, and all other places where a python could blend in with the scenery; we duly added large python to our list of possible dangers. When we buried this one's remains away from camp, it took three men to roll it into the hole.

This incident brought to mind a horror story I had been told not long after my first arrival in the Philippines. According to the story, an officer had gone horseback riding in the jungle on Corregidor; his horse had returned alone to the post, half-crazed with fear. When a search party retraced the path taken by the officer, lying across it the men found a huge python that was obviously engorged with a large object. The python was killed and cut open: inside was the body of the officer. The search party speculated that the python had been waiting in the branches of a tree, and when the officer passed, it dropped down on him, knocking him from the horse, which would account for the state the horse was in when it returned to the post.

309

The next day, Juan, Reyes, Valdez, four of the other men, and I made the hike to Manuri, arriving just before lunchtime. As had become our habit, we refreshed ourselves by bathing in the stream and washing our clothes. Soap was no longer available in the barrio, but Teniente Leaño brought us some ashes to use in its place. This worked very well. We never did find out what kind of tree or shrub produced these ashes, but they certainly seemed to do the job.

During lunch, I told Leaño about the twenty-foot python that had supplied us with part of a meal. He said he had heard the shot and thought we had shot either a pig or an Ilongot. He asked me if I had eaten any of the python's liver, and I said I had had my share. He said, "That's good. Now you will live to see your family and friends in the States." I replied that I was confident I would outlive the war.

CHAPTER 37

The Betrayers of Captain Cushing

Later in the day, the conversation in Teniente Leaño's home turned to a discussion of the pro-Japanese, or fifth columnists. We had been keeping a log of all fifth columnists: who they were; their activities; and the help they had been giving to the Japanese forces. Our intelligence information came as always via the bamboo telegraph; from friendly tenientes; and also from Señors Villanueva and Rodriquez. On the west side of the Cagayan River, most of the people in the barrios surrounding Jones couldn't be trusted; they were fence sitters and could go either way: pro–Phil-American or pro-Japanese.

Juan began talking to Teniente Leaño about the people in Fugo Sur who had been involved in the betrayal of Captain Cushing and his men: specifically, the Hernandezes and several of their neighbors.

There have been many stories, and many names put forward, in the matter of Cushing's betrayal. At the time, Teniente Leaño had interrogated many of the barrio people who had witnessed the shooting. Without a doubt, they were betrayed by the Hernandez family, with the help of several neighbors.

On 19 September 1942, Cushing and three of his men finished their noon meal in the Hernandez hut and rested for a while before leaving. In the meantime, the Japanese had been informed that Cushing was in Fugu Sur trying to make contact with Lieutenant Colonel Nakar or any American officer of the 14th Infantry. (Nakar was not captured until 29 September.) As Cushing and his men left, they were hit by a volley of fire from the rifles of six Japanese soldiers and an equal number of BC.

Captain Cushing and two of his men were hit by the first volley. One man escaped but was later caught and executed. Although wounded, Captain Cushing continued to fire until he ran out of ammunition. The number of times he was hit depended on who told the story. He died a hero, and before his betrayal, he had done more to destroy and harass the enemy than any single officer in northern Luzon.

The rumor that Captain Cushing saved the last bullet for himself was false. He fired his last shot at the enemy and died of his wounds before the Japanese soldiers reached him. The Japanese admired Cushing for his bravery, and they gave him a military funeral. He is buried in Jones, Isabela.

The following is an excerpt from Colonel Horan's diary:

> "Walter Cushing was one of the many miners who received a commission. His knowledge of demolition was the cause [of] destruction of enemy convoys which included more than a thousand enemy casualties. I recommended him for major before he left the 121st Infantry headquarters on a mission to Manila. He left thinking his rank to major would be approved."

Horan surrendered to the Japanese while Cushing was in Manila, and the captain assumed command of the 121st Infantry upon his return.

While Colonel Horan was a prisoner, Cushing was in direct contact with him and offered to help him escape. Horan declined the offer on the grounds that the consequences for other prisoners of war and for the Filipino population could be disastrous. He asked Cushing to carry on the guerrilla warfare and to gather intelligence information to be forwarded to Australia. When Cushing left for the province of Isabela, he knew Colonel Nakar was in possession of a radio transmitter.

It was during this contact with Horan while he was held prisoner that Cushing was told Horan had received no reply to his recommendation to promote Cushing to major. Cushing's official status was captain and commanding officer of the 121st Infantry Regiment; however, most Filipinos referred to him as Major Cushing.

I told Teniente Leaño, Lieutenant Reyes, Sergeant Valdez, and Sgt. Juan Reyes that those responsible for the betrayal and deaths of Cushing and his men should be executed. Leaño volunteered to go with my soldiers to eliminate the traitors; but, I said this was our job. After reestablishing that the principal betrayers of Captain Cushing had indeed been Hernandez and his two sons, I ordered Reyes, Valdez, and Juan to execute them. I gave the order in May 1944, nearly two years after the event, and nearly two years after our original raid, when, not knowing all the details, I had restricted the retaliation to the taking of food supplies only. We would take necessary action against the other neighbors involved in Cushing's betrayal at a later date.

We began to plan the raid. I asked Teniente Leaño if there were some way we could get Mrs. Hernandez out of the family's hut on the night the retaliatory execution was to take place. He said that wouldn't be a problem; Mrs. Hernandez was a midwife and there were many women in the surrounding barrios who were with child, including a relative of his, on our side of the river, who had used Mrs. Hernandez as her midwife several times before. This relative, he said, was now pregnant again and was using another midwife. Leaño said he would ask his relative to contact Mrs. Hernandez to act as the midwife when the time came, which he thought would be soon.

Next we selected the complete team for the raid. Juan, Lieutenant Reyes, Sergeant Valdez, and two Ilocano soldiers, whom Valdez would pick, would be our hit men.

Before we left Manuri the next morning, I asked Teniente Leaño to notify Teniente Reyes or Juan (whom I would send back to Dabubu after we arrived back in our camp) when Mrs. Hernandez would be needed as midwife so the exact time of the raid could be set. Leaño said he would like to see it happen immediately. He was truly a loyal Phil-American patriot. We bid him good-bye and left for our camp.

That afternoon I told Vea, Dolatre, and Dannug of my order to eliminate three of Cushing's betrayers. The order was entered in our daily log, including the names of the men who would participate in the raid. I was pleased that Lieutenant Reyes had volunteered because I had anyway intended to ask him to lead the raiding party. I wanted to

313

go, but I thought it best that the Philippine men take care of their own betrayers.

I discussed the plans with Lieutenant Reyes, Sergeant Valdez, Juan, and the two men Valdez had picked. We decided it would be best to have someone enter Fugu Sur looking for rice, to be sure no Japanese or BC were in the barrio. Before the raid was made, this precautionary step would be coordinated with Teniente Leaño. There was very little danger involved; but, the timing was important.

It was decided that the team would go upstream, north past Fugu Sur, then they would double back on foot. They were to take meat along to give Hernandez's dogs to prevent their barking. They would approach the hut, call out Hernandez's name and ask for his wife, saying she was needed. As soon as Hernandez answered that his wife was out, they would throw in a hand grenade and spray the hut with rifle fire. Finally, they would need to go into the hut to make certain Hernandez and his two sons were dead.

The following day, after we had gone over the plan a number of times, Juan returned to Dabubu accompanied by the two Ilocano soldiers chosen by Valdez. Juan was to remain in the barrio, while the other two were to return to camp when word came from Teniente Leaño; and if there were any supplies available, they were to bring them back at the same time.

Several weeks later, Valdez's two soldiers returned with supplies, and with word from Leaño that Hernandez's wife was out of the barrio of Fugu Sur and would be away from home for at least three days. There had been no Japanese patrols in the area of that barrio for over a week. Tenientes Leaño and Reyes thought the raid should take place that very night or certainly the following night, if no enemy patrols were in the area.

Positive they could complete the mission that same night, the men of the raiding party left at noon for Dabubu to pick up Juan. I wished them good luck and said I would pray for their safe return. I told Lieutenant Reyes to take all necessary precautions, and not to take any unnecessary chances; I wanted no casualties.

That night I found it impossible to sleep. Sometime after midnight several of the listening posts called out to say they had heard shooting.

Noting the time, I planned to check with the five men upon their return to see if they had fired their weapons at that particular time.

Late the following day, Lieutenant Reyes and his group returned with three sacks of rice, some camotes, peas, and dried fish—and with the report that they had followed the plan to the letter, even down to feeding the few barking dogs in order to silence them.

Reyes recounted that when they had arrived at the Hernandez hut, he called out asking for *lalaki*, or man. Hernandez had shouted back from an open window, "*Wen* apo." (Yes sir.)

The lieutenant said that they were looking for Mrs. Hernandez because a family near Jones needed her services. When Hernandez answered that his wife had already gone and asked who Reyes and his men were, Reyes yelled, "We are here to take care of you and your sons for betraying Captain Cushing."

One of the group threw a hand grenade through the open window, and Sergeant Valdez sprayed the hut with BAR fire.

When Reyes and his men kicked down the door and entered the hut, they found Hernandez and his two sons on the floor, dead; so, they searched the premises and collected up five sacks of rice and some other food the family had hoarded. Before leaving, they left this note on the senior Hernandez's body:

> This is in revenge for the betrayal
> of Capt. Walter Cushing.
> Guerrilla Forces, Isabela Province

On the way back, the raiding party left two of the sacks of rice with Teniente Reyes.

When I asked Lieutenant Reyes what time the raid took place, he said a little after midnight. This tallied with the time I had written down after the listening posts reported hearing shots, and it was good to know they were so alert. Now I told them to be doubly alert every minute of the day and night; the raid might very well bring the BC or Japanese back into the jungle to search for us.

Juan had remained in Dabubu to watch for any signs of enemy reaction. About a week later, he returned to report that a patrol of twenty-four Japanese and four BC was patrolling the barrios on the river's west side on a regular daily basis. This patrol had ventured over to the east side only once; when I asked Juan why he thought that was, his opinion was the same as mine: the patrol was afraid of being ambushed on the east side. Indeed, I intended later to do exactly that.

I asked Juan to return to Dabubu the following morning to get information on enemy strength in Jones, with the figure broken down into numbers of Japanese soldiers and of BC. I also wanted information on the rice and other food supplies on the west side of the river; and, above all, I wanted a list of former soldiers and officers who could be trusted.

Rumors were circulating that the American forces were closing in on the Japanese to the south of the Philippine Archipelago. On Luzon, the Japanese were moving their troops towards the west coast; to the Lingayen Gulf, the two Ilocos provinces, and the Subic Bay area. This meant there wouldn't be too much of a defense set up in the Cagayan Valley. What defense there was would consist mostly of motor patrols, and this, in my judgment, was to confuse the guerrilla forces about the enemy's exact locations and numbers. Originally, we were fooled; however, our spies informed us that these motor patrols were the same Japanese forces that had originally been in Jones. The Japanese were now covering the entire Cagayan Valley with one regiment, or less than half the troops they had had previously in the Jones area alone. There were no enemy troops left in the Pinappagan area.

We received word by way of the bamboo telegraph that there were large numbers of organized guerrilla forces in northern Luzon, and they were trying to contact Major Roberts. I told the men, if we didn't hear or receive orders from Roberts in the next month or two, we would gather what trustworthy men and officers we could in the Jones area and go to join the other units. It was my opinion, based on whatever information I could gather, that I could build up my force to about 175 loyal officers and enlisted men willing to fight. I knew if we split into small units for the purpose of travel, we would have no problem crossing enemy lines. We could avoid patrols by skirting municipalities and using the bamboo-telegraph route; and, we would be abetted by friendly pro–Phil-American civilians.

About a week and a half later, Juan showed up in camp with more detailed information about enemy strength. The figure varied from five hundred to fifteen hundred Japanese troops, and included one hundred permanent BC.

It was confirmed via the bamboo telegraph that the enemy forces were being concentrated in strategic areas. Only a few small garrisons remained in the outlying municipalities. For the most part, municipalities were being patrolled by motorized units, and barrios were not patrolled at all anymore.

Teniente Leaño sent a man to Pinappagan who verified that there were no Japanese there. He did hear that Major Roberts, one American corporal, six Filipino soldiers, and one Filipino officer, Captain Dingcong, were safe in the immediate vicinity. The barrios in that area were supplying them with rice, and on occasion the men would stay overnight in one or another of them.

Juan gave me a list of approximately a hundred loyal soldiers and three officers who were ready to join us. According to his information, these men still had their weapons and some ammunition, which they had hidden from the Japanese, and they were ready to join our force anytime we needed them. He also said the Japanese finally were admitting the Americans would be trying to retake the Philippines; however, they insisted the Imperial Forces would drive us back and sink our navy.

We were hearing rumors now that American submarines were bringing supplies to some of the Visayan islands to the south of us. We also heard that supplies were being landed in northern Luzon. Since such supply drops had to be coordinated for locations and times, there had to be operational radio contact between MacArthur's headquarters and some of the guerrilla units.

I called a meeting of all the officers and men that night and told them my plans for moving north to the mountain provinces and joining up with the guerrilla forces there. Then I told Juan I was going to give him a message for Major Roberts, telling him my plans. Juan was to return to Dabubu now and report back to me in a week. If I still hadn't heard from Major Roberts by then, Juan was to deliver my message. This was sometime during June 1944.

CHAPTER 38

Major Roberts Arrives

Juan returned three days later with a message from Major Roberts ordering me to send an officer to Pinappagan to guide him to my headquarters or camp. His messenger was waiting at Teniente Reyes's hut.

I had two officers. As usual, Lieutenant Reyes volunteered, saying he needed a change of scenery. He left immediately for Pinappagan, via Dabubu, taking Sergeant Dannug with him. I was to meet them, and Major Roberts, at Teniente Reyes's place on their return, and the lieutenant was to send a runner ahead to notify me of their expected arrival time.

About a week later Juan showed up, informed me Major Roberts would be in the barrio the following day, and said his father wanted me to stay with him until the major's arrival. I left Lieutenant Vea in charge of the camp.

Juan and I made good time. It was cloudy and looked like rain. The monsoon season was beginning. We reached the barrio in mid-afternoon. I took a bath in a nearby creek. After so many months of wearing cut-off shorts, I felt a little strange in the remnants of my khaki trousers and shirt, carefully saved against future need. Torn and ragged as these were, however, and considering my two and a half years in the jungle, I felt fairly presentable for the meeting with my commanding officer.

I decided to wait for Major Roberts in another hut, some distance from Teniente Reyes's, in the event something had gone wrong. I was in the habit of taking necessary precautions rather than unnecessary risks.

After lunch the next day, I spotted Major Roberts heading toward the teniente's hut. I called out to him. He turned and we looked at each other. It was an emotional meeting. He looked thin and haggard and was barefoot. We shook hands. He said, "It's been a long time." "Yes sir," I said, "but we have something to look forward to now: the landing of American troops and going on the offensive against the Japanese."

I asked him if he had heard of an American colonel who had already organized a division of guerrilla forces. Roberts said he'd heard rumors of large guerrilla units in the mountain provinces but had received no messages or contact from any colonel. I mentioned the bamboo telegraph that had been set up throughout northern Luzon, and how we were getting our information via this telegraph. I reported the number of men I had in the jungle and that I had lost two men since I last saw him: Emilio, who had died of beriberi; and Koopmann, one of his own air-warning men, who had surrendered.

I told him that after the Pinappagan raid, I had proceeded to Dumabato, one of the designated rendezvous areas. There I had joined with Lieutenant Reyes and thirteen of our men; we had headed north through the jungle to our present location near Dabubu, which had been another designated rendezvous area. Here, we had located Lieutenant Vea and his men. I reported I now had a total of forty-six men, including two officers, who had been my responsibility for the past two and a half years.

I said I also had a list of over a hundred other men and a number of officers who were loyal and on whom we could depend. I told him about the circumstances of Captain Cushing's death, and that we had killed three of the civilians responsible for this.

Major Roberts asked me why Koopmann had surrendered. I explained, and I added that I had warned the men about surrendering because the Japanese did not keep their promises of amnesty. Poor Koopmann had found that out. I relayed the report I had received that the Japanese had used him for bayonet practice.

I told the major there were very few Japanese in the municipality of Jones and suggested that if he wasn't going to take any action against the BC or Japanese patrols, I would rather keep my troops in the jungle. We could move back to Campsite One, which would put us closer to the barrios and food supplies. I told him about our five

319

alternate campsites. He asked, "Why all the campsites?" I said I well remembered the raid at Pinappagan; the alternative sites had allowed us to shift location whenever danger threatened. At times moves had to be made not only because of the enemy threat, but also to get us closer to our sources of supply. This also kept my men alert: moving from one campsite to another was, in fact, good training for them.

I asked him what his plans were for the immediate future. He said he would let me know. I could see he was tired from his hike.

Juan called us for the evening meal, an especially good one in honor of Major Roberts. Roberts asked about our supply of food. I said there wasn't too much available on this side of the river, but the Spaniards had helped us. He asked, "Which Spaniards?" I said, "Señor Villanueva and Señor Rodriquez." I told him about my battles with malaria, beriberi, jaundice, and dysentery. He told me he had had beriberi but had gotten over it.

By the time we finished eating it was after dark. Both Roberts and I were tired, and we decided to say good night to our host. Major Roberts asked me how safe it really was to sleep in the hut. I explained that in the barrios, the bamboo telegraph was our security. I reassured Roberts and said I wouldn't consider sleeping in Reyes's hut unless I knew it was safe to do so. I added that since Pinappagan, this was probably only the fourth night I'd spent in a barrio and that the jungle had been my home all during this time. Satisfied, Roberts found a corner, as I also did, and we slept.

The next day we discussed in much more detail the fifth columnists' activities on the west side of the Cagayan River. I said we had a list of all the known betrayers, informers, and spies.

I described the bamboo-telegraph route to him, and told him that the Japanese were aware of the existence of such a route, which meant that occasionally the guerrilla forces would change it, whenever the Japanese caught a messenger. Civilians would carry messages hidden about them, either in the linings of their clothing or hat bands, or inside bamboo walking sticks. The best method, however, was the one favored by Teniente Leaño: wrapping the message in a cigar where it could be lit—literally allowing the messenger to smoke his way out of danger if he were caught.

I expressed my desire to contact the mysterious American colonel in northern Luzon who had been trying to contact the major for a long time. I suggested that we could gather the 170 officers and enlisted men we had and move north, following the bamboo-telegraph route. In order not to endanger any of our lives, we could divide up into small units, which would make it easier to get our men through the enemy lines; also, it would be easier for civilians to supply food to smaller groups. I suggested groups of twenty to twenty-five men, with an officer and an NCO in charge of each group; I suggested we could move out at two- or three-day intervals and use rendezvous areas.

Major Roberts said he felt moving such a number of troops might jeopardize too many lives, both civilian and military; he preferred his own idea of remaining in the area, gathering and training the men here. He added that he would give my plan some thought.

I told him that his plan would present several problems. First, the training of that many men would have to be done within the protection of the jungle, not in the barrios, which would be quite difficult considering the terrain. Second, the barrios would not be able to supply enough food to feed a group of 170 men; I had had a hell of a time trying to feed 45 men. Furthermore, the jungle would only be suitable to training in guerrilla tactics and general defensive warfare; but if all the rumors about a division being organized in northern Luzon were true, most of our fighting would be offensive. Major Roberts finally decided to get more information.

A week later we heard a large number of planes approaching from the northeast and flying toward the southwest. They had American insignia, and Roberts identified them as United States Navy bombers; there were approximately sixty of them headed in the direction of Clark Field and Manila. (I had known they were American planes before I saw them from the sound of the engines.)

The morale of the people improved 100 percent. Even the fence sitters were now loyal Phil-Americans. We continued to get word that groups of Huks and small bandit units from southern Luzon were terrorizing and looting the small outlying barrios and, more often than not, raping the women. None of these marauding bands had reached our barrios—yet—but I felt we should wipe them out if they entered our area to plunder and rape. Roberts suggested we talk to the outlaws first, attempting to reason with them, perhaps coming to some agreement so that we could induct them into the 14th Infantry. I said I couldn't and wouldn't depend on their loyalty. I wanted to gather only the 170 men I knew were loyal and could be trusted; however, the major had already made up his mind and there was nothing I could do to change it. I told him if after talking to them, he still wanted these men in the 14th Infantry, he could put Captain Dingcong in charge of them; for myself, I didn't want a damn thing to do with them; they were murderers and rapists, and the barrio people hated them for good reasons.

Sometime after we discussed this, Major Roberts received a second message telling him to report to Col. Russell W. Volckmann, commanding officer of all USAFIP–NL (United States Army Forces in Philippines–Northern Luzon). The USAFIP–NL had been organized and trained during the Japanese occupation; food for its members was supplied by the civilian population.

I told Major Roberts we had heard rumors of this large guerrilla force in northern Luzon toward the end of 1943. We had discussed several options: if the major hadn't contacted us, we were either going to gather what loyal soldiers we could and join the guerrilla forces in northern Luzon or organize a large guerrilla force of our own and strike the enemy wherever possible.

One day when we were in Manuri, Roberts asked me if I knew anything about a BAR. I said, "I should! I was a Browning-automatic rifleman in the army for nearly a year, and I can disassemble and reassemble the weapon blindfolded."

So saying, I got Sergeant Valdez's weapon, loaded it, aimed, and fired. I wasn't using the sling, missed my aim, and landed on my back. The major said I should have had the BAR on safety. I said I knew it was on automatic and loaded; but, I had forgotten to take into account my physical condition. I should have fired it with my arm in the sling and from a prone position, not a sitting one, to counterbalance my weight loss. It was a little embarrassing, but we all enjoyed a good laugh. The demonstration did remind the men how to disassemble and reassemble the weapon, and, above all, that one should use the sling if one didn't have the strength to fire the weapon without it!

In July 1944 we received word from Teniente Reyes that some of the marauding troops had shown up across the Cagayan River in one of the nearby barrios. According to Reyes's information, there were fifteen enlisted men and one officer in the group. Roberts decided to make contact. I said some of my soldiers and I would go along with him. The major sent word to the officer in charge of these troops he wanted to talk to him; word came back that he agreed to talk. We crossed the river and contacted the young lieutenant who was in charge of this small, lawless guerrilla unit, whose members, neither Huks nor bandits, would rather harass and kill their own people than fight the Japanese.

After some questioning by the major, the lieutenant told us he was under the command of a major in Mountain Province, and his orders were to wipe out any civilians who had collaborated with the enemy. Even after a lengthy discussion, the lieutenant still insisted he had orders to kill all collaborators. I interrupted the conversation to tell the lieutenant I had been living in the area for the past two and a half years with forty-four men, and through the intelligence information we had gathered, I had compiled a list of every collaborator, traitor, spy, fifth columnist—or whatever one wanted to call these betrayers. There were, however, some civilians who had collaborated with the Japanese who were actually double agents and supplied us with both food and intelligence information. I asked, "What if you killed one of these people who have been helping us?" The lieutenant said, "If you give me the list of the real collaborators, we will take care of them for you." Not impressed with his blustering, I said, "No, I've had it up to my neck with you." I added that his best bet was to "get your ass back on your horse" and report back to his commanding officer. Then Major Roberts wrote out a message, giving it to him with strict orders to deliver the message to the major in Mountain Province. The lieutenant left looking like a whipped dog.

By this time, we were well into another monsoon season—my fourth since the war began. Roberts and I were supervising the training of our men in offensive warfare; squad, platoon, and company tactics; deployment of troops; use of cover when available; and above all, such life-or-death techniques as not to bunch up, an unfortunate human tendency in both offensive and defensive warfare.

In October 1944, Major Roberts at last decided to report to Colonel Volckmann's headquarters. He made a trip to Pinappagan before proceeding north to Mountain Province. I requested that he leave Captain Dingcong in the Pinappagan area with his eight or nine men, and the major agreed to do that. At Pinappagan he also suggested that during his absence, Dingcong find and train some of our soldiers from the 14th Infantry who were dispersed by Colonel Nakar and were living in the Pinappagan area.

Major Roberts returned from Pinappagan with two misfit soldiers. One was an American corporal, and the other, a Philippine soldier who had thrown his rifle away when we were first raided at Pinappagan.

I told the major I wasn't too pleased about these two men. Roberts admitted the corporal had disobeyed orders while with him after the raid, almost causing a disclosure of their hideout in the Pinappagan area. But, he said he thought I could teach both men some discipline. I said I was sure I could, but if either one of them stepped out of line or disobeyed an order, thereby endangering the lives of the rest of the men, I would take severe disciplinary action.

Shortly after this, Roberts left for Volckmann's headquarters with a guide and some Philippine soldiers who had come with the guide. He left word with Captain Dingcong and with me that he would return as soon as possible; during his absence, Dingcong was to remain in the Pinappagan area and I, in the area of Jones.

CHAPTER 39

Jungle Justice

Lieutenant Reyes and Sergeant Valdez now requested orders to eliminate a few of the known spies on the west side of the Cagayan River. I gave the order, with the proviso that the spies were to be tried by the barrio people. Tenientes Leaño and Reyes were well informed, as was Juan, about the identity of these collaborators. We checked the list of names, which Sergeant Dannug had, against the names Juan and the two tenientes had. We came up with a total of ten men, in three different barrios on the west side of the river, whose collaboration had resulted in much loss of life. There were more than ten others in those barrios who were guilty of lesser offenses, and in the municipality of Jones there were as many as fifteen—including the mayor, chief of police, and Lieutenant del Rosario, who had betrayed Colonel Nakar.

Lieutenant Reyes, Sergeant Valdez, and Juan picked fifteen of our best men. Their orders were to cross the river, pick up all ten of the major spies, and return with them to Manuri.

About 15 November, the group left early in the morning and returned that evening with the spies, everyone of whom had been taken by surprise. The other known collaborators were warned not to inform the Japanese garrison in Jones. Afraid for their lives, they heeded the warning; they even thanked Lieutenant Reyes for sparing them from the fate they knew awaited their former friends. Lieutenant Reyes then gathered a number of witnesses who were to accompany them to Manuri.

I told the tenientes, Lieutenants Reyes and Vea, Sergeants Valdez,

Dolatre, and Juan that if the ten men were found guilty, they were not to be tortured or mistreated under any circumstances, and they were to be executed by a firing squad.

The trial took three days. Eight of the ten were sentenced to death by firing squad, including the neighbors who had helped the Hernandez men betray Captain Cushing. Two men were released with a warning. The executions took place at dawn on the morning of 20 November 1944. After that we had no further trouble with collaborators.

We were now being supplied from both sides of the river. Farmers had planted rice at the beginning of the rainy season, and each family had a crop of rice again.

One day, while we were sitting on the south side of a small river that empties into the Cagayan, an enemy patrol of eight men spotted us. Seeing that we outnumbered them, they turned and fled, heading toward Jones. We decided to cross to the north side of the small river and go into the jungle because we knew the Japanese would be back with a larger force. As we left, we covered our footprints; then we crossed the river and started to walk backwards, barefooted. For a distance of about one kilometer, whenever possible we walked in streams. We knew the Japanese would not follow us too far into the jungle. Planting bamboo spears in camouflaged areas and streams along the way, as usual, we then moved back to Campsite Five.

The following day we watched from inside the jungle while about fifteen Japanese searched the area where we had left our deliberately misleading footprints. The search party crossed the river, but the deceptive tracks led the men to suppose we had crossed back over again. When some of the party stepped on the sharp bamboo spears we had placed in the stream, they screamed like banshees; all fifteen quickly headed back to the opposite side of the river.

I told the men I wanted to take some Japanese alive in order to get information from them, but that we would have to wait until they cut the size of their patrols.

About a week after this incident, we heard that a supposed guerrilla, or in other words bandit, force was terrorizing the barrios on the west side of the river. I took my men, crossed the river, and entered the barrio of Tangao where I asked the teniente to send word to the so-called guerrilla unit's leader, who claimed to be a major, that I wanted to discuss joining his group.

The teniente found a messenger, and I told him to be sure to tell the "major" I had only five men with me. I had reliable information that the group, which I was certain was an outlaw one, consisted of no more than twelve men; I doubted its leader would be able to resist such bait.

After the messenger left, I kept five men with me and sent the others off to take cover around the teniente's hut. Unless the outlaws made a move to open fire, none of us was to fire at them.

At last, late in the afternoon the "major" and all his men came riding into Tangao on small but sturdy Carameta ponies (a type of native pony used in Manila to pull rickshawlike carriages, or *carametas*, and named after these conveyances by the American soldiers). With their long unkempt hair and generally wild appearance, the bandits looked pretty fearsome, which I imagined was their intent; psychological fear can be a formidable weapon. I just visualized them without their long hair, and they looked to me like any other Filipinos. Once over that hurdle, I greeted the "major," feeling not the slightest intimidated and rather enjoying the situation.

The bandit leader, perhaps not quite so cocksure as he would have wished, said he had heard of me; but, I was supposed to command more than five men. I explained that discrepancy by blaming the local propensity for exaggeration.

With considerable arrogance, he now said he wasn't interested in having an American in his unit, but if any of my men wanted to join his group, they could; he would even provide them with ponies.

Naturally, I asked where he would get more ponies.

"From the farmers, of course." He was beginning to lose patience.

This gave me the perfect opening: I asked what he used for money. At that, the "major" sprang the trap by saying, "Don't you know there's a war on? We need horses and food, and we take what we need."

Quite mildly under the circumstances, I asked who his commanding officer was.

"You're talking to him and you also ask too many questions."

I apologized.

His sneer changed to a look of great menace, and he leaned toward me and announced, "I told you I take what I need. I need more weapons, and I want yours."

"Okay," I said. "I don't want any trouble."

In a lower voice, I said, "Reyes, would you provide the 'major' with more weapons."

At a small prearranged motion from Reyes, my men emerged silently from their hiding places, their weapons trained on the bandits. The Tangaoans, who had been standing around listening to the exchange, scattered; but, as they left, the men drew their bolos.

The "major" didn't have to relay my next words to his men; they threw down their arms and scrambled to dismount. Nor did their leader need the two seconds I gave him in which to do the same.

Now I called for the barrio people to come forward so that the bandit leader could explain to them why their barrio and the others had been pillaged and the women raped. When the "major" tried to explain it all by saying he had heard that all these barrios were inhabited by spies and traitors, I confronted him with the fact that I knew he, like most of his men, was Tagalog.

Then I asked him what he was doing this far north of Manila. I said I suspected he and his men had been driven from the Manila area for robbing and raping, but I invited him to speak out in his own defense—if he could.

He said these stories were all exaggerated.

I said, "Not according to our information. However, my men have orders to let you go after they take your weapons." Sergeant Valdez had already disarmed the group; now we also confiscated the ponies.

Next the "major" asked for an escort to the vicinity of Santiago, and when I asked him why his group needed an escort, he replied that he was afraid the civilians might kill him and his men.

I pointed out that if they hadn't gone about looting and raping, they would have nothing to fear, adding, "I can go into any barrio in the area and be welcome because I always treated the people with respect." Then I turned to the teniente and asked him if his people wanted these men in Tangao. The answer was of course no.

The "major" started to plead with me, but I turned my back on him and walked away. My men followed, leading the ponies and carrying the confiscated weapons and ammunition. As we left Tangao, we heard screams. I am sure not one bandit got away that day.

About a week later the BC and a few Japanese soldiers came to Tangao to ask about the killing of the bandits. (We surmised that the Japanese had received the information through their own intelligence network.) The teniente said they had been booed while drunk. When the Japanese asked for the bandits' rifles, the teniente told the patrol leader that an American with a lot of guerrillas had entered the barrio, taken the rifles and ponies, and headed north toward Jones. The leader of the patrol said he wanted to see the buried bandits. After uncovering about five graves, the Japanese could see they had all been booed to death. The rest of the teniente's story must have satisfied the patrol leader too; he took his men back to Jones.

The Japanese started to patrol both sides of the river in groups of as many as twenty men, but they did not venture into the jungle. They also mistreated the people, demanding to know who was feeding the guerrillas.

Now Lieutenants Reyes and Vea, and Sergeants Valdez and Juan Reyes suggested we capture a few men from their patrols and teach them a lesson in maltreatment. I said we would do just that as soon as the Japanese cut back to a patrol-group size smaller than fifteen or twenty men.

In about a week they did cut back to patrol groups of four to six men. We made arrangements with Teniente Leaño. If a small patrol did come in, he was to give the men enough basi to get them drunk; then, we would try to capture some of them on the trail between Manuri and the barrio of Daligan on their return to Jones.

We didn't have to wait long. Leaño sent word that there were four Japanese soldiers in his barrio. The people of Manuri were giving them a good meal and the basi was flowing freely.

Our new headquarters, Campsite Six, which was established during Roberts's stay with us, was located just inside of the jungle, midway between Dabubu and Manuri and would now be used as a base of operations. We sent word back to Leaño to keep the Japanese patrol in Manuri long enough to give us time to skirt the barrio and catch the men on the trail leading to Daligan, nearly opposite Jones on the east side of the river.

Taking all of my men and using Juan as point, I moved us out quickly so that we could get into a good position for capturing all four Japanese alive. It took us about three hours to reach a spot we thought offered the best cover and concealment within a few feet of the trail. I sent Juan back to notify Teniente Leaño that we were all set to intercept the patrol.

Juan had no sooner arrived in the barrio than he was told by one of Leaño's neighbors that the Japanese were ready to return to Jones by way of Daligan. He took one of the ponies we had left in Manuri and headed back with the message. After the pony had been staked out in the jungle, I deployed the men in such a way as to cut the patrol off at the flanks and the rear if its four men tried to escape.

Lieutenant Reyes, Sergeant Valdez, and I waited with the lead group. After about a twenty-minute wait, we heard the four coming along the trail singing. Our rear-guard and flank-protection men let them go by. When they got to our position we stood up with rifles aimed and shouted, "Hapon surrender." Two of them dropped their rifles; the other two started to raise their rifles to fire and were killed with two shots. We approached and took all their weapons and ammunition—and some basi they were carrying.

I let Lieutenants Reyes and Vea, and Sergeant Valdez question the two men. The questioning went on for half an hour without results. I wanted to find out the exact number of Japanese and BC in Jones; where all their main headquarters were; the names of the regiments or divisions; and the names of the commanding officers of these units. The captives wouldn't talk. My instructions were to get the information without harming them, but, with that proviso, to use whatever methods were necessary to accomplish this. Valdez instructed Juan, who meanwhile had remained hidden, to get a large clay pot from Manuri. We did not want Juan to be seen by the Japanese because we still needed him in his capacity of spy.

Valdez had fashioned a thin rattan rope, and he tied the thumbs of one of the Japanese together, mounted the pony, tied the other end of the rattan around his own waist, and took off at a slow trot. He told the

Japanese, when he was ready to talk to let him know. Sergeant Valdez kept the horse at the trot for about five minutes before the Japanese soldier decided he would talk.

The man gave us a figure of about five thousand for the number of troops in Jones, which we knew was a barefaced lie.

About this time one of my men showed up with the clay pot Juan had procured. The men gathered some rocks, set the pot on top of these, filled it with cold water, took the other prisoner, and sat him in the pot. Then they built a fire. Lieutenant Reyes and Sergeant Valdez told both prisoners their stories had better match; we meant business. Valdez got back on the pony and took off at a gallop; the Japanese soldier, who was still tied to Valdez's waist, was able to run only a short distance before he fell and began screaming. He was really ready to talk; so was the soldier who was sitting in the now-lukewarm water.

We questioned the two men separately. This time we learned there were two hundred Japanese, and about the same number of BC, in Jones. Their Isabela headquarters was in the vicinity of the capital city of Ilagan, and they patrolled the valley most often by truck. They had heard their officers say the Americans were on the way back to retake the islands. The Japanese were concentrating their forces near the coast in the Lingayen Gulf area, and along the north coast on the Babuyan Channel between Aparri and Abulug.

The headquarters for these units was the capital city of Tuguegarao in the province of Cagayan. The Japanese noncommissioned officer whom we had captured wasn't too familiar with troop movements in the province of Nueva Vizcaya or the mountain provinces.

I asked him if he ever had heard of a Corporal Koopmann. He said yes, but that this corporal tried to escape and was bayoneted. I said that Koopmann had gone in to surrender carrying a white flag of truce, but he had been used for bayonet practice. Neither Japanese answered when I said Koopmann had believed their offer of so-called amnesty.

Next we asked about Colonel Nakar. They said he was executed because he spit on the Japanese flag, and his betrayers included one of our own former officers; the chief of police of Jones; the mayor of Jones; and several Filipino soldiers.

At last we asked about the betrayal of Captain Cushing. The

enlisted man said Cushing wouldn't surrender; when he fired his weapon at the Japanese and BC, their bullets hit him many times. He died fighting, and he and his men killed several Japanese and BC during the shootout. He added that one of Cushing's men got away but later was captured, tried to escape, and was killed. I asked if he didn't mean butchered, but he didn't answer me. I asked, "What did you do with Captain Cushing's body after he was killed?" His answer did not surprise me: "We gave him a military funeral. He was a brave man and caused the death of fifteen hundred Japanese soldiers by using dynamite to catch Japanese convoys in the narrow mountain passes."

Lieutenant Reyes asked what we were going to do with the prisoners. I said, "Take them with us to the camp at the edge of the jungle." I knew they would try to escape, and I told Sergeant Valdez to give them the opportunity and also to pass this information on to the men. I said, "You know what to do if they try to escape." That night I was awakened by two shots. I got up. Lieutenant Reyes and Lieutenant Vea were already up. The Japanese prisoners had tried to escape. I said, "Good, that's two less to feed."

CHAPTER 40

Ambush: Our Last

The next morning I told the men I was sure by now the Japanese major in command of the Jones garrison would assume the patrol had been killed.

I decided to send Teniente Leaño to Jones to ask the major for protection against guerrilla retaliations in the barrios on the east side of the Cagayan River. He was to tell the garrison commander that, since the barrios were supplying the Japanese with food and information, he would like to have Japanese soldiers stationed in each of them. If this couldn't be done, he would ask the major either for rifles and ammunition so that the barrio people could protect themselves against the guerrillas, or for a daily, large-size patrol.

It was a bold plan, but I was sure that the Japanese major would say no to each request. Leaño could give him the information that, ever since the American planes had flown over the Jones area, the guerrillas were seen quite frequently at the edge of the jungle from Manuri to Palacian Grande. I didn't believe the major, at this stage of the war, would risk sending a large patrol into the jungle, undoubtedly to lose more of his men; but—there was that matter of saving face.

I discussed the plan with the men and they were of one opinion: that the Japanese would indeed try to save face by patrolling the Jones' barrios in large numbers but would not risk coming into the jungle after us. If they did come in, we would apply the same tactics that we had used in the past. My plan would be to ambush them on the barrio trail leading to, and from, Jones.

I sent a runner to bring Leaño to our camp. After his arrival we informed him of our plan. Without hesitating, he consented to give the information and requests to the Japanese major.

After two days, Leaño returned and told us the major had said no to the first two requests but had agreed to patrol the barrios of Jones. We now had to wait and see where—and when—the patrol would go.

About a week later, Juan and the two tenientes showed up at Campsite Six very excited. They said, now that the Americans had landed on Leyte and would soon invade Luzon, some of the BC were deserting the Japanese: they didn't want to be caught fighting for a lost cause.

The three men also reported that the Japanese major had orders to hunt down and destroy the guerrilla forces—with a patrol made up entirely of BC. Evidently, his commandant didn't want to risk losing more military personnel.

I asked how many BC were in Jones and the tenientes and Juan estimated from fifty to two hundred. The truck patrols were continuing, and continuing to confuse our estimates; I intended to ambush these at a later date.

I sent Juan out to contact about fifty of the most trustworthy men, and one officer, Lt. Benjamin Aviles, who had been living in Palacian Grande. I wanted all the men who would participate in the ambush to have access to rifles, a supply of hand grenades, and automatic weapons if any were available. I told Juan to have the men clean their weapons and have them ready for use. I asked Juan if, with the help of Lieutenant Aviles, a Corporal Antonio, and a Private Pedro, he could assemble that many men. He was sure he could.

I said to tell Aviles we would be waiting on the trail, just inside the jungle east of Virgoneza in two days. Aviles wasn't to enter any of the barrios with a large group of men but was to enter the jungle somewhere north of Virgoneza. He and his men were to travel in groups of two to three being careful not to attract any attention. They were to be unarmed.

Juan left with his father, who said he knew where there was some ammunition hidden and would get it for us. I now asked Teniente Leaño to go back to Jones, contact Señor Villanueva, get what information he had for us, and return the following evening.

334

The next evening the teniente returned and said the Japanese major had been called to Ilagan but would return to Jones in a few days. Señor Villanueva had heard that under the major's command, the BC were to patrol all of the Jones' barrios. Leaño also said Villanueva had been informed by a Japanese NCO that about fifty BC had deserted.

I was now sure the Japanese major would leave Jones with a large number of men in his patrol. We would, of course, ambush this force.

I discussed the ambush plan with my officers and men. We would let the enemy patrol get as far south as Palacian Grande before ambushing it, and I especially wanted the Japanese commander, his officers, and noncoms picked off first. After losing their leaders, I knew the rest of the men would panic and run. My concern centered around what route the major would take.

He might decide to proceed upriver on the west side to Fugu Sur, cross the Cagayan River farther south or opposite Palacian Grande, then follow the trail north, next to the jungle, to Virgoneza, Qumalabaza, Dibuluan, and on to Bantug and Jones; or, the patrol might leave Jones, go by way of Bantug to Dibuluan, then to Manuri, back to Dibuluan, continue on as far south as Palacian Grande, and return by the same route; or, it could cross the river to the west and use the trail north to Jones. Obviously, we needed accurate information on this aspect of the major's plan.

My own plan was to divide my men into four equal groups. Sergeant Valdez, Juan, and I would be with the first ambush unit; Lieutenant Aviles would be with the second; Lieutenant Vea would lead the third; and Lieutenant Reyes and the remaining men would form the fourth, or clean-up unit.

I intended to ambush the search party between barrios, and from the edge of the jungle. Each ambush unit leader would send four men from his group across the river directly opposite his unit's position, in the event any of the enemy decided to cross. After my group ambushed the patrol, we would harass it from the rear. When it reached the second, third, and fourth units, this same tactic would be used until the patrol, or what was left of it, surrendered, or escaped all the way into Jones.

Juan and Teniente Reyes returned to camp with Teniente

335

Leaño—and with a good supply of ammunition; and, they said they were sure they could get even more of this. Juan said he had carried out my instructions. The men he had contacted all had weapons, and there were a hundred more men who wanted to go on this ambush with us. I said fifty would be enough.

I went through our plan, drawing it out on the ground, and asked Juan and the tenientes if they knew of any good ambush areas between the barrios. The tenientes volunteered to show us some and arranged to meet us just inside the jungle a little north of Virgoneza at noon the next day.

The following day Tenientes Reyes and Leaño, and Juan, with Lieutenant Aviles and the fifty men, arrived at the rendezvous about an hour after lunch. I had known some of Aviles's men in the past, and it was good to be reunited with them. Using Lieutenant Reyes as my interpreter, I explained our ambush plans.

I asked the men to raise their hands if they had any automatic weapons; two men, both former sergeants, had. Then I asked about mortars: they had none. But, they did have about twenty hand grenades. I said they were to carry about twenty rounds of ammunition and to be sure to pick up all the enemy rifles and ammunition after the ambush; the BC carried the same kind of weapons that we did: either the old Enfield or the Springfield rifle.

Lieutenant Reyes drew our plan on the ground for Lieutenant Aviles and the new men and explained that the password, as usual, would be "Lillian." Of the fifty men with Aviles, six were NCOs: the two sergeants who had the BARs, and four corporals.

Teniente Reyes then left with Lieutenant Aviles and his men to show them their ambush location. Lieutenant Reyes and Lieutenant Vea, with their men, left with Teniente Leaño. Sergeant Valdez, Juan, our men, and I headed south inside the jungle toward Palacian Grande where we found an ideal ambush spot just a few kilometers north of that barrio. We made sure each man knew what position he would hold at the time of the ambush.

After they were shown their various ambush positions, the new men were instructed to return home and wait until they heard from Juan. We didn't know how long we would have to wait for the next en-

336

emy patrol—and the implementation of our plans for ambush—but our plans were now completed and every soldier knew his job. When the men got the word from Juan, they were to bring their weapons, carrying them inside hollow bamboo poles. They all grinned and said that was just where they had been hiding them.

Lieutenant Aviles stayed at Campsite Six to get better acquainted with us and those of our men that he would be taking along on the ambush patrol as part of his unit.

After breakfast about four days later, we received word that the Japanese major, one other Japanese officer, some BC officers, and about one hundred BC enlisted men had left Jones before daybreak, going south toward the barrio of Fugu Sur on the west side of the Cagayan River. Orders were given to Lieutenant Reyes and Lieutenant Vea to take supplies of food and move their men into position. Runners were sent to tell Aviles's men to report to their units.

My intention was to ambush the patrol on its return to Jones. I wasn't sure whether the group would return to Jones on the east or west side of the Cagayan River; but, from the intelligence we had received earlier, I was sure the major and his men would cross the river to the east in the Palacian Grande area; therefore, I chose the ambush areas on the east side of the river.

After checking our weapons and ammunition, we left camp. Besides my pistol, I carried a rifle on this patrol. We dropped Lieutenant Aviles off at his ambush site, where some of his men were already in position.

Valdez and I moved out at a fast pace with our men following. Within an hour after leaving Lieutenant Aviles, we were in position and ready. With a corporal in charge, four men were sent to the opposite side of the river. They had one bangkâ, and we had two.

It was nearly noon when we spotted the Japanese patrol across the river. It had taken them a long time to travel such a short distance from Jones. They must have stopped at nearly every hut on the way down to question people to see if they had any knowledge about the guerrilla forces and their hideouts.

As soon as the Japanese patrol left a hut, our intelligence agents would cross the river and give our units that information. We noted

337

that the patrol had been walking two abreast, using a point of four men, with no flank protection. I was sure the patrol would use the same formation on our side of the river.

I sent two runners to Palacian Grande to watch, and they returned in about an hour and said twelve bangkâs had been used to ferry the patrol to our side of the river; we could expect it in an hour, if the major took the trail to Jones.

I told my two sergeants, Valdez and Juan, and one of the corporals to pick off the two Japanese officers. We passed this word along to the men to prevent everyone from firing at the same officers. Valdez, Juan, and I would be the first to fire. The Japanese patrol was carrying several automatic weapons. I told my men with hand grenades to lob their grenades at the enemy automatic riflemen. We had also counted five BC officers; other men would try to pick these off.

A little later we heard the sound of hobnail boots. Next we spotted the point; the main column followed closely with a BC officer in the lead. I don't know why, but I remember the thought flashed through my mind as I looked at him that the war was over for him. Not much later, we spotted the two Japanese officers nearly at the end and on the far side of the column.

I looked at Juan and pointed at the two; he nodded. We took aim and fired at the same time that Valdez opened up with a burst from the BAR. Both officers dropped. Several of the men lobbed their hand grenades. The enemy patrol started for the river: some men tried to swim but were picked off by our men in position on the other side; others threw down their weapons and surrendered; the rest took off on the trail north, only to get shot at from across the river. About fifteen minutes later we heard Lieutenant Aviles's group open fire.

We took fifteen prisoners; there were fifteen wounded; twelve of the enemy were dead, including the two Japanese and three BC officers. I had the fifteen prisoners dig a slit trench, and we buried the dead.

I gave one officer's sabre to Juan and one pistol to Sergeant Valdez. I kept the major's sabre and pistol. This was the same major who had hounded me for over two years. (When I returned home, I gave the sabre to the American Legion, Fred Weller Post Number 186, Eureka, South Dakota.)

I had the prisoners make litters and carry six of their most seriously wounded; the rest could walk. We picked up all the weapons and ammunition and headed north. Our prisoners carried a white flag we had made.

We could hear firing from Lieutenant Vea's position. Then, in a short time we reached Lieutenant Aviles's position. He had buried his group's victims—four enlisted men—and had six prisoners, four of whom were wounded. We collected two more BARs and the BCs' Springfield rifles.

About an hour later we heard more shots, which I knew were coming from Lieutenant Reyes's unit. Our four-man unit on the opposite side of the river was moving north in line with us. The men were anxious to cross over to our side, but we called to them that they could cross back when we made contact with Lieutenant Reyes's unit.

When we arrived at Lieutenant Vea's position, he had eight prisoners, including four wounded, and his group had killed four. They had already buried the dead and made litters to carry the wounded.

We reached Lieutenant Reyes's position about an hour and a half later. He said he and his men had chased the remainder of the enemy troops halfway to Jones. He had eleven prisoners, five of whom were wounded, and six enemy dead.

Out of an approximate total of 120 enemy troops, 26 were killed, 28 were wounded, and 40 were captured. We had collected over a hundred weapons, including three BARs and other weapons thrown away by the retreating soldiers. I asked the BC sergeant how large the patrol had been. He said there were about 115 enlisted men and 5 officers, which meant only 26 had escaped to Jones.

I knew it was impossible for us to guard and feed the prisoners and, especially, take care of their wounded, so I decided to let them return to Jones.

After we had taken the prisoners' names, ranks, and serial numbers, we told the BC sergeant we would let him return to Jones with the other prisoners. He was to give the following message to all those who were loyal to the Japanese forces in Jones, especially the mayor and the chief of police: they would be tried when the Americans retook Luzon.

I made the prisoners take an oath never again to bear arms against the loyal Filipino or American soldiers. We gave them a guide as far as Bantug, which was just across the river from Jones.

The sergeant and his men asked if they could join us, but I told them, as far as I was concerned, I could never trust them. I said to tell the Japanese if they wanted Hieb and his soldiers, we would be waiting for them in the jungle.

"We heard many of your comrades are deserting. Is this true?" I asked. The sergeant said it was true, and that the desertions had begun after the landing of the American troops on Leyte. I asked him why he hadn't deserted. He said he wished he had. He was sure to desert now—if the Japanese didn't shoot all of them for their failure to kill or capture us. I told him he should be thankful we were giving his group an escort as far as Bantug. "For your own good, I hope you desert." I added. The sergeant saluted and said he and his men would take my advice.

I had all my new men follow us to Campsite Six. It was late when we arrived. The prisoner escort arrived back a few hours later. When I asked if there had been any problems, the men told me that without the escort, none of the prisoners would have reached Jones alive, because the civilians along the way said they were traitors and would have killed them. Three of the wounded had died on the way to Bantug.

I began training the men daily in offensive warfare, squad, platoon, and company tactics. All the surrounding barrios were supplying us with rice, camotes, bananas, papaya, and fish—but, we were now a force of ninety-six, and all this food still gave us only two meals a day.

News reached us that most of the BC had deserted the Japanese, and the deserters were returning to their homes, for the most part in the Manila area. The Japanese didn't send any more patrols into the jungle; their commander in Jones wanted no part of us. For the first time, we enjoyed freedom of movement in all the barrios. I planned to wait for our chance and then send an ambush party north towards Echague to ambush one of the Japanese truck patrols that were still active in that area.

A few days after the ambush I received a message from Colonel Volckmann ordering my men and me to report to Major Roberts, who was now in the vicinity of Laoag, the capital city of the province of Ilocos Norte, commanding the 15th Infantry. With the message, I also received the order dated 28 November 1944 promoting me to captain. I noticed on the same order that Captain Dingcong had been promoted to major; and, after leaving me, the messenger was to proceed south to Pinappagan to give Major Dingcong his copy of the orders.

I notified all the men who were still living in the barrios to report to me in two days in Manuri with weapons, grenades, and whatever ammunition they had. I showed Tenientes Leaño and Reyes where we had hidden the Japanese weapons and gave them permission to keep them. A message came from the mayor and the chief of police in Jones begging for their lives. They said they would act as double agents if we would forgive them for their past mistakes.

I told Tenientes Leaño and Reyes to go along with the two traitors' plan until the time came when the island had been secured. Then they could try them, using all the loyal barrio tenientes in the Jones area for judge and jury.

After some questioning, the BC sergeant captured in our last ambush had told us that Leyte had been taken by the American forces under the command of Gen. Walter Krueger.

Out of the seventy thousand to seventy-five thousand Japanese defending the island of Leyte, only about five thousand, including their wounded, survived. The guerrilla forces on Leyte had been of great help to the Americans. I had asked the sergeant where he got all this information. He said, "On one of the Japanese shortwave radio sets."

General MacArthur was now the Southwest Pacific Supreme Commander. The president of the Philippines, Sergio Osmeña, was with the American troops who had made landings both at Tacloban and Dulag after destroying most of the Japanese fleet in Leyte Gulf. It was on the second day after the 20 October landing that MacArthur, some of his staff, and President Osmeña waded ashore and MacArthur made his historic "I have returned" radio address to the Philippine people and the world.

PART FIVE

FROM THE JUNGLES TO V-J DAY

CHAPTER 41

On the Move Again

My work in the Jones area was completed. Our sojourn in the jungles was over. My thoughts went back over the long months that had added up to two and a half years since the raid on our camp near Pinappagan: the seemingly endless days of gnawing hunger when the mind refused to focus on anything but food; the frustration of inaction and isolation; the constant threat of being discovered or overwhelmed in our jungle campsites; and the mind-numbing, weary treks through miles of dense jungle terrain. Now it was all behind us. We were ready to take up a new kind of battle, no longer as guerrilla fighters, but as an army of men. We would be joining other groups such as ours, made up of men who had been waiting for the tide to turn; men like us, ready to fight the Japanese Imperial Forces and free the islands.

At the invitation of Tenientes Leaño and Reyes, we met in Manuri for one last feast together. To my surprise, my friend Juan, who had helped me reach Dumabato after the raid on Pinappagan, was there with his wife. The tenientes from the surrounding barrios joined in the celebration, bringing enough food to see us through at least three days in our coming journey to join the other guerrilla units. During the speeches that night, many hearty expressions of thanks were given to everyone who had helped us through our ordeal. I had come to love and understand these people. There were not many dry eyes, including my own, and I told the villagers, "I am sure the Lord will bless you for your kindness to my men, and to me, and I will take with me fond memories of such good Christian people. I will always remember you in my prayers."

345

We shook hands all around and embraced the many people whom we had come to know as friends and brothers. We bid all the tenientes good-bye, and I told them I hoped if we saw each other again, it would be when their homeland was once again free, and the Japanese had been driven from the Philippines.

The officers, NCOs, and I discussed the route we would take to join our fighting forces in the mountain provinces. There were several civilian guides who would take us as far as Echague. Starting from Manuri, we would skirt the barrio of Bantug on the jungle side, then proceed north to Dammang, which was a friendly barrio. The people there would help us cross the Cagayan River and bring us around or through the town of Echague; from there we would head straight northwest until we got to the mountain province of Ifugao, whose people had remained loyal. Majors Blackburn, Burnett, and Praeger operated in this area, and the Japanese feared their soldiers.

As we left Manuri early the next morning, all the barrio people turned out to wave good-bye. Tenientes Reyes and Leaño insisted on going with us as far as Dammang. Making the journey were 168 enlisted men and 6 officers, including, Lts. Leonardo Galima, Enriquez Cruz, Benjamin Aviles, Gervacio Reyes, and Pedro Vea; and myself, now a captain.

We wanted to reach Dammang in time to ferry the men across the Cagayan River under cover of darkness, and, if possible, pass through or around Echague, to get as far northwest of there as possible before daybreak.

As we skirted Bantug, opposite Jones, Teniente Leaño went to see if he could find out how many Japanese soldiers or BC were left in Jones. He returned with the information that there were less than fifty Japanese soldiers and only about twenty BC left in that municipality. He had also verified that many of the BC had deserted after our last encounter with them.

Juan and both tenientes went on into Dammang to make arrangements for feeding us and getting us ferried across the river. We arrived in the Dammang area well before dark and set up camp just inside the jungle about one kilometer from the barrio. Sergeant Valdez went to contact the tenientes and Juan to find out what intelligence they had for us concerning the number of Japanese in Echague.

About an hour later, the sergeants returned with an invitation from the teniente of Dammang to come into the barrio after dark for supper, after which the people of the barrio would get us safely across the river. Dammang was one of the message centers for the bamboo telegraph, and the people could be trusted. Spies had also been sent to Echague, and the teniente would let me know if there were any Japanese soldiers there.

A short time later, Dammang's teniente turned up. I had met him once before, in Jones in 1942; he was a friend of Villanueva. According to his spies, he said, the only troops in Echague were the BC, who numbered not more than twenty—and were afraid of the civilians when not protected by the Japanese. Some of the BC had been deserting and the desertions increased when they heard what had happened to their comrades in Jones, where a force of "over one thousand" guerrillas had attacked them!

Laughing, I said, I hoped that number would grow to two thousand by the time the rumor reached their division headquarters. I knew the Japanese could not, and would not, spare any of their own forces to go after any more jungle-based guerrillas. They were concerned with gathering their troops in preparation for meeting the American landing forces and fighting the consolidated groups of guerrillas that had already formed units.

Assembling the officers and NCOs, I told them we would go through the town of Echague that night, making a forced march until morning, which would put us some distance north of Ramon. There we would cross the Magat River into the province of Ifugao. The guides thought it was possible to reach the area where we expected to cross the Magat River sometime the following morning, and from there other guides would take us to our next destination.

After supper in Dammang, we crossed the Cagayan River, using about fifteen bangkâs. I had said good-bye for the second time to Teniente Reyes and Teniente Leaño. They were brave and courageous men, and to this day I carry with me heartfelt gratitude

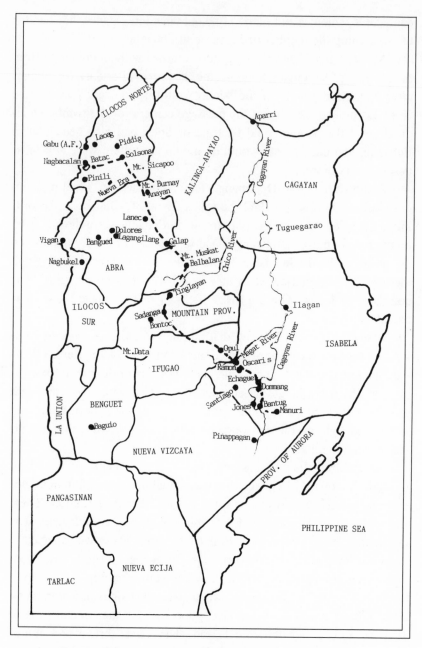

*Route, Manuri to Batac, Headquarters, 15th Infantry,
Philippine Army*

for the part they played in helping my men and me survive. They were true patriots.

I had also thanked the teniente of Dammang for the food and the two guides, one of whom had gone on ahead of us into Echague, where he had relatives, to check out any unfriendly forces, and to see if any BC outposts had been set up. As we neared the town, the guide returned to report there was one outpost consisting of three men, and it was manned all night and had one telephone line to the BC headquarters in Echague, and one to Ilagan. I asked if he knew where the lines were located. He said his relatives did, and if we would take care of the sentries on the main highway, they would cut the lines.

Lieutenant Aviles volunteered to go with four other men to take care of the sentries. I said to go ahead, but not to fire any shots and to use just boloes or bayonets. Aviles and his men would tell the sentries they were on their way to Santiago to visit relatives and get rice. They would say they had come from the Jones area where the guerrillas were very fierce and had taken all their rice supplies. While they took care of the sentries, the rest of us would be infiltrating through the town using the other guide.

Before Aviles left, I wrote out a message which he was to pin on one of the dead sentries. He and the men with him who had been living in the barrios during our stay in the jungles had been waiting a long time to fight back; he smiled after reading it and put it in his pocket. The message read as follows:

> This is in payment for helping the Japanese Imperial Forces. We suggest that the remaining Japanese Constabulary desert before the same fate befalls them.
> Guerrilla Forces
> Jones Area

Our guide began leading us through Echague. Lieutenant Reyes was in the first group of ten. The guide knew which building the BC was using as its headquarters and gave it, as well as the outpost, a wide berth. In half an hour he was back, ready to take the next group through. Aviles hadn't returned, and I was getting edgy. But by the time the guide returned for the third group, Aviles and his men had appeared and reported the mission accomplished. I asked the guide if the telephone lines were cut. When he said, "Wen apo," I said, *"Tayo na."* (Let's go.)

Everyone was barefooted; most of the men had been wearing the hobnail shoes of dead Japanese soldiers, and the noise of that many men wearing hobnails could have alerted the remaining BC. There was also a chance that barefooted, we could mislead the BC into thinking we were headhunters.

As we arrived on the other side of town, we rejoined the other groups, and I gave the men permission to put their shoes on at our next rest stop if they wished; from now on, the rear guard would be dragging branches to cover our footprints.

We made good time, and I called a rest halt after about an hour and a half. I put my shoes back on, but I noticed most of the men preferred to remain barefooted.

By morning we had reached the Magat River and crossed it in the bangkâs provided by the people from the barrio of Oscaris, which is just north of the town of Ramon. The barrio teniente told us there were no Japanese or BC in Ramon.

We had marched about forty miles in two days. On reaching the barrio of Opul, where the teniente kindly supplied food for us, and guides to take us on to our next destination near Sadanga, we rested for a day. Sadanga, which is near the town of Bontoc, would be a good two-and-a-half-day hike.

I had been feeling some symptoms of an incipient malaria attack, and I think I needed the rest more than the men did. I wasn't exactly in top physical condition, and soon we would be climbing, leaving the valley behind, and heading into the mountain provinces, Igorot country. The Igorot people consisted of five tribes: the Benguet, Bonto, Kilinga, Ifugao, and Apayao. Each tribe name corresponds to a province or a subprovince of the same name.

The Igorot tribes were very friendly toward the American guerrilla forces, and the two new guides who joined us after the first day of walking and climbing out of Opul were Igorots from the Ifugao tribe. Besides their own dialect, both of them could speak and read English, Ilocano, and Tagalog. They wanted to join our unit and go into the province of Ilocos Norte with us. I nicknamed one of the G-stringed, bolo-armed young men Mickey because I couldn't remember the correct pronunciation of his name, which sounded like Mickey. The nickname stuck for as long as I knew him. The other young man's name was Alfredo Duwang.

I asked them why some of the officers who were operating in the mountain provinces hadn't inducted them into the army. They told me their parents had let their older brothers join the guerrilla units but would only allow them to act as guides for the army because they were needed to help their families work the land.

Our young guides could outwalk any of us. We were moving steadily up into mountainous terrain, and when I would ask them how far it was to the next barrio on the other side of the mountain, they would always answer *idiay* (there, or close by). If the distance was somewhat farther, the sound of the word was drawn out; thus, iiidiiiaaay meant a long distance. If our guides had been walking alone, the distance for them would have been idiay; for us, however, it was iiiidiiiiaaaay!

We reached Sadanga, which was located on the Chico River, sometime in the afternoon of the third day. The barrio people knew we would be arriving and had prepared food for us. This was the first time I tasted dog meat, and after what we had eaten in the past, it tasted all right.

We rested at Sadanga for a day because there was more mountain climbing ahead of us. I was still not feeling well, and the Sadangans gave me some bark tea, the local remedy for malaria. This didn't seem to help much, and I only hoped the attack wouldn't be too severe, because it usually took me several days to recuperate, and I was always left in a weakened physical condition for some time afterwards.

CHAPTER 42

An Unwelcome Order and Christmas Again

The following day I received a message from Major Roberts asking me to meet him in the town of Nueva Era, Ilocos Norte. That same day I also received a message from Lt. Col. Romulo A. Manriquez, commanding officer of the 14th Infantry, ordering me to transfer all officers and enlisted men under my command to the commanding officer of the 14th Infantry—himself—by order of Col. Russell W. Volckmann. The messenger informed me that Major Dingcong had already reported to Lieutenant Colonel Manriquez.

This was just not my day! I had trained many of these men on the island of Negros; we had been together ever since; and, they were damned good soldiers. A bond had grown between us. We had become a unit as we faced adversity together, and these men had proven their steadfastness and courage. They were men who could be depended upon to do their duty. Each one of them knew that the life of every other man depended upon his obedience to duty; each had proven trustworthy, had met the enemy, had been tested under fire, and had prevailed. We had drawn strength from each other, and we had become an effective fighting force with a special quality.

I was sick at heart knowing I would have to relinquish my command of these men. The only other choice I had would be to have them follow me to Major Roberts, commanding officer of the 15th Infantry at Nueva Era. However, if I did that, I would be open to a court-martial. Ill with the onset of a malaria attack, and sickened by the decision I had to make, I got very little rest that night.

The next morning I had all my officers and men report to me. I read them the two messages I had received the day before. I told them if I disobeyed the order from Lieutenant Colonel Manriquez and had them report with me to Major Roberts, nothing would happen to them; however, I could be court-martialed for disobeying Colonel Volckmann's orders.

I said, "I have been in the army nearly twelve years, and I believe in following orders, regardless of how unjust they may seem. I have known most of you since we left Negros. You are top-notch soldiers, as good as any I have ever trained. I am proud of you and I will miss you. I know you all understand the necessity for obeying orders."

I suggested they take one more day of rest and then leave with their guides to report to Manriquez. With that, I bid them goodbye with my prayers for their safety and God's blessings on them, and the hope that they would soon see the day of their country's liberation.

Lieutenant Reyes called the men to attention. They all saluted. I returned the salute with tears in my eyes. It was the same for the men. Further words could not express what we had shared together.

I attempted to get some rest, and some relief from the malaria attack with the local medicine, but this still wasn't working. Shivering and shaking, I asked Mickey to see if he could find some blankets. That night I broke out in a sweat and knew I would get some relief before morning. I wrote out my message to Lieutenant Colonel Manriquez and finally managed to get a few hours sleep.

In the morning I called Lieutenant Reyes, read him the message I had written, and asked him to deliver it to Manriquez. It read as follows:

> To: C.O. 14th Infantry
> In compliance with instructions from Colonel Volck-
> mann, I am regretfully transferring 168 men and offi-
> cers under the command of Lt. Reyes, an outstanding
> officer, to your command. I recommend all of the offi-
> cers for promotion, and any enlisted men they recom-
> mend. I have trained and have known most of the

officers and enlisted men since September of 1941 and
know them to be outstanding soldiers.

Capt. Harley F. Hieb

When Lieutenant Reyes and the men were ready to leave, I shook
hands with each soldier as he passed by. It was hard to hold back the
tears, and the men felt as I did and understood. I wished them "Godspeed and good luck." My prayers went with them. Lieutenant Reyes
thanked me for the wording of my message to Manriquez.

I was feeling quite a bit better the next day but was still weak. I
asked Mickey if he could deliver a message to Major Roberts and told
him, if the major wanted him as an orderly, he had my permission to
stay; but first, he would have to get his parents' consent.

Mickey was sure they would give it, and while I took a few more
days to recover from the malaria attack, he returned to his parents'
home to speak with them. Several days later he returned with three
other men, two of whom carried old Springfield rifles with plenty of
ammunition; all three wore G-strings and carried bolos.

I had my .45 pistol, a Springfield rifle, and a couple of hand grenades—and Alfredo Duwang, Mickey, and the other three Igorots: a
far cry from the experienced troops I had trained and with whom I had
started the march from Manuri.

I checked the map. The guide who had brought the message from
Roberts said he was from Solsona, Ilocos Norte. He said he would
take us to Roberts's headquarters by way of Solsona. I said, "Hell,
that's out of our way. We would have to travel north, then after reaching Solsona, we would have to backtrack south to reach Nueva Era." I
suspected the guide was not too familiar with the other mountain trails
I had suggested and wanted to take a route home that was familiar to
him, and along which he had made friends carrying messages in the
past. However, no doubt his was also the safest route; so, I decided to
go with him to Solsona.

We had to cross the very high, rugged Cordillera mountains, and
the guide told me that in my physical condition, it would take us five to
six days to reach Solsona. I decided to wait one more day before

leaving. It was now 18 December 1944. I hoped we could get there by Christmas Day. I would send Mickey to Major Roberts with a message after we reached our destination.

The first day of the trip, we began at a slow pace to give me time to get some strength back in my legs; but even so, in spite of frequent, though short, rest stops, we made pretty good time. At Tinglayan, the villagers had a meal waiting for us, and after the usual obligatory glass of basi, I was ready to call it a day. I was sound asleep the minute I lay down, exhausted from a tiring day's hike.

When we left Tinglayan early in the morning, I told the guide that we would try to make it to the barrio of Balbaban. The hike was another long one for me but an easy one for the others.

The next morning we headed northwest crossing Mount Muskut. It took us all day to reach the barrio of Galap.

I had picked up my share of leeches that day; at Galap the barrio teniente had me strip down, and after sending my clothes to be washed and boiled, he checked my body for more leeches. When he found one, he would take a hot knife and hold it close; the bloodsucker would feel the heat, let go, and drop off. I was scorched a little bit in the process, but at least I was rid of the leeches. The hot knife worked better than the smouldering-stick method I had used once in the jungle of Manuri.

The next day after an early breakfast, we were once more on our way. We were now in the province of Abra, where there were some Japanese occupying a few of the provincial towns, but none in the outlying barrios. I told my five men and the guide to question any civilians we came across in order to find whether we were getting back into enemy strongholds. We were told the Japanese were supposed to have a large number of troops in Bangued, the capital city of Abra, which was nearly due west of Galap.

We headed north, passing through a number of barrios, and arrived at Lanec after dark. After supper, I excused myself, explaining to the teniente that I was tired and would like to rest because we wished to get an early start in the morning; we still had some very rugged terrain to cross, and it would take us several more days to reach our destination. He took us to a large frame building where we were to quarter for the night. In the morning I sent a runner ahead to Anayan with the following message:

> To the Teniente of Anayan:
> We will arrive at barrio Anayan today. Request prepared meal for party of seven. Also request food supply for the remainder of our journey to Solsona. We should reach your barrio about midafternoon. After eating and resting we will continue toward Solsona.
> Capt. Harley F. Hieb

When we reached Anayan the teniente had received my message and had an excellent meal ready. The next morning, he kindly furnished new guides and two *cargadors* (carriers) to carry our supplies.

That day we again walked until dark, eventually reaching an abandoned building where we decided to shelter for the night. We had climbed to the upper floor and were settled in, resting, when we were awakened late in the night by the sound of voices. It sounded like two men talking—in Japanese.

I made a motion to my men to be quiet. We looked down through the cracks in the bamboo flooring and saw two unarmed Japanese soldiers. We were ready for them, and if they had decided to come up the stairs, they would have been dead on arrival. We waited until they lay down and went to sleep. Mickey and Alfredo crept down the ladder and poked their rifle barrels into the bellies of the soldiers. When they saw the armed, G-string–clad Igorots standing over them, the two Japanese jumped up and raised their arms. My other Igorots tied them up, and Mickey and Alfredo took turns guarding them.

In the morning we searched the two and untied their hands; I asked them what happened to their weapons. I couldn't understand them, nor could they understand me, but it seemed as though they might have been captured and then escaped. Using sign language, I asked where they were getting their food. They understood this question and indicated they had been stealing. I had them take their clothes off, and we searched them again, thoroughly. I wanted to be quite sure they weren't carrying any knives or other concealed weapons. We went through their clothing and found only some military script. I told them to get dressed and told my men we would use them as cargadors.

It was now 24 December—Christmas Eve. We passed through several barrios and received more supplies, including some rice cookies, which I enjoyed. When people asked me why we didn't kill the Japanese soldiers, I said we would do so only if they tried to escape. I noticed my Igorots glance at each other, and I suspected they were hoping the prisoners would attempt to escape, thus supplying the excuse to kill them.

That day we crossed Mount Burney, intending to make it to the foot of Mount Sicapoo before dark. We ate late in the afternoon and began our ascent. After about an hour's climb, we found a hut and decided to spend Christmas Eve there. The guide was sure we would be able to reach Solsona by midafternoon of Christmas Day.

This would be my sixth—and, I was positive, my last—Christmas in the islands. I hoped to get a letter out to my parents and one to Elaine. I knew supplies were coming in by submarine, and I thought maybe that meant there was a chance for mail to go out. I found myself reminiscing about home and Elaine; but eventually, I fell asleep.

I hadn't been asleep very long when one of the Igorots woke me. Before he could tell me, I knew. "I'll bet the Japanese soldiers tried to escape," I said. He answered yes. I said I hadn't heard any shots. The Igorot said, "We need our ammunition. We boloed them." I didn't answer.

It was Christmas Eve, and my men had boloed two prisoners to death who I was sure hadn't tried to escape. Killing armed enemies in the battle for the defense of life and country, or traitors who have betrayed compatriots or causes, is required of a soldier in wartime; but, killing unarmed prisoners is not. I wondered again how much longer the war would go on.

I didn't get any more sleep that night, and in the morning, I asked the Igorots what they had done with the Japanese soldiers. They said they had buried them under some rocks. It was Christmas Day.

We climbed Mount Sicapoo and started down the trail to Solsona. As we neared the town, we met some civilians from the outlying barrios who told us there were no Japanese in Solsona; however, some

357

were still occupying the capital city of Laoag. We arrived in Solsona in the afternoon.

The whole town came out to greet us, and a big Christmas fiesta had been prepared. My first request was for a hot bath, a shave, and a haircut, and soon a hot tub of water was ready—and the first bar of soap I had seen in two and a half years. I stayed in the tub, scrubbing myself for over an hour, while my clothes were being washed and ironed, and my boots shined. After I finished scrubbing, the barber went to work; then I got back in the tub again to get all the hair washed off. By that time my clothes and shoes were ready. I dressed and went to meet the mayor and all the town dignitaries, plus some of the barrio tenientes. The mayor asked if I would say a few words to the people of his town. I said, "I would be glad to, but I am neither orator nor politician. My job for the last eight years has been instructing soldiers in infantry tactics."

I told the townspeople I was happy to be in Solsona, and that this was my sixth Christmas in the Philippines since my arrival from the States in 1939. I told them that without the help of the kind Philippine people, I would have been buried somewhere on the island a long time ago. I said, "I would like to thank the people of Solsona, all the people of Luzon, really, who helped the guerrilla units of the 14th, 15th, and 121st Infantry regiments survive the war. The Philippine people are my brothers and sisters. I have nothing but love for you and admiration for the sacrifices you have made for the past three years. I thank God we are together on this Christmas Day to celebrate the birth of Christ. May the Lord bless all of you on this Christmas Day."

The mayor said it was time to eat, and maybe they could get me fattened up and in better physical condition. The meal I enjoyed that evening was the best I had had since my first meal with Señor Villanueva so long ago in Jones. It included chicken, duck, pig, rice, camotes, all kinds of fruits and vegetables—and of course basi to top it off. I felt like I had gained four pounds that night. Everyone sang Christmas carols, and then I thanked my hosts and said good night.

It was almost nine o'clock before I awakened the next morning to the pleasant experience of finding my breakfast waiting for me. I decided to rest in Solsona for a few days to regain my strength before going on to Nueva Era, Ilocos Norte, where Major Roberts and his executive officer, Capt. John Patrick O'Day, were located, according to what information I could gather.

I wrote the following message to Roberts:

> To: Major Roberts
> Commanding Officer 15th Infantry
> Merry Christmas. I am sending this message with Mickey—my Christmas present to you. I picked him up in the province of Ifugao because he wanted to join the army. He will make you an excellent orderly. He speaks English, Ilocano, and the mountain dialects. However, if you do not want him, send him back. I am also sending a copy of a message I sent to Lt. Col. Romulo A. Manriquez, Commanding Officer, 1st Infantry, by order of Col. Russell W. Volckmann ordering me to transfer all my officers and enlisted men to the commanding officer, 14th Infantry, USAFIP-NL. This was a personal blow to me after training 168 men and using some of them in guerrilla warfare. I have been resting in Solsona for the past few days. I have 4 Igorot bolomen with me: 2 with no weapons; 2 with Springfield rifles. If any changes have been made request new instructions be forwarded. I will wait here until I hear from you.
>
> Hieb

Mickey and the guide left with my message on 28 December. The guide said they should reach Nueva Era in a day and a half and he would try to be back by New Year's Day.

On 1 January 1945, the townspeople and the people from the surrounding barrios joined in the celebration of the New Year. There was dancing, plenty of food, and plenty of speech making.

On 2 January the guide returned with a message from Major Roberts telling me to report to the forward command post near the town of Batac.

The mayor of Solsona furnished me with a guide who knew where the forward command post of the 15th Infantry was located. I reported there to Maj. Harry Roberts on 5 January. My new assignment was as the regimental S–3 (Plans and Training officer). It was work I understood and knew. The regiment was not nearly up to strength, and although they were good, loyal civilians, some of the officers the major had commissioned were without any military background: one was a former governor; one, a congressman; a number had been small-town politicians who had stayed loyal to the guerrilla forces. They were fine people, but we needed experienced personnel; what bothered me was that we had such available, but the more experienced had been overlooked, or deliberately bypassed, in favor of less experienced, but influential, civilians.

I expressed my feelings on this subject only once to my commanding officer. On a day when I had set up some field exercises for one of the battalions, I said the officers should have been picked from the enlisted ranks. We had a number of excellent Philippine Scout NCOs who could have done one hell of a better job as officers than these civilians dressed as officers. I said, "I am sure they are all good, honest, patriotic men; but, they are not officer material." The only reply I got was a look that clearly indicated who was in command.

I told Major Roberts I would do my best to see that all the senior and the subordinate officers, with their enlisted men, got enough training in offensive warfare to make a respectable showing in any battle they might encounter. I knew the men were familiar with hit-and-run tactics—but the days for those were bygone. It was a new ball game now. I told the major I hoped time would be with us, so we could turn the regiment into a first-class fighting organization.

CHAPTER 43

The Battle for Ilocos Norte

We both knew the landing on Luzon by the American forces was imminent. Our orders were to clear out and destroy all enemy forces from the provinces of Ilocos Norte, Abra, and Ilocos Sur. We would be facing ten thousand well-trained, battle-experienced Japanese troops. Considering the fact that we were once again working with troops who were inexperienced in this type of warfare, it was an assignment that carried a tremendous responsibility. Major Roberts ordered me to supervise the training of these men, adding that on the positive side, he suspected the Japanese thought we outnumbered them.

We spent the next three days in the field training in offensive tactics. The men learned quite a bit in the short time I had to spend with them; but in my estimation, they were still not ready for offensive warfare.

On 9 January, we received orders to execute D-day missions. Our mission was to demolish and destroy all bridges between Vigan and Laoag, and also any bridges to the south of Vigan and to the north of Laoag.

On 12 January, the demolition party headed by Capt. Perfecto R. Doña, together with Lt. Larry Soliven and his demolition platoon, destroyed the important Tipcal Bridge. One highway from this bridge led to Batac, the other to the Currimao-Paoay-Balacad road.

The demolition of the Carasgas Bridge at Batac took place on the same day. That party was headed by Lt. Jose Ibalio, assisted by Sergeant Macagba, and was supported by armed men under the command of Lieutenants Bayag and Sarco. The same team destroyed the Mausag

War Zone, Ilocos Norte and Abra

and Darat bridges on 14 January. This prevented the enemy from using motorized troop carriers and put them back on their hobnail boots.

The enemy was slowed down further by our roadblocks on other highways of approach; the construction of booby traps; the mining of roads; and the destruction of their wire communications.

At the same time that our demolition teams were committed to slowing down the enemy forces, Roberts ordered the remainder of the regiment to eliminate all enemy-held positions. The 3d Battalion was assigned the province of Ilocos Sur, including Highway 3, to as far south as the capital city of Vigan.

Our only radio was the one at our rear command post, which was located in the area of Nueva Era, about midway between our location and that of the 3d Battalion; it was used only when messages were sent to higher headquarters.

We were to attack, drive out, and destroy all enemy troops from the towns surrounding the Ilocos Norte capital city of Laoag. We were also to clear the airfield just south of Laoag.

Within several days we had driven the enemy from the town of Batac; there were few enemy casualties because most of the Japanese troops fled north to Laoag. There was very little resistance to the rousting of Japanese forces from some of the smaller towns in the area just south of Laoag. The battle for the airfield itself was another story. Two battalions were committed to this task.

Up to this point, all of the towns and barrios in Ilocos Norte had been liberated with the exceptions of Laoag and Gabu Airfield. Casualties inflicted on the enemy since 9 January were about one hundred killed, and about the same number wounded. Thus far, we had suffered very light casualties.

There were three large-scale raids on the Japanese-held airfield; these resulted in slightly more than one hundred more enemy casualties. The first raid took place at midnight on 24 January and was led by Maj. Simeon M. Valdez, a capable and courageous officer who was the commanding officer, 1st Battalion, 15th Infantry. He had served in Bataan, and after the war, he was elected by Ilocos Norte to serve in the Philippine Congress.

Valdez was assisted by Sergeant Macagba, an S–2 agent, and

approximately five hundred bolomen under the command of Alfredo Duldulao. As a result of this raid four ammunition dumps were destroyed and the fires caused by 280 exploding drums of gasoline could be seen for miles around.

The second raid was conducted on the night of 26 January by Sergeant Macagba, with the commander of the bolomen, Duldulao, and seventy of his men. This time two transport planes, one fighter pursuit plane, two army trucks, and 350 drums of gasoline were destroyed.

The last raid, which I took part in, was conducted by S–2 agents from the 2d Battalion, 15th Infantry, again with Sergeant Macagba and Duldulao and his bolomen. We burned the Japanese quarters along the runway; destroyed and burned 50 drums of gasoline; and took away one complete airplane radio set, two .20mm MGs (machine guns), four .45-caliber MGs, and plenty of assorted ammunition. Eight Japanese soldiers were killed and one was captured. The Japanese withdrew their forces to Laoag.

The next military operation was the taking of the capital city of Laoag. I was with the 1st Battalion when we found two enemy .75mm artillery pieces, together with a supply of ammunition. I suggested to the battalion commander that we use these on the Constabulary headquarters: the headquarters for the Japanese forces in Ilocos Norte. He thought this was an excellent idea.

There were several scouts with us who were originally from the 26th Cavalry Philippine Scouts, and they had some knowledge of the .75mm weapon. To man the pieces, I gave the two scouts a couple of soldiers who made a number of dry runs and then decided to fire a shot. We were on the side of a hill overlooking the city. The first shot fell very short. I told the sergeants I could do better by barrel-sighting the weapon; and, I think that's what they did with the second shot, which seemed to land close to our target. The battalion was now advancing in a skirmish line, using the support from our two captured artillery pieces.

We entered the city the following morning, 13 February, expecting house-to-house fighting; however, we encountered no resistance. The first round of artillery from our .75mm had hit the church courtyard, doing no damage. In fact, none of our rounds did any damage, but they had scared the daylights out of the Japanese, who had been getting hit from two sides, by the 1st and 2d battalions, and had decided to evacuate the city the night before.

Several days later when I tried to contact Major Roberts, I found he had left to meet a PT-boat skipper. In the meantime, the regiment staff officers and the battalion commanders wanted to know whether to harass the enemy from the rear, or go around and establish a line of defense in order to inflict casualties, or sit tight and wait for Major Roberts to return.

According to our intelligence reports, the enemy had about eight thousand men and officers in the field. If this force was allowed to proceed unhindered, it would join with the other enemy forces to become a very formidable army. Unable to contact Major Roberts and confronted with the time element involved in the next course of action, I, as S–3 officer, had to make a decision.

I decided to cut off the enemy's escape by putting up lines of resistance. I asked the two battalion commanders and the S–2 officers if we could get around the enemy troops and establish a line. The officers were familiar with the area and said it could be done. We checked our maps and decided to establish our main line of resistance along and across Highway 3, with the 2d Battalion directly south of Batac in the area of Pinili. The 1st Battalion was to tie in on the right flank of the 2d Battalion, with each battalion holding one company in reserve.

The line would extend from west to east, which would cut off any breakthrough to the south. This is where the Japanese 79th Infantry Brigade was located, in the Vigan-Tangadan area, and where our 3d Battalion, under the command of Maj. Gaudencio Silloña, assisted by Capt. John Patrick O'Day, was now engaging the enemy. Our objective was to prevent the 3d Battalion, in Ilocos Sur, from being overwhelmed by the addition of any more enemy troops to the force they were already battling.

Our first encounter with the enemy was in the Battle of Nagbacalan–Paoay Lake. An ambush on the retreating Japanese, our attack caught them by surprise, and we estimated about one hundred enemy soldiers were killed, and about the same number wounded. Our losses were very light with only two killed, five wounded, and one missing.

The second encounter, on 20 February, was in the Battle of Lawa Bridge. In this encounter, G and E companies of the 2d Battalion received heavy fire from the enemy, whose men were trying to penetrate our line but were repulsed. This encounter cost the enemy fifty killed. Our losses were again light: one killed; two wounded.

The third encounter was in the Battle of Tipcal Bridge and Mabusag River. This battle marked the first time that the 2d Battalion companies made a coordinated frontal attack against the enemy. The companies had the following positions: E and F companies occupied the position 150 yards west of Highway 3 as far as the seacoast; G Company occupied and defended the positions 150 yards east and 150 yards west of the demolished Tipcal Bridge.

A heavy exchange of gunfire opened the battle; Japanese in large numbers tried to outflank our positions. Our .50-caliber MGs prevented them from crossing Tipcal Creek at our right flank. The Battle of Tipcal Bridge and Mabusag River inflicted a heavy toll: 150 Japanese were killed and twice that number were wounded.

On 23 February, the 2d Battalion, keeping two platoons in reserve, took up positions on high ground. The battalion dug in on our main line of defense south of Batac in the Pinili area along Highway 3; the 1st Battalion tied in on the right flank of E Company.

I sent a message to the 1st Battalion's commanding officer, Major Valdez, telling him to expedite his tie-in on the right flank of the 2d Battalion and reminding him to keep one company or several platoons in reserve.

I was wondering what had happened to the eight thousand enemy troops. There was no word from our civilian intelligence agents. I was sure enemy supplies, especially the food, must be low. All the towns and barrios had been told to evacuate their inhabitants when the Japanese approached and to leave no food behind. This in itself, I thought, could have slowed down the enemy troops.

As I was speculating on the situation, Major Roberts showed up, mad as hell. He dressed me down for deploying the troops without written combat field orders. I heard him out.

I told him that in the absence of both himself and his executive officer, Captain O'Day, a decision had to be made because of the time element involved; we couldn't just sit and wait.

I didn't think he should have been dressing me down for doing what any loyal officer would do for his commanding officer. I had consulted the other officers and had made what was in my judgment the right decision for the situation. There was still plenty of time to write out a combat order, if he wished, showing our location and the deployment of each battalion and its reserve units, with all necessary instructions.

The major said it would be a good idea if we put it in writing for his signature. I said, "Yes, sir. If something goes wrong, you can hold me responsible." And I added, "There has been a lack of communication in our regiment." He answered, "We have only one radio set." I said, "I realize that, but you could let me know where I could locate you if you are needed." He answered, "Let's drop it. I have okayed your battle plan." Major Roberts then left to check on the 1st Battalion.

My runner had returned with a message from Major Valdez stating that he was now making contact with the right flank of the 2d Battalion and would deploy his men to the east of us, using a platoon from each company as a reserve unit.

We also received word from one of our intelligence agents that the main body of enemy troops was within half an hour's walking distance from our position. I sent word to Valdez to warn his men not to expose themselves; they were to allow the enemy to approach within less than one hundred yards before opening fire; we wanted this to be a surprise attack.

Exactly one half hour after the intelligence agent reported their position, the Japanese forces came into view. They were using one company of what I estimated to be about two hundred men as a point. There was a distance of about five hundred yards between the point and the main body. When the point got within one hundred yards or less, our men opened up with every weapon available. Part of the enemy's main body deployed into a skirmish line; the rest was out of effective rifle range. We were getting very little fire from the point company. The Japanese were concentrating on their main skirmish line, moving forward and yelling "banzai." Our men were taking a heavy toll of these troops. If we had had the manpower, the time would have been ideal for a counterattack.

I sent a runner with a message for Major Valdez suggesting it might be a good idea to move one reserve platoon to the right flank of our men. I could see there was very little firing coming from that direction. This was accomplished immediately, and again, the Japanese shifted their movement more to our right. Nearly the entire Japanese point—two hundred men—had been wiped out. And we had pinned down the Japanese main line of resistance.

The banzai attack had slowed down, and the Japanese were bringing up some of their reserve forces. I knew they would break through somewhere between the 1st and 2d battalions, our weakest point. They were running and firing, killing some of their own forward men to keep the rest moving and prevent retreat. They made another banzai attack, finally breaking through our lines to move in retreat in an easterly direction towards Abra.

Not only did we inflict a great number of casualties that day; we also cleared the province of Ilocos Norte of enemy troops. Now it was a matter of mopping up the deserters and the wounded. All in all, it was a great victory for Major Roberts, commanding officer of the 15th Infantry; Ilocos Norte was the first province on the island of Luzon to be liberated from the Japanese.

During and after the mopping-up operation, one of our civilian agents had a report that some Japanese stragglers had been spotted at Gabu Airfield. I sent out a night patrol and decided to go along with it. We reached the airfield after dark and found one Japanese soldier who had been critically wounded by one of our men. Another Japanese soldier came out of the bushes with his hands raised. The dying soldier asked for a drink of water, which we gave him. The leader of the patrol asked me, "What shall I do with him? He won't live until morning. He's lost too much blood." I answered, "Do what you have to." A shot was fired, and the enemy soldier's suffering was over. We returned to Batac with our one prisoner.

CHAPTER 44

A Step Up and
A Welcome Friend

The following day I finally met Capt. John Patrick O'Day, who was the executive officer of the 15th Infantry. In a heavy Irish brogue he asked me if I had any idea of the whereabouts of Major Roberts. I said I wasn't sure, but the chances were he might be in Laoag.

I told O'Day we needed to check Gabu Airfield for mines. He said that would be easy: he had five civilian prisoners with him that he wanted tried by civil court. Before he took them to Laoag, he suggested, we should get a herd of carabao and have the prisoners drive it across the field, covering every inch of it.

It took all day to complete the job.

Major Roberts eventually showed up. He had reorganized one battalion and his staff; and, as I suspected he might, he had commissioned several civilians. During his absence, he had received orders from higher headquarters that he had been promoted to the rank of lieutenant colonel. This promotion in rank may have been not only because he was commanding a regiment, but also in recognition of the successful liberation of the province of Ilocos Norte.

He assigned me as commanding officer of the 2d Battalion. The present battalion commander was to take over one of the companies within the battalion. I felt having the former commanding officer assigned as one of my company commanders might create an uncomfortable situation and expressed my feelings to Roberts about this. Roberts said he hoped I could handle it. I told him he had nothing to worry about and thanked him for giving me the opportunity to command a battalion.

When Captain O'Day returned from Laoag a few days later, the two of us had a very long conversation, ranging over our respective situations that had resulted in our finding ourselves in our present positions. Formerly, he had commanded the 15th Infantry and lost the command to Roberts. I told him I had had 168 soldiers and lost them to Lieutenant Colonel Manriquez.

O'Day told me he had been a police officer in Brooklyn, New York, before coming to Luzon seventeen years ago. When the war started, he was working in the gold mines in the Baguio area and had worked his way up to superintendent.

Referring to the time prior to Roberts's takeover of his command, he asked me if I had heard any unsavory reports about him and his men. I told him I was aware of one none-too-flattering rumor that was circulating concerning an incident he and his men supposedly had been involved in.

According to that rumor, O'Day and his men had been unloading supplies from a submarine when they were surprised and ambushed by a Japanese patrol that had been informed of their presence by some villagers. Although wounded, O'Day escaped with his men, only to return later and massacre the entire village for the betrayal.

After I repeated the rumor, O'Day faced me directly and swore to me he had never harmed any women or children, that he and his men had only punished known fifth columnists, "the dirty bastards," as he called them, who betrayed their own people. I told him I would take his word for it, and we shook hands.

I found O'Day likable and easy to converse with. He questioned me about the amount of time I had in the service; I told him twelve years, and that I was an instructor in infantry tactics. To further questioning, I told him about my escapes from the Bataan Death March and the raid on our camp near Pinappagan. He seemed especially intrigued by my account of the events that took place after that raid. He was curious about how it happened that I ended up with the responsibility for maintaining forty-six men and officers in the jungle, trying to gather enough food to stay alive, and dodging and ambushing Japanese patrols.

During our conversations, he told me he had had one sister, but she had died while he was in the Philippines, and he had no place to call home when he returned to the States. I said, "John, you will always be made welcome in my home by my parents, even if I don't make it back." He copied down my name and address and said, "Don't be surprised if you see me after the war."

I told him about the girl I was engaged to, and that I was trying to mail some letters I had written to her and to my parents. He took these and said he would see what he could do about getting them out. (They were the first letters I had written since the war began.) Sometime later O'Day left for Ilocos Sur.

On 1 March a field order was issued by Lieutenant Colonel Roberts for the 1st and 2d battalions to proceed to Lagangilang and Dolores, both in the province of Abra. Lagangilang was the designated area for the 1st Battalion and the regimental command post; my designated area for the 2d Battalion was the town of Dolores. My orders were to secure all the towns, and their barrios, in the surrounding area. Roberts left for Ilocos Sur to check on the 3d Battalion; his staff was to set up his forward command post in the vicinity of Lagangilang.

Before we left for our new assignment, we were issued new weapons: Tommy guns, BARs, and some carbine semiautomatic rifles—one of which I now started to carry in addition to my .45 pistol.

The 1st and 2d battalions had some rugged mountains to cross on the way to Abra. To make it easier to obtain food, we would be taking separate routes. The 2d Battalion moved south to Nueva Era, then in a south-by-east direction to Dolores. The 1st Battalion, under Major Valdez, followed the route I had taken when I first arrived in Ilocos Norte, going to Solsona, then cutting straight south to Lagangilang. My battalion arrived in the vicinity of Dolores the first week of March.

CHAPTER 45

The Battle for Bangued

We continued to harass Japanese patrols, keeping the enemy on the defensive and off balance. This kept patrols out of the towns and barrios occupied by the 1st and 2d battalions. I could now contact the forward command post in Lagangilang by radio to keep headquarters informed of the situation as it developed. The Japanese started to consolidate their forces in the vicinity of Bangued. E Company was ordered to take the junction at Suyo along Highway 6 leading into Bangued.

The following messages, taken from the carbon copies still in my possession, represent some of the daily communications sent to my company and platoon leaders by means of which the various units were apprised of necessary shifts and changes.

> To: C.O. "F" Co.   26 March 45
> Send your 3d platoon to Muden to Lt. Barangan. He can show them the lay of the land around Bangued. Also send me an overlay of your position and where your 37mm is located. Hope to hear some action in your area. Good luck.
>
>   Hieb

> To: Lt Valeros   26 March 45
> 2d Bn Hq Dolores.
> Am sending some men over who you can assign to Capt Barangan. They know the terrain he is operating in and may be of great help to him. If you can't use them all, send the rest to regt.
>
>   Hieb

To: C.O. "F" Co.   26 March 45
Have 2 squads of the 3d platoon patrol Cabuloan. I
understand there is a lot of rice left in that barrio and
the Japs sometimes go there. These 2 squads should
patrol every day. The people want to get their rice
from said barrio.

Hieb

To: C.O. "F" Co.   27 March 45
I have given permission to the chief SS [Secret Ser-
vice], Mr Viste, that his bolo men can go with your
patrol so they can gather their rice.

Hieb

To: C.O. "E" Co.   27 March 45
1st Bn near Pidigan are sending patrols to barrio In-
duyong. Warn your men to be on lookout for friendly
troops. Make contact with 1st Bn patrols.

Hieb

To: C.O. 1st Bn.   27 March 45
Received a message giving your location. We are now
near Highway 6. Our line running south from a point
near Pelican. Be on the watch for friendly patrols.
Good luck.

Hieb

To: C.O. "E" Co.   27 March 45
Keep me informed of new developments tonight.
Have talked to wounded soldier. Doc believes he will
be all right. Am sending a strong patrol to the highway tonight so they can make a surprise attack in the
morning north of your position.

Hieb

To: C.O. "F" Co.   28 March 45
Your panels will be changed today. Information received that Japs are again patrolling Cabuloan. Believe you should keep 2 squads in the Cabuloan area.

This will build a complete ring around the Japs in Bangued. Get Lt Fabian from hq to fix the 37mm.

Hieb

To: Lt Valeros.   28 March 45
Call regt and find out if the SWP [Special Weapons Platoon] of "F" is needed there. If not send about 2 squads of said platoon to Capt Barangan who badly needs them for his left flank.

Hieb

To: C.O. "F" Co.   28 March 45
Have notified regt about the SWP of your Co and will have them send 2 squads to you to fill out your left flank. Are there any Jap casualties? We have been fighting Japs for 2 days. 3 of our men are wounded.

Hieb

To: C.O. "E" Co.   28 March 45
Send me a good sketch of your position and the position of the enemy. Also the strength of the enemy and type of arms they are using. Will send a combat patrol from "H" Co to hit the enemy from their rear and flank. Are there any Jap casualties? Good luck.

Hieb

To: C.O. "E" Co.   28 March 45
Hold your line and I will have a platoon of "H" Co flank the enemy tonight or will have them come up on rear of Japs. I believe if you hold your fire that will worry Japs as to what we intend to do.

Hieb

To: C.O. "E" Co.   28 March 45
Received your message. Good if you can advance. I pray you can run the Japs back across the Highway. I still plan to send 1 platoon from "H" Co. Keep me informed of your position so I can notify the platoon before they move out.

Hieb

374

To: C.O. "E" Co.   28 March 45
Am sending Lt Barroga with 1 platoon to strike the
Japs on their flank. The men you saw on high ground
were our S–2 men. Hold your position and watch for
the platoon of "H" in the morning. Keep me informed
of anything new. Do not get careless. Watch your
flanks.

Hieb

To: C.O. "E" Co.   28 March 45
Notify your squad on the hill that 1 platoon of "H" Co
will be there this eve. It is impossible for me to notify
the platoon from "H" Co as they may be about to
reach the top of the mountain by now. Be sure your
squad does not fire at the platoon from "H" Co or the
surprise attack will be in vain.

Hieb

To: C.O. "E" Co.   29 March 45
Has the platoon of "H" Co made their flank attack as
ordered? When attack comes off advance your Co.
Are you still holding your position? The C.O. 15th
wants to know why the Japs again control the junction
after I had notified him we control the said junction. If
there are only 35 Japs they could easily be driven out
by your Co.

Hieb

To: C.O. "F" Co.   29 March 45
Has Lt Fabian reported to you to repair the 37mm?
What was all the shooting about in Bangued early this
morning? We have heard your 37mm fire for the past
2 days. Are you patrolling barrio Cabuloan? Have the
2 squads from your SWP reported to you? Keep me
informed.

Hieb

To: Lt Barroga.   29 March 45
Try and drive the Japs from the hill you mentioned in
your message to Capt Doña. If this can't be done, give
Cpl Pableo 1 of your best squads to ambush the Japs

375

on the road south of Suy. Keep your men there until I call for you. Your food and water will be sent to you. Cpl Pableo will show you the position of our friendly troops.

Hieb

To: Capt Doña.   29 March 45

Give me your exact location on this map. Do you know if there are any Japs left at Bancag where the building was burned? If not, I will move some men in that area which commands the road and it may command the Pidigan-Bangued junction. Also, if possible, give me the position of the platoon from "H" Co. I will keep that platoon on the hill for the time being.

Hieb

To: C.O. "F" Co.   1 April 45

Sorry I cannot spare any 30-caliber ammunition as we are short here. Have radioed Roberts and told him to supply you from the regt. Keep moving in on the Japs. I believe a great number of them have withdrawn to Pidigan. Keep me informed.

Hieb

To: C.O. "H" Co.   1 April 45

Do not withdraw your guards or outposts. I will have them follow you when Capt Doña arrives here.

Hieb

To: C.O. "E" Co.   1 April 45

Withdraw your men to Langiden but leave outpost you have on the east side of the Abra River. Your men should be informed they are not coming back to stay as they may have to return tomorrow because "H" Co is short men.

Hieb

To: Lt Daga.   1 April 45

I will send 2 squads as soon as "E" comes in from the field which may be in about 2 hours. Do you still

376

have the squad from "H" Co? How many armed men
have you in the combat section with you?

Hieb

To: C.O. "H" Co.   2 April 45
Believe it is some distance from Capt Barangan's position to the road. But if you believe it is the best place
for the .50-caliber MG, mount it. However, it should
be mounted wherever you have a good field of fire.
Will send the squad that was with Lt Daga to you in
the morning. I hope to hear a good portion of the road
has been taken by "H" Co.

Hieb

On 1 March the 3d Battalion launched an attack from Ilocos Sur
against the enemy forces in the Tangadan mountains. At the same time,
the Japanese were retreating from Vigan, the capital city of the province
of Ilocos Sur, and joining with those forces in the Tangadan area.

Meanwhile, E Company (2d Battalion) lost the junction at Tayup
along Highway 6, and the Japanese took over again there. Facing the
now-combined superior force, we continued to harass the enemy daily.
At this point, while the 1st Battalion was held in reserve, I split my battalion into three combat companies to confuse the Japanese; they
didn't know whether they were facing a regiment or a division.

The regiment forward command post received word that Roberts
would be joining us in a few days. In the meantime, I ordered the company commanders to keep the pressure on and to continue harassing
the enemy; I had decided to take Bangued, the provincial capital of
Abra. The first step toward this objective would be to take Casamata
Hill, which overlooked the highway and guarded the eastern entrance
to the city. I was sure when Roberts showed up, we could initiate the
attack on the hill, and I planned to call in an air strike to aid us in our
assault. According to our intelligence reports, the enemy was well
dug-in there and able to overlook the whole area from bunkers and
trenches.

Several days later, after being briefed at the regiment forward
command post, Roberts joined me and gave the orders to advance on
Casamata Hill and take it.

The morning of the planned attack didn't have a very auspicious beginning. For whatever reason, and I didn't bother to ask what it could possibly be, our chaplain was playing Russian roulette with a Japanese pistol and shot himself between the toes. As I was in the process of bawling him out for being so stupid, a sudden intuition flickered through my mind that from here on, the rest of the day was probably on the downhill slide. I wasn't far wrong.

I moved my battalion out, and we crossed the Abra River with E Company leading using one platoon as point. I had split E into two columns, one on each side of the road; F and G companies followed, each with flank guards out to the right and left. I was holding H Company in reserve. We advanced steadily, making good time and cleaning out small pockets of Japanese along the way.

Roberts and I were with the point, E Company, as we approached Casamata Hill. I decided to set up my forward command post behind some trees in the area about 250 yards from the enemy position, and about 50 yards to the rear of E Company, which was our main line of resistance. Captain Doña, the E Company commander, moved his troops into a skirmish line while the remainder of the battalion took cover along the sides of the highway. We were getting heavy machine-gun fire from the enemy, and I told Roberts we would probably take some heavy losses even if we tried flanking the enemy positions.

To soften up the enemy lines, I suggested an air strike, which would give us an excellent chance to move in and take the hill. Roberts agreed to call for an air strike. White panels that were very easy to spot from the air were laid out as markers to guide the planes and indicate where our lines were established.

We heard our planes coming in and circling our position. They couldn't possibly miss the white marker panels, and at the same time E Company was laying down a heavy line of fire, which also pinpointed the enemy's line of resistance. After circling the enemy, the planes unloaded their bombs and then circled low for strafing runs.

The first run went very smoothly, and then the planes circled for another one. As they came in for the second strafing, some of the Japanese we had bypassed as we moved toward the hill opened fire on the planes. When he received fire from an area he knew we were occupying, the flight leader must have assumed we had lost our position and been driven back while his planes were on their way to give us air support—and that we had left our marker panels behind.

On their second run, the planes strafed the highway where my battalion was dispersed. Fortunately, the men knew how to take cover. Fire power from the planes sprayed down the highway as far as I could see, even beyond the battalion command post. Using a tree for protection, I watched to see a strip of roadway being ripped up as the bullets tore into it. On their next run, I saw the planes circle, getting ready to come in from another direction, this time across the highway.

One of the runners, Corporal Belvador, and I sprinted across the road. I yelled at the corporal to keep both ends down when we hit the protection of the embankment on the other side. As it passed overhead, one of the planes strafed the panels, shredding them. The instinct to look up was too strong for Belvador, however, and he was hit right between the eyes, never even knowing what hit him.

My troops were boiling over with fury and kept asking what had gone wrong. I knew what had caused the mistake, but there wasn't time to explain; I limited myself to saying I would never ask for close air support again as long as I was commanding officer of the 2d Battalion. Our casualties were light considering the circumstances, but morale was understandably low. I told Roberts I thought the best thing to do was withdraw, regroup, and try to take the damned hill another day. He agreed.

As we withdrew, I sent one platoon from Captain Doña's E Company to hunt down the bypassed Japanese who had given us all the trouble and confused the air-strike planes. I gave the platoon leader of the combat patrol assigned to the task their approximate location and told him to try to take them prisoner if possible: I wanted to know just how many Japanese we were facing on that hill.

We withdrew to the barrio to our rear and dug in. We waited for a Japanese reaction, but they decided not to counterattack. The platoon leader who had been sent to flush out the bypassed Japanese soldiers returned with the report that they had located four enemy soldiers who were killed when they refused to surrender. One of our men had received a slight flesh wound. They had picked up all the Japanese weapons, but only a very little ammunition. That explained why the enemy troops had not made a counterattack. They were obviously running low on ammunition, and probably on other supplies too. The next conclusion was easy: since the Japanese were not being resupplied by ship- or airdrop, their days on northern Luzon were numbered.

Two days after our withdrawal from Casamata Hill, we were given another chance to take it, and the capital city of Bangued as well. I advanced my troops the same way I had when we had tried to take the hill earlier. This time, however, I was going to hit the enemy's flanks. While the frontal attack was underway, Captain Doña was positive E Company could take the hill. In fact, he was so sure, he took along the American and Philippine flags to raise after he and his men reached the summit.

We received no enemy fire until we reached our former forward command post. Doña had his company in a skirmish line, moving forward a squad at a time while several platoons from H Company harassed the Japanese on their right and left flanks.

By noon that day Casamata Hill had been taken. Captain Doña raised both flags on the summit and a big shout went up from all the men in the 2d Battalion. Doña, his arms raised high in triumph, lingered so long on the summit to savor the victory that I began to worry he would be picked off by the retreating Japanese.

We pursued the enemy troops and drove them out of the city of Bangued. The men were justly proud of their accomplishment. Their confidence had been restored.

CHAPTER 46

Mopping Up in Abra

After the fall of Bangued, I was ordered to cover the right flank of the 3d Battalion, south of the Tangadan area, and to keep contact with the left flank of the 1st Battalion. After Bangued had fallen, the 1st Battalion was committed to pursue and attack the rear of the 79th Japanese Imperial Infantry Brigade under the command of General Araki. The 15th Infantry, USAFIP–NL, totaling about three thousand enlisted men and officers, had outmaneuvered and encircled an enemy force of about eight thousand.

Before I left Bangued, I was asked by its people to appoint a governor or mayor. I said it was not my job, but in the absence of Colonel Roberts, I would appoint anyone the mayors of the surrounding towns and the barrio tenientes recommended. They selected a retired high school principal who was a loyal Filipino. I told the people I would appoint him governor on a temporary basis until Roberts returned from Ilocos Sur where he had gone after the fall of Bangued. We left the capital in good hands.

In the meantime, we kept a steady pressure on the Japanese forces, enclosing them inside a smaller and smaller perimeter.

The following are some of the messages sent to my company and platoon leaders during the battle for the province of Abra.

> To: Lt Bayog "E" Co.   5 April 45
> Move your platoon into Pidigan after bombing by our planes. Hold the town if you can. Am sending two S–2 agents who were in Pidigan last night and report no Japs there. Use these two agents as guides. Am

sending a sketch of what I want done so you will know how the new line will look. If you get to Pidigan look around in that area. Your food will be sent to you. Keep me informed.

Hieb

To: C.O. "H" Co.   5 April 45

Will send the rest of "E" Co tomorrow to take Pidigan after the bombing. You will have to swing your line with the help of 1 platoon from "E" Co. Your message is not very clear. Where are these 90 to 100 Japs? You say 4 Jap outposts with 7 men each that would make 28. Where are the rest? Give me a sketch of your position and enemies including their outposts. (Bombing will be tomorrow.)

Hieb

To: Lt Bayog "E" Co.   6 April 45

OK Bayog if bombing doesn't come off today take a strong combat patrol into Pidigan tonight. Do you need a grenade launcher for this work? I can get one from "F" Co if you desire. How many Japs do you believe are in front of Lt Quirante's position? Can you give me a sketch of the enemy's position and yours?

Hieb

To: C.O. "H" Co.   6 April 45

If any order for transfer has been made it has not come to my knowledge. These men that you have in your Co (the 5 enlisted men mentioned) will not be transferred at this time. You still have over 100 armed men plus 2 platoons of "E" Co. Lt Bayog will send a strong combat patrol to Pidigan tonight. I again requested by radio to have bombing tomorrow.

Hieb

To: Lt Quirante & Lt Bayog.   7 April 45

Congratulations on your promotions. The C.O. with the staff is in appreciation of your hard work and may we expect you to continue your good work. As soon as the bombing is finished, Lt Bayog with 2 platoons will move to Pidigan on attack, drive out the enemy, and hold the town. Immediately also, Lt Quirante will send strong combat patrols to destroy the Jap outposts in front of his line.

Hieb

To: C.O. "H" Co. 7 April 45
You have already told me a number of times that you located the enemy outpost. Your patrols are combat now and not reconnaissance. Use your judgment. Don't expect bombing of enemy outpost. You should know they would not waste a bomb on an enemy outpost. Harass the enemy!

Hieb

To: 1st Lt Bayog "E" Co. 7 April 45
Move into Pidigan but take panels with you. You can return after harassing the enemy there. Find out what damage has been done by our planes. Inflict as many casualties on the enemy as possible. You can send out patrols after your return from harassing the enemy lines to your front. Keep me informed.

Hieb

To: C.O. "H" Co. 7 April 45
Turn over your command to your most reliable officer for about 1 hour and report here for instructions. Expedite! Rush!

Hieb

To: 1st Lt Bayog "E" Co. 7 April 45
Withdraw your men after getting all palay [rice] that the bolo men can carry and any other supplies which were left by the Japs. Pidigan may be bombed again tomorrow. If all palay can't be carried burn what is left so the Japs can't recover it. You have done a good job. Report to my CP when you come back but leave your men in position as before. Get all information possible about the Jap positions.

Hieb

To: C.O. "H" Co. 9 April 45
Am sending the radio personnel to you. All [S-3] combat reports will be sent by radio. Let's hear a lot

383

of action from "H" Co. Use radio only for important matters and sending in your combat reports. Will send you the new disposition of 1st Bn in a few days.

Hieb

To: C.O. "E" Co.   12 April 45
Remember your panel display is changed. Am sending a few supplies. Send out strong combat patrols into enemy territory. Also send a patrol down highway to Narvacan. This patrol can be a squad. I am leaving for Narvacan this morning to get food supplies for the battalion.

Hieb

To: C.O. "E" Co.   12 April 45
Have your patrols reported in? Have them occupy the high ground to your front as shown to you this P.M. I will send an overlay to you, then show me on said overlay the disposition of your troops. My CP is now at barrio Mission to your rear. Give me one more runner from Co. Make contact with Lt Valdez of "E" 66th on your left flank tomorrow morning.

Hieb

To: C.O. "E" Co.   13 April 45
Make contact with the right flank of the 3d Bn. According to their situation map, their right flank has advanced ahead of your line. Move your line forward.

Hieb

To: C.O. "F" Co.   13 April 45
Take the hill that you mentioned to me this morning and contact the right flank of "E" Co.

Hieb

To: C.O. "E" Co.   15 April 45
Move your company up on the ridge if possible before dark and before the Japs can reinforce their troops.

Hieb

To: C.O. "MP" Co.   21 April 45
Received your overlay and map. Your line is accord-

384

To: C.O. "MP" Co.   21 April 45
Received your overlay and map. Your line is according to my field order. Do not send out combat patrols until contact has been made with "G" and "F" Co's. Lt Suero of "F" Co is now in Kagatungan (see your map). He is moving north towards Dalimag to contact the enemy. The enemy is reported to be in Dalimag, so watch your right flank until contact can be made with "F" Co. "G" Co is not here yet but may be in today. I will have the C.O. of "G" Co contact you upon his arrival. Get civilians in your area to help you with whatever is needed. Your supplies will follow.

                                                                    Hieb

To: C.O. "F" Co.   23 April 45
The 2 wounded officers will be replaced. Make Sgt Ver and Cpl Nacino acting platoon leaders. Ver has already been recommended for commission. The corporal will be recommended if he proves himself as a leader. I have ordered the "MP" Co to extend their line more towards Dalimag. "E" Co will be in Dalimag tonight. Telephone lines will be run to your command post tomorrow.

                                                                    Hieb

Now that we were on the offensive, we were suffering more casualties. The enemy was entrenched in well-constructed bunkers and connecting trenches and tunnels. The regiment now had an air control officer with a radio jeep to direct our planes in making their strikes on the enemy positions; however, I never asked for air support in my sector again.

On one of the air strikes against the enemy's fortifications in the 3d Battalion sector, a five-hundred-pound hung bomb on a P-38 fighter plane did not release on its target until the plane swung out of its dive. The bomb dropped on a 3d Battalion platoon that was on the flank of the 2d Battalion and wiped out 95 percent of the platoon. My connecting flank platoon lost four men. It was an accident, but it served to reinforce my reservations about using close-in air support. Again I expressed my feelings on the subject to Roberts.

We continued to receive enemy probes of our lines, but we kept heavy pressure on the Japanese.

In the latter part of April, Japanese troops made a banzai attack on my battalion, finally breaking through F Company lines; but in the process they suffered heavy casualties. The 2d Battalion then pursued and harassed the Japanese as they fled up the Abra valley.

In anticipation of enemy movement from the Tangadan area, elements from all three battalions of the 15th Infantry were placed at strategic positions in order to follow the enemy movement south and east. When the confused Japanese forces reached the trails east of Villaviciosa, our troops resorted to guerrilla tactics in harassing them; this type of hit-and-run warfare confused them further. Hundreds of dead Japanese soldiers were strewn along the hills and trails, while their wounded and sick were left behind to surrender or starve.

The enemy rear guard of about three hundred crack troops was assigned to cover the retreat of General Haraki, Colonel Sugiki, and Colonel Marsubara. A wedge was cut into the enemy rear guard by E Company of the 2d Battalion, costing the enemy a great number of casualties when the troops tried to rejoin their main body; only about twenty enemy soldiers succeeded. It was a very much weakened enemy that crossed into Abra on a retreat to Bessang Pass.

The battle at Tangadan had ended with heavy losses inflicted on the enemy. We also took our losses, but the ratio was ten Japanese for each one of our soldiers lost.

CHAPTER 47

Bessang Pass and Victory

The enemy was pursued by the 3d Battalion to the foothills of Bessang Pass. The 2d Battalion was moving into its new sector in the mountains guarding the pass. The Japanese were well dug-in with fortified bunkers, connecting trenches, and tunnels where they kept their artillery pieces.

Prior to relieving the 121st Infantry, we were given a few days of rest. We bivouacked in an area behind a nearby hill. While we were in the bivouac area, I set up a perimeter of defense with outposts. One night, one of the outposts started to fire on what was thought to be enemy forces. Soon the whole outer perimeter was firing. I had the devil's own time getting them to stop. The next morning all we found in front of one of the outposts was a dead carabao.

After calling a meeting with all the officers, I told them the next time anything like that occurred, if the person who fired the original shot couldn't produce a dead Japanese, I would take severe disciplinary action against him. I said I was aware we had passed small pockets of enemy soldiers, but they were not about to attack and were merely trying to reach their own forces before they starved to death.

Several nights later, I heard a shot, and then a loud burst that sounded like a hand grenade exploding. I got out of the foxhole dug inside my tent and went outside. The sentry walking post nearby was very excited. He had fired at two men who hadn't been able to give him the password. When we investigated, we found two dead Japanese soldiers. They were not carrying rifles; all they had was one hand grenade, which had exploded and killed them when the sentry hit it while

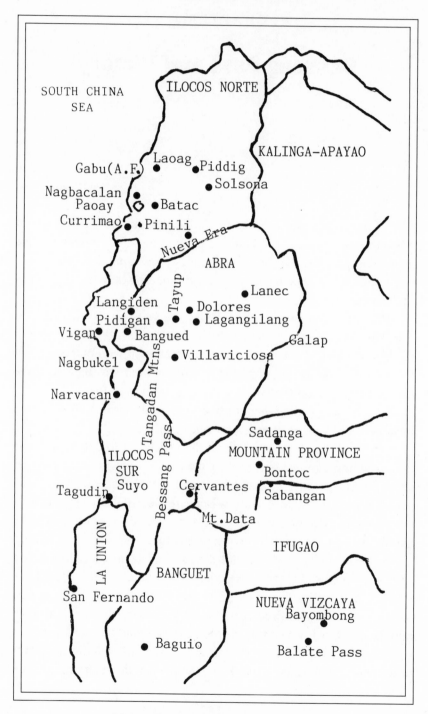

Mount Data Area, Northern Luzon

firing at them. I complimented him for being so alert, and so did everyone else in the camp.

The next day, during the evening mess call there was a commotion in the mess line. I sent my orderly to find out what it was all about. He came back in a few minutes and told me two unarmed Japanese soldiers were lining up for chow. I had to laugh. I told them to feed the two soldiers and then take them to regiment headquarters, under guard, for interrogation.

A few days later the 15th Infantry replaced the battle-worn 121st Infantry. My mission as commanding officer of the 2d Battalion was to repulse any enemy attack and drive them back, which we did. The enemy again tried to penetrate our line, and we drove them back again. They then tried to find a weak point in the 1st Battalion, but again they were repulsed and driven back.

At this point, the 2d Battalion was pinned down. I made an inspection of the front lines to see what was holding up Captain Doña's E Company. The captain asked for one more day to give him a chance to dislodge the enemy. I agreed and decided to return to the command post in the meantime to ask for artillery support. Captain Doña's position was on a long razorback ridge where in some places no more than a platoon could be deployed. With the Japanese so well dug-in, it looked like it would take some close artillery support to dislodge them. In some areas their bunkers were only fifty yards in front of E Company. Because of the enemy proximity to his position, both Doña and I were worried about the accuracy of close artillery support, or possibly having to pull back while it was being called in.

While I was pondering the situation, Roberts showed up. He wanted to know what the hell was holding up Company E. I said, "The Japanese." He looked at me a little more closely and said, "What's the matter with you?"

I was still feeling weak and feverish from a malaria attack I had had after returning from inspecting the line; and that, along with Doña's problem, hadn't left me feeling very diplomatic. I told him Doña had requested I wait another day before calling for close artillery support in order to give him another chance to dislodge the enemy. I explained in detail the course of action I was considering, which was

389

to pull Doña's forces back about fifty yards, have them dig in, call for artillery-support bombardment of the enemy fortifications, and then try to advance. I added that I was under the weather from another malaria attack, but that I usually recovered from these attacks in a few days and would be all right.

Roberts said if I was sick, I should get transportation and report to the hospital; his attitude seemed to me to be that I had picked a hell of a time to have a malaria attack. Then he asked if I had a man who could guide him to E Company. I said, "Any man in my command post can do that."

After the colonel left, I was beset by the feeling that I was letting my troops down, and this bothered me mightily. I didn't need such aggravation on top of the fever from the malaria, especially while I was trying to map out Doña's position for the artillery support.

Later in the day, O'Day, now a major, showed up. He took one look at me and said, "You look like hell!" I could always say what I was thinking to O'Day, and I said, "I wish Roberts had said that. He left here after making me feel like I was letting my troops down by having a malaria attack while there's a war going on."

O'Day told me he was going to replace me while I got rid of the damned malaria. I said I would go with him to Captain Doña's position. He said, "Hell no, not in your condition." I insisted; and he finally consented. As we neared the top of the hill, I almost collapsed. I was weaker than I had realized, and now I couldn't stop shaking. O'Day sent me back with my runner, and that night I stayed at the forward command post.

The next day Roberts came back and gave me a direct order to report to the hospital. A short while later, a driver with a Jeep arrived, and I was taken to the 7th Evacuation Hospital. The doctor there weighed me—the scale read 101 pounds—and asked me a lot of questions. When he found out I had been in the Philippines since 1939 and had survived the Japanese occupation, he said I had enough points to be returned to the United States.

I asked him what he was talking about when he mentioned points. He explained points were given for each month of combat or overseas service. It seemed to me he was leading up to saying I was in such poor health that he was going to give orders to the effect that I was physically unfit for further frontline duty. I had to appear to agree with him; so, I said I was sure I qualified to be returned to the States, but I wanted to get a few days' rest to regain my strength and then go back to see my men before I would be ready to return home. I spent about a week in the 7th Evacuation Hospital, then went by Jeep to Base X to get some much-needed clothing.

I was feeling quite a bit better, and the thought of some new clothes was giving me a real lift. When I got to the clothing supply area, I had a run-in with a major who refused to issue me any clothing unless I had a requisition order. I figured the rags I was standing in should have been all the requisition order I needed. Exceedingly angry, I went directly to Base X headquarters and asked for permission to see the commanding officer. I was told the general had gone out for lunch, but I could wait until he returned. I waited.

When the general returned, I was told he would see me. I reported to him and told him about the problem I was having getting clothes issued to me. I surely looked like an apparition in the tattered remnants I wore. I even showed him the holes in my boots.

The general had heard of some of our guerrilla activities during the Japanese occupation. He asked all sorts of questions: how many men I had had with me; how I had existed in the jungles; and what my present assignment was. Then he reached into his desk drawer, brought out a bottle of good bourbon, and poured a drink for both of us. He called in his aide and told him to go with me and see that I was put in proper uniform. I thanked him. He said he couldn't understand why I didn't take advantage of the opportunity to return to the States. I said, "I want to be here when the Philippine people are liberated, and I want to finish what I was in on from the start." He said, "God be with you and good luck." I left with his aide, got all the supplies I needed, took a shower, and changed clothes. Clothes may not make the man, but they did a lot for my morale that day.

The following day, the Jeep driver and I headed back to the front lines. As we neared them late that afternoon, I noticed American engineers rebuilding and widening the road leading to Bessang Pass. I had the driver stop and asked one of the soldiers operating a heavy grader

391

whether Bessang Pass had been taken. He said no, but that he was sure it would be in the next few days. I heard artillery fire, and I knew it wasn't ours. He said the Japanese had been firing at the engineers frequently to slow them down. He said they had not had any casualties themselves, but they had captured several half-starved Japanese soldiers. I thanked him for the information and we continued on our way.

As we rounded a bend in the road, an artillery shell landed in front of us. I told the driver to step on the gas and get around the next hill before the Japanese could zero in on us. All told, about three artillery rounds were fired at us before we got out of range.

I reported to the adjutant at regimental headquarters. The adjutant said Roberts had gone back to division headquarters and was to return that day. The next morning I reported to regimental headquarters to be briefed and brought up to date before taking back my command. I was told Roberts had already gone up to the front. I asked for a guide to help me find him, and we proceeded along the road that went right by my command post. We continued past the long razorback ridge where E Company had been stalled when I reported to the hospital. As we rounded a curve in the road, I spotted Roberts with his runners and part of his staff. They were all sitting on an open, grassy, forward slope of a hill to the left of the road. It was a dangerous position to be in with the Japanese artillery still in the mountain tunnels and overlooking our entire front.

I joined the group and reported to Roberts that I was in good health and ready to take back my command of the 2d Battalion. I mentioned to him that the Japanese still had their artillery in the tunnels. He said he was aware of it, and he asked me how I knew. I told him they had tried to bracket-in on my driver and me as we were rounding the curves on the mountain road leading to his command post. He said, in the light of that information, my standing up in the open was making him more than a little nervous. I didn't sit down and told him why.

"Colonel, I want to be on my feet if any artillery rounds come in. The Japanese have field glasses and can see you sitting on the ground. I have my cover spotted, and if they open fire, I can move a helluva lot faster from a standing position than you can from a sitting position."

He remarked that it sounded like I was ready for combat again.

The thought crossed my mind that Roberts had been catching hell from Colonel Volckmann for not having taken Bessang Pass within the time schedule we had been given; and consequently, he was perhaps so preoccupied he didn't know what he was doing.

That afternoon I was brought up to date on the locations of the three battalions in a thorough briefing by the regiment S-3 and S-2. The 2d Battalion had taken some enemy positions during my absence.

I was also given the attack plans. We, the 2d Battalion, were to make a frontal attack, with the 1st Battalion advancing along Highway 4 toward Bessang Pass. The 3d Battalion was to make a flanking attack on Hill 99 after our American support artillery laid down a heavy barrage of artillery fire to soften up the enemy positions.

The next morning, I picked up a guide and moved along the razorback ridge that had been so difficult for E Company to take. There were enemy bunkers, entrenchments, and tunnels all over the area. The stench of death persisted. Huge green flies buzzed everywhere, attracted by the dead bodies. I arrived at the E Company command post and informed Major O'Day I was ready to take over the command of the 2d Battalion.

I made an inspection of my companies and gave the company commanders the battle order for the day. We started our offensive using our own regimental 88mm-mortar platoon for close heavy-weapons support.

The fighting that day was an incredible test of physical courage. The men had to make their ways up the sides of the pass in the face of direct fire from the Japanese entrenchments above them. The enemy rolled hand grenades down on the troops clinging to the rocky surface; and, as they moved upward, the troops threw their own grenades up into the enemy's tunnels and trenches. In spite of the persisting fire power, the men kept going; two days later the regiment poured through Bessang Pass, while the remnants of the Japanese 19th Division withdrew to the east.

The Battle for Bessang Pass, 14 June 1945, was the hardest-won battle that my battalion fought. Much credit should be given to the 121st and 66th Infantry regiments for their help. After it was over, our troops moved through the pass and kept going east to capture the town of Cervantes, where we were given a short rest period.

My 2d Battalion had seen more action and had been in more difficult situations than either the 1st or 3d battalions. We were now held in reserve while the 1st and 3d located and cleaned up any of the enemy troops still holding defense pockets. I knew my men and officers appreciated the rest.

After the capture of Cervantes, the 15th Infantry had been ordered to attack eastward, and to take and hold the junction of Highway 4 and the mountain trail running from Baguio to Bontoc. While the 15th Infantry had been pushing the Japanese to the east, the 14th Infantry Regiment, under Colonel Manriquez, and the 11th Infantry, under Colonel Blackburn, were hitting the Japanese from the rear. Meanwhile, two divisions of American forces, one moving east on our right and one moving north through Balate Pass, pushed Yamashita's forces into a small compressed pocket in the mountains of northern Luzon.

It was now mid-July, and during this respite while we were being held in reserve, I finally received answers to the letters I had sent to my parents and to Elaine. I was thrilled and happy to hear from Elaine. It had been six years since I last saw her; and, probably more than three years had elapsed since anyone back home knew whether I was dead or alive. Yet Elaine had waited for me!

I remembered again how special she was, and how fortunate I was to have met her. I had never relinquished the hope that she would wait for me, but the knowledge that I was most likely listed as MIA, if not worse, had given me occasional qualms. Three years was a long time to cling to nothing but a hope, especially considering the odds against its fulfillment. Elaine and my mother, however, had remained convinced that I would come home.

Elaine, I now learned, was in the Marine Corps and was stationed in Washington, D.C. Her parents, William and Rose Marr, had sent my letters on to her. My parents had also sent her parts of my letters to them. Later I found out that although my parents had received my first letter in April 1945, they were not notified by the War Department until 9 June that I was alive and had been taken off the MIA list. I also received notice during this time of my promotion to major, back-dated to 19 June 1945.

One day, while we were waiting for orders to move forward, Lt. Col. Arthur Murphy, chief of staff, USAFIP–NL, arrived by Jeep from division headquarters looking for Colonel Roberts's headquarters. I gave him the location and said I would send a guide along with him. This was the first time I had met Murphy, and he was pretty irate. He informed me that he had been sniped at by some Japanese soldiers my troops had bypassed. He thought we ought to be patrolling the road. I told him it would take several divisions to cover the area from my position to division headquarters, and all I commanded was a battalion. Nonetheless, he was still bristling when he left.

Later, when I met Colonel Volckmann, I asked him if Murphy had ever mentioned our conversation that day in the vicinity of Cervantes. He said Murphy had, but Volckmann reassured me by adding that he knew it was impossible for us to eliminate or kill all the enemy forces while we attacked and moved forward. He told me to forget I had ever had a conversation with Murphy.

During our stay in Cervantes, I had a gunsmith in my battalion shorten the barrel of a carbine rifle that had been hit on the side by a grenade fragment. I had him file down the sear, or latch, and cut off the forward portion of the barrel, shortening it considerably. He reconstructed the stock so that I could wear it as a sidearm; it was now an automatic weapon instead of a semiautomatic rifle. The men made a holster, which I could wear on my web belt.

I tried the weapon out by firing a burst and found it had less recoil than the .45 automatic. I was very pleased and thanked the men who had worked so hard on it. I never carried my .45 pistol again after trying out the reconstructed carbine, which from then on I hardly ever let out of my sight. There were quite a few men who would have liked to buy it from me. Two forward observers, one an air officer and one an artillery officer with my battalion, offered me a considerable amount of money for it, but I told them it was doubly valuable to me because it was a gift from the men, and it was going back to the States with me.

The 2d Battalion was again committed. With the help of Major Valdez's 1st Battalion, we had pushed the Japanese forces back to the

395

road junction near the town of Sabangan, which we had been ordered to attack and seize. After Colonel Roberts called in an air strike on the entrance to the town, our two battalions were directed to enter from the south. The Japanese had left a large number of dead as their remaining forces got away and headed toward Mount Data to the south.

I was ordered to pursue an attack south along the mountain trail known as Highway 11, in the direction of Mount Data. We were making progress daily, but the going was rough. Small pockets of well-dug-in Japanese could hold us up for several days. Major Valdez's battalion finally passed through our battalion position and gave us some relief.

I developed another bad case of malaria and was ordered back to the hospital. This time I was flown back most of the way by a light spotter plane. I was taken to the 47th General Hospital. I had been there about ten days when I requested a return to my unit. The request was denied. They said I was on my way back to the States. I told the medical officer in charge I had promised to return, and that I wanted to go back to pick up some personal belongings. He finally consented.

On the day I was taken back to my battalion by plane, Hiroshima was bombed. It was 6 August 1945. The Supreme Allied Headquarters reported by radio to the world that the casualties in Hiroshima were 129,558 killed, injured, or missing—and another 170,000 homeless. The blast destroyed 60 percent of that city, which in 1940 had had a population of 343,700.

I arrived that night by Jeep at our regimental forward command post but was unable to locate Colonel Roberts. I then proceeded to the forward command post of the 2d Battalion. Maj. Celedonio A. Anchetta had been in command of the 2d Battalion during my absence. I bid my men and officers good-bye and returned to the hospital.

It was evident the war was all but over. It could only be a matter of days before the Japanese surrendered. Three days later, on 9 August, Nagasaki was bombed. One-third of that city was destroyed and 60,000 were killed or wounded.

On 2 September 1945, the Japanese government accepted the terms of unconditional surrender. The formal signing took place aboard the battleship *Missouri* in Tokyo Bay.

I was evacuated in mid-September to the 126th General Hospital on the island of Leyte for further treatment. I had seen it through from beginning to end—from the bombing at Clark Field outside Manila to the bombing of Hiroshima and Nagasaki to V-J Day. I thanked God it was over. I was ready to go home.

APPENDIX

RESTRICTED
COMMONWEALTH OF THE PHILIPPINES
ARMY HEADQUARTERS
APO 401

GENERAL ORDERS)
: 10 December 1945
NUMBER 246)

AWARD OF THE GOLD CROSS

1. Award of the Gold Cross. By direction of the President, under the provisions of Circular No. 86, this Headquarters, dated 22 July 1945, the Gold Cross is hereby awarded by the Chief of Staff, Philippine Army, to the following-named officer:

Major Harley F. Heib[sic], O-888099 INF. For conspicuous courage and gallantry in action, during the period from 9 April to 27 April 1945. As Commanding Officer of the 2d Battalion, 15th Infantry Regiment, he led his men from Tagudin, Abra to the vicinity of Nagbukel, Ilocos Sur, by a necessarily circuitous route of almost sixty miles across a mountainous terrain, in order to counter-attack the flank of the enemy who were then enveloping the right flank of the 3d Battalion which was deployed abreast of Highway No. 6 and was attacking the Japanese main line of resistance. After an exhausting forced march to its new zone of action, the 2d Battalion was commited [sic] to attack on the Japanese left flank at a point about one and one half kilometers North of Barrio Rizal. By an intelligent appreciation of the tactical situation, Major Harley F. Heib[sic], led his men to attack so aggressively that heavy casualties were inflicted on the enemy. With a display of conspicuous courage in the face of the withering fire of the enemy, Major Heib[sic], continued to lead the vigorous attack until the Japanese were forced to abandon their elaborately constructed fortifications, tunnels, pillboxes and caves, and thus saved the 3d Battalion from complete annihilation.

By order of the Secretary of National Defense:

OFFICIAL: R. JALANDONI
                           Brigadier General, Philippine Army,
                           Deputy Chief of Staff.

s/t LUIS RAMOS,
Colonel, AGS,
The Adjutant General.

DISTRIBUTION
"A" "L" "X" "C" "F"
                    R E S T R I C T E D
A TRUE COPY: dac
29 June 1951
F.S. LAGMAN
1st Lt, AGS
Asst Adj Gen

USAFIP–NL

Total strength of all guerrilla forces organized in December 1944 under the command of Col. Russell W. Volckmann and designated as the United States Army Forces in the Philippines–Northern Luzon.

Commanding Officer: Col. Russell W. Volckmann
Chief of Staff: Lt. Col. Arthur Murphy

Headquarters and Headquarters Detachment	377
Total Regimental Strength	15,490
11th Infantry Regiment	
14th Infantry Regiment	
15th Infantry Regiment	
66th Infantry Regiment	
121st Infantry Regiment	
Engineer Battalion	973
Field Artillery Battalion	600
Land Communication Service	44
Medical Battalion	808
Military Police	1,273
Quartermaster Battalion	405
Replacement Battalion	1,231
Service Troops, Headquarters Company	
Signal Company	210
Total	21,411

The above information was obtained from *Guerrilla Days in North Luzon*, published by the USAFIP—NL (Volckmann's Guerrilla Forces), Camp Spencer, Luna, La Union, Republic of the Philippines.

15th Infantry, USAFIP–NL
2d Battalion

I would like to express my sincere regrets for not having available a source in order to list all of the company officers' names and those of the NCOs and privates who contributed so much toward making our battalion such an able and efficient fighting force.

Maj. Harley F. Hieb, AUS	Commanding Officer
1st Lt. Benjamin Carpio, PA	Executive Officer
1st Lt. Lawag Fonacier, PA	S–1 Adjutant
2d Lt. Filologo M. Macagba, PA	S–2 Intelligence
1st Lt. Fermin B. Sumagit, PA	S–3 Plans, Training, and Operations
2d Lt. Santiago B. Barangan, PA	S–4 Supplies and Logistics
1st Lt. Nemesio B. Cuesta, PA	C.O., Hq and Hq Co.

E Company

1st Lt. Julian Bayag, PA	Company Commander

F Company

Capt. Cornelio Barangan, PA	Company Commander

G Company

1st Lt. Larry G. Soliven, AUS	Company Commander

H Company

1st Lt. Jacob F. Quirante, PA	Company Commander

Number of Casualties
6 January 1945 to 15 August 1945

KIA	WIA	MIA	TOTAL
73	157	0	230

(Total men lost by the 15th Infantry Regiment for the period of 6 January 1945 to 15 August 1945: KIA 280; WIA 568; MIA 6; Total, 854.)

Masaya, Jones, Isabela
May 31, 1948

Captain Harley F. Heib[sic]
323 Liedle Ave. W.
Eureka, South Dakota
U. S. A.

My dear Sir,

This is to inform the Captain that one of his boys who suffered with him through thick and thin has not been recovered yet as member of the 14th Infantry, AUS by the Recovered Personnel Division, PHILRYCOM. I have filed my request for consideration as member of the 14th Infantry, AUS and they require certificates from officers who were with us.

In this connection Sir, may I request your favor of providing me a certificate to the effect that I was a member of the 14th Infantry, AUS and was inducted into the unit on July 14, 1942. I know that with your certification as an American Officer will hasten the favorable action of RPD, PHILRYCOM on my request.

Other boys of the same unit like Abundio Curutan, Patrocinio Balminero and others have been recovered and are now enjoying the Gl Bill of rights granted to AUS veterans. I hope that with your certificate I shall be enjoying the same privileges as they are now having.

Enclosed is a certificate I typed which if the Captain will find it alright will sign it if not then the Captain is requested to make one which is his own making.

Lastly, but not the least, I extend my greatest and warmest regards to him and to his family if he got one already. I am thanking the Capt. in advance, I am.

Very sincerely,

ENRIQUE S. DANNUG

323 Liedle Ave. W.
Eureka, South Dakota
17 June 1948

Mr. Enrique S. Dannug
Massaya, Jones, Isabela

My Dear Mr. Dannug:

I was certainly happy to hear from you, in fact, I have thought of the people who helped us in our time of need many times, however, you may remember that I have always had a poor memory for names. Of course, when I received your letter and saw your name I remembered who you were. I did have a list of my friends' names in the Islands, however, I believe they were misplaced or lost.

I wish you would give all my friends in and around Jones my best wishes and regards, also give them my address as they may want to write.

Enrique, do you recall keeping some records and a diary for me? If you still have them in your possession, I would certainly appreciate very much if you would send them to me.

Were the people who helped us ever reimbursed by the Government? Did your father ever collect for all the receipts we gave him? There are a million and one questions I would like to ask, but will wait until you answer this letter.

I sincerely hope the signed certificate will help you obtain the G.I. benefits. If there is anything more I can do, please let me know.

I've been married two years and we expect an addition to the family next month.

Will write more in my next letter.

Sincerely,

Harley F. Hieb 0–890424
Major, Inf. AUS.

323 Liedle Ave. W.
Eureka, S. D. USA
17 June 1948

CERTIFICATE

I certify on my official oath that I know personally and officially ENRIQUE S. DANNUG who was a member of the 14th Infantry, AUS under the late Colonel Guillermo Nakar.

ENRIQUE S. DANNUG was with the 1st Bn., 14th Infantry, AUS when the unit was reorganized and inducted into the Army of the United States.

That said inductee was given Army Serial Number in the Army of the United States—10626966 upon his induction on July 14, 1942.

That ENRIQUE S. DANNUG was inducted in the grade of SERGEANT, his rank in the Philippine Army.

Said inductee was loyal to his unit throughout the war.

That I know of the above facts as I was with the 14th Infantry at that time.

Harley F. Hieb 0-890424
Major, Inf. AUS.

27 May 1950

Major Harley F. Heib[sic], Inf., USAR
0890424, Eureka, South Dakota
United States of America

Dear Sir:

This letter will be a surprise to you as did the letter of the Dept. of the Army to me. When I requested that office to forward my first letter to you, I did not expect that they will give me your address instead. As a way of explanation therefore, I wish to state here that recent development regarding our status had forced me to "move heaven and earth" for your address. I approached all persons whom I thought had your address but to no avail. My only resort then was to send my letter through the Dept. of the Army who instead gave me your address. I explained in my letter to that office the urgency of my contacting you and I am indeed very grateful for their advice. I assure you that your address will remain in my possession.

Since it had been a long time when you bid your troops goodbye, I deemed it proper to introduce myself. My identity will also serve the purpose for which I am writing this letter.

I was the orderly of . . . in the 14th Inf., AUS when he was the Regimental Signal Officer of the unit stationed in Dumabato, Pinappagan, Nueva Vizcaya. . . . and Cpl. Harold B. Koopmann were then quartered with you in Dipintin, Pinappagan. I was with you when you hunted down the headhunters who beheaded the schoolmaster, Mr. Domingo. I was with you during the induction of the unit into the AUS. You will remember, sir, that after the attack against the CP which preceded the capture of Col. Nakar, I joined you.

Sir, in a letter of the AGRD dated 9 March 1950, they notified me that they revoked the confirmation of my status in the AUS on the alleged ground that I was not physically present during the induction. To you who actually witnessed the event when several men of Lt. Gervacio Reyes and me were inducted into the AUS in the schoolhouse knows that such allegation is absolutely wrong. The AGRD obviously committed a grave mistake for which I cannot entirely blame them. I am well aware of the fact that the AGRD drew their conclusions from the processing papers made when we returned to military control. In my processing papers, I stated only the bare truth, confident that in my case, it sufficed. I did not elaborate in my statements because I always believed that the truth no matter how bare needs no elaboration to be the truth. Unfortunately, the AGRD found my statements not sufficient, as in several other cases. Major Dingcong had already protested against the revocation of several members who were actually in the CP. It would had been convenient for me to approach him, but he was not with me when I got inducted. It would be useless to see him regarding this matter so I am writing to you instead. Sir, I know you will help me, knowing you will not allow the truth be defeated by mistaken inference.

The Vet. Adm. in Manila advised me to contact you for the affidavits of American officers of the United States Army who had actually seen me physically and personally present during the induction. With your support, sir, the Vet. Adm. promised to effect my reinstatement into my real status. The AGRD also promised to review and correct the mistake committed to my prejudice with your support. I have a strong faith in the American sense of justice, in the principles for which I fought and with which I now invoke my right. In this faith, I am confident of your support and in the reinstatement of my name to its rightful place among the roster of those who had faithfully serve in the defense of your country and mine. I believe that I won the privilege to be in the AUS and I believe most sincerely that you will help keep that privilege.

Sincerely yours,
Benjamin Dolatre
Ex. Sgt. 10626018

SPECIAL ORDERS   DEPARTMENT OF THE ARMY
NUMBER 152   Washington 25, D.C., 13 November 1956

EXTRACT

35. LT COL HARLEY F. HEIB[sic] 0890424 AUS (LtCol Inf–USAR) upon his appl is ret fr active svc 31 Jan 1957 under prov sec 5 Cong appr 31 Jul 1935 as amended by Sec 3 act Cong appr 13 Jun 1940 sec 202 act Cong appr 29 Jun 1948 and act Cong 16 Jul 1953 (PL 126 83d Cong) after more than 23 yrs active Fed Svc. He is rel fr asg and dy, Oakland, Calif, 31 Jan 1957 and at proper time WP his home. PCS. TDN. PHHGSIA. 2172010 701–115 P 1011–02 S99–999 for tvl of off. 2172010 701–211–14 P 1311–02, 03, 07 S99–999 for tvl of depn transportation of authorized HHG including packing and crating and unpacking and uncrating. SPN 567.

By Order of Wilber M. Brucker, Secretary of the Army:

OFFICIAL: MAXWELL D. TAYLOR
                             General, United States Army
                             Chief of Staff

JOHN A. KLEIN
Major General, United States Army
The Adjutant General
A TRUE EXTRACT COPY:

M. A. GOGOLA
CWO W–4, USA

APPENDIX

HEADQUARTERS
U.S. ARMY PERSONNEL CENTER
Oakland 14   California

AMPCS–CO 201, Heib[sic], Harley F., Lt Colonel 0–890424
24 January 1957
SUBJECT: Letter of Commendation

TO: Lt Colonel Harley F. Heib[sic], 0–890424
      U.S. Army Personnel Center
      Oakland 14, California

1. On the occasion of your retirement from the military service and your departure from the Personnel Center on 31 January 1957, I wish to commend you for the outstanding and superior manner in which you performed your duties, most recent of which was Commanding Officer of Troop Command.

2. You have performed many duties during your long tenure with this command, each one contributing to the overall efficiency, welfare and morale of the command. I have particularly noted your untiring efforts, complete loyalty and interest right up to the date of your retirement which is in keeping with the best traditions of the United States Army.

3. Your retirement and resultant loss to this organization will be keenly felt. I would like to take this opportunity to thank you for your fine support.

4 Best wishes for good health and a long, happy retirement which you so justly deserve.

L. A. AYERS
Colonel TC
Commanding

Bibliography

Ancheta, Celedonio A., and Ricardo A. Arcilla, eds. *Exigencies Of War: With a Brief Biography of President Ferdinand E. Marcos.* Manila: Philippine Historical Association, 1965.

Arnold, Robert H., Colonel, USAR. *A Rock and a Fortress.* Sarasota, Fla.: Blue Horizon Press, 1979.

Enriquez, M. Jacobo, and J. Ben Quimba. *Pocket Dictionary: English-Tagalog-Ilocano Vocabulary*, Rev. ed. Manila: Philippine Book Company, 1980.

Harkins, Philip. *Blackburn's Headhunters.* New York: W. W. Norton & Company, 1955.

Horan, Col. John P. Personal Diary: "The First Five Months of Guerrilla Warfare in Northern Luzon."

Knox, Donald. *Death March: The Survivors of Bataan.* New York: Harcourt Brace Jovanovich, Publishers, 1981.

Netzorg, Morton J. *The Philippines in World War II and to Independence (December 8, 1941–July 4, 1946): An Annotated Bibliography.* Department of Asian Studies, Data Paper no. 105. Ithaca: Southeast Asia Program, Cornell University, 1977.

Ongpauco, Lt. Col. Fidel L., AFP (Ret). *They Refused to Die: True stories about World War II heroes in the Philippines 1941–1945.* Quebec: Levesque Publications, 1982.

Schultz, Duane. *Hero of Bataan: The Story of General Jonathan M. Wainwright.* New York: St. Martin's Press, 1981.

USAFIP Area Command, Historical Records Section. *Guerrilla Days in North Luzon: A Brief Historical Narrative of a Brilliant Segment of The Resistance Movement During Enemy Occupation of the Philippines 1941–1945.* Luna, La Union: USAFIP, NL (Volckmann's Guerrilla Forces), 1946.

United States Army Forces, Pacific, General Headquarters. Military Intelligence Section, General Staff. "The Guerrilla Resistance Movement In The Philippines." Intelligence Series, vol. 1. Tokyo, 1948.

Volckmann, Col. Russell H. *We Remained: Three years behind the enemy lines in the Philippines.* New York: W. W. Norton, 1954.

Vreeland, Nena, Geoffrey B. Hurwitz, Peter Just, Philip W. Moeller, and R. S. Shinn. *Area Handbook for the Philippines.* 2d ed., DA Pam 550-72. Washington, D.C.: Foreign Area Studies, The American University, 1976.

Willmott, H. P. *Empires in the Balance: Japanese and Allied Pacific Strategies to April 1942.* Annapolis: Naval Institute Press, 1982.